THE WELSH CHURCH FROM REFORMATION TO DISESTABLISHMENT 1603–1920

THE WELSH CHURCH FROM REFORMATION TO DISESTABLISHMENT 1603–1920

GLANMOR WILLIAMS

WILLIAM JACOB

NIGEL YATES

FRANCES KNIGHT

UNIVERSITY OF WALES PRESS
CARDIFF
2007

British Library Cataloguing-in-Publication Data
A catalogue record for this book is available from the British Library.

ISBN 978-0-7083-1877-5

Typeset by Columns Design Ltd, Reading
Printed and bound in Great Britain by Anthony Rowe Limited, Chippenham, Wiltshire

Contents

Preface

The image of the ruined nave and west front of Llandaff Cathedral at the beginning of the nineteenth century, which adorns the front cover of this book, is one that has summoned up for generations of Welsh churchmen and historians a picture of the state of the Established Church in Wales for much of the period between the Reformation and its eventual disestablishment in 1920. The aim of the contributors to this book is to dispel that image and to replace it with one that more accurately reflects the truth as revealed in the vast surviving documentation from this period in the National Library of Wales and in the university libraries and local record offices of the principality.

The popular image of religion in Wales between the early seventeenth and the late nineteenth centuries is one that was born out of the acrimonious debate about disestablishment at the end of this period. Anglicans and Nonconformists, for different reasons, colluded in their dismissal of the Established Church before the middle years of the nineteenth century as one that had failed the people of Wales. They differed, of course, in their analysis of the contemporary situation. Whereas nonconformists argued that the desertion of the Established Church by a majority of the population of Wales was an argument for its disestablishment and disendowment, reformers in the Established Church argued that they had learned the lessons of the past and that an Established Church revitalized by them could now offer religious leadership to the people of Wales. The result of both arguments was that the Established Church of the past stood condemned, and it was a condemnation which has been accepted by most Welsh historians over the succeeding century and more, and which still appears, almost undiluted, in popular books on Welsh history. Recently there has been some questioning of the myth by scholars in Wales, but it has tended to be very tentative and limited in its impact. Note has, on the whole, not been taken of the substantial reinterpretation of the religious history of other parts of the British Isles and of mainland Europe in the period 1600–1900 over the last thirty or forty years. The aim of this book is to apply the same revisionist techniques to the primary sources of Welsh religious history and as far as possible to let them speak for themselves rather than being filtered through the prejudices of the Church's detractors in the past. Another, and equally important aim, is to interpret Welsh religious history in the broader context of British and European religious history, and not to view what was happening in Wales from too isolationist a perspective.

This book is not intended to be a history of 'The Church in Wales' in the three centuries before disestablishment, nor does it attempt to be an all-embracing history of religion in Wales in this period. It is rather something between the two. It is primarily a study of religious establishment. That means that it includes a detailed analysis of how that establishment operated at diocesan and parochial levels. Religious dissent is dealt with extensively, but in the context of how it impacts on the religious establishment, and no attempt has been made to discuss the internal developments within non-Anglican churches after the early nineteenth century when Wales becomes, for the first time, a genuinely religiously pluralist society. The third aim of this book, and one which has to a large extent determined its approach, is to provide a comprehensive account of the religious development of Wales between the early seventeenth and early twentieth centuries to complete the important work begun by Glanmor Williams in *The Welsh Church from Conquest to Reformation* and *The Reformation in Wales*, and to provide the link between them and several recent studies of the churches in Wales during the period since disestablishment.

The death of Glanmor Williams, early in 2005, shortly after the completion of his two chapters, has robbed Welsh religious historiography of its greatest living practitioner, and I and my fellow contributors would like to dedicate this volume as a fitting memorial to someone that was for us both a mentor and a friend. I remember, in particular, his kindness to me as a young researcher in Wales more than thirty years ago and again the excitement of his presentation of his initial findings for his contribution to this book delivered as a paper to a day school at the University of Wales, Lampeter, in 2003.

As the person who exercised the role of general editor in preparing this book for publication I should like to thank my other colleagues, William Jacob and Frances Knight, for the enormous amount of work they have put in to complete their contributions promptly. We very much hope that the book will become a standard text on Welsh religious history in the way that the earlier work by Glanmor Williams has, and that it will spread knowledge of Welsh religious history beyond the borders of the principality. We acknowledge with gratitude the decision of the University of Wales Press to publish this volume, and that of the Centre for the Advanced Study of Religion in Wales at the University of Wales, Bangor, to include it within their series of publications on Welsh religious history. We are also grateful to all the libraries and record offices that have made their resources available to the contributors, especially the National Library of Wales.

An especial expression of thanks must go to Abi Gardner, of the University of Wales, Lampeter, who drew the maps and plans in Figures 1–4, and to those who have permitted the reproduction of illustrations of which they own the copyright: the Dean and Chapter of Llandaff Cathedral (front cover and Illustration 12); Lord Newborough (Illustration 1); the Royal Commission on the Ancient and Historical Monuments of Wales (Illustrations 2–6 and 8–10); Thomas Lloyd (Illustration 7); and the late R. W. Soden (Illustration 11).

I am also particularly grateful to my wife, Paula, who undertook the final stages of coordinating the typescripts of the four parts of this book and preparing them for the press, and to Sarah Lewis of University of Wales Press for all her help and advice, and especially for her tolerance of the delays that occurred in delivering the final text to the publisher.

Nigel Yates
University of Wales, Lampeter

Editor's Foreword

Despite the secular nature of contemporary Wales, scholarly interest in the religious past is far from abating. Historians and theologians are currently engaged in a range of studies on many aspects of the development of church, religion and society from the very earliest centuries to the present.

The flourishing state of the discipline is represented in the latest volume in the Bangor History of Religion Series. *The Welsh Church from Reformation to Disestablishment 1603–1920* is an admirable, well-planned and much needed synthesis which is set to become the standard history of Welsh Anglicanism for our generation. Its authors are eminent in their field and the study will serve as a memorial to our pre-eminent social historian of Welsh religion, the late Sir Glanmor Williams. Its four sections cover the periods from the Elizabethan Reformation to the advent of disestablishment, when the link between the Welsh dioceses and the see of Canterbury was severed to create the autonomous Church in Wales. Although majoring on Anglicanism, there is much on the establish church's response to Dissent, Victorian Nonconformity and the ongoing impact of the Evangelical Revival, while the Welsh experience is compared with and contrasted to parallel developments within the Church of England. In all, this is a worthy addition to what has become the standard series of academic studies in the history of religion in Wales.

The Centre for the Advanced Study of Religion in Wales, established in 1998, continues to provide a focus for research and scholarship on all aspects of the nation's religious past. Through its publications including its monograph series, its Welsh language volumes and *The Welsh Journal of Religious History* as well as sponsoring meetings and colloquia on specific subjects, it persists in fulfilling its aim of fostering a better and wider understanding of the religious past and its bearing on the present and the future.

D. Densil Morgan
Centre for the Advanced Study of Religion in Wales
University of Wales, Bangor

Tables

TABLES

Figures

Illustrations

Abbreviations

DNB	*Dictionary of National Biography*
DWB	*Dictionary of Welsh Biography* (London, 1959)
ICBS	Incorporated Church Building Society
JHSCW	*Journal of the Historical Society of the Church in Wales*
JWEH	*Journal of Welsh Ecclesiastical History*
JWRH	*Journal of Welsh Religious History*
LPL	Lambeth Palace Library
NLW	National Library of Wales
NLWJ	*National Library of Wales Journal*
PP	Parliamentary Papers
SCH	*Studies in Church History*
SPCK	Society for the Promotion of Christian Knowledge
SPG	Society for the Propagation of the Gospel
WHR	*Welsh History Review*

Part I

1603–1660

1

The Early Stuart Church

Throughout the long reign of Elizabeth I from 1558 to 1603, the queen had sought to maintain a firm hand over the content of doctrine, the nature of worship and the organization of the Church within her kingdom. As Supreme Governor of that Church she had, in general, successfully countered all the efforts of the two main factions which aspired to bring about fundamental change in the structure of belief and worship. Although neither her Roman Catholic adversaries nor her Puritan critics had been completely eliminated, each had been kept firmly within bounds. Nevertheless, in 1603, as the queen drew near to her end, a crucial issue, which for much of her reign she had never been willing to resolve publicly, one way or the other, still remained undetermined. Who was to succeed her on the throne? By the 1590s this was as much a religious question as a political one. Was her successor to be a Protestant or a Catholic? Would it be James VI of Scotland, or a representative of the Spanish royal family? Elizabeth had never given a clear-cut indication of her wishes in this matter; presumably because she had not wished to enhance a potential successor's position at the expense of her own; a rising star might easily eclipse the setting orb. Yet, during Elizabeth's last days it was becoming increasingly obvious that James Stuart was likely to be her successor; and so, indeed, it ultimately proved to be. When Elizabeth died on 24 March 1603 James VI of Scotland became also James I of England. Ironically enough although, beforehand, both Protestants and Catholics had looked expectantly to James to provide them with favours, neither party derived much joy from their new monarch. The Hampton Court Conference of 1604, convened specifically to settle religious questions, advocated changes, it is true, but they were not far-reaching enough in either direction to please Catholic or Puritan.

In his attitude towards Wales James I was well-disposed.[1] He basked in the warmth initially shown towards him by his Welsh subjects,[2] many of whom viewed him as the rightful heir of what they conceived of as the 'Welsh' dynasty of the Tudors[3] and looked for similar benefits at his hands as they had received from his Tudor predecessors. Moreover, James regarded the harmonious union of Wales with England as a precedent that might be repeated just as successfully in the case of Scotland. Furthermore, neither the Catholic nor the Puritan element was especially strong in Wales. The one outstanding Puritan produced there, John Penry (1563–93), had been executed when he was only thirty years old and, having spent most of his short public life outside Wales, had made virtually no impression on his own country. On the other hand, the Catholics were considerably stronger in parts of Wales, since, as proverbial Welsh wisdom maintained, 'it is much easier to light a fire on an old hearth'. This was especially true of the diocese of St Asaph, where there had been 250 openly recorded recusants in 1603, and of Llandaff, where there had been 351, which gave it a higher proportion of recusants to Anglican churchgoers than any other diocese in England or Wales.[4] Interestingly, and perhaps somewhat unexpectedly, the most devoted groups of Roman Catholics and of Protestants had been found in much the same areas of Wales – Wrexham and Flintshire in the north-east and Monmouthshire in the south-east. As early as 1604, within a year of James's coming to his throne, the Elizabethan penal laws against Roman Catholics were re-enacted. The alarm aroused by the Gunpowder Plot of 1605 led to still more severe legislation in 1606, when two new statutes were passed: the one imposing stiffer fines on recusants and the other requiring officers of local government to be stricter in compiling their lists of offenders. The fines imposed on the Catholic recusants were ostensibly very punitive, though only a small proportion of them was collected. The Catholics, many in whose midst were women, as they had been in the previous century, stood their ground staunchly. They continued to be found in their traditional centres of strength such as Denbighshire, Flintshire, Monmouthshire, the Vale of Glamorgan and in the area around Milford Haven.

Little support was, however, forthcoming for Catholic plots against the king's person. Neither the Watson Plot nor the Bye Plot of 1603, nor even the Gunpowder Plot of 1605, elicited much backing from Wales, although the Whitsun Riot of 1605 on the Herefordshire border with Wales seems to have stirred considerable excitement among Catholics in that area.[5] In 1610 the Oaths Act was directed particularly against women devotees, who often formed the hard core of recusant resistance. The women tended to reject Anglican worship while the men went through the motions of church attendance to avoid being fined. The net effect of the more stringent legal code was to make the watch being kept by local authorities on suspected Roman Catholics appreciably more sharp-eyed. This vigilance was reflected in the increased numbers of them being recorded in the gaol files of the Court of Great Session and the Recusant Rolls, even if nothing like all the fines ostensibly recorded were, in reality, collected.

In spite of all the pressures applied to them during James's reign, Roman Catholics maintained their numbers remarkably well in their accustomed strongholds.[6] Throughout the early Stuart period, the problem of recusancy continued to be broadly similar to what it had been in Elizabeth's reign – the dogged and unyielding commitment of a handful of faithful Catholic families to maintain their beliefs from generation to generation in face of a hostile government and public opinion. Most of them were drawn from yeomen and substantial farmers; people of sufficient means to maintain an independent point of view. Many of them, too, were the tenants of substantial landowners; as was said of a Monmouthshire tenant, 'his religion is part of his copyhold, which he takes from his landlord and refers it wholly to his discretion.'[7] To such landlords they continued to look for protection as well as patronage. The survival of the old faith continued to depend on the courage and steadfastness of the rank and file, directed by the influence of a select group of upper-class believers and the zeal of dedicated priests. Among the latter, two of the most active were Fathers Robert Jones (1566–1615) and William

Griffith (*flor. c.*1600–10) who, between them, virtually reconstructed the Catholic missionary effort in Wales and the Marches. Another significant figure was Father John Salisbury (1573–1625), a descendant of the celebrated north Wales family of that name, and author of the inspirational book, *Eglurhad Helaethlawn o'r Athrawiaeth Gristnogawl* ('A Full Explanation of the Christian Doctrine', 1615).[8] He lived from 1615 to 1625 at Raglan Castle, home of the Earl of Worcester, the most powerful of Welsh Catholics. During those years, Salisbury was Jesuit Superior of the North and South Welsh District. It was he, too, who in 1622 set up the District Headquarters at Cwm in Llanrhuddol, just over the English border between Herefordshire and Monmouthshire. Salisbury was extremely active as head of the Jesuit College at Cwm and in preparing young priests at the outset of their lives of active service to their church. It is noticeable, nevertheless, that numbers of recruits for the Catholic priesthood were declining in the seventeenth century. Even in the diocese of Llandaff, where sixteen young men had offered themselves as candidates for the priesthood during Elizabeth's reign, only four came forward between 1603 and 1625. Figures for the other Welsh dioceses showed a similar decline.[9]

Both the Catholics and the Puritans, therefore, had been tamed, and James I had been securely seated on his throne and firmly established as Head of the Anglican Church. Even so, there still remained a great deal in the state of that Church in a 'dark corner of the realm' such as Wales that continued to be in need of reform. Its condition worried earnest churchmen for many decades, down to the 1640s and even beyond. At a very late stage in Elizabeth's reign, contemporary observers had commented with deep disquiet on the widespread ignorance, indifference and the residue of pagan and Catholic trends that they perceived on all sides among the Welsh population. John Penry, for example, believed that 'most people never think of any religion, true or false'.[10] The unknown author of the Catholic classic, *Y Drych Cristnogawl* ('The Christian Mirror', 1585) maintained that there were whole shires in Wales 'without a single Christian living within them, people living like animals, most of them knowing nothing about morality, but only keeping Christ's name in their memories, without knowing more about him than animals do'.[11] It was not to be wondered at that in such circumstances beliefs and practices deriving from ancient folk-religion as well as from medieval Catholicism should persist: vigils for the dead, veneration of the saints, visits to holy wells and the like. Bishop Marmaduke Middleton of St David's in 1583 had denounced his flock as having been 'for the most part, trained up in erroneous amity and wretched superstition',[12] while as late as the 1630s, authors desirous of reform, like Vicar Rhys Prichard (1579–1644), Robert Llwyd (1565–1653), Rowland Vaughan (1590–1667) or Oliver Thomas (1598–1653) would be denouncing those vestiges of earlier Catholic and pagan practices and beliefs that they found it so difficult to uproot and the apathy and ignorance of their parishioners. There were congregations scolded by the poet George Herbert (1593–1633) for needing 'a mountain of fire to kindle them'.[13] As late as 1646 John Lewis of Glasgrug (*flor.* 1646–56) could refer to the 'swarm of blind superstitious customs that are among us, passing under the name of harmless customs', such as 'calling upon saints in their prayers, peregrinations to wells and chapels'.[14]

Resort to the practitioners of magic was also commonplace among the Welsh, like most of the peoples of Europe in this period. In the Middle Ages the Church was believed to have at its disposal a vast reservoir of supernatural resources and, in spite of the anti-magical tenor of official teaching, it had nevertheless tended to pander to the popular appetite for the other-worldly and spectacular, and that at a time 'when the role of the priest and the magician was by no means clearly distinguished in the popular mind'.[15] The ranks of diviners and sorcerers had swollen considerably in the sixteenth century as the magical powers attributed to priests had eroded. Every district in Wales had its own *dynion hysbys*, its 'wise' men and women; its wonder-workers, charmers and others deemed to be able to pronounce curses, cast spells or foil them, intone divinations, detect thieves, cure animals or humans of their ailments, with all these procedures having some religious aura about them. That great Puritan writer Morgan Llwyd (1619–59) put into the mouth of the Eagle in his *Llyfr y Tri Aderyn*

('Book of the Three Birds', 1656) a series of questions suggesting that astrology could foretell the future, that 'making the sign of the cross on the forehead kept away evil and that sorcerers were the guardians of many great mysteries'.[16] As the Church increasingly ceased to be associated with the supernatural powers once associated with it, fewer people were attracted to its services.

Attendance at church services continued to give rise to deep concern among church authorities. Admittedly, the large majority of the population – possibly as high as 80–85 per cent – made their Easter communion; but on ordinary Sundays parishioners, particularly among the poorer classes, were very remiss about coming to church. Contemporary poets and moralists, like Thomas L1ywelyn (*flor.* 1580–1610) or Vicar Prichard, condemned the ale-house as a prime source of temptation for many members of the population, dejectedly contrasting the deserted church with the crowded tavern. The latter they identified as the wellspring not only of drunkenness but also of gluttony, foul language, adultery, prostitution, brawling, gambling, unlawful games and all manner of sinful behaviour. Many other people, who ought to have been in church, were lured from places of worship by sports, dancing and similar merry-makings, which were normally conducted on Sundays. Robert Llwyd of Chirk referred caustically to the decadence of his age, with its addiction to the taverns, playing fields, bowls, football, tennis and the like.[17] Bishop Godwin of Llandaff (1601–17) censured those heedless semi-pagans of his diocese who 'horribly profaned the sabbath by playing unlawful games at the time of divine service, often in the churchyard'.[18] Although many of these sports had been legally allowed in 1617 by James I's 'Book of Sports' and again by Charles I in 1633, there was probably much truth in Dr Thomas Richards's mildly sardonic remark that one could 'hardly associate' the authors of godly Welsh books 'with a warm welcome for such pastimes'.[19]

Many among the parishioners, however, had other less wayward reasons for being absent. Among the poorer farmers and labourers, who had little choice but to exercise perpetual care over crops or livestock, it was work which kept them busy out of doors on Sundays. There were also many who found the journey to church long and difficult. Hence it was that parish churches to be found in towns or compact nucleated parishes were the best attended. Many of the Welsh parish churches, by contrast, were situated in places which could only be reached after a lengthy and inconvenient journey and were made all the more inaccessible during winter months, when the weather was at its most inclement, with rivers and streams swollen, and the rough and ill-tended trackways of hill and moorland Wales at their most impassable. The church buildings themselves were cold, dark, draughty and sometimes in a state of poor repair, in sharp contrast to the warm and welcoming taverns.

The people whose attendance at church was most urgently desired by the authorities of Church and state, as is evident from contemporary sources in England and Wales, were the heads of households. Indeed, it appears not too much to claim that in most Protestant countries it was not the 'priesthood of all believers' so much as the 'priesthood of all householders' that was being aimed at. Amongst the heads of households were to be found a relatively broad band of social types: minor gentry, freeholders, professional men, merchants, and others of the same kind. Included among them also were the more substantial tenant farmers, men of sufficient standing to bear office as parish constable or churchwarden. They were not only expected by public opinion to be good Christians themselves but were also charged with the duty of enforcing belief and morality on those who came under their authority: wives, children, servants, apprentices, tenants, labourers, the poor and the beggars.[20] It was assumed – in theory at least – that their regular attendance at church should be supplemented by a bonus of inestimable value in the eyes of enthusiastic pastors: regular domestic devotions, when bibles, prayer books, primers, catechisms and other uplifting works might be read and meditated upon.

James I found the position of the king within the Church of England, and the episcopalian nature of that church, to be distinctly more to his liking than the dispositions in its Presbyterian counterpart in which he had been brought up in Scotland. He delegated responsibility for maintaining worship in accordance with the Book of Common Prayer and encouraging regular attendance at the parish churches very largely to the bishops and the clergy. James enjoyed, in particular, the measure of control over the choice of bishops with which he was now endowed as Head of the Church of England. There was, however, a notable difference between his selection of bishops for Welsh dioceses and that which his Tudor predecessor had exercised – possibly because he could not count upon such well-informed advisers as far as Wales was concerned as had been available to Elizabeth; James had no William Cecil or Gabriel Goodman to whisper in his ear.[21] Whereas Elizabeth's Welsh bishops were almost all Welsh-born, or at least had Welsh connections, that was manifestly less true of the Jacobean bishops. A number of them were neither Welsh themselves nor had any Welsh associations. In the diocese of Llandaff, for instance, following the departure of Bishop William Morgan to St Asaph in 1601, three Englishmen were presented in succession to the diocese: Francis Godwin (1601–17); George Carleton (1617–19); Theophilus Field (1619–26): and then a Scot, William Murray (1627–39).[22] Not until 1640 was a Welshman, Morgan Owen (1640–5), appointed bishop of the see. One of the Llandaff bishops, George Carleton, was not unaware of his own lack of appropriate qualifications for the diocese to which he had been called. He confessed that he could do little good there because of his ignorance of the Welsh language and also on account of the opposition of some 'great men who hate the truth'. He had the honesty to admit that he had accepted the diocese only because the favours of princes were not to be rejected.[23] Not all the early Stuart bishops were as frank as Carleton.

On the other hand, in north Wales the choice of bishops was much more commendable, some of the best of them owing their appointments to the influence of Archbishop Laud. During the reigns of both James I and his son most of the diocesans were Welshmen. At St Asaph, the excellent Bishop William Morgan was succeeded by Richard Parry, who proved to be a conscientious bishop and a diligent scriptural translator (see below). A native of Flintshire and an Oxford graduate, he had served first as chancellor of Bangor and then as its dean before becoming bishop of St Asaph in 1604. He remained as bishop there until 1623, when he was succeeded by Bishop John Owen, who held the see until 1642. Owen, too, revealed himself to be a dedicated bishop, though deeply concerned by the unconcealed activities of recusants in his diocese and the growing influence of St Winifred's Well as a focus for the congregation of Roman Catholics from within his bishopric and from outside it. He reported to the archbishop in 1633 on the 'number and boldness of the Roman Catholics . . . much encouraged by the superstition and frequent concourse of that party to . . . St Winifred's Well'.[24]

In the diocese of Bangor, Bishop Henry Rowland (1598–1616) turned out to be one of the best bishops of the age. A Caernarfonshire man by birth and an Oxford graduate, he was a good scholar, greatly interested in education, and the founder of Bottwnog Grammar School. He also established scholarships at Oxford and was, in general, a conscientious bishop. He was succeeded by Lewis Bayly (1616–31), also of Welsh birth and an author best known for his famous book, *The Practice of Piety*, which went through no fewer than seventy-one editions by 1792, and was very successfully translated into Welsh by Rowland Vaughan of Caer-gai, running to six editions.[25] Bayly, however, had a somewhat chequered career in Parliament and was the subject of some criticism in his own diocese, but was, on the whole, a caring bishop. Another good bishop was William Robert (1632–65), who was appointed to his see as a result of Laud's influence. He was a generous benefactor to his diocese and the Church. He found the situation to be extraordinarily difficult during the Civil Wars, but managed to live long enough to recover his lost possessions after 1660.

Most of these bishops were intent on trying to maintain the higher standards which had been attained by the end of Elizabeth's reign, especially among the higher clergy, and the increased number of graduates who had been installed among them in the dioceses at large. They were justly praised for their efforts by a distinguished historian of the diocese of Bangor in the following terms:

> The list of distinguished and clergy was remarkable and cannot be equalled in a similar period of time either before or since. The age may be called the golden age of the Church in Wales, not on the ground that the Church or its organization

> were free from great imperfections, for such was not the case, but because . . . the Church inspired teachers who wrought their Church and their country great good.[26]

All of the higher clergy, virtually without exception, and many others beneath them were now university graduates and some among them were scholars and authors of distinction.

In the diocese of Bangor, Edmwnd Prys (?1544–1621), archdeacon of Merioneth and a highly gifted scholar and poet, immortalized himself as the translator into Welsh of the metrical psalms (see below). Dr John Davies of Mallwyd (*c.*1567–1644), also a luminary of Bangor diocese, was an accomplished biblical translator and rendered other books into Welsh. He acted as Bishop William Morgan's right-hand man and was indispensable as Bishop Richard Parry's aide, and also a Welsh grammarian of the utmost distinction. In the diocese of St Asaph lived Robert Llwyd (1565–1655), vicar of Chirk. He was best known for his admirable translation of Arthur Dent's *Plain Pathway to Heaven* into Welsh as *Llwybr Hyffordd yn Cyfarwyddo'r Anghyfarwydd i'r Nefoedd* (1630). He was one of a small group of clerics who aimed at raising contemporary standards of religion by providing readable Welsh translations of popular religious books. He also did a great deal to assist and encourage his bishop, Richard Parry, to translate into Welsh the version of the Bible published in 1620.

Down in south Wales, in the diocese of St David's, one of the outstanding figures was Robert Holland (?1556–?1622). Settled in the south-western diocese, where he held a number of livings, he became a prolific author of Welsh books. The most celebrated among them was his translation, with the help of George Owen Harry, of James I's own book, *Basilikon Doron* (1604). But the best-known of the St David's clergy by far was undoubtedly the chancellor of the diocese, Rhys Prichard (*Yr Hen Ficer*, the Old Vicar) (1579–1644), vicar of Llandovery and author of *Cannwyll y Cymry* ('The Welshman's Candle'), which became, along with Edmwnd Prys's metrical psalms, one of the most popular collections ever of Welsh poetry.[27] Although *Cannwyll y Cymry* was never set forth in print during its author's lifetime, his poems were widely popular, in oral and manuscript versions, throughout south-west Wales, where they were learned and memorized. The chancellor of Llandaff diocese, Edward James (?1569–?1610), was another to whom his fellow countrymen owed an incalculable debt for his splendid translation into Welsh of the famous sermon collection, the *Book of Homilies* (1606).

A continuing weakness, however, among the higher clergy in Wales, just as in England, was the universal practice of pluralism. With many of these clerics now being increasingly drawn from among the younger sons of gentry families, there was a tendency among them to gather into their own possession two or three of the best livings, possibly even more, in order to maintain their own lifestyle appropriately. This, in turn, generally meant hiring poorly paid stipendiary clergy to 'care for the cure of Souls'. These curates were themselves often obliged to hold a number of such livings, often at some distance from one another. The consequence was that poverty and neglect were widespread among the parish clergy and serious in their effects. The average level of parochial income was very low.[28] Some Reformation changes had themselves had the effect of extinguishing earlier sources of income, such as pilgrims' offerings, the sale of candles, or masses for the dead. The century from 1540 to 1640 was one of rapid inflation, followed by the disasters of the Civil Wars. The pressures may not have borne too heavily on those parsons who farmed their own glebe and collected all the tithe that was due to them. They probably lived at best on the scale of minor gentry or at least of substantial yeomen. Many others were not nearly so fortunate, however. Those who felt the pinch of poverty most keenly were the incumbents of impropriated livings, once in the hands of the monasteries, but which now, for all practical purposes, had passed into the possession of the local gentry. The southern dioceses were particularly hard hit by the practice. Llandaff was especially impoverished in this respect,[29] which meant that many of its clergy received incomes which were worth only about one-third to a half of their real value. The unbeneficed clergy were even worse off and were obliged to take charge of two or three of these livings in order to scrape together a remuneration on which they were barely able to live.

The conditions just outlined were the long-standing problems of the medieval and the Tudor Church in Wales and were being only very slowly improved by the passage of time. The truth was that the Welsh Church had always found it difficult to cope with its responsibility for adequately instructing its congregations. There had always been, and still were, too many of its clergy, notably among the unbeneficed, who were, for the most part, too under-educated and too badly rewarded appropriately to fulfil the duties of catechizing, teaching and preaching laid upon them. Back in the earliest days of the Reformation, in 1546, Sir John Pryse of Brecon (1502–55), author of the first book to be printed in Welsh, had felt compelled to admonish those many clerics who either could not, or would not, reveal to their parishioners those spiritual truths that the latter ought to know for the sake of the health of their souls. This deficiency Pryce attributed chiefly to the poverty and ignorance existing among the clergy and to the absence of any printed books in Welsh among them to help them feed their flocks in accordance with their duty as spiritual pastors.[30]

Yet thanks to the strenuous efforts of a small band of pioneers there had been a distinct improvement. In 1630, close on 100 years after John Pryse had published the first Welsh book, when Robert Llwyd came to dedicate his own volume, *Llwybr i'r Nefoedd* ('Pathway to Heaven') to his bishop, Robert Parry, he believed himself able to paint a much more encouraging picture of the clergy in his diocese:

> you will find that many of your under-shepherds are training and guarding their flocks with care and tactful diligence. Some are full of energy and whole-hearted . . . some gathering smooth and serviceable stones from God's Word to hurl at the spiritual Goliath . . . some driving vigorously . . . against the priests and worshippers of Baal, and others eminent for their learning and talents . . . distinguished gifts of pure doctrine, eloquence of speech and boldness to overthrow sin and iniquity.[31]

Such a roseate impression of the St Asaph clergy was doubtless too self-delusory on Llwyd's part to be applicable to all the clergy of the four dioceses of Wales; yet it needs to be borne in mind if only as a counter-weight to all the equally overstated comments made by Puritan critics, which are prone to be quoted as if they were the plain, unvarnished truth.

The difficulties of the clergy were intensified by two other sets of circumstances: first, the widespread illiteracy existing among the mass of the population; and second, the absence of a printing press in Wales. It is very difficult to tell just how many of the people of Wales were able to read in the early seventeenth century, but it is almost certain that it could not have been more than 20 per cent of them, at best, and the actual figure may have been as low as 10 per cent. Adding to that difficulty was the absence of a printing press. Indeed, the former may well have arisen from the latter – because there was no printing press, there was little opportunity for people to learn to read. Wales was economically such a poor country and the printing industry so capital-intensive that the money simply did not exist to establish it. Neither did Wales enjoy the advantages of a buoyant trade and industry which might have brought in their wake busy commercial routes, prosperous cities and towns, flourishing schools and universities, and produced enough of those well-heeled middle classes and successful artisans that might be expected to provide the natural sources of supply for a market of bookbuyers. If in these circumstances, therefore, writers of Welsh origin aspired to publish their books they were obliged to look to London to seek out the services of printers. This proved to be so costly and troublesome an exercise that Welsh authors had little choice but to look for well-to-do patrons to pay for the printing costs or else, as often as not, to foot the bill themselves. Seeing a book through the press in London was a more than ordinarily expensive operation. The London printers invariably complained that they found the Welsh language very strange and difficult to set, which, of course, added to the costs – and to their errors! A Welsh writer generally found that he usually had to stay in London, where accommodation was always very expensive, to supervise the passage of his work through the press and correct as many of the multifarious printer's errors as he could. The inevitable outcome of such a laboriously produced and error-strewn finished product among an already limited Welsh reading public was a necessarily slow and restricted circulation and readership.

Simultaneously pouring from the press, of course, was a prolific stream of literature in English in the shape of bibles, prayer books, texts, commentaries, sermons, and other devotional books of every kind, of which educated Welsh people might avail themselves. A minority of the Welsh were familiar with English and literate in it. English had been used in Wales since medieval times, but most of the Welsh still were only able to manage their own language.[32] The last decades of the sixteenth century and the first of the seventeenth century had seen considerable progress in this respect. The key to the propagation of Protestant doctrine and worship in Wales, as in a number of European countries, lay in the successful translation into the vernacular of the Bible and the service book, together with the spread of literacy and regular preaching. The paramount achievement of the Welsh Church in the sixteenth century had been Bishop William Morgan's magnificent translation of the Welsh Bible (1588) and the Book of Common Prayer (1599). Regular reading of these texts in the Welsh parish churches, week in and week out, over the year had familiarized those who heard them with the teaching, vocabulary and worship of the Church. Preaching sermons based on the vernacular scriptures, although admittedly much less frequent than might have been desired, all helped to engender among the hearers a genuine attachment, which contributed markedly to the anger felt by many when the use of the Prayer Book came to be banned by the Puritans. Among the clergy responsible for conducting these devotions in the early Stuart period, university graduates and former pupils of grammar schools were increasing in numbers.[33] Although not all of them were preachers, it was from their midst that the most effectual pulpit performers were drawn. Great emphasis was placed upon the effective use of the pulpit, as may be gauged from the increasing tendency on the part of the corporations of towns like Haverfordwest or Swansea to pay for sermons delivered by visiting lecturers.[34]

Religious literature, too, was being produced and circulated with growing enthusiasm. During the reign of James I major steps forward were again taken in the field of biblical translation. In England, in 1611, the Authorized Version of the

English Bible, stemming from decisions reached at the Hampton Court Conference (1604), was published and, on the strength of its intrinsic merits, superseded all other translations of the Bible into English. Its appearance quickly spurred on two Welsh translators – Bishop Parry of St Asaph and his brother-in-law, Dr John Davies of Mallwyd, to bring out a broadly comparable Welsh version in 1620.[35] This translation incorporated all the merits of the Authorized Version and it owed most to the superb gifts of Dr Davies as a linguist and represented an improvement on even William Morgan's masterpiece of 1588. One of its translators, Bishop Parry, summed up not only his own and Dr Davies's reactions but also those of all other contributors, who had had an earlier share in the work since the first New Testament and Book of Common Prayer had appeared in Welsh in 1567:

> And if it should be given to me to please my God and my King and help the Welsh people, I shall attain what was uppermost in my prayers, what was my chief care in my work and will be a comfort to me as long as I shall live.[36]

Soon after the Bible of 1620 came from the press, there appeared in 1621 an edition of the Book of Common Prayer, revised in accordance with the text of the Bible of 1620. The superb quality of the Welsh embodied in both works owed most to the flawless scholarship of John Davies, one of the most masterly Welsh grammarians of all time. For centuries, these texts were to be those that were the best known to all Welsh-speaking congregations in parish churches and to the denizens of those private households in which domestic worship was offered. They represented a major advance in making Protestant services intelligible to worshippers, by whom they were warmly received. In contrast to the praise heaped upon the Bible for its contribution to keeping the Welsh language alive and vigorous, much less has been heard in favour of the Book of Common Prayer. Its role has been passed over with very much less comment, possibly because it played no part in the Nonconformist worship familiar to the majority of the Welsh population from the early nineteenth century, whereas the Bible was at the heart of it.

Bound up along with the Prayer Book of 1621,which was to prove seminal in the development of religion in Wales, was Edmwnd Prys's metrical translation of the Psalms. Prys was a great master of the Welsh language and its traditional verse forms, and he now deployed his talents to splendid effect in rendering many of the Psalms into intelligible Welsh verse. Here, for example, is his version of Psalm 51:

> Duw, crea galon bur,
> Dod imi gysur beunydd;
> I fyw yn well tra fwy'n y byd
> Dod ynof ysbryd newydd.
>
> Bydd dda wrth Seion fryn,
> O Arglwydd hyn a fynni,
> Ac wrth Gaersalem, dy dref tad,
> A gwna adeilad arni.
> (Create in me a clean heart, O God.)[37]

Prys's translation proved to be exceptionally popular among the people, not only in the age in which they appeared but also for centuries afterwards. No fewer than ninety-five editions of the work appeared between 1621 and 1865, i.e. an average of one edition every two and a half years.[38]

Ten years after the publication of the Bible of 1620, another hardly less formidable breakthrough was achieved, when the first modestly priced edition of the Welsh Bible was published. *Y Beibl Bach* ('The Little Bible') of 1630 was specifically intended for family and domestic use and was published at the very much lower price of 5*s*., though it should be remembered that this was the average cost of a sheep at the time. The *Beibl Bach* was the fruit of an initiative undertaken by two earnest Protestants – 'church Puritans', as they were known – both of Welsh extraction: Thomas Middleton (1580–1631) and Rowland Heylin (?1582–1631), both of whom had successfully made their way in the world of trade as London merchants. Their intention in publishing this edition of the Bible was to make it, in their own words, 'a familiar friend' in Welsh homes: 'it must dwell in thy chamber, under thine own roof, as thy friend, eating of thy bread, like a dearest companion and chief adviser.'[39] Admirable intentions! But, alas, judging by some of the comments passed in the 1640s, even after the publication of *Y Beibl Bach*, it seems that bibles were still at a premium in Wales. Thus, Vavasor Powell declared in 1646 'that there was not one in five hundred families who possessed one', and another observation made in 1649 estimated the figure at one in twenty.[40] It would be unsafe to take these figures at face value; Puritan authors were better known for resounding phrases than statistical exactitude in their calculations. Yet, despite the wide discrepancy between these two estimates, it is evident from both sources that possession of a bible was regarded as a great rarity. The Puritan author, Oliver Thomas, contrasted the Welsh unfavourably with the English on this score; whereas bibles were so scarce among the former, among the latter there was 'hardly one who could not read and even among men and women of the lowest classes; tinkers and coopers and the like, having their Bibles and familiar with them'.[41] It should, however, be borne in mind that the aim of Middleton and Heylin in drawing upon the resources of the prosperous and well-intentioned among Welsh businessmen in London and elsewhere with a view to publishing bibles and other religious works in Welsh for distribution among the deserving poor at greatly reduced prices, or even free, had thereby opened a path that was so painstakingly to be trodden by their later followers in the Welsh Trust, the SPCK and the Welsh circulating schools with unswerving devotion.

Another essential part of the Church's panoply of instruction, and one that could be employed in reading and instruction at home and at work as well as in church, was the Catechism, copies of which might be printed as separate publications as well as being included regularly in each edition of the Book of Common Prayer. Complaints had often been heard in the sixteenth century that the practice of catechizing children was being neglected, but it would appear from the number of the editions of the Catechism being printed in the seventeenth century that it was now being more regularly used.[42] Among the more popular publications of this kind in use at this time was the volume known as *Llyfr Plygain* ('Book of Matins'). Its contents brought together in a single volume a curious miscellany of items, many of a secular nature. But it also included the Catechism, the Athanasian Creed, and a number of psalms. It was originally published late in the sixteenth century, but at least four editions of it appeared during the first half of the seventeenth century: in 1607, 1612, 1618 and 1633 (the last edited by Dr John Davies of Mallwyd), a further thirteen editions of it being issued in the years down to 1791.[43]

The sermon, as was to be expected, was an indispensable medium for instruction and inspiration among parish congregations. That fiery brand among early Puritan evangelists, Vavasor Powell, was so convinced of the sovereign worth of the sermon that he was emphatically of the opinion that he would not give up a sermon for the printing of a thousand books![44] That was not untypical of Vavasor's colourfully exaggerated eloquence when striving to make his point. Powell was, no doubt, all too conscious of complaints that had been voiced for nearly a century about the infrequency of sermons, especially those being preached in the Welsh language. He seems to have been the only one among his own contemporaries who knew anything about John Penry, that most devastating of Welsh critics of the absence of sermons in Welsh. Penry had pilloried the Elizabethan clergy mercilessly for being 'dumb dogs' who never preached and the bishops who abused their office for presenting such inept men to livings.[45] Such criticisms were too harsh, however; the best Elizabethan bishops, like Richard Davies of St David's (1561–81) or William Morgan of St Asaph (1601–4), not only untiringly preached themselves but also unceasingly impressed upon their clergy the need for regular preaching. Certainly, towards the end of the sixteenth century and the beginning of the seventeenth there had been notable progress in this direction. Robert Llwyd's effusive praise of the efforts of the St Asaph clergy has earlier been quoted (see above) and recent work on clerical education during the period has revealed the substantial increase in the numbers of graduates and preachers in all the Welsh dioceses.[46]

All this notwithstanding, hard-hitting complaints were still being aired about a dearth of preachers and sermons, especially in the Welsh language. Bishop Bayly of Bangor, in a report dated 1623, told of many churches in his diocese where there was a deplorable lack of preaching, as well as a neglect of other priestly duties, such as the christening of children, visiting the sick, and burying the dead.[47] In 1630, in sharp contrast to Robert Llwyd's encomium about the clergy of St Asaph, a clergyman from the same diocese presented a very different view. Oliver Thomas was a committed Puritan and an industrious author, who claimed in his book, *Car-wr y Cymry* ('A Lover of the Welsh', 1631) that there were between 40 and 60 churches in Powys whose congregations had never heard a sermon. Similarly, Vavasor Powell asserted in 1641 that there were not, 'upon strict inquiry, so many conscientious and constant preachers as there were of counties in Wales'.[48] It would be risky to accept these estimates literally without making allowances for a tendency to overstatement on the part of Puritan authors; yet it seems impossible not to accept that the country was suffering from a shortage of sermons, especially those being preached in the Welsh language, at this time.

No small part of the reason for the lack of sermons lay in the inability of a number of the clergy to prepare their own discourses – either because they were too meanly educated to do so or else because they were unable to preach in Welsh. Such deficiencies in clerical education and the link between them and the absence of sermons had long been recognized in England, where as early as 1547, a *Book of Homilies*, a collection of authorized sermons composed by some of the foremost clerics of the Anglican Church had been set forth in print, so that they might be used in the pulpits by other clerics. It is impossible to estimate accurately how much use of the *Book of Homilies* was made in Wales; not very much, it is tempting to suppose, since impoverished Welsh-speaking parishes were hardly likely to have spent much money on English books. In view of the acute shortage of Welsh-language preachers and the urgent need for a similar publication in Wales, the early appearance of a Welsh translation of the *Homilies* might have been anticipated, yet it was not, in fact, until 1606 that Edward James, a protégé of William Morgan and chancellor of Llandaff diocese, published the Welsh version of it. Although James produced an excellent translation, the style of which owed much to Morgan's flowing prose as its exemplar, it does not seem to have met with much success. Whereas forty-four editions of the English *Book of Homilies* appeared between 1547 and 1657, it was not until the nineteenth century (1817) that a second imprint of the Welsh version was deemed to be worth undertaking.[49]

Most of the prose literature on religious subjects written in Welsh during the first half of the seventeenth century consisted of translations. At first sight, that might appear to be surprising, since it is notoriously difficult for translators to avoid following too closely the idioms and speech rhythms of the original authors whose work they are translating; but, on reflection, the practice becomes more easily understood. The prime motive of the Welsh littérateurs was to ensure the religious well-being of their readers rather than to enhance their own literary reputation. So they translated those classics – usually written in English – which had already won a secure place in the respect and affection of the reading public; the work of those men who were described by one of the Welsh writers as 'powerful and effectual workers in the vineyard of the spirit'. In that way, the translators were surer of themselves and of their readers. As David Rowlands (*flor.* sixteenth century) put it, 'it became an accustomed practice in all languages to translate works of godly and devoted men to add to knowledge, enlarge understanding and purify morals and Christian practice.'[50] Nearly all the works in question were aimed at raising the level of day-to-day belief and conduct. Most of what they contained was evidently directed at those heads of households charged with being good Christians themselves and with fashioning in the same mould 'their children and their households to bring them up securely in the faith'.[51] Authors expressed their intention of writing in a plain, unadorned style, 'contenting myself', to quote Robert Llwyd, 'with such words as the commonalty of the country are familiar with and understand'.[52] Not that such protestations should lead it to be supposed that they wrote in debased fashion. On the contrary, by 1640, Welsh prose had reached a pitch of high mastery. Three generations of writers had created a new, pliant and virile prose, which conveyed to those of their countrymen who were literate and interested the core truths of the Christian religion. Just how many of the Welsh population could read at this time cannot be said with any great certainty. It seems doubtful whether they numbered more than 10 to 20 per cent, but there were probably many others who may have been illiterate but were nevertheless anxious to listen to those members of the literate minority who were sufficiently concerned and well-disposed to read to them.[53]

Welsh poetry, like Welsh prose, also had its distinct contribution to make to the religious life of the age. This was particularly true of the *canu rhydd* (free-metre poetry). The kinds of poetry devised in the free metres were much beloved of the Welsh at this time. Erasmus Saunders, a cleric of south-west Wales (1674–1734), was later to describe his fellow countrymen as 'being naturally addicted to poetry; so some of the more skilful and knowing among them frequently composed a kind of Divine Hymns or Songs'.[54] Poems of this kind that were especially well loved were the *cwndid* of south-east Wales and the *halsingod* of south-west Wales. The two most influential among these free-metre poets of the early-seventeenth century were Edmwnd Prys and Rhys Prichard. The phenomenal success achieved by Prys's translation of the Psalms has already been referred to above. Much the same might be said of Rhys Prichard's verses. What had led the Old Vicar to turn religious instruction into verse on behalf of ordinary people was the sight of their 'ignoring sincere preaching but remembering vain songs'.[55] So he poured forth a mass of popular religious verse in plain language and easily memorizable metre. At first, he had had no intention of printing these verses. However, although designed for oral transmission, they soon became so popular that they were widely copied into manuscripts, the availability of which encouraged many of the illiterate to learn to read. As long as the large majority of the populace remained illiterate or, at best, semi-literate, these poems were, perhaps, the most effective medium of religious teaching. The Vicar himself confessed:

> Ni cheisiais ddim cywreinwaith
> Ond mesur esmwyth perffaith.
> Hawdd i'w ddysgu ar fyr dro
> Can un a'i clywo deirgwaith.

(I never sought any artistic composition but a smooth and easy measure, easily and quickly learned by anyone who heard it three times.)[56]

Much of Prichard's widely circulated verse was somewhat uninspired and pedestrian stuff; but at his best he could strike a genuinely poetic note, as, for instance, in the following stanzas:

> Och! Pa galon na thosturia,
> Chwipio Christ am bechod Adda.
> Lladd bugail am fai'r defaid,
> Crogi'r Prins i gadw'i ddeiliaid.
>
> Gwerthu'r Meistr i brynu'r gweision,
> Lladd y Mab i gadw'i elynion.
> Mwrdro'r meddyg, brathu'i ystlys,
> Gael ei waed i helpu'r clwyfus.

(O what heart would not feel pity! Flogging Christ for Adam's sins; slaying the shepherd for the sins of the sheep. Hanging the prince to save his subjects. Murdering the physician, wounding his side, to shed his blood to help the injured.)[57]

At a more rarefied and sophisticated level, there flowered the exquisite English verse of Welsh-born poets like George Herbert (1593–1633) and Henry Vaughan (1622–95), although it has to be admitted that few of their own countrymen had ever heard of their poetry, let alone read it. All the same, in its own fashion it bears moving testimony to the affection in which the Church was held by men of their standing and its power to shake them to the depths of their being. Even though their verse may have been unknown to most Welsh people, there is no reason to suppose that the poets' profound regard for the established religion was not shared by many others who remained mute and inglorious.

It is also worth remembering at this point that the Roman Catholic communities, although small and still under heavy pressure, were also able to make widespread use of vernacular literature in their devotions. Printing recusant books in English or Welsh was a hazardous operation, which called for access to printing presses on the Continent, since the king's government exercised strict control over those located in England. If and when such printing was successfully accomplished in Europe, there still remained the formidable task of smuggling the 'contraband' books into the realm and getting them circulated clandestinely among the faithful. Catholic authors were often obliged to resort to publication by means of manuscripts copied by devoted Catholic scribes, such as Llywelyn Siôn (1540–1615),[58] who devoted their whole lives to the laborious and perilous task. Their reward was the knowledge that several hand-written copies of much-treasured texts like *Directori Cristionogawl* ('Christian Directory') or *Sallwyr Iesu* ('Jesus' Psalter') were going the rounds of Catholic communities at the same time. These works were nearly all translations composed by their authors in the same sort of plain, intelligible style as that adopted by their Protestant adversaries. It was intended that they too should be understood by the 'unlearned', i.e., those who had had no formal education but were not necessarily illiterate, and certainly not uninterested. These Catholic books were the output of a handful of dedicated priests like Robert Gwyn (*flor.* 1568–1600) or Rhosier Smyth (1541–1628).[59] Such works might often be read aloud at Catholic services when no priest was available to officiate. In addition to these prose offerings, a number of Welsh Catholic poems survive from the period. These were original compositions, not translations, and were much appreciated by those who read or heard them. This Catholic literature has a double interest. It not only underscores the value of Welsh literature in maintaining Catholic beliefs but it also reveals the shared inheritance of Catholics and Protestants in the ancient literary patrimony of Wales and their inextinguishable pride in it.[60]

After Charles I had succeeded his father in 1625 there seems at first to have been an upsurge in Catholic numbers – possibly because persecution had lost something of its edge during the king's 'personal rule' from 1629 to 1640, when he no longer had to placate a Puritanly inclined House of Commons. None the less, the feeling of alarm which an apparent increase in the size of the papist minority could awaken in the minds of the population was quite disproportionate to the actual number of recusants involved, although Catholics might be emboldened to stand forth more openly and in greater numbers as a result of a somewhat more conciliatory attitude on the part of the king. The most highly publicized example of that increased Catholic temerity in Wales was witnessed at St Winifred's Well in Holywell, Flintshire, on the saint's day in November 1629, when an estimated 1400–1600 people, including two members of the peerage, a number of knights and many squires and gentry, as well as crowds of commoners, foregathered there. This open demonstration of strength and confidence on the Catholic side greatly alarmed the bishop of St Asaph and many other Protestants, both inside and outside Wales, at the increasing influence that the ancient well-shrine appeared to be exercising over the Catholic faithful in Wales and the North and Midlands.[61] Extensive fears of the extent of sympathy for the papist cause believed to be harboured at court, combined with the alarm signals sounded by Catholic victories in the Thirty Years War (1618–48) in Europe, served to intensify concern at what was interpreted as being evidence for a secret Catholic 'Fifth Column', made all the more sinister by the proximity of Catholic Ireland to Wales. What added further to the fears of Welsh Protestants was that the most powerful landowner in Wales, the Earl of Worcester, was an openly avowed Catholic.

The differences between Charles I and his father as rulers were becoming readily apparent. Although Charles was far less given to theorizing about the 'Divine Right of Kings' than his father, he was, in practice, much more stubborn and less conciliatory. Relationships between him and those of his subjects who were politically conscious and articulate tended to deteriorate markedly between 1625 and 1629. These differences found expression in the early Parliaments of Charles's reign. Added to the political discontents was a growing divergence between the king and Parliament over matters of religion. Charles was a tolerant man by nature, but he was married to a Catholic wife, Henrietta Maria, which led to a widespread supposition that he was overly sympathetic to her co-religionists. Certainly, Catholics had grown in number during Charles's reign – in Wales as well as in England – but this increase seems to have been more apparent than real, and attributable less to royal sympathy than to the more careful scrutiny and reporting of recusants on the part of those officials responsible for their detection. Although Charles himself remained a staunch and devoted Anglican, he had, unlike his father, abandoned Calvinist beliefs. Like his archbishop of Canterbury, William Laud,[62] Charles had adopted Arminian beliefs and High Church attitudes. From 1629 to 1640 he ruled without once summoning Parliament, and during these years, his religious stance became increasingly unacceptable to those of his subjects who were Puritan in sympathy.

Puritans drew their inspiration from an emphasis on the most distinctively Calvinist aspects of belief, worship, morality and organization. These included an emphasis on what Puritan enthusiasts perceived to be the unique authority of God's Word and the centrality of preaching it; simpler and more scriptural forms of worship, discipline and organization; the immediate responsibility of each individual believer for becoming convinced of his or her election to salvation by predestined divine decision, and the obligation thereafter resting upon them to make manifest the fruits of grace in everyday conduct and morality. Such attitudes also tended to embrace the rejection of all High Church trends in the direction of 'idolatry' and other such external signs and symbols. Puritan values and attitudes of this kind made their liveliest appeal wherever religious and social circumstances had favoured the earliest nourishment of Reforming opinion; wherever Protestant sermons had been most frequent and fervent, literacy prevalent, habits of Bible reading and household devotions regular and deep-rooted, mistrust of the pretensions of bishops and priests to authority over laymen widespread, claims for the validity of personal experience forcefully upheld, and the Puritan work-ethic eagerly adopted.[63]

Such characteristics were commonly found in the towns and counties of eastern and southern England. They could hardly be expected to flourish anything like as vigorously in what Puritans were wont to describe as the 'dark corners of the land' such as Wales. As the early Cardiff Puritan, William Erbury (1604–54), put it so pessimistically, 'Wales is a poor oppressed people and despised also.'[64] Yet even in Wales, if palpably less pronounced and influential, these Puritan characteristics were by no means entirely absent. Some traces of preliminary conditioning for the advance of Puritanism had clearly been observable in the early seventeenth century in those places where the English language was commonly spoken and English bibles more widely distributed; where there had been more fervent preaching in both languages, and greater insistence on the place of the Bible and its authority, a tentative programme of the publication of mildly Puritan literature in Welsh, and the dissemination of Prys's translation of the Psalms and the poems of Vicar Prichard and others like him, a quasi-Puritan awareness showed signs of early growth.

Some of the most flourishing centres of Puritan allegiance were to be found in the same sort of places where recusant loyalties were also apparent, most notably along the former Marches between England and Wales. That becomes easier to understand when it is recalled that these regions had a long tradition of lax management; here, where administrative boundaries and the jurisdiction of dioceses, no less than lordships, were less sharply demarcated and less rigorously observed, it was not easy to enforce discipline. When frontiers were loosely defined, it was often comparatively easy to slip from one zone of responsibility to a neighbouring one. Earlier examples of the way in which the unorthodox and heretical could exploit the possibilities were provided by the activities of the fifteenth-century Lollards. Late Renaissance Roman Catholics were to repeat the process of eluding the authorities in the Tudor and early Stuart eras. So did Puritans in the seventeenth century. In the same districts there also survived long-established patterns for more lawful, regular and busy trafficking by land and sea on the part of merchants, traders, officials, labourers and other travellers. Many Welsh people were attracted from the south Welsh seaboard to ports on the other side of the Bristol Channel, notably to Bristol itself and Gloucester. Similarly, from inland Welsh counties they were drawn to towns and cities along the English border, especially to Chester, Oswestry, Shrewsbury, Ludlow and Hereford. By the end of the sixteenth century there was a colony of Welsh expatriates to be found in almost every one of these border towns, big and small. In these urban centres, in Wales and in England, there usually existed industrious and mostly literate social groups, to some of whose members Puritan doctrines tended to make a well-defined appeal. There was a lively exchange not only of material goods but also of religious ideals which, in turn, spread into Wales. There, such values might often be stimulated by the sermons preached by eager Puritan preachers or lecturers, paid for by town corporations or interested individuals in places like Wrexham, Cardiff, Swansea or Haverfordwest.[65]

By the 1630s, when bishops in Wales sought to carry out those inquiries enjoined on them by Archbishop Laud more rigorously in their dioceses, they uncovered unmistakable shoots of Puritan sympathies. The diocese most attracted to such aspirations was Llandaff, and especially the county of Monmouthshire, from which a number of the early pioneers were drawn. The apostle of the first Puritan church in Wales was a Monmouthshire man, William Wroth (1576–1641), an Oxford graduate, who was made rector of Llanfaches, a small parish lying between Chepstow and Newport, on 17 July 1617, at the presentation of King James I. For nearly twenty years before he came under censure from his bishop in the 1630s, Wroth had, by means of his eloquent preaching and the example of his personal sanctity, succeeded in converting many from what a Puritan source criticized as their 'sinful courses in the world'. These converts he subsequently gathered into 'the gospel order of church government'.[66] Among the multitudes who rapturously came to Llanfaches were believers not only from other parts of Monmouthshire but also from Welsh counties like Glamorgan and Brecon and, in addition, from the English border shires. One of those most deeply swayed was William Erbury; son of a merchant from Roath near Cardiff, and a graduate of both Oxford and Cambridge universities, Erbury was ordained deacon in 1626 and served for some years as a curate at Newport. Having become vicar of St Mary's, Cardiff, in 1633, he preached Puritan doctrine with all the fervour of his somewhat excitable and unstable mind. His curate there was Walter Cradock (?1610–59), yet another Monmouthshire man, an Oxford graduate, and a preacher of exceptional gifts. He was to become a leader so venerated that Puritans in later years were oftentimes known as 'Cradockites' in Wales.

It was soon after becoming archbishop of Canterbury in 1633 that Laud had revived the Court of High Commission. In 1634 Charles I, as result of his archbishop's willingly accepted persuasion, instituted a new and more vigorous drive against Puritans. He now issued instructions to each of his bishops requiring them to present an annual report 'so that we may see how the whole church is governed and our commands obeyed'. Earlier, in 1633, Bishop Murray of Llandaff had been able to certify that he 'had not one refractory, nonconformist or schismatical minister' and only 'two lecturers and they are both licensed preachers'. But in 1634, in pursuit of the king's commands, Murray described both Erbury and Cradock as having preached 'very schismatically and dangerously'. Erbury was given a stern warning not to persist with such activities, while Cradock, adjudged by his bishop to be a 'bold, ignorant fellow', had had his licence to preach taken away from him.[67] He now left Glamorgan and found a more congenial habitat in Wrexham, where he spent several months in 1635–6.[68]

In the neighbouring diocese of St David's, reports of similar activities were presented. Puritan lecturers were being encouraged in the major boroughs and trading centres of Haverfordwest and Tenby, both of which had large populations of English-speakers and had been long-term centres of advanced Protestant sympathies.[69] In 1634 the bishop of St David's, Theophilus Field, suspended an unnamed lecturer for 'inconformity', and in the following year dismissed others of the same kind for comparable offences. In 1636 Field drew attention to the vexatious conduct of one Marmaduke Matthews (1603–83) on the eastern edge of his diocese in the deanery of Gower. Matthews, a native of Llangyfelach near Swansea, and an Oxford graduate, was vicar of Penmaen in Gower, and was charged by his bishop with having preached against the 'keeping of all holy days, with divers others, as fond, of profane opinions'. In 1638, Matthews, seemingly weary of sustained episcopal pressure on him, emigrated to New England, where he became a Puritan pastor.[70]

Nor were parts of north Wales, especially in those areas close to the English borders, lacking in Puritan sympathies. Although Bishop Parry of St Asaph had reported in the year 1634 that his diocese was untouched by nonconformity, he had overlooked one important fact: that in the town of Wrexham, the largest urban centre in his diocese and the most populous town of north Wales, the eminent Puritan author and lecturer, Oliver Thomas, was busily engaged in making converts. It was to Wrexham that Walter Cradock decamped from Cardiff in

1635 and remained there for eleven months, in the course of which he drew large crowds to hear him preach as early as six o'clock in the morning. He was to be joined by the adolescent and prodigiously gifted Morgan Llwyd (1619–59) from Ardudwy, at once to become one of his most promising disciples. It was Cradock, too, who converted Vavasor Powell (1617–70), a Radnorshire man, who was later to develop into one of Wales's best-known and most outspoken Puritans.[71]

In spite of the attachment of Wrexham people to Oliver Thomas, Walter Cradock was not allowed to remain long in their town, being driven out by the opposition of some of the more orthodox citizens. Wrexham, however, remained a dynamic centre of Puritan activity, and it may very well have been in that town that the bishop of Hereford had arrested an anonymous Puritan conventicle of 'mean persons' in 1640. In the preceding year he had already felt compelled to complain of a company of 'Brownists' (i.e., the followers of Robert Brown, d. 1633) – a term often used to denote believers in a tendency to separatism – on the borders of his diocese, 'in that part . . . adjoining to Wales'. He castigated them for preaching 'dangerous errors and stirring up the people to follow them'. He also added the significant note, 'when they hear of an inquiry, they slip over the border to another diocese.' We may have here a reference to the origins of the Baptist church associated with the Olchon Valley.[72]

It was to Brampton Bryan, over the border in England, home of that major benefactor of early Puritans, Sir Robert Harley (1579–1656) and his wife, Brilliana,[73] that Walter Cradock and his converts, Llwyd and Powell, appeared to have retired for a time to find protection and encouragement. It was not long, however, before Cradock and Llwyd were drawn southward again by the magnetic attraction of Llanfaches, lovingly referred to by Puritans as 'Antioch, the mother church of that Gentile country'.[74] Here, William Wroth, 'Apostle of Wales', having appeared before the Court of High Commission, and being compelled to yield up his benefice, had in November 1639 gathered his people into a 'gospel order of government' along lines formulated by Puritan communities across the Atlantic in New England. The church at Llanfaches was not overtly separated from the Church of England. Its leaders considered themselves as being 'separated from the world and not the saints'.[75] However, the Laudian canons laid down in 1640 permitted no compromise, and Wroth's church at Llanfaches is generally regarded as the first Nonconformist church to be established in Wales.

The precedent created by Wroth and his followers was followed in other parts of Wales. Not far away, in the county of Glamorgan, William Erbury established another independent church before the outbreak of civil war in 1642. A third church is mentioned in a late but well-informed source on the early development of Puritanism in Wales – the account written by a Welsh Puritan leader, Henry Maurice, as late as 1675. Maurice assigns priority among the Welsh churches in Glamorgan to the 'saints of Merthyr' (Tydfil), and also to 'the church that meets at Swansea, gathered at first by Mr Ambrose Mostyn'.[76] The church at Merthyr was reported to have been constituted about 1642, but little can be gleaned about its earliest beginnings. By the 1650s, however, Merthyr was unquestionably a robust and self-assertive centre of Puritan beliefs.[77] That church founded by Ambrose Mostyn was better attested. Mostyn was a scion of the well-known Mostyn family of Flintshire and an Oxford graduate who was appointed a lecturer in the parish of Pennard (Gower) in April 1642. It was the only lectureship of its kind to be set up in Wales by the Long Parliament; but before Mostyn could achieve anything very much, civil war had broken out in August 1642. In the meantime, up in Mostyn's native north-east Wales, the Puritans of Wrexham and the surrounding district were more lively than ever, with the yeomen and traders of the neighbourhood being notorious for their addiction 'to gadding to sermons'.[78] The truth was that Puritan believers, active and enthusiastic as they might be in some limited districts, were no more than a tiny minority of the population of Wales as a whole. The large majority remained loyal in their allegiance to the Church 'by law established', even though so many of them continued to be woefully ill instructed and badly informed about the nature and teaching of that Church. They were its adherents far more by inheritance and usage than from conviction or belief.

2
The Civil War and Interregnum

During the years from 1640 to 1642 both political and religious tensions between Anglicans and Puritans inevitably intensified. The Laudian canons of 1640 insisted on the acceptance by all the king's subjects of the doctrine, ceremonies and government of the Anglican Church, and laid down that the whole population must attend their parish churches to receive communion. There were some, even in areas so little attracted to Puritan ideals as Wales, to whom such orders were objectionable in whole or part, and demarcation disputes become more heated, leaving little room for compromise. Religious disagreement was widened by the growing political hostility between king and Parliament; to such an extent that, in August 1642, Charles I raised his standard at Nottingham and declared war on his disaffected subjects. At the outbreak of hostilities, much the greater part of the Welsh people, including nearly all the clergy, sided with the king. Although there were in most Welsh counties individuals and families with inclinations towards the Parliamentary and Puritan cause, including those who primarily had their own private interests to serve by lending such support, the large majority favoured the Crown. Most of them were also, to a greater or lesser degree, in favour of the Established Church, the Book of Common Prayer, and the accustomed forms of worship. In the words of the leading Welsh poet, Huw Morus:

> Ti fuost gyfannedd, yn cynnal trefn santedd,
> Ac athro' r gwirionedd, cysonedd i sain.[1]

> (Thou wast a dwelling-place, maintaining a holy order, a teacher of truth, constant in its intention.)

Among the staunchest supporters of the Crown were the Roman Catholic recusants, presumably because they took it for granted that, however disappointing King Charles had been in his treatment of them, he was very much less hostile to them than Parliament and the Puritans were likely to be if they triumphed. Numerically the Roman Catholics may not have been as strong as has frequently been suggested. Open recusants numbered only about 4.6 per cent of the Welsh population, although the people of Wales amounted to something of the order of 6.8 per cent of the population of England and Wales as a whole.[2] However, the numbers of recusants in the official returns were almost certainly considerably lower than they should have been. They should have included in addition many sympathizers, some of whom were actual believers and many others who were known to be to be very well-disposed. All of these succeeded in concealing their real allegiance from the none too efficient officials who carried out inquiries into their loyalties and activities. Furthermore, in their midst, the recusants could count on the unconcealed loyalty of the Earl of Worcester, generally regarded as the wealthiest of the king's supporters and a man who was later to claim that he had spent £900,000 of his own money in support of the king's cause during the course of the wars.

Wales was important to the Crown for two main reasons: first, as a recruiting ground for troops; and second, as a source of money. Not that the thousands of Welsh infantrymen raised for the king's armies proved to be all that valuable, mainly because the poor fellows were, for the most part, ill trained, poorly armed, badly led and indisciplined. Consequently, they suffered disproportionately heavy losses in battles that were to prove to be much the bloodiest conflicts ever fought in the island of Britain, leaving them deeply disillusioned by their experience of warfare.

In the meantime, the tiny minority of convinced Puritans in Wales were obliged to keep their heads down well below the parapet and make themselves as inconspicuous as possible. A number went into hiding and some were imprisoned. A leader as prominent and articulate as Vavasor Powell, as might be expected, found himself being hounded so persistently in Breconshire that he felt he had no choice but to flee to London for safety. Walter Cradock's people at Llanfaches deemed it necessary to seek sanctuary with their Baptist brethren meeting at Broadmead Church in Bristol. That proved to be no permanent resting-place for them, however, when the Royalist armies captured the city in July 1643. Having managed to evade seizure by a hair's breadth, Cradock and what remained of the Llanfaches church were forced to escape hotfoot to London, where they joined the Puritan church of All Hallows the Great, meeting in Thames Street.[3] Back home in Wales, the goods of some of the Puritan faithful were being seized by Royalists, which led Parliament to establish the Committee of Plundered Ministers to protect their interests. That Welsh stalwart, William Erbury, always took pride in relating how he had been the first to benefit from that committee's labours.[4]

As the war proceeded, however, there was movement in the opposite direction in the shape of Anglican exiles fleeing from Puritan pressure in England to seek safety in Royalist Wales. They numbered among them fugitives as eminent as Archbishops John Williams and James Ussher, and Dr Jeremy Taylor. Archbishop Williams found refuge in his native north Wales where, in Dr Thomas Richards's words, 'he committed virtually all the sins of a delinquent by deserting his province of York, helping the commissioners of the King in North Wales and fortifying Conway Castle at his own expense'.[5] Archbishop Ussher sought sanctuary at the Stradlings' home, St Donat's Castle, where he found his hosts' magnificent library very much to his taste.[6] Jeremy Taylor, chaplain to Lord Carbery at Golden Grove, Carmarthenshire, from 1645 onwards, made the most of his peaceful surroundings to write some of his finest books there (see below).[7]

Parliament, for its part, bestirred itself in trying to raise clerical standards in Wales in the hope of advancing the Puritan cause there. The Committee for Plundered Ministers came into existence in December 1642 to replace the earlier Committee for Scandalous Ministers; and County Committees, also, were set up wherever that proved possible. Their purpose was to expel, as and when they could, those ministers considered to be below the required standard. In Glamorgan, they deemed thirty-five incumbents to be unsatisfactory, and a further eighteen in Monmouthshire, all of whom they ejected. On the other hand, many incumbents adjudged to be 'good men' were left in their livings unmolested.[8] Parliament was also much concerned to take account of the need for more Welsh preaching in Wales. A Committee of the House of Commons was set up in June 1644 to appoint Welsh-speaking preachers who would accompany the Parliamentary commander, Sir Thomas Middleton, on his campaign into the Severn Valley. County Committees were also instructed to ensure that there should be preaching in Welsh as well as in English in those districts for which they were held responsible. Parliament further recognized that a successful ministry was dependent to a considerable extent on the finances available to its 'oppressed' servants. Thus, in 1643, £300 was set aside out of income derived from the lands of Llandaff diocese. This sum was intended to provide stipends for the three itinerant ministers of south Wales, viz., Walter Cradock, Henry Walter and Richard Symonds; while in 1648 the Committee for Plundered Ministers authorized payment of £120 to Morgan Llwyd and £100 each to Vavasor Powell and Ambrose Mostyn, their counterparts in north Wales. Walter Cradock, himself one of the most silver-tongued of all Parliamentary preachers, went into ecstasies about the success attained by the Puritan preachers at work during these years, proclaiming in 1646: 'The gospel has run over the mountains between Breconshire and Monmouthshire like fire in the thatch.'[9] The House of Commons, the House of Lords, and the Committee for Plundered Ministers had undoubtedly exerted themselves to some effect and, between them, had appointed 130 ministers in Wales during these years.[10] But not all of them reached those standards so rapturously trumpeted by Walter Cradock. There is no reason to doubt that some among the newcomers were self-seeking converts, and the fact remains that a large majority of Welsh livings were retained in the hands of episcopal clergy, only a minority of whom would be considered to be effectual preachers by any standards.

In the course of the military campaigns fought between 1642 and 1646, both sides had suffered setbacks; the Royalists to a considerably greater extent than the Parliamentarians. The outcome was that the pressures on Wales had increased conspicuously: casualties among the troops were very heavy; a number of towns, fortified places and churches suffered severely; and the cattle, cloth and coal trades – mainstays of Welsh economic life – were seriously disrupted. Royalists and churchmen did not hesitate to voice their grievances; those of the county of Glamorgan, for example, deplored the situation 'in which schismatics of several kinds are of greatest trust, with some in chiefest places of government in this county, whereby our souls and lives, our liberties and estates, must be at their desire'.[11] Catholic recusants may have felt most aggrieved of all, if the reactions of Dorothy Wynn, wife of Griffith Wynn, of Llannor, Caernarfonshire, are an accurate yardstick. In the Quarter Sessions of that county, Dorothy was alleged to have said 'oftentimes', with undisguised bitterness, 'that she hoped to wash her hands in the Protestants' blood'.[12] No doubt, the disasters of warfare had raised the emotional temperature to fever pitch among dedicated partisans on both sides.

By 1646, however, the Parliamentary armies had clearly won the First Civil War. In the same year the House of Commons endorsed the recommendation of the Assembly of Divines, which had been sitting at Westminster since 1643, that the Book of Common Prayer should be banned and replaced by a new Presbyterian text, the Directory of Worship, throughout the whole of Wales. This new book was not everywhere well received or used – not even among Puritans, especially in the ranks of the army. These dissensions among the Crown's enemies enabled King Charles I, defeated in the field, to take advantage of the opportunity to exploit the differences between his opponents and to play one off against the other. The situation in Wales was not unfavourable for such manoeuvres; and, indeed, it was there that the Second Civil War broke out in 1648. The combination of the forces of the Parliamentary malcontents and the king's supporters were once more no match for Cromwell's troops; and in 1648 Colonel Pride and his men undertook a 'purge' which sent the conservative members of the 'Rump Parliament' packing. Charles I himself was executed in January 1649. For two or three years beforehand, and still more, perhaps, after the audacious execution of the king by his Puritan enemies, a whole flood of divergent religious ideas and doctrines, to which Welsh religious radicals had not remained immune, had inundated the realm. Episcopal jurisdiction was abolished, censorship collapsed, and a proliferation of books, sermons and pamphlets swarmed from the press. The effects were apparent among some of the foremost Welsh Puritans. William Erbury had fallen under the spell of the Seekers, a small sect who believed that no true church had existed since the spirit of Antichrist had appeared in the world, but that God would, in his own time, single out apostles and prophets to found a new church.[13] Vavasor Powell and Morgan Llwyd had been captivated by the teachings of the Millenarians; and John Miles brought back with him from London in 1649 strict Baptist principles. When all these prophets and many others besides were let loose to preach and propagate in Wales, the country was to undergo a tumultuous and confused decade in the 1650s.

Following Colonel Pride's purge of the conservative members of the Long Parliament in December 1648 and Charles I's execution in January 1649, the remaining fifty or so members of the Rump Parliament moved to take action intended drastically to change the nature of religious life in Wales. Nor was it the only such 'backward' region on which Parliament's attention was focused; radical measures were also applied to the northern counties of England, to Ireland, and to New England. The outcome, as far as Wales was concerned, was the passing on Friday 22 February 1650 of the Act for the Better Propagation and Preaching of the Gospel in Wales.[14] This was the most important piece of devolutionary legislation relating to Wales since the Act of Union 1536–43, or the Act for the Translation of the Bible and the Prayer Book of 1563. It came as a response to petitions sent to Parliament from both north and south Wales, and it was also the result of pressure being applied to Parliament, by three individuals in particular. The first of these was Major-General Thomas Harrison, one of Cromwell's best officers, a man with strong Millenarian sympathies, who had been appointed to the south Wales command in 1649. The second was Hugh Peter, a fiery Cornishman and an ardent Puritan chaplain, who had earlier written an influential book which stressed the need for improving the state of Wales. The third was the tireless and impassioned pulpit orator, Vavasor Powell.

Those Puritan authorities entrusted with the responsibility for carrying out the Act had two principal objectives in view: first, the institution of a Puritan ministry throughout the whole of Wales; and second, the establishment of a number of schools, mostly in market towns, for the education of children and, in the process, their indoctrination in the practices and ideals of Puritans. During the previous century or more there had, of course, been a number of Parliament-directed initiatives in religion; but this one differed from all the others insofar as there existed no executive arm in the person of a monarch to enforce it with royal authority. To carry through the proposals, therefore, 71 commissioners were appointed – 29 of them to act in north Wales and 42 in the south. Headed by Major-General Harrison, many of the commissioners were army officers and a number of them already had earlier experience of administration. In the next three years – the Act lasted only until 1653[15] – they were to constitute the 'military middle class' which ruled Wales.

The Act also set up a body of 'approvers', consisting of twenty ministers of religion. Fourteen of these had previously had experience of preaching and ministering to the needs of their congregations. Many of them were Englishmen by birth, and most of those among them who were Welsh came from the more Anglicized districts of Wales and could hardly be described as being well fitted to appreciate some of the distinctive problems of ministering to the Welsh-speaking population of the north and west of the country. Neither could they be said to have been united in the doctrines and beliefs they held. All of them, it is true, were 'Puritan' in sympathy, but that umbrella term covered a multitude of divers shades of opinion. Some were Independents (itself a term that embraced many different beliefs); others were Presbyterians; some were committed Baptists (believers in the baptism of adult believers); and yet others were former clergymen of the Church of England, now converted (in name at least) to one or other of the many kinds of Puritanism.

The commissioners were given extensive powers to enable them to fulfil the duties allotted to them. Any five or more of them might hear such complaints of delinquency or non-residence as were alleged against any clergyman, and expel him if he was found guilty. They were also empowered to inquire into the circumstances in which a cleric might be accused of holding more than one living and oblige him to choose which one of those livings he wished to retain. In addition, they were authorized to issue certificates to clergymen giving them permission to preach. Twelve or more of the commissioners were allowed to take stock of the income accruing from church livings in order to be able to set aside allowances for the support of the wives and children of those clergymen who had been dismissed.

Furthermore, the commissioners, or any five of them, were given authority to hear all complaints of misdemeanours, oppressions or injuries in Wales. They were authorized to bring those accused of such wrangling before them in order to pass judgement in their cause. This was, indeed, a very wide-ranging brief which, for all practical purposes, made the commissioners responsible for the local administration of Wales. Some of them already derived added authority from the powers they enjoyed as members of the Council of State, military commanders, members of the Committee for Compounding, Members of Parliament or high sheriffs.

To assist the commissioners in carrying out their duties, another body of twenty-four approvers was set up. Its primary task was to select, in the words of the Propagation Act itself, 'godly and painful men of approved conversation [i.e., behaviour] . . . to preach the Gospel in Welsh'.[16] The approvers were admirably equipped to carry out such a responsibility, since they included in their midst many of the most celebrated Puritan preachers in Wales, including stalwarts of the calibre of Walter Cradock, John Miles, Morgan Llwyd, Ambrose Mostyn and Vavasor Powell.

This brought them to the very core of their responsibilities, i.e., the ejection of many of the existing clergy and their replacement by appropriate successors. The grounds for removing many of the previous incumbents were immorality, continuing loyalty to the king and the Church of England, and the refusal of allegiance, though all of these could be, and no doubt were, interpreted very loosely. In all, 278 of the existing clergy are known to have been removed – a far larger number than had ever been turned out in the previous religious clearances of the Tudor era.[17] This figure, even so, does not include any of the unbeneficed clergy, of whom, if previous experience is any guide, there may well have been some hundreds. Of their fate we can learn little or nothing; but it seems conceivable that some of them, at least, may have been recruited into the ranks of the new incumbents. The fate of the ejected clergy showed wide variations: some had private means or family support to fall back upon; others became schoolmasters and/or authors; some were dependent on the good will or charity of former parishioners. Some accepted their fate docilely and merged into the background; many conducted Anglican services in private houses; others were bolder and held such services more or less openly in churches, especially in those more remote areas where there was little supervision or opposition. There was evidently a good deal of sympathy for the ejected clergy among the local population; and, in any case, there was a desperate shortfall of adequate successors to replace those who had been turned out.

It was, as the commissioners and approvers soon discovered, much easier to pull down an old Anglican edifice than to replace it with a new Puritan structure. So pressing was the shortage of fitting replacements that the approvers had little option but to fall back on the tried and trusty practice of itinerant preaching. Some of the approvers themselves were among the most gifted exponents of the art and readily returned to their former routines. Walter Cradock went back to mid-Wales; John Miles was very active among the Baptist churches he had founded in south and south-east Wales; Ambrose Mostyn adopted Wrexham as his base; while Vavasor Powell, most energetic of them all and sarcastically dubbed 'the metropolitan of the itinerants',[18] ranged over Breconshire, Radnorshire and Montgomeryshire. Some highly promising newcomers were also welcomed to the ranks of the itinerants: Stephen Hughes (1622–88), the 'apostle of Carmarthenshire', and Charles Edwards, author of *Hanes y Ffydd Ddiffuant* ('The History of the Unfeigned Faith', 1677), one of the most attractive of Welsh prose writers as well as being a gifted preacher. In all, there were some 63 itinerants at work; the large majority of them labouring in south Wales, with only

12 of them posted to the north. Along the borders between England and the shires of Radnor, Brecon and Monmouth there were 30; in Glamorgan and Carmarthenshire 23; and in Pembrokeshire and Cardiganshire 5. Some of them were well known and successful preachers; but others were old soldiers, farmers and former craftsmen, and scarcely fitted by experience or training for their present role. Some of them could preach only in English, which inadequately served to meet the needs of the majority of the population. Most limiting of all, there were nothing like enough of even this miscellaneous company of messengers to fulfil the high-flying ambitions of those who had framed the Propagation Act. It was all very well for a Puritan enthusiast like Vavasor Powell to proclaim ecstatically that 'no generation since the Apostles' days had had such powerful preachers and plenty of preaching as this generation had',[19] but his sternest critic, Alexander Griffith, a vitriolic Anglican pamphleteer, could write of '700 parishes unsupplied with any recognized preacher and one could ride ten or twelve miles on the Lord's Day where there are twenty churches and not one door opened'.[20] Both these commentators, sincere upholders of their respective viewpoints as they might be, were also polemicists, it must be remembered, and prone to exaggeration and one-sidedness in their judgements.

In addition to trying to establish a Puritan ministry in Wales, the other twin thrust of the commissioners' energies was delivered in the field of education. In this respect, they were following in the footsteps of sixteenth-century reformers, Catholic and Protestant. The Puritans, like their predecessors, were anxious to try to dispel the endemic ignorance existing among the population and, particularly, to raise the level of literacy in their midst. They recognized the urgent need for a dramatic expansion in the educational facilities available in Wales and, to this end, embarked on the first experiment in state-supported schools. Some of the former assets of the Church of England were diverted to fund the key project of setting up some sixty schools in Wales, mostly in the main market towns. The money was also used to remunerate the teachers who staffed these schools. To add to the effectiveness of these establishments, the commissioners left in being the existing grammar schools, of which there were about a dozen in all,[21] and any private-venture schools to function as before. Twenty-six of the new schools were established in north Wales, and twenty-eight in the south. Although such a balance of numbers between north and south was equitable enough, it conceals the fact that there was an overwhelming concentration in the eastern half of Wales and a gross neglect of the western sector. For example, there were eleven schools in Denbighshire and not one in Merioneth; and while Montgomeryshire and Breconshire had eight and nine respectively, Caernarfonshire and Anglesey had to make do with one apiece. Education was free in these schools, and some girls, as well as boys, were taught. The schoolmasters placed in them were generally expected to be committed Puritans, and some of them went on to become ministers and, in the process, to acquire an increased remuneration. Other teachers, however, were recruited from the ranks of Anglican clergymen who had been ejected from their former livings. Evidence for the nature of the curriculum and the standard of the teaching in these schools is painfully scanty; but the chances are that there were wide variations between one school and another. It is also worth remembering that there were a number of schools in being besides the state-sponsored and grammar schools. These were maintained on a private-venture basis by former Anglican clergymen or schoolmasters, like the one which Hugh Gore, a deprived clergyman and a future Anglican bishop in Ireland, maintained in Swansea.[22]

One thing, however, is quite certain: after 1658 many of the schools went downhill, with numbers of their teachers leaving and others becoming sadly disillusioned. By 1660, only twenty-six out of the original fifty-four were left in existence. Yet the schools had not been by any means an unqualified failure. It may be true that the principle of state support for education did not take firm root until the nineteenth century, but the need for more schools and increased learning had once again been spelled out in terms too plain to be ignored, A number of the leading pioneers of the 1650s had been so convinced of the desperate nature of the need that they would again take up the cause – this time on the basis of voluntary support – in the 1670s. The Independents Stephen Hughes and Charles Edwards and the Anglican William Thomas were to be some of the most prominent standard-bearers in the ranks of the Welsh Trust, founded by Thomas Gouge (1600–81),[23] in the years 1674–83, while Bishop Gore founded a boys' grammar school in Swansea.

The Propagation Act itself, which had set up the Puritan schools in the first place, lapsed in 1653. In that same year, Oliver Cromwell was persuaded by some of his more enthusiastic followers, like two of their foremost Welsh representatives, Vavasor Powell and Morgan Llwyd, to establish the Parliament of Saints ('Barebones Parliament'). It proved to be a short-lived expedient, however, and one with which Cromwell speedily lost patience. In December 1653 he proclaimed himself Protector of the Realm – to the intense indignation of zealots of Vavasor Powell's persuasion. In 1654 a new system of church government, called a Commission for the Approbation of Publicque Preachers, or the 'Triers', as they were generally known, was set up.[24] Consisting of nine laymen and twenty-nine ministers, it was based in London. It was made up in the main of moderate men and was representative of the differing strands of opinion within Puritanism, but it had only two Welsh members – Walter Cradock and George Griffith. Ahead of these Triers in Wales lay an enormous undertaking from the Puritan point of view. Some idea of the formidable responsibilities confronting them may be gleaned from the deeply unsympathetic opinions formulated by General Fleetwood in April 1654, when he declared that the people of Wales, with 'envenomed hearts against the ways of God . . . the forwardest and greatest promoters of the King's interests in time of war . . . little better than the Irish, are particularly to be looked after'.[25] The earlier system of itinerant preaching was now to be abandoned, and an attempt made to place ministers in settled parishes. But the number of those available to fulfil such obligations continued to be sadly inadequate, and Puritan incumbents still remained the butt of stinging criticism on the part of Royalist bards like Huw Morus or prose writers such as Rowland Vaughan of Caer Gai. Nor was it easy to envisage how it would be possible to encourage and train qualified new recruits, even though enthusiasts like Major-General James Berry or John Lewis of Glasgrug were keen to set up a national college for the purpose. Unfortunately, their well-meant promptings met only with inadequate support and scant success.

The eleven years between the execution of Charles I in 1649 and restoration of his son, Charles II, to the throne in 1660 formed an interlude that was characterized by wide and hotly debated differences, many experiments and much heart-searching in the religious life of England and Wales. Those who sympathized in general with Puritan aspirations, whatever the nature of their private beliefs, had been immensely heartened by their military triumph in the civil wars and the removal of the king. A great outpouring of religious enthusiasm of many different kinds had thereby been released: ardent preaching; unfettered discussion and disputation; and the unrestricted publication of a torrent of books and pamphlets (if the cost of printing them could be met) had diffused new ideas far and wide in England, ripples from which radiated to some extent into Wales.

A good example of the newly awakened fervour is the dissemination of Millenarian ideals, especially in the shape of Fifth Monarchy tendencies. Millenarianism, i.e., a belief in the second coming of Jesus Christ on earth and the founding of his reign of a thousand years, had long flourished in some places and at some periods in the Middle Ages;[26] but it became much more influential still as a result of the emphasis on the authority of the literal interpretation of the Scriptures in Protestant circles. Zealots such as the Fifth Monarchists derived their name from their conviction that the appearance of the Fifth Monarchy, i.e., the kingdom of Jesus Christ, was imminent. Four great empires, it was thought, had already appeared – those of Assyria, Persia, Greece and Rome. The fifth, the Millennium of Christ's rule on earth, was believed by some contemporaries to be at hand. Their hopes for this dénouement were intensified by their fervently literal interpretation of the two great apocalyptic books of the Bible – the Book of Daniel and the Book of Revelation. Calculations based on biblical texts to work out the precise year in which this great cosmic event was to happen yielded ingenious results, but varied in their estimates of the actual year of destiny – forecasts ranging between 1656 and 1666. These eschatological speculations stirred many Welsh Puritans to the depths of their being, chief among them being Vavasor Powell and Morgan Llwyd. The latter was convinced that the 'pillars of the world are shaking and fire and tempest rage in every land about'.[27] Wales became a stronghold of Fifth Monarchists, whereas elsewhere they were usually an urban faction. The high hopes of the Fifth Monarchy men reached their peak in 1653, when Cromwell dismissed what remained of the Rump Parliament and replaced it with the Parliament of the Saints. However, the extreme views being ventilated in the new assembly, and the bitter divisions which appeared amidst its members within weeks, led to severe disillusionment and the speedy dissolution by Cromwell of the Parliament. In Wales it was Vavasor Powell who stood forth as Oliver Cromwell's most extreme opponent. He denounced the Lord Protector as an apostate and a blasphemer; and at one point he claimed to have no fewer than 20,000 saints feverishly waiting the call to arms. In 1656 he published a pamphlet entitled *A Word for God*,[28] which was a categoric indictment of the wrongdoings committed by Cromwell's regime. It was presented to the Protector by one of Powell's supporters, but it carried the endorsement of only 322 supporters, ludicrously fewer than the thousands of whom Vavasor had earlier boasted. Among the 322 signatures was Morgan Llwyd's name, but, much to the latter's annoyance, it had been included without his consent. An immediate answer to Vavasor's thunderings in *A Word for God* was penned by Walter Cradock under the title of *The Humble Representation and Address to his Highness of Several Churches and Christians in South Wales* (1658).[29] Signed by 762 individuals, more than double the number of those who had subscribed to Vavasor's outburst, it enthusiastically commended the Lord Protector's godly endeavours and denounced the disloyalty of traitors like Powell.

During those years of the Commonwealth, the religious scene appeared to be one of Puritan control and direction, but closer scrutiny reveals much confusion and no little contradiction. Morgan Llwyd, possibly the greatest of all the Welsh Puritans, writing of his fellow believers, spoke much that was applicable to many of his countrymen:

Men's faces and voices differ much,
Saints are not all of one size;
Flowers in the garden vary, too,
Lest one monopolize.
Let us hold fast with head and heart and ford the living stream
Abide with God, and Christ will guide us and keep us from extreme.[30]

It might, indeed, have been better for Wales if many more of its sons and daughters had heeded Llwyd's caring and tolerant voice. But most of his compatriots preferred to cling determinedly to what they believed to be the truth, no matter how much bitterness towards others that might engender. Among them were those who clung in their hearts to Anglican ways and the Book of Common Prayer, and who continued to worship as best they might, in public or in gentlemen's houses. Available to give them guidance were a large number of expelled Anglican clerics. Some were men of such distinction as Jeremy Taylor at Golden Grove; others like Hugh Lloyd, Hugh Gore, Francis Davie or William Thomas were, all of them, to be consecrated Anglican bishops in the Restoration Church. The last-named, having been sequestered for his loyalty, then taught school at Laugharne, where he sometimes read the Book of Common Prayer and preached, although not without disturbance from an itinerant Puritan preacher.[31] William Thomas was doubtless only one among many to undergo experiences of this sort – preaching and providing services to Anglican loyalists as and when he might. A number of these expelled clerics, in order to maintain themselves, their wives and families, turned to schoolmastering. Others employed their talents as authors. Jeremy Taylor wrote some of his finest works, among them *Holy Living* (1655) and *Holy Dying* (1657),[32] while he was chaplain to Lord Carbery. Another Anglican writer in the 1650s, but one of a very different sort, was Alexander Griffith (d. 1676), unsparing antagonist to Vavasor Powell, who published his best-known work, *Strena Vavasoriensis* ('Vavasorial Prediction') in 1654. But, sarcastic as he could be, the anti-Puritan Griffith became sufficiently reconciled to his *bêtes noires* to serve as one of their schoolmasters from 1658. There were also Anglican authors who published in Welsh. One of the best-known of these was Rowland Vaughan, who had issued his first and most celebrated book as far back as 1630, *Yr Ymarfer o Dduwioldeb*, a translation of Bishop Bayly's *The Practice of Piety*. Not until 1656 did a second edition of it appear, and then Vaughan published nothing further until 1658, when he brought out no fewer than five works in the same year. No explanation has ever been offered for this quite unusual publishing pattern, but it would seem that his long silence was at least partially due to the alarms and excursions of the civil wars and the Puritan supremacy. But it may also be, on the other hand, that it was the death of Cromwell and the weakening of Puritan authority that precipitated the spate of books he issued in 1658. Yet what he wrote in *Prifannau Sanctaidd* does not suggest he felt himself to be unduly muzzled by Puritan control: 'O! who can look without mourning and sighing upon the parties and sects of schisms and heresies, the which Satan hath harvest kindled today to put to silence right doctrine and its professors and to set up the priests of Baal from the refuse'.[33] This was written, as Sir Thomas Parry percipiently noted, at a time when Puritans were in control of country and church. Rowland Vaughan's words, however, help us to appreciate not only his own attributes, but also the loyalty of the majority of the Welsh people to the Church of England and also to explain why it was possible to re-establish that church so early in the 1660s.

Another long-standing and long-suffering group which survived the years of Puritan rule that were even more harrowing for them than for the Anglicans were the Roman Catholic believers. Of all the dissentient groups which were kept under tight control by their Puritan overlords, the most hard-pressed of all were the Romanists. Even Oliver Cromwell, who was reputed to be in favour of freedom of conscience, expressed his views on papistry in this unsparing fashion in 1649: 'I meddle with no man's conscience. But if by liberty of conscience you mean liberty to exercise the Mass, I judge it best to use plain dealing and to let you know that where the Parliament of England has power, that will not be allowed.'[34] Nor had the Roman Catholics done their cause any favours in the public mind by becoming associated with Irish Catholics. Nevertheless, they were unyieldingly devoted to their faith; they had also, over the generations, become adept at knowing how to maintain in secret their worship, sustain their priests and their congregations, and keep up their lines of communications with one another in face of severe persecution. They continued successfully to do so in the 1640s and 1650s, in spite of the martyrdom of two of their priests – Philip Powell, a Benedictine, executed at Tyburn in 1646, and Thomas Vaughan, put to death at Cardiff, also in 1646[35] – and fines and disabilities of many kinds. The feature of Catholic activity which appears to have dwindled perceptibly during the years of the Interregnum, however, is the production of Catholic literature. We have no evidence of any new prose or poetic works appearing during this period. Even so, there were many books and manuscripts which had long been circulated under cover among the devout, and it seems probable that they continued to be treasured by believers and sent the rounds in secret in their midst. Furthermore, the relatively rapid appearance of two major Catholic publications in 1661 and 1662 suggests that work on them had long been proceeding even during the years of oppression. This was the more remarkable when it is recalled how intense were the dislike and suspicion of Roman Catholics. Even a man of disposition so kindly and all-embracing as Morgan Llwyd could exclude them from his sympathy. For him the pope and Beelzebub were birds of a feather:

> A thousand years great Beelzebub and Pope, his son and foole,
> Made Christendom their slaughterhouse, the Church their dancing stool.[36]

In spite of all the differences of belief and emphasis among the Puritans there were, perhaps, four main trends among them which could be distinguished: the Presbyterians; Independents; Baptists; and Quakers. Not that any one of these was undivided within itself or necessarily sharply segregated from the others. For instance, some Baptists often worshipped in company with Independents, and even among the Baptists themselves there might be division. There were those who were strict or 'closed' Baptists, who insisted upon 'closed' communion, received only by those who had undergone adult baptism. But there were also 'open' Baptists, who believed in the validity of adult baptism, but who were willing, nevertheless, to commune with believers of Independent or Presbyterian persuasion. Perhaps it was inevitable that there should be variations of belief and practice amongst a miscellaneous mass of believers, acknowledging no overarching episcopal or other authority, but owning to a firm belief in the authority of the Scriptures, the autonomy of the individual congregation, and the importance of private conscience.

Surveying the general scene back in 1643, it might have been supposed that the Presbyterians were likely to emerge as the dominant Puritan sect. At that point, the Parliamentary armies had arrived at the agreement with the Scottish Presbyterians known as the Solemn League and Covenant, by the terms of which, in return for Scottish military assistance, Presbyterian Church arrangements similar to those enforced in Scotland were to be established throughout England and Wales. Even in 1646, Parliament endorsed the opinion of the divines meeting at Westminster that the use of the Book of Common Prayer should be forbidden in all churches in England and Wales and should be replaced by the Presbyterian Directory of Worship. However, well before this juncture, it had become plainly apparent that it was the Independents who were likely to emerge as victors, even in Wales. Those zealous itinerant preachers who had swept through south Wales 'like fire in the thatch', in Walter Cradock's graphic phrase, were Independents almost to a man. So, too, were most of the leading evangelists in Wales; pre-eminent men of the stature of Cradock himself, Ambrose Mostyn or Morgan Llwyd. Of crucial significance was that the Directory itself, the prescribed Presbyterian book of worship, never, in fact, seems to have been translated into Welsh, a crippling limitation, although the suggestion had understandably been made that there ought to be a Welsh version. Nevertheless, in the most comprehensive bibliography of all Welsh books ever published, no copy of a Welsh edition of the Directory is mentioned,[37] and no reference to such a work appears to exist anywhere else. In the evident absence of such a Welsh translation, one is, indeed, bound to wonder how it was that many churches were able to get through the service. Did they use the forms provided in the English book, which must have been highly unsatisfactory, if not unintelligible, to many of the congregation? Or did the minister paraphrase the English forms in Welsh to the best of his ability? Did they use the Book of Common Prayer – it will be remembered that under the terms of the Propagation Act of 1650 a number of incumbents were ejected for refusing to give up the Prayer Book? Or were there some who were reduced to wholly extempore worship?

At all events, the Presbyterians, never having managed to secure an early footing in Wales, made little or no impact on the country. Not until 1653 did they achieve any real success, and then only in the north-east, in the English-speaking part of Flintshire. This was when Philip Henry, best known as a great diarist,[38] arrived there to become tutor to the children of Judge Puleston of Emral. Although Philip Henry was not ordained until 1657, he exercised considerable influence in the neighbourhood, partly as a result of his own attractive personal qualities and partly because of his powerful preaching. He held forth not only in his own church of Worthenbury but also farther afield at Gresford, Wrexham, Ellesmere, Penley and Wolverhampton. Despite Henry's own tolerant and likeable attitude, the Presbyterians did not appear to be anxious to press westwards into Wales. They seemed to be more preoccupied with their own interests on the border and over on its English side. That may well have been chiefly owing to the fact that they had few, if any, Welsh-speaking ministers at their disposal. The outcome was that, although there may have been formidable isolated sympathizers with Presbyterian ideals like Sir Thomas Middleton or John Lewis of Glasgrug, they remained as individuals, scattered here and there all over Wales outside English Flintshire. But although there were no gathered congregations, Presbyterians remained on friendly terms with other Puritans in their neighbourhood. There were other people, however, with whom Presbyterians found it difficult to establish what they would probably have regarded as a friendly rapport. In June 1657, for example, even in the parish of Worthenbury, where Philip Henry's influence was at its most persuasive, the survival of old pre-Puritan customs was unmistakable when a company of parishioners assembled in the church to deck it with flowers, just as they had been accustomed to do before ever the Presbyterians had appeared on the scene.[39]

The majority of the Puritans would have been defined in the somewhat imprecise terminology of the age as 'Independents'. Most of the best-known ministers, the foremost leaders, preachers and authors were avowed Independents. In spite of the significance they attached to individual gathered congregations of true believers and their mistrust of governmental control over the Church, they had no difficulty in accepting the financial support offered to them by the commissioners appointed under the terms of the Propagation Act of 1650. Even when that statute had lapsed in 1653 some of the leading figures among the Independents settled down in convenient centres where, supported by the government, they continued to evangelize fervently. To take but one example: Ambrose Mostyn adopted the long-established stronghold of Wrexham as his base. From there he preached with great effect in neighbouring towns, at places as far-flung as Welshpool and Oswestry. Again, it was at Usk that Walter Cradock settled and eagerly seized all such opportunities as were offered to him to preach in mid-Wales. Stephen Hughes, from his parish at Meidrim, took virtually the whole county of Carmarthenshire as his mission field. Morgan Llwyd, on the other hand, withdrew to the Llŷn peninsula, but although he there 'lost his voice', he devoted most of his energies to an impressive outburst of authorship. Between 1655 and 1657 he produced no fewer than seven books in Welsh and two in English as well as a large body of verse in both languages.[40] His most famous books were *Llythyr i'r Cymry Cariadus* ('Letter to the Beloved Welsh') and *Llyfr y Tri Aderyn* ('Book of the Three Birds'). The latter is usually – and rightly – regarded as the greatest as well as the most celebrated of all his writings. It presents a dialogue between three birds: the Eagle, representing the government and the administration of the land, especially that of Oliver Cromwell; the Raven, who is a symbol of the earthly elements to be found within the state Church; and the Dove, who stood for the true Christian i.e., the sincere Puritan. Later on, Llwyd came under the influence of the German mystic Jacob Boehme, and was also strongly attracted to the Quaker doctrine of the inner light.

It was the Independents, also, who were primarily responsible for the new edition of the Welsh Bible, published in 1654. It was a work desperately needed in view of the acute shortage of bibles available in the Welsh tongue at the time, and also of the unique importance placed upon scriptural authority in Puritan belief and worship. In 1659, too, it was the Independent minister Stephen Hughes who organized arrangements for the publication of the verses of Vicar Prichard, the first printed version of them certainly known to have been issued. It is distinctly paradoxical that Hughes, a wholly committed Puritan, should so enthusiastically have taken in hand the first publication of the verse of the equally loyal Anglican, Rhys Prichard. However, Hughes was to continue with his publishing efforts throughout the course of the remaining twenty-eight years of his life spent during the Restoration era (1660–88).[41] Although it was Independents who were responsible for most of the considerable body of Welsh religious literature published during the 1650s, one of the worrying facts about it is that we do not know, and have no obvious means of finding out, how many copies of these works were published, although it seems fairly certain that no edition would consist of more than 1,000 copies and many may have been numbered only in hundreds. We have even less information about the number of people who were in a position to purchase and read these books, or about how many of those who were illiterate listened to them being read for their benefit by others sufficiently educated and well-disposed to do so.[42]

Turning from the Independents to the Baptists, it is known that believers in adult baptism were reputed to have existed in the Olchon Valley on the borders of Herefordshire as early as 1633,[43] and in 1646 there is a description of an enthusiastic believer who was described as having been 'apreaching' and 'diping' and to have 'rebaptized hundreds' in the counties of Radnor and Brecon.[44] It was not until 1649, however, that the first recognizably Baptist church was constituted in the Gower village of Ilston. Its founder, John Miles (1621–83), was a Herefordshire man by birth, and one whose knowledge of

Welsh may have been scanty or even non-existent. He graduated at Oxford and later appears to have become a chaplain in the Parliamentary armies. Having settled in Gower *c.*1647 or 1648, he and a colleague may well have been invited, or even encouraged, to go to London by the members of the strict Baptist Church who met at the Glass House in Broad Street, London. He was certainly dispatched back to Gower by the Broad Street congregation to undertake the task of evangelizing in what the London Baptists designated as that 'dark corner'. Miles proved himself to be possessed of unusually effective powers as a preacher and particularly as an organizer. He not only founded a successful church in Ilston but also managed to set up a number of other flourishing Baptist churches in the area between the town of Carmarthen and the Herefordshire border. He succeeded in maintaining unity among the six churches he had founded by establishing a quasi-Presbyterian organization, which was to prove the method of government adopted by the Welsh Baptist denomination of the future. Although each church enjoyed autonomy, that did not imply independence for each congregation. They were held together in a General Meeting (an Association or *Cymanfa*), which met annually in different places, and to which each individual church sent representatives. This system was developed to keep the Baptists united and to safeguard them against heresy and the danger of disintegration, to which the freedom of the Independents rendered them more than ordinarily liable. John Miles may, indeed, be credited with the achievement of a large degree of cohesion among the early Baptists, but there still remained wide and serious differences among them. One of the most critical of these was whether or not genuine Puritan believers who had not undergone baptism as adults should be allowed to join in communion with those who had done so. There were those like Captain Jenkin Jones of Llanddeti, who was a very widely known Baptist, who held that people of other sects should be allowed to commune with Baptists and, indeed, urged those who believed as he did not to join any of Miles's 'strict' Baptist churches. It was, none the less, Miles's vision which, thanks mainly to his own firm insistence, was to carry the day among Welsh Baptists.[45]

The most extreme sect among the Puritans was that of the Society of Friends, as they called themselves, or the Quakers,[46] as they were generally known by others. They were founded in 1653 at Swarthmore in Yorkshire by a humble English cobbler, by name George Fox (1624–91). Their central doctrine was that of the inner light of the spirit, through which every genuine believer was led by divine inspiration to the truth for himself. Consequently, the Quakers tended to be hostile to any form of established authority in Church or state. Among those to whom this new and revolutionary doctrine made a compelling appeal was Morgan Llwyd, who dispatched two members of his congregation to Swarthmore with the object of discovering as much as they could about Quaker teaching. One of the two was John ap John (1625–97), a yeoman of Ruabon, who was later to become the chief apostle of Quakerism in Wales.[47] He accompanied George Fox's envoy, Thomas Holmes, on the latter's mission to Wales in 1654. Holmes, who knew no Welsh, necessarily concentrated in the main on those leading market towns with considerable English-speaking populations, such as Abergavenny, Cardiff, Swansea, Tenby and Haverfordwest. This was followed up in the next year (1655) by a mission, of which John ap John was the leader. In 1657, George Fox himself came to Wales on a wide-ranging journey, in the course of which he aroused a great deal of interest and made many converts, especially among those who were able to understand English. With their ardent appeal to enthusiastic individuals, the Quakers appeared to be filling the gap left by the decline of Millenarian movements like that of the Fifth Monarchy men, who had struck a responsive note amid the most radical members of the Puritan congregations. Certainly, the Quakers made no concessions to established conventions or orders. They rejected all the sacraments of the Church and refused to pay tithes or take oaths. They insisted on wearing hats in church, were wont to create disturbances and uproar at the conventional services held in the churches, or 'steeple-houses' as Quakers called them, and were not averse from resorting even to violence. It was no wonder that these radical reformers and their somewhat outlandish behaviour should have created consternation among the stricter and more orthodox Puritan sects, all of which were affronted by them and uncompromisingly opposed them. As early as 1656, the Baptist John Miles published a condemnatory tract, entitled *Antidote against the Infection of the Times*, in which he sought to expose what he believed to be the errors of Quaker ways. None the less Quakers continued to make numerous converts in various parts of Wales, notably in those districts where English-speakers existed in considerable strength. Had they succeeded in recruiting larger numbers of fluent Welsh speakers to propagate their teachings, they might well have been able to draw in many more converts.

The death of Oliver Cromwell in 1658 proved to be a devastating blow to the Puritan regime in Wales no less than in England. The removal from the scene of the Lord Protector meant the disappearance of a strong secular arm which, for the best part of a decade, had controlled government in the interests of the Puritan sects. Oliver was succeeded by his much more ineffectual son Richard, who soon proved himself to be of a calibre quite inadequate to fill his father's very formidable shoes. The results were predictable. Opponents of the regime took fresh heart, while those of its adherents who were at best no more than lukewarm, began seriously to think of ways in which they might come to terms with any successor dispensation – almost certainly it would be a royalist one! – which would take over, and how they might safeguard any gains they had acquired in earlier years. There followed some two uneasy years of angst and uncertainty, in the course of which royalist hopes and conspiracies gained increasing strength and support until, on 25 May 1660, King Charles II was welcomed back to the country and restored to his father's erstwhile throne.

What was the condition of religion in the Wales to which the new ruler had successfully established his hereditary right? Neither the ardour of the 'saints' nor the armed might of the Commonwealth had been able to win over a majority of the Welsh people to Puritan convictions or lifestyle. Most of them were still attached to worship according to the Book of Common Prayer, combined in many instances with a liberal sprinkling of older habits and customs, among which regular attendance at church and a thorough knowledge of Christian doctrine did not figure very prominently. Nor had the hasty and ill-coordinated evangelizing efforts of the Commonwealth, associated as they were with an unpopular political and military programme, made good the deficiencies, however well intentioned they may have been. A predominant core of Anglican-cum-Royalist loyalty lay at the new king's disposal. Particularly was this true of the gentry, whose command of the allegiance of the lower classes remained firm, essentially unshaken by the upheavals of the civil wars and Puritan rule.

An infinitely smaller group numerically, which had also been totally unmoved by Puritan proselytization, was that tiny fraction made up of the Roman Catholics – probably not numbering more than 3,000–4,000 in all, who indomitably maintained their loyalty to papist doctrine. For a hundred years before 1660 they and their predecessors had never known anything but ostracism at best and persecution at worst. Frowned upon by rulers in Church and state, and suspected of disloyalty and treason, they had always had to maintain their faith largely under cover and in secret. They would continue to tread much the same path between 1660 and 1688, even though they inwardly hoped for more generous treatment from the new king and especially his brother James.

The Puritan sects still remained no more than a small minority among the Welsh population as a whole. Even so, none of them elicited much sympathy from the Royalist and Anglican majority. Moreover, as has already been seen, they were deeply divided among themselves. Those regarded as the most radical in their midst – by antipathetic Puritan sects as well as Anglicans – were the Quakers and the Baptists. It was hardly to be wondered at that they should seem to the Royalists the most dangerous and irreconcilable of their opponents.

The king himself was adjudged to be a man not wholly unfavourable to some measure of religious toleration, as the Declaration of Breda, issued in April 1660, seemed to indicate. When he landed at Dover on 25 May 1660 to take up anew his father's lost crown, he was enthusiastically welcomed by the majority of his Welsh subjects. Even among the Puritan minority there were some leading figures who continued to hope that a *modus vivendi* might be found in a church settlement broad enough to accommodate all but the most die-hard sectarians. The well-known Welsh Presbyterian minister, Samuel Jones (1628–97) of Llangynwyd, expressed his conviction that, in spite of all the tempests, 'the ark of the Church, when God himself is both master of the storm and anchor to it, shall at length rest on Ararat'.[48] But the venom and hatred stirred up between 1640 and 1660 by long years of civil war and Puritan rule could not easily be dispelled. The early measures adopted by the king's government during the last six months of 1660 against those believed to be most hostile to the new regime gave an indication of what was to follow. Baptist ministers were evicted from livings; Quakers and Roman Catholics were fined and imprisoned. The Savoy Conference of 1661, which it was hoped would find a solution to the problems of religious differences, broke up in failure. The election of the hard-line Cavalier Parliament, which met in 1661 and in the next year passed the Act of Uniformity, sealed the fate of any hopes of toleration cherished earlier by some Puritans that there might be only one Protestant Church within the country. In the light of these developments the preceding decades could now be seen as having brought into being a hard-core minority of Puritans who could neither be compelled nor persuaded to unite with their Anglican brethren. Neither could the still steadfast minority of Roman Catholics. Henceforth, all would go their separate ways, for the most part morbidly suspicious of one another's intentions.

Notes to Part I

1. The Early Stuart Church

1 A. H. Dodd, 'Wales and the Scottish succession', *Transactions of the Cymmrodorion Society* (1937), 201–25.
2 E. G. Jones, *Cymru a'r Hen Ffydd* (Caerdydd, 1951), ch. 2
3 G. Williams, *Religion, Language and Nationality in Wales* (Cardiff, 1979), ch. 2.
4 *Idem*, *Wales and the Reformation* (Cardiff, 1997), pp. 374–5.
5 R. Mathias, *The Whitsun Riot* (London, 1963).
6 Jones, *Hen Ffydd*, ch. 2.
7 Williams, *Wales and the Reformation*, p. 267.
8 T. Parry, *A History of Welsh Literature*, trans. H. I. Bell (Oxford, 1962), p. 238.

[9] Jones, *Hen Ffydd*, ch. 2.
[10] J. Penry, *Three Treatises concerning Wales*, ed. D. Williams (Cardiff, 1960), p. 32.
[11] Williams, *Wales and the Reformation*, p. 320.
[12] Ibid., pp. 280–1.
[13] *Idem*, *The Welsh and Their Religion* (Cardiff, 1991), p. 147.
[14] T. Richards, *The Puritan Movement in Wales, 1639 to 1653* (London, 1920), p. 12.
[15] K. Thomas, *Religion and the Decline of Magic* (London, 1971), p. 234.
[16] Richards, *Puritan Movement*, p. 11.
[17] *Rhagymydroddion, 1547–1649*, ed. G. H. Hughes (Caerdydd, 1951), p. 138.
[18] Williams, *Wales and the Reformation*, p. 33.
[19] Richards, *Puritan Movement*, p. 19.
[20] Williams, *Welsh and their Religion*, ch. 5.
[21] Ibid., p. 193.
[22] *Glamorgan County History, IV: Early Modern Glamorgan*, ed. G. Williams (Cardiff, 1974), pp. 240–1.
[23] Ibid., p. 239.
[24] G. Williams, 'St Winifred's Well', *Flintshire Historical Society Journal*, 26 (2003), 32–5.
[25] *DNB*, s.n. Lewis Bayly.
[26] A. I. Pryce, *The Diocese of Bangor in the Sixteenth Century* (Bangor, 1923), p. 81.
[27] R. B. Jones, *'A Lanterne to their Feet'* (Llandovery, 1994).
[28] G. Williams, *The Welsh Church from Conquest to Reformation* (Cardiff, 1962), ch. 8.
[29] *Glamorgan County History, IV*, pp. 242–5.
[30] G. Williams, 'Sir John Prys, Brecon', *Brycheiniog*, 12 (1998–9), 240–1.
[31] D. R. Thomas, *History of the Diocese of St Asaph*, 3 vols (Oswestry, 1908), I, p. 105.
[32] Ll. B. Smith, 'Pwnc yr iaith yng Nghymru, 1282–1536', *Cof Cenedl*, 1 (1986), 1–34; 'Yr iaith yng Nghymru'r Oesau Canol', *Llên Cymru*, 18 (1995), 79–91.
[33] W. P. Griffith, *Learning, Law and Religion, 1540–1640* (Cardiff, 1976), pp. 117–18.
[34] J. D. H. Thomas, *A History of Wales, 1485–1660* (Cardiff, 1972), pp. 117–18.
[35] E. Rees, *Libri Wallie*, 2 vols (Aberystwyth, 1987), I, pp. 22–3.
[36] J. G. Jones, 'Richard Parry, Bishop of St Asaph', *Bulletin of the Board of Celtic Studies*, 26 (1974–6), 175–90.

[37] *Y Llawlyfr Moliant Newydd* (Abertawe, 1955), p. 14; see also G. A. Williams, *Ymryson Edmwnd Prys a Wiliam Cynwal* (Caerdydd, 1986), pp. xci–cxvi
[38] Williams, *Welsh and their Religion*, pp. 168–9.
[39] *Rhagymadroddion 1547–1649*, pp. 122–5.
[40] Richards, *Puritan Movement*, p. 9.
[41] Williams, *Welsh and their Religion*, pp. 44–5.
[42] Rees, *Libri Wallie*, I, p. 131.
[43] Ibid.
[44] Richards, *Puritan Movement*, p. 9.
[45] Penry, *Treatises*, *passim*.
[46] Griffith, *Learning, Law and Religion*, pp. 117–18; see also R. T. Jones, *Vavasor Powell* (Abertawe, 1971).
[47] Richards, *Puritan Movement*, p. 9.
[48] Ibid., pp. 8, 10.
[49] G. Williams, 'Llyfr yr homilïau', in *Grym Tafodau Tân* (Llandysul, 1984), pp. 182–9.
[50] *Idem*, *Welsh and their Religion*, pp. 159–60.
[51] Ibid., p. 160.
[52] Ibid.
[53] Ibid., pp. 34–5, 43–5.
[54] E. Saunders, *A View of the State of Religion* (Cardiff, 1949), p. 164.
[55] Williams, *Welsh and their Religion*, p. 165.
[56] Ibid.
[57] Ibid., p. 44.
[58] *Idem*, *Wales and the Reformation*, pp. 261, 274.
[59] *Idem*, *Welsh and their Religion*, pp. 152–4.
[60] Ibid.
[61] Williams, 'St Winifred's Well', pp. 44–7.
[62] See H. R. Trevor-Roper, *Archbishop Laud* (London, 1962); on the rise of Arminianism in the Anglican Church in the early seventeenth century see N. Tyacke, *Anti-Calvinists: The Rise of English Arminianism c.1590–1640* (Oxford, 1987).
[63] Useful general works include R. J. Acheson, *Radical Puritanism in England, 1550–1640* (London, 1990); C. Hill, *The World Turned Upside Down* (London, 1975); G. F. Nuttall, *The Puritan Spirit* (London, 1967); G. H. Jenkins, *The Foundations of Modern Wales 1642–1780* (Oxford, 1987); M. R. Watts, *The Dissenters from the Reformation to the French Revolution* (Oxford, 1978).
[64] G. H. Jenkins, *Protestant Dissenters in Wales, 1639–1689* (Cardiff, 1992), p. 10.

65 W. S. K. Thomas, *Stuart Wales* (Llandysul, 1988), pp. 59–63.
66 Jenkins, *Dissenters*, pp. 12–13.
67 *Glamorgan County History, IV*, pp. 252–3.
68 Richards, *Puritan Movement*, pp. 26–7.
69 *Pembrokeshire County History, III*, ed. B. Howells (Haverfordwest, 1987), ch. 4.
70 Richards, *Puritan Movement*, p. 27.
71 A. H. Dodd, *History of Wrexham* (Wrexham, 1957), p. 52.
72 T. M. Bassett, *The Welsh Baptists* (Swansea, 1977), pp. 13, 20, 23–4.
73 *DWB*, s.n. Harley family, appendix.
74 *Glamorgan County History, IV*, p. 255.
75 Jenkins, *Dissenters*, p. 13.
76 *Glamorgan County History, IV*, p. 255.
77 Ibid., pp. 286–7.
78 Dodd, *Wrexham*, pp. 51–3.

2. *The Civil War and Interregnum*

1 Thomas, *History of Wales, 1485–1660*, p. 200.
2 Philip Jenkins, *A History of Modern Wales, 1536–1990* (London, 1992), p. 114.
3 Jenkins, *Dissenters*, p. 14.
4 Ibid., pp. 14–15.
5 Richards, *Puritan Movement*, p. 33.
6 R. Dunning (ed.), *St Donat's Castle and Atlantic College* (Cowbridge, 1982), p. 26.
7 For Jeremy Taylor, see below p. 47.
8 Thomas, *Stuart Wales*, pp. 52–6, 66–7.
9 Thomas Rees, *A History of Protestant Nonconformity in Wales* (London, 1861), p. 7.
10 Jenkins, *Dissenters*, p. 15.
11 Thomas, *Stuart Wales*, p. 45.
12 Jones, *Hen Ffydd*, p. 61.
13 F. L. Cross (ed.), *The Oxford Dictionary of the Christian Church* (Oxford, 1957), p. 1237.
14 Richards, *Puritan Movement*, p. 121.
15 Ibid., p. 94.
16 Ibid., pp. 51–9.
17 Williams, *Wales and the Reformation*, chs 6, 7 and 9.
18 Thomas, *Stuart Wales*, p. 67.
19 Richards, *Puritan Movement*, p. 121.
20 Thomas, *Stuart Wales*, p. 64.

[21] L. S. Knight, *Welsh Independent Grammar Schools* (Newtown, 1926).
[22] R. A. Griffiths (ed.), *The City of Swansea* (Stroud, 1990), pp. 23–4.
[23] *DNB*, s.n. Thomas Gouge.
[24] Thomas Richards, *Religious Developments in Wales, 1654–62* (London, 1923), pp. 4–7.
[25] Ibid., p. 147.
[26] N. Cohn, *The Pursuit of the Millennium* (London, 1957).
[27] Jenkins, *Dissenters*, p. 13.
[28] Richards, *Religious Developments*, pp. 213–34; see also Jones, *Vavasor Powell*.
[29] Ibid., pp. 130–2.
[30] Quoted in G. F. Nuttall, *The Welsh Saints 1640–1660* (Cardiff, 1957) p. 17.
[31] David Walker (ed.), *A History of the Church in Wales* (Penarth, 1976), p. 76.
[32] See above, p. 35.
[33] Parry, *Welsh Literature*, p. 244.
[34] Jones, *Hen Ffydd*, pp. 12–13.
[35] T. P. Ellis, *The Catholic Martyrs of Wales, 1535–1680* (London, 1955), pp. 150–3.
[36] Jones, *Hen Ffydd*, p. 72
[37] Rees, *Libri Walliae* makes no mention of any copy.
[38] Philip Henry, *Diaries*, ed. M. H. Lee, 1802.
[39] R. T. Jones, *Congregationalism in Wales* (Cardiff, 2004), pp. 53–6.
[40] *Gweithiau Morgan Llwyd*, eds T. E. Ellis and J. H. Davies, 2 vols (Bangor, 1899 and 1908).
[41] G. Williams, 'Stephen Hughes (1622–88), Apostol Sir Gâr', *The Carmarthenshire Antiquary*, 37 (2001), 21–30.
[42] Williams, *Welsh and their Religion*, pp. 166–72.
[43] Bassett, *Baptists*, p. 13.
[44] Ibid., p. 14.
[45] G. Williams, 'John Miles and the Baptist denomination in Wales', *Minerva: The Journal of Swansea History*, 7 (1999), 11–18.
[46] T. Mardy Rees, *A History of the Quakers in Wales* (Carmarthen, 1925).
[47] N. Penney, *John ap John and the Early Records of the Friends in Wales* (London, 1907).
[48] Samuel Jones, quoted in Williams, *Welsh and their Religion*, p. 49.

Part II

1660–1780

3

The Restoration Church

The Restoration

The restoration of King and Church was generally greeted in Wales with enthusiasm. The nobility and gentry of north Wales complained of the previous regime: 'under the pretence of propagating the Gospel, [they] have for a long time shut up our Churches, converting the endowments of the Church to their own use, and sown the seeds of false Doctrine and Schism amongst us.' They besought the king to restore 'all those good and wholesome laws' for the government of the Church passed by Elizabeth and the first two Stuarts.[1] Many had been educated at Jesus College, Oxford, under the high church Francis Mansell before the war and influenced there by high church teaching.[2] Dissenters were regarded as potential rebels. In the north houses of Baptists and Fifth Monarchists were plundered and in the south Quakers were mobbed. In Carmarthenshire in May 1660 meetings of gathered churches were harassed, and in the autumn the leaders were arrested and congregations dispersed.[3] In the north-east at the Denbighshire Great Sessions in 1660, 45 people from Denbigh were presented for 'depraving the Booke of Comon Prayer', 15 from Gresford and over 50 from Wrexham were presented for absence from divine service, and 27 were presented at the Quarter Sessions at Ruthin.[4] Fears of unrest and rumours of plots by radicals and dissenters continued throughout the 1660s.[5]

William Roberts, bishop of Bangor, survived the Commonwealth and at his first visitation of his diocese after the Restoration he was accompanied by 'divers worthy, noble and loyall Gentry' including the high sheriff. Bishops were rapidly nominated to succeed the three bishops who had died during the Commonwealth: George Griffiths to St Asaph on

22 September 1660, Hugh Lloyd to Llandaff on 8 October and William Lucy to St David's on 15 October. None were obvious candidates for preferment on the national stage, but all three had strong local links, which was a strong commendation in comparison with the previous regime. Lloyd had been archdeacon of St David's, and held livings in Glamorganshire in the 1630s; Lucy had been archdeacon of Brecon, and Griffiths had been chaplain to a previous bishop of St Asaph, a prebendary of the cathedral, and an incumbent in Montgomeryshire, and was an upholder of the Welsh language and traditions. Lucy further promoted his popularity by giving generous terms to purchasers of leases of episcopal estates.[6] Successive bishops of Bangor during the rest of the century had strong Welsh backgrounds: Robert Morgan, who succeeded in 1666, had been rector of Llanddyfnan and Trefdraeth in Anglesey, and spoke Welsh; Humphrey Humphreys had been an incumbent in the diocese and was a Welsh-speaker; Francis Davies and William Lloyd of Llandaff had been incumbents in that diocese.

Of 130 clergy who lost their livings following the Restoration seventy-eight left by the end of 1661. Many were removed by the Act of September 1660 for Confirming and Restoring of Ministers, which restored to their livings clergy removed under the Commonwealth, and prohibited the return of those who had 'declared against infant baptism'. Only thirty-one ministers were removed as a result of the Act of Uniformity in 1662. Most withdrew quietly. The counties where there were significant numbers – Glamorgan 23, Breconshire 14, Montgomeryshire and Cardiganshire 13 each, Denbighshire and Pembrokeshire 11 each, and Monmouthshire 10 (of whom thirty-four subsequently conformed) – were those where Puritanism had prospered.[7] New appointments rapidly followed the withdrawals. At St Asaph in December 1660, immediately after the bishop's consecration, there were eighteen collations or institutions, and nineteen between March and May 1661; this compared with three each month between September and October 1662.[8] Many clergy were confirmed in parishes to which they had been appointed during the Commonwealth.[9] There were sixty institutions and collations in Bangor between July1660 and November 1663.[10] In Llandaff Bishop Lloyd appointed local men to parishes in his gift, and ordained local men to titles in their home parishes. Five prebendaries appointed to the cathedral in 1660 were Glamorgan-born, including his two sons-in-law, who assisted him; the archdeacon, who headed the chapter, was a Glamorgan man. At Chepstow he collated a native of the town to replace a popular and influential Nonconformist.[11]

The restored Welsh bishops were fearful of, and therefore intolerant of, dissenters: fears of another rebellion haunted them. Successive bishops of Bangor, where there were few dissenters, firmly opposed dissent, as did Lloyd at Llandaff and Lucy at St David's. Lucy claimed in *A Treatise of the Nature of a Minister* against Independents, published in 1670, that if dissenting civic leaders who maintained dissenting preachers were 'forced to pay such sums to the amendment of poor vicars in market towns I durst say I would make this a happy diocese from such scandalous sectaries'.[12] Puritans held office in boroughs and towns into the 1680s in south-east and south Wales. Swansea, Carmarthen, Brecon, Cardigan and Haverfordwest all had dissenting schools.[13] The consistory court in the archdeaconry of Brecon failed to secure attendance by non-attenders at their parish churches, who appear to have ignored excommunications pronounced against them.[14]

William Lloyd, on becoming bishop of St Asaph in 1680, resolved to win over dissenters by argument rather than coercion. During his primary visitation, in September 1681, at Welshpool he disputed for a day with a group of Quakers, and subsequently arranged a formal debate at Llanfyllin town hall, where he was accompanied by clergy, justices of the peace and deputy lieutenants. Four days later he met a group of Presbyterians at Oswestry, and publicly debated in the town hall about episcopal ordination from 2 until 7 or 8 p.m. He held further debates in 1682. However, when persuasion failed, he applied compulsion, and clamped down on dissenters during the Rye House Plot.[15]

Although enforcement of the penal laws was patchy, dissenters were always fearful. In Denbighshire, John Carter, who was imported as a military governor into the locality by the previous regime, remained as a deputy lieutenant. In Anglesey, by contrast, not a single Interregnum justice was reappointed.[16] In Cardiganshire Sir John Vaughan of Crosswood was relatively tolerant in implementing the Clarendon Code, commenting: 'as long as persons conform outwardly to the law we have no inquisition into opinion,' and in Carmarthenshire Sir Rice Williams of Edwinsford was lenient.[17] There is little evidence of much action by justices against dissenters in Breconshire,[18] or in Glamorgan, where the Mansells of Margam patronized Puritan clergy and employed ejected clergy as tutors.[19]

Action against dissenters was sporadic. At Northop in Flintshire a group of people were prosecuted for gathering in the parish church and insulting the vicar, and attempting to prevent him entering the reading desk. In 1663 the churchwardens of Wrexham presented 68 people at the Quarter Sessions for not attending church. Twenty-six people were presented in 1664 at the Great Sessions in Denbigh for absenting themselves from church, and 27 from Bromfield and 12 from Chirkland as 'Nonconformists'.[20] In 1666 the lord lieutenants of north Wales counties harried dissenters following the discovery of a plot in London.[21] Radical groups – Quakers, Fifth Monarchists and Baptists – suffered most persecution, and migrated in significant numbers. Later, James II's attempts to win the support of dissenters were regarded by the majority in Wales with horror.

The Background

Wales in this period was a fragmented society. Internal communications were poor, especially between north and south. Bristol, Shrewsbury and Chester respectively were more convenient centres for south, mid- and north Wales than anywhere in Wales itself. There were marked differences between north and south, and between upland and lowland areas. In 1800 possibly 90 per cent of the population spoke Welsh, and perhaps 70 per cent were monolingual,[22] but north Walians claimed not to understand south Walians and vice versa. Welsh Members of Parliament did not act as a bloc as Scots members did. After the abolition of the Council of Wales in 1689, apart from the Courts of Great Session, which heard cases before two judges twice a year in four circuits, the Established Church was the only body serving all Wales, and the only body formally to use the Welsh language. There was no university, few bookshops and no theatres in Wales.

The population of Wales in the mid-eighteenth century was estimated at about 45,000. There were few significant towns. Wrexham was the largest in the mid-eighteenth century with 6,720 inhabitants, followed by Swansea with 6,040 and Carmarthen with 4,576. Market towns were the trade and social centres, but were small.

Wales was a predominantly rural and poor society, of small farmers and labourers. John Loveday commented on the poverty of dress of the Welsh compared with the English, noting that in south Wales women wore neither shoes nor stockings, and that although women in the north wore no shoes, they were better dressed than in the south.[23] Industry grew slowly: in the south before 1760, mostly in the vast and poor upland parishes where Merthyr Tydfil later became the largest town in Wales. Sir Humphrey Mackworth developed coal mining on his estates at Neath and lead mining and lead and copper smelting in Cardiganshire. Iron smelting was developed in the 1720s at Caerphilly, Machen and Tredegar. John Loveday noted coal mining around Llanelli in the 1730s. In the north-east, lead mines were developed at Halkyn, Holywell and Mostyn; and on Anglesey in the 1780s Parys mountain employed 1,200 miners. These concerns attracted English labour as well as that from Welsh farms. All such developments, however, were small-scale.

The lesser Welsh gentry had suffered economically for their Royalism during the Commonwealth, and were alienated from the non-Welsh-speaking, mostly London-based, great magnates. During the century many landed families failed to produce male heirs, and their estates were consolidated and passed to heirs based in England. The gentry were, in any case, concentrated in the lowlands and the borders.

There was social fluidity. Griffith Jones, the son of a blacksmith, married the sister of a baronet and great magnate in south Wales, Sir John Philipps. Howell Harris, the son of a small farmer, was accepted as an honorary member of the local gentry. His close involvement with Madam Sydney Griffith aroused scandal, not because she was a member of the gentry but because both were married. His brothers who went to

London did well; one became an assay master at the Royal Mint, and another was a London tailor who was sufficiently successful to buy the Trefeca estate and in due course serve as high sheriff.

Politically Wales was largely Tory. Parliamentary seats were dominated by a small group of county gentry who tried to avoid the expense and animosity of contested elections. Although there were only 15 or so nonjuring clergy in Wales – 2 in the diocese of Bangor, 3 in Llandaff, 6 in St David's and 4 in St Asaph,[24] there were strong Jacobite sympathies among the magnates and leading gentry, including the dukes of Beaufort in the borders, Sir Charles Kemyss in Monmouthshire and Glamorgan, Sir John Philipps in Pembrokeshire, and Lord Bulkeley on Anglesey and in Caernarfonshire and Merionneth. Montgomeryshire was reckoned a Stuart stronghold. The White Rose Circle in the north-east included not just Tory squires but the magnates Sir Watkin Williams Wynn of Wynnstay, and Sir Robert Grosvenor of Eaton Hall. The Society of Sea Sergeants, including the leading gentry in the south-west, was reckoned a Jacobite organization. However the attachment to the Stuart cause did not provoke political rashness. Despite the Pretender's proximity in Manchester in 1745, Sir Watkin Williams Wynn and the rest did nothing to jeopardize their positions.[25]

Despite its remoteness and isolation, there were close links, at all levels of society with London, which was a Mecca for Welsh craftsmen, servants and labourers, as well as merchants and drovers and, increasingly, for clergy; many Welsh gentry settled in London.[26] The first annual St David's Day celebration in London was held on 1 March 1715, when George Lewis, rector of Dolgellau, preached to the Loyal Society of Antient Britons in St Paul's, Covent Garden. The following year there was a feast at Haberdashers' Hall and subscription forms for the proposed new edition of the Welsh Bible were distributed. From 1734 there was a Welsh charity school on Clerkenwell Green.[27]

London was a major focus for raising capital and gathering technical skills for industrial development in Wales: Sir Humphrey Mackworth raised the money there for his mining enterprises.[28] Immense sums of money were also raised for the promotion of the Gospel in Wales by London philanthropists, many of whom were Welsh-born. Thomas Gouge raised funds for his Welsh Trust from London clergy and merchants, as well as Welsh gentry, to provide bibles in Welsh and schools.[29] Many initiatives for improvement in the Established Church in Wales, and providing Bibles, Prayer Books and devotional and instructional literature were, as we will see, London-based and -funded. London Dissenters also raised money for their co-religionists in Wales, and took a keen interest in their well-being. The Congregational Fund, established in London in 1695, gave grants of £30 and £20 in 1696 to share among churches in south Wales. Grants from them and the Presbyterian Fund supported ministerial students at Brynllywarch.[30] Howell Harris, the Methodist revivalist, was strongly supported by his London-based brothers, and acquired a body of London friends and supporters through spending significant periods supervising Whitefield's Tabernacle during Whitefield's absences. Harris was the chief Welsh distributor of London-based revivalist magazines, many of which were printed and edited by a London Welsh printer, John Lewis.[31]

Dissent

Nineteenth-century Congregationalist historians claimed a heroic seventeenth-century Independent past for Welsh dissent.[32] The Compton Census of 1676 which provides a guide to the number of dissenters from the Established Church does not support this. Thomas Richards claimed that dissenting groups were of some size, and that incumbents making the returns thought it their duty to play down the strength of dissent. Anne Whiteman, however, suggested that incumbents seem to have done their best to give truthful answers about numbers of absentees from Holy Communion, and that their knowledge about their parishioners should not be underestimated. A complicating factor was defining dissent in relation to 'partial conformity' by those who attended both a dissenting meeting house and their parish church. Dissenters' attendance at parish churches might fluctuate widely in relation to the risk of persecution, and especially the popularity or otherwise of the incumbent or the curate, compared with the dissenting minister.[33] Even a deprived minister like Samuel Jones of Brynllywarch who withdrew from Llangynwydd in the summer of 1662, had his children baptized at his parish church.[34] Calamy observed of the Nonconformist Stephen Hughes:

> His Moderation and lively Preaching recommended him to the Esteem of the sober Part of the Gentry, by whose Connivance he often preach'd in the publick Churches, which were much throng'd by the vast Numbers that came to hear him from the Neighbouring Parishes.[35]

The distinction between a conforming Anglican and a dissenter may, in many instances, have been difficult to draw. Some people attended both their parish church and a meeting house. Dissenting congregations probably gave the impression of large numbers because they gathered congregations from a wide area.

The conflict model of the nineteenth and early twentieth centuries for relations between the Established Church and dissent does not satisfactorily describe the late seventeenth- and eighteenth-century experience. Anglicans and dissenters cooperated in the Welsh Trust. The few cases of dissenters refusing to pay church rates in the diocese of St David's during the first half of the eighteenth century suggests an amicable situation between dissenters and their parish churches.[36] Anglican authorities did not necessarily approve of this. At Llanybri near Llansteffan, in Carmarthenshire, Edward Tenison, archdeacon of Carmarthen, in a visitation in 1710 discovered that the impropriator, the Earl of Northumberland, had leased the ruined church to the principal of the dissenting academy in Carmarthen to use as a Presbyterian meeting house. Tenison also criticized the incumbent of Pencader, Carmarthenshire, who lived in Carmarthen, for allowing stone from the ruined church to be removed to build a dissenting meeting house.[37]

Geraint Jenkins has pointed out that dissenters were a tiny minority, about 1.15 per cent of the population, compared with about 6.5 per cent in England and Wales as a whole. Following the Declaration of Indulgence in 1672 185 licences for meeting houses were granted in Wales – 136 in the south, and forty-nine in the five northern counties.[38] Many of these were only rooms in houses. In 1676 in St David's diocese 2,368 Nonconformists were recorded, mostly in the archdeaconries of Brecon (1361) and Carmarthen (597); 217 in Bangor; 635 in St Asaph; and 895 in Llandaff, mostly concentrated in six deaneries – Abergavenny (189), Chepstow (195), Groneath (118), Llandaff(180) and Newport (173).[39] Dissenters were few in north-west Wales. In the north-east dissent was well established in only three deaneries – Bromfield, Vale and Mauchin. Wrexham had over a third of the dissenters in the diocese of St Asaph. Except in the major urban centres – Wrexham, the most populous town in north Wales, and Swansea – dissenters did not form a significant proportion of the population.[40] By 1715 there had been significant growth, or people were being more open about their allegiances. Michael Watts estimates that then 5.74 per cent of the population of Wales were dissenters, and that two-thirds were in Carmarthenshire, Glamorgan and Monmouthshire.[41]

Dissenters were not a coherent group. In the border counties of Breconshire and Radnorshire in the late seventeenth century, they comprised seven groups: Arminian or General Baptists based at Llanddewi Ystradenni in Radnorshire; 'closed communion' Baptists at Llanigon and Olchon, led by Thomas Powell; 'open communion' Calvinistic Baptists at Llysdinam in Llanafan Fawr, associated with Thomas Evans; Quakers; two separate congregations including Independents and Baptists, one led by Henry Maurice at Llanigon, and the other being the remains of Vavasor Powell's church in Radnorshire; and a congregation led by John Weaver of New Radnor. After the Toleration Act in 1689 denominational differences became more distinct and church organizations more rigid.[42]

In north Wales in 1738 in the diocese of St Asaph the visitation returns suggest that there were only 151 families of dissenters in sixty-six of the 117 parishes for which returns survive.[43] However, in Llandaff diocese in 1763 twenty-two dissenting ministers were recorded, of whom seven were over sixty, and only three under forty-five. Dissent was strongest in upland areas, and almost non-existent in lowland areas. Guy notes that few clergy showed outright hostility to dissent.[44]

Independents were the largest Welsh dissenting group after the Restoration. In 1675 Henry Maurice reported twelve Independent churches in Wales, each with several meeting places, which probably accounts for the seventy-two meeting house licences for Independent congregations granted under Charles II's Declaration of Indulgence in 1672, mostly for private houses, and the forty-four Independent preachers licensed. They were mostly on the borders and in the south – in Wrexham, Montgomeryshire, Radnorshire, Brecknockshire, Carmarthenshire, in Swansea, Glamorgan and Monmouthshire.[45] In 1715 there were twenty-six churches in Wales.[46] In Bangor diocese, in the visitation of 1749, it was noted that there were only two Independent meeting houses, of which one lacked a 'teacher', and the other had just two families.[47]

Craftsmen and yeomen were the backbone of the churches, with a few well-to-do members.[48] There was strong emphasis on the community and independence of a church. The leadership of a church comprised the pastor assisted by teaching elders, governing elders and deacons. Those to be ordained had to be members of the church, and were ordained by the congregation.[49] Although Calvinism was pervasive among Welsh Independents, there could be tensions, as at Wrexham in 1710 between moderate and extreme Calvinists, which might reflect personal tensions within the church. There were also divisions over Arminianism in south-west Wales in the 1730s.[50]

Howell Harris, the Calvinistic Methodist revivalist, was initially welcomed into Independent meeting houses, but his emphasis on the certainty of salvation as essential, his tendency to emotionalism, and his desire to control and judge members of his societies offended many Independents. Revivalism influenced some churches, through the use of Dafydd Jones's translations of Isaac Watts's hymns from the 1740s, and the secession of some Methodist exhorters and societies. However, it was only after 1780 that revivalism took hold of Welsh Independency.[51]

Academies were established for the education of the sons of members of Independent congregations at Brynllywach from *c.*1670, Abergavenny from 1697 until 1702, at Oswestry and then Shrewsbury from 1700 and at Carmarthen from 1704.

Carmarthen became the premier academy, supported by grants from both the Congregational and Presbyterian Funds. It was an important resource for educating ministers. However, in 1757 it split over concern about Samuel Thomas's Arianism; the portion sponsored by the Congregational Fund moving to Abergavenny and the portion sponsored by the Presbyterian Fund remaining in Carmarthen.[52]

In *c.*1715 there were twenty-five Presbyterian congregations in Wales of which seventeen were in Carmarthenshire, where they apparently comprised 13.8 per cent of the population,[53] and two in Denbighshire. Their meeting house in Wrexham was demolished in riots in 1715–16 after the Hanoverian succession.[54] Contemporaries, especially Anglican clergy, had difficulty distinguishing Presbyterians from Independents, and Densil Morgan has suggested that from 1714 Presbyterians and Independents were completely indistinguishable.[55] In the visitation of the diocese of St Asaph in 1738 fifty-two Presbyterian families were noted, and two meeting houses, at Llanbrynmair, with twelve families, where the rector noted, 'My own people go too frequently to the meeting, but always communicate with me', and at Llanwyddelan.[56] In 1749 Bishop Drummond noted eight Presbyterian meetings.[57] The increase in numbers of meeting houses may result from clergy noting every location where meetings were held, rather than churches. In the diocese of Bangor, at the visitation in 1749, incumbents noted four meetings, three of which were recorded as not having 'teachers'.[58] In 1761 the bishop of Llandaff was petitioned for licences for meeting houses from Presbyterian congregations in Bassaleg and Chepstow.[59]

The Committee of the Dissenting Deputies in London, the coordinating body for dissenters in England and Wales, kept a watchful eye on the affairs of Welsh dissenters, and received more complaints from Wales than from any English counties. Complaints particularly related to the refusal of justices to register meeting houses. Following a complaint of the Montgomeryshire justices' refusal in 1740, the committee sought advice from the attorney-general, who provided it, and returned his fee. Then, and following subsequent complaints they, on the basis of the advice, applied for a writ of *mandamus* from the Court of King's Bench to the various county justices against whom complaints were made, to require the justices to register the meeting houses. Even in 1765, when it was alleged that the applicant from Anglesey was not a 'regular' dissenting minister and that the proposed meeting house 'had been used by Enthusiasts of the Wildest sort who stripped themselves in their Worship', a licence was granted. All complaints to the deputies were taken up with the respective bishop or the chancellor of the diocese or, when it was complained in 1745 that it would be difficult to get any lawyer to take up the case of an alleged insult against a dissenting minister in Caernarfonshire, with the Custos Rotulorum.[60] Dissenters may have been a minority, but they were not easily oppressed.

The Quakers began advancing in Wales from 1654, when John ap John, who had been a member of Morgan Llwyd's Baptist congregation at Wrexham, and had divided the congregation, began organizing missions. Their radicalism raised fear and hostility, and all other groups closed ranks against them.[61] Quakerism spread largely through the fragmentation of existing congregations, especially when millenarian hopes were dashed by the political changes in 1653–4. In Merioneth the defections were startling – three justices of the peace became Quakers and held meetings in their houses.[62] After the Restoration Quakers were the most persecuted Protestant dissenting group because of their refusal of the oath of allegiance.

They continued to make modest advances until the 1680s, Bishop Lloyd, as has been noted, debating with them at Welshpool in the hope of winning them. During the 1680s there was wide-scale migration of Welsh Quakers to Pennsylvania. In 1682 a group of families comprising about forty people from the area around Bala in Merioneth sailed from Liverpool in May, and a second party left in September 1683 comprising about a hundred people, at least half of whom were from Merioneth, settling on land purchased by John ap John. In 1698 a party of sixty adults and two children, probably from Radnorshire, left from Carmarthen for Pennsylvania.[63] A number of Quaker apologetic treatises were published in Welsh in the 1690s in an attempt to establish themselves in Welsh-speaking areas and to recruit new members. This provoked sharp responses from Anglican clergy. Despite there being few Quakers left in Wales, at the Yearly Meeting in 1702 it was again agreed to sponsor the translation and publication of books in Welsh, and £18.5s. was raised to translate and print current Quaker best-sellers at Thomas Jones's press in Shrewsbury. However, only a trickle of books was published.[64] Four meetings survived in the eighteenth century in Cardiganshire and Carmarthenshire. In north Wales, at Dolgellau in the diocese of Bangor, two families of Quakers were noted in the parish in 1749, and at Llangelynnin, Merioneth, a man and his wife and two small children were noted as Quakers and 'having a meeting now and then, at their own house for themselves and those of their kidney'.[65] In St Asaph in 1738 only twelve Quaker families were noted in the diocese.[66]

Baptist congregations had begun to be established along the Marches by soldiers during the Second Civil War, but they were not a homogeneous group. Some churches were the fruit of the Act for the Better Propagation and Preaching of the Gospel in Wales of 1650, established by Hanserd Knollys, the London Baptist leader, in Montgomeryshire, and by John Miles at Ilston and Llantrisant in Glamorgan, and at Carmarthen, Hay and Abergavenny. These were all five Calvinist in doctrine, and despite some differences were agreed on closed communion, and formed an association. They gathered their congregations from wide areas, and members mostly met in district house groups, with elaborate rules to ensure that each church was united from time to time to break bread. Their gathered, rather than communal, nature, and the emphasis on adult baptism, meant that they were seen as socially divisive and undermining family life, in what was still a communitarian society. They were kept in touch by general meetings, comprising elders and messengers from each church.[67]

Baptists, with the Quakers, bore the brunt of the persecution of dissenters after 1660. Ministers like John Miles who had accepted settled livings were expelled. Vavasor Powell, who had ministered in Merioneth and Montgomeryshire, was arrested and intermittently imprisoned until his death in 1670. Failure to baptize children at a parish church resulted in excommunication, involving loss of civil rights and ineligibility for burial in a churchyard. Many more prosperous Baptists conformed to avoid loss of civil rights and persecution. In 1690 the Hay congregation meeting at Olchon had about thirty members, the church at Llantrisant had between fifty and sixty members, but no minister, the church at Abergavenny had eighty members, and the church at Carmarthen had disappeared.[68] However, a new church at Rhydwilym established in 1667 by William Jones, an ejected Independent minister, had 113 members drawn from thirty-eight parishes across Pembrokeshire, west Carmarthenshire and Cardiganshire.[69] The Baptists kept their testimony alive in the old centres after 1660, and old members were replaced by new members. In 1700 a Welsh Association was formed, which included three new churches founded since 1689, at Blaenau, Glandwr and Trosgroed.[70]

John Miles emigrated to New England in 1663, and in 1701 a number of the Rhydwilym congregation emigrated to the Delaware River. Emigration continued into the 1720s, and some of the most experienced and ablest ministers migrated. Some branches of churches became separate churches, so that in 1714 there were 14 churches, of which 5 were in Glamorgan and 3 in Carmarthenshire.[71] By 1760 there were 19 churches and by 1770 21.

The exclusivism of the doctrine of election and the strictness of Baptist fellowship inhibited their growth but made isolation and social ostracism a virtue, which assisted their survival. Marrying out, drunkenness, and attending Methodist meetings were frequent grounds for expulsion. At Llanwenarth church, out of 185 members between 1714 and 1760 forty were excommunicated, of whom eight were received back. The membership of Baptist churches tended to be tradesmen and farmers, although some churches consisted mostly of labourers.

After 1760 membership began to grow. It was reckoned that there were 530 'clear gains' in membership between 1762 and 1770 discounting losses from death and expulsion, and a gain of 1,126 between 1770 and 1780 (compared with an estimated membership of 1,601 in 1760). The Methodist revival contributed to this. In the late 1730s there were contacts between representatives of Baptist churches and Howell Harris, but Harris was put off by their exclusivism, and they by his emphasis on experience and the individual. A few of Harris's converts joined the Baptists when Harris and Daniel Rowland separated in the 1750s, but in the 1760s and 1770s numbers influenced by

Methodism came into membership – sixty-five were incorporated into membership at Newcastle Emlyn between 1765 and 1774. Former Methodists often wanted emotional preaching and singing, which led to splits in some congregations.

In 1776 a Baptist mission to north Wales was initiated, using Methodist techniques, at the instigation of Thomas Llewellyn, a London educationalist and manager of the Particular Baptist Fund, with the support of Methodists and English Baptists. In 1749 only two Baptist meeting houses had been recorded in the diocese of Bangor.[72] After two pastors undertook a twenty-one-day preaching tour into Caernarfonshire and Anglesey, followed up by pairs of preachers from south Wales, at monthly intervals, disaffected Anglicans, Methodists and Independents were attracted, and a new church was established at Llangefni in 1779. In general the mission was successful where Independents had put down roots in the seventeenth century, and where Methodists had been active since the 1750s.[73]

The character of the Welsh Baptist movement, however, changed in the last quarter of the century, partly, despite resistance, owing to the evangelical revival. A significant turning point was Joshua Thomas's *Hanes y Bedyddwyr Ymhlith y Cymry* ('History of the Baptists among the Welsh People', 1778) which identified Baptists with the earliest British Church, and was positive about Methodism, emphasizing Welshness, a generosity of spirit towards other Christians and hope for a better future.[74]

The Compton Census recorded 217 'Papists' in the diocese of St David's, 19 in Bangor, 275 in St Asaph, 551 in Llandaff and a total of 1062 for the whole of Wales.[75] Only 926 were reported in 1767.[76] Most of these were on the Monmouthshire/Herefordshire border, around Raglan and Abergavenny, and in Flintshire, around Holywell. Abergavenny and Monmouth were allegedly largely Catholic towns, and fifteen priests were reported in the 1670s in the north Monmouthshire countryside. The *Herbert Correspondence*[77] listed nine priests in 1675, and noted that Mass was said 'publicly and constantly', and that Roman Catholic magistrates protected them. In 1678 a wave of anti-popish propaganda swept across much of Wales. In a report to Parliament on the 'state of Popery' in Monmouthshire Sir John Trevor claimed that priests were maintained in twelve houses. In the 1680s it was claimed that 100 pilgrims were seen at St Michael's Chapel on Skirrid Fawr near Abergavenny.

After the Popish Plot, Bishop Croft of Hereford eliminated the Jesuit mission at Cwm, destroying the main base for Roman Catholic influence, and two Jesuits and a secular priest were executed. It was alleged in the context of the plot, that there were numerous priests in Monmouthshire and that magistrates did not enforce the law against papists.[78] A survey of 1706 listed 746 recusants in Monmouthshire, suggesting a serious underestimate by the Compton Census.[79] Monmouthshire continued to be a centre of Catholicism. Gentry families at Llanarth, Courtfield and Perthyr maintained chaplains and supported a mission at Abergavenny, where the baptism register between 1740 and 1750 recorded names of people from twenty-five parishes in the county and three from neighbouring counties. When an alleged Roman Catholic was elected town clerk of Monmouth in 1730, the election was challenged, but he was supported by a petition of thirty burgesses.[80] Monmouthshire recusant gentry in exercising rights of patronage to parish churches seem to have appointed incumbents sympathetic to their views, and often of their own surname. The incumbent of Rockfield, who was presented by the recusant Powell sisters, allowed Bishop Prichard's burial in the chancel of the parish church.[81]

The earls of Powys were a major influence, employing Jesuit chaplains from the 1670s until the last earl's death in 1748. Two bursaries were offered annually, of £20 each, for a boy from south Wales and a boy from north Wales to the English Jesuits' school at St Omer. In Montgomeryshire, a priest was based at another Powys property, Buttington Hall, near Welshpool, where a Roman Catholic school begun under James II did not survive 1688, when the chapel was broken up by a mob. A priest was subsequently appointed to Welshpool by the Vicar Apostolic in 1763.[82]

The Popish Plot did not eliminate recusancy in south Wales.[83] The influence of the strong Catholic presence that emerged in the west Vale of Glamorgan in the 1680s is seen in the various offices Catholics held after 1689,[84] and in an increase in the number of Jesuits in the south Wales district from five to twelve between 1704 and 1733.[85] There were very few Roman Catholics in west and north Wales, and allegedly only eight Catholics in mid-eighteenth-century Caernarfonshire, six of whom were migrants.[86]

The first Vicar Apostolic of the Western District, Philip Michael Ellis, went into exile with James II, and a successor, Matthew Prichard was not appointed until 1713. He came from the Perthyr congregation, where he made his base. He was succeeded on his death in 1730 by his coadjutor, William York, who was succeeded in 1764 by Bishop Walmesley, who had been coadjutor since 1756. In 1773 Walmesley reported nine priests in Wales, and 750 Roman Catholics, 475 of whom were in Monmouthshire. Mass centres continued with resident priests at Holywell, Abergavenny, Perthyr, Monmouth, Brecon, Chepstow and Usk, and domestic chapels at Talacre, Llanarth and Courtfield. He reckoned that most Catholics were 'poor' and included few people 'of quality'.[87] In 1764 Fr Gregory Powell issued two catechisms in Welsh, and in 1776 a prayer book in Welsh, suggesting that the Roman Catholic community was largely Welsh-speaking.[88]

Where Roman Catholicism survived, it generally retained the allegiance of a whole community, gentry families and their households and tenants, and the professional and commercial classes who owed their livings to them.[89] For gentry families, long-standing social relationships within county communities tended to transcend religious divisions, and Catholics seem to have cohabited in comfort and security with Anglican neighbours.

Despite their small numbers, Roman Catholics continued to be regarded as a threat. One of the motives for providing schooling for the poor was to protect the Welsh from the temptations of popery.[90] Although, like all dissenters in Wales, in terms of the total population, Catholics were a small minority, locally they appeared significant. Concentrated in the parishes around Powys Castle and Holywell, they seemed very numerous in small communities, just as, in parts of Carmarthenshire, Glamorgan and Monmouthshire, gatherings of Protestant dissenters from a wide area could give an impression of a larger presence than was statistically the case.

4
Episcopal Administration

Bishops

From the late seventeenth century, as Parliament became more prominent in government, bishops' votes in the House of Lords became more important in achieving majorities for ministries in the House, and it was expected that bishops would regularly attend the Lords during annual parliamentary sessions. As a result sees more convenient for London came to be regarded as desirable and Welsh dioceses were seen as remote and inaccessible. Thomas Sherlock, on his first visit to Bangor in 1728, wrote to a friend ' 'tis pity this Bprick shou'd be only a bridge to a better. It may not be so to me and if it is not, I can like everything here, but the distance from the Parliament house.'[1]

However, bishops visited their dioceses during the summer recess of Parliament most years. The Ordination Register at St Asaph shows bishops ordaining in their cathedral most summers.[2] At St David's bishops ordained in their diocese, at Brecon or Carmarthen, every year between 1705 and 1758 except in 1732 and 1734.[3] Bishops of Llandaff ordained every year in their diocese between 1663 and 1679, but thereafter their palace at Mathern became uninhabitable and they seldom ordained in their diocese, though from 1704 until 1736 bishops of Llandaff held the deanery of Hereford *in commendam* and conducted ordinations in Hereford Cathedral, which may not have been much less accessible from parts of the diocese than Llandaff.[4] At Bangor all recorded ordinations were in the cathedral between 1689 and 1780, except between December 1713 and July 1722, when a register may be missing (for the Lists of Institutions continue throughout the period, suggesting that all administration was not neglected) and between 1750 and 1756.[5] This is as good a record as that of most bishops of

English dioceses, and better than some, especially elderly and ailing bishops.[6] The only surviving complaint about a bishop's failure to ordain in his diocese, by James Harris, vicar of Llantrisant in 1701, was because of the 'great Age' of bishop Beaw.[7]

It was not merely the remoteness of Welsh dioceses that led bishops to hope for translation. The relatively modest endowments of Llandaff and St David's made them a financial burden to their occupants. In fact all the Welsh dioceses were among the nine poorest dioceses of the Established Church.[8] Bangor was reckoned to be worth £120 a year in about 1671, Llandaff about £400 a year in 1660, St Asaph about £300 a year in *c.*1705 and St David's about £405 a year in 1688; by 1762 Bangor and St Asaph were reckoned at £1,400, St David's at £900, and Llandaff at £500.[9] However, annual income fluctuated, depending on payment of 'fines' for granting new leases on property, and income from tithes. In order to fund the duties of the bishop, as well as provide a personal income, additional offices were held *in commendam* to supplement income from the endowments of sees. Bishop Griffith of St Asaph was granted a dispensation to hold the archdeaconry of St Asaph, and the rectories of Llanrhaeadr-ym-Mochnant and Llanymynech and Llandrinio *in commendam* which were reckoned to be worth £260, £150, £70 and £120 respectively. Bishop Lloyd of St Asaph acquired other livings to be held *in commendam* – vicar of Llanyfydd in 1680, rector of Llanarmon-yn-Ial in 1686, rector of Eastyn or Queenhope and rector of Llanymynech in 1685, rector of Whitford in 1686, rector of Bangor Monachorum in 1690 and rector of Marchwiel in 1691.[10] George Hooper was reluctant to accept St Asaph in 1703, fearing he would be less well off if he had to give up his existing lucrative preferment. However he struck lucky, for a new vein of lead was discovered in a lead mine on one of the episcopal estates. In 1712 Bishop Fleetwood secured an act for the abolition of the onerous tax of mortuaries payable to the bishop by incumbents newly beneficed in the diocese after the death of a predecessor, in exchange for the augmentation of the income of the see by the first sinecure in the bishop's gift to fall vacant.[11] At Bangor the archdeaconries of Bangor and

Anglesey were annexed to the bishopric. In Llandaff the treasurership of the cathedral was annexed to the bishopric, and the bishop usually held at least one good English living; Bishop Beaw was rector of Adderbury in Oxfordshire, where he generally lived, and where he conducted ordinations, and Bishops Tyler, Clavering and Harris were successively deans of Hereford.

Securing the income and rights of the see could be difficult. Lloyd at St Asaph was unsuccessful in attempting to recover the advowson of Llangollen and the manor of Meliden, which had been alienated.[12] Bishop Ottley of St David's proceeded against his predecessor Philip Bisse, on his translation to Hereford, for dilapidations on the palace at Abergwili and the bishop's house in the College at Brecon. The case took four years to settle, and Ottley got less than half what he claimed. He also claimed that Bisse, while receiving £500 a year in rents between 1710 and 1713, had received a total of £1,660 in fines for the renewal of leases during the period, while Ottley only received £229 in fines between 1713 and 1715.[13] At Ottley's death in 1723 his executors found he was owed rents amounting to £110 of his average income.[14] Sherlock found at Bangor: 'The revenue of the Bprick has been much neglected; the mannours are leased to some great gentlemen in the country wch are thereby much the greater: and the Bishop much the poorer.' However he found the local people generous in kind: 'I abound in venison, fat sheep and fat beef, wch come and are likely to come in plenty for present. I have already a buck and a half, half a fat oxen, several whole sheep, lobsters, ducks and fresh wine.'[15]

Attempting to maximize income from episcopal estates could be risky, for tenants might become hostile. The attempt by Bishop Watson of St David's to obtain the best income from his estates in the 1680s and his vigorous and tactless handling of tenants contributed to the revolt of his diocese and his deprivation for alleged simony.[16] It was difficult to manage estates from London. Bishop Moss of St David's put the income of the see on a steadier footing by employing one of the clergy as his local agent, and, seeking rents reflecting real values rather than high fines and low rents, employed one of his tenants to survey the episcopal lands to establish clear boundaries.[17]

Expenses of office were considerable. Payment of the taxes of First Fruits and Tenths and legal fees for degrees, consecration, confirmation of election, homage, restitution of temporalities and enthronement, and fitting up the episcopal residences meant that during the first years in a see a bishop was likely to have little money to spare. Working expenses were also high, including travel to and from and living in London during parliamentary sessions. In their dioceses bishops were expected to live as great magnates, to maintain proper state in their palaces, to entertain the gentry and provide accommodation for influential travellers, and hospitality for visitors, and to give charity to the poor and contribute generously to local subscriptions. Bishop Beaw of Llandaff, when he lived at the palace at Mathern in the 1690s noted: 'Bread and Beer were freely distributed at my doors every day. My Gates stood open to all comers . . .'[18] Henry Prescott, the registrar of St Asaph diocese, noted, at John Wynne's first visit to the diocese as bishop, that he dined most days with the bishop, and that 'company . . . crowds his Table every day'.[19] John Loveday visiting St Asaph in 1732 commented on the hospitality of Bishop Tanner, and that 'the Country is continually sending him in Provisions of all kinds'.[20] To omit such shows was a false economy, for customary respect would be forfeited.

There has been much criticism, by contemporaries and historians, of bishops of Welsh sees for the relatively short tenure of their sees. St David's had 19 bishops during the course of 120 years, St Asaph 17, Bangor 16 and Llandaff 14. This bears comparison with the two worst-endowed English dioceses, Bristol and Oxford, which had nineteen and fourteen bishops respectively. Long tenure of a see could be disadvantageous in an age when there was no provision for retirement. Elderly bishops might linger in poor health, unable to give much attention to their dioceses. Bishop Lucy of St David's was housebound for his last five years. The 'great Age' of Bishop Beaw of Llandaff and his failure to 'Exercise his Episcopal Functions especially in Ordination and Confirmation of Children for several years' were complained of by one of his leading clergy in 1701, five years before his death.[21] Bishop Bull, appointed to St David's at the age of seventy-one, was unable personally to undertake the triennial visitations in 1705 and 1708.[22] Welsh-born and Welsh-speaking bishops were as likely to accept translation as English-speaking bishops. John Wynne of St Asaph accepted translation to Bath and Wells, Humphrey Humphreys of Bangor to Hereford and John Evans of Bangor to Meath.

It has been suggested that the only long episcopate at Llandaff during our period, that of Bishop Beaw, was the result of his political disfavour at court,[23] but the well-connected Shute Barrington, son of a viscount and brother-in-law of a duke, was thirteen years bishop of Llandaff. The perceived remoteness of Bangor and of St Asaph, as previously noted, was perhaps the major deterrent to bishops staying long. Some tenures, however, were scandalously short. John Thomas was nominated to St Asaph in November 1743, but before his consecration, in January 1744, Bishop Reynolds of Lincoln died, and Thomas asked Bishop Sherlock of Salisbury, whom he was due to succeed at Bangor, to lobby the Duke of Newcastle, who managed ecclesiastical patronage on behalf of the ministry, to recommend him to the king for Lincoln. Thomas pointed out that though the value of the two sees 'was nearly the same', Lincoln was more accessible from London. When Thomas Gilbert was nominated to Salisbury in 1748 after eight years at Llandaff, he wrote to Newcastle that "twas a matter of great comfort to be so happily deliver'd from his present disagreeable situation', although his successor, Edward Cresset, wrote to Newcastle, 'The situation of Llandaff is so convenient to me that I shall never desire to leave that neighbourhood' and he even resigned his deanery of Hereford. When, in 1761, John Ewer had not proceeded to take up his nomination to Llandaff two months after he had accepted it, Newcastle commented that such delay 'does not seem decent' and resolved not to offer Ewer any other vacancy.[24] While one might sympathize with men reluctant to go to the considerable expense of taking up appointment to a poor diocese, or keen, even at the major expense of translation to another diocese, to improve their lot, to move with such alacrity was cavalier treatment of the clergy and people of a diocese.

In comparison with most English dioceses, with the exception of St David's, Welsh dioceses were small, as well as poor, and young and able men may have felt disappointed that their capacity was not being further extended. Shute Barrington, after seven years at Llandaff, felt frustrated and restricted.[25] While some bishops did not remain in their dioceses long enough to contribute much, Welsh sees seldom suffered from the decline in health and long old age of their bishops. It could be advantageous to have a young bishop, keen to make his mark and attract the attention of a ministry's ecclesiastical advisers, for preferment to bishoprics was usually on merit.[26] Welsh dioceses may have benefited from the energetic episcopates of aspiring younger men.

Most bishops brought relevant experience to their appointments. Of the 76 men who served as bishops in Welsh dioceses during the period, 28 had been fellows of colleges, 8 had been bishop's chaplains, 16 had been deans, 17 had been archdeacons. Some were distinguished scholars. Humphrey Humphreys of Bangor was considered one of the outstanding scholars of Welsh history and literature of his generation.[27] Bull of St David's was an eminent patristics scholar and theologian, and a leading apologist for the Established Church against Roman Catholic claims.[28] John Wynne of St Asaph was principal of Jesus College, Oxford, and had produced an abridgement of John Locke's *Essay concerning Human Understanding* for the use of undergraduates.[29] Even Benjamin Hoadly, briefly at Bangor, was no mean scholar. Thomas Tanner of St Asaph was a distinguished scholar and antiquary.

Bishops of Welsh dioceses were conscientious in their primary duty of ordination. As we have seen, they usually conducted ordinations in their dioceses each year so that candidates did not need to travel to London or elsewhere to be ordained. The registers suggest that, in only ordaining at the canonical ember seasons, bishops of Welsh sees were more observant of the Canons than some English bishops, many of whom had frequent 'special' ordinations, out of season. There is no evidence that bishops in Wales did not exercise caution in selecting ordination candidates, as recommended by Archbishops Sancroft and Tenison. Bishop Bull at St David's required candidates to appear before him for examination a month before the ordination. Ottley's examining chaplains reported to him in detail about candidates. Ottley carefully monitored testimonial letters presented by candidates, and checked their dates of birth, and the proposed stipends. Bishop Trevor's examining chaplains catechized candidates in detail about their knowledge and Methodist tendencies, and deferred candidates for lack of learning and suspicions of Methodism.[30] Most bishops of St David's probably sympathized with Bishop Lloyd of St Asaph's protest to Sancroft that the prohibition against ordaining non-graduates was

> not practicable in our Welsh dioceses. We have a great many more cures of souls than we have graduates in this country: and as most of the people understand nothing but Welsh, we cannot supply the cures with other but Welshmen. But yet of those whom I have ordained the graduates have not always been the best scholars.[31]

Although it was alleged in the 1680s that there were men roving the Welsh borders and Wales with forged letters of orders,[32] there is no evidence it was the fault of the bishops.

Bishops Humphreys of Bangor, Lloyd of St Asaph and Bull of St David's, at least, were of the circle around Archbishops Sancroft, Tillotson and Tenison who were keen to raise standards of pastoral practice among clergy. Bishop Lloyd summoned a synod of the clergy to St Asaph in June 1681 to consult them about what 'things are amiss in the Church and how every fault might be mended, and what is well may be improved'. They met at 7 a.m., so that he could preach and administer Holy Communion before beginning business, and they dined with him. He announced the appointment of rural deans and issued a request to incumbents to compile a *notitia* in standard form for their parishes listing names of 'housekeepers', numbers in each household, and ages of those under sixteen. Some lists indicate the stage in Christian education which children had reached and others note those who had been catechized or confirmed. Lloyd at his synod in 1691 emphasized the importance of keeping the lists up to date. In 1683 the topic was the 'more decent and orderly administration of the holy offices'. Lloyd kept a close eye on his clergy and dealt summarily with any allegations of officiating at clandestine marriages, drunkenness and immorality. It was claimed he knew every priest in the diocese.[33]

Bishop Fleetwood compiled a *notitia* of St Asaph in 1708, which listed the names of incumbents, their degrees, the value of the living, the patron and the taxes payable for each parish, and also had transcribed a '*Notitia* of ye Diocese from a Parchment Book written about 1560'.[34] Humphrey Humphreys, who claimed to know every parish and clergyman in Bangor when he was promoted from dean to bishop, in 1700 gave 'a strict charge to his clergy to meet frequently . . . That the clergy of each Deanery unite together' to consider Archbishop Tenison's circular letter about standards of pastoral care. He was 'personally present at one or other of ye Meetings, the Clergy throughout ye whole Diocese being associated'. He instructed

> That the meetings should be either in Church or the Minister's House or some other private house, and not in an Alehouse if possibly it can be avoided. But if it cannot be avoided I desire that no Ale be drunk in the room of meeting; and that as soon as the business is over all depart to their respective homes without any sitting to drink.[35]

John Evans continued Humphreys's reforms at Bangor. Bishop Watson at St David's in the 1680s pressed for the repair of churches and parsonages and insisted on the residence of the clergy, against much opposition from clergy.[36] Bishop Bull at St David's set out his high standards for the clergy in his diocese in *A Companion for Candidates for Holy Orders: or The Great Importance and Principal Duties of the Priestly Office* and *The Principal Parts and Branches of the Pastoral Office with Rules and Directions for the Due Performance of Each of Them*, which became standard handbooks for clergy, remaining in print for over 150 years. Bull revived the office of rural dean with responsibility to exercise surveillance over 'the conversation and diligence' of both clergy and laity.[37] Bishop Ottley at St David's encouraged the repair of parsonage houses. All the bishops of the Welsh dioceses were actively involved with the SPCK and its 'Welsh policy'. Bishop Tyler of Llandaff in 1718 set up a commission of inquiry 'to Inform ourselves ye true, clear, improv'd yearly value of Every Benefice' to assist the identification of the poorest benefices for augmentation by Queen Anne's Bounty.[38]

Visitation of parishes by the bishop or his deputy was a central aspect of the management of a diocese.[39] Bishops of the Welsh dioceses, especially of St Asaph and Bangor, were unusually diligent compared with bishops of English sees, in that often they visited every parish personally. Bishop Lloyd of St Asaph in 1685 and Bishop Humphreys of Bangor in 1690 issued visitation questionnaires to clergy and churchwardens in Welsh. In July 1716 Henry Prescott, the registrar of the diocese of St Asaph, recorded the Welsh-speaking Bishop Wynne's progress through his diocese, staying with the gentry or the leading clergy. At Llangollen, for example,

> The 2 Bayliffs of the Town attend his Lordship here. About 10 he goes to the church. Mr Humphreys has a good discourse chiefly on the Liturgy. A numerous Clergy call'd, my Lord has a long and affectionat Charg on the 3 Heads of the present King's right, of Obedience by virtu of the oaths to him, and the Clergys duty to teach and inculcate these to their people. A crowded dinner, extravagant Exhibicions go on after noon.[40]

The next day the bishop confirmed in the church. The bishop's charge additionally illustrates his role as a local representative of the Crown. The year after the 1715 rising, among the uncertainly loyal clergy and gentry of north Wales, amongst whom the registrar was numbered, such a charge was not out of place. The dinner provided an opportunity for clergy to meet one another, and for the bishop to meet them, which could be a restricted experience if he spoke no Welsh and they were nervous in English. In 1716 and 1719 Wynne visited nearly all the parishes in the diocese, and in 1724 124 of the 140 parishes and chapelries.

The standard of completion of the returns for Thomas Tanner's primary visitation of St Asaph are of outstanding quality compared with most English dioceses.[41] At Bangor in 1739 Thomas Herring of Bangor undertook what he called 'a perilous' primary visitation, reporting: 'I determined to see every part of my diocese, to which purpose I mounted my horse and rode intrepidly but slowly though North Wales to Shrewsbury.' In 1749 Bishop Pearce of Bangor reported to the Earl of Hardwicke: 'since my arrival here I have been upon visitation . . . of my whole diocese.' He noted that

> As my horse, Who was a native of Merionneth had never been used to any but such rough and stoney ways he carried me very safe and had (as I found) peculiar skill to step from one stone to another without once stumbling on the whole journey . . . Our roads for several miles was rather a pair of stone stairs than a path; and whereas we might have gone off from the rough pavement we should have run the hazard of being set foot in a bog.[42]

Visitations in the vast diocese of St David's were a marathon and strenuous experience for bishops.

Churchwardens were required, at a visitation, to report defects in the parish, including moral offences, and anything wrong with the church building or its furnishings. Bishop Maddox of St Asaph in 1738, in citing the clergy in preparation for his primary visitation, asked them to assist their churchwardens to prepare their presentations, and to 'point out to them (if need be) what needed to be presented, and to check what had not been put right since the last visitation'. Presentments of torn surplices, damage to the pulpit cushion, and lack of a bier, as well as for leaking gutters and roofs, broken windows and damaged churchyard walls in the archdeaconry of Carmarthen in the 1750 visitation of St David's suggest that careful attention was paid to details by parish officers. When, from the 1730s, bishops, in preparation for a visitation, began to issue questionnaires to be completed and returned by the clergy, much information was elicited about parishes, including numbers of families in the parish, whether or not the incumbent was resident, whether there was a curate, the pattern of Sunday and weekday services, the language used, the frequency with which Holy Communion was celebrated, numbers of communicants at Easter, and other times, any schools in the parish, numbers of dissenters, Roman Catholics and, in due course, Methodists.

Rural deans reported regularly to the bishop.[43] Where rural deans' reports of their inspections of parishes survive, as at St Asaph from 1709 onwards, and St David's in *c*.1717, they show meticulous attention to detail, including the incumbent's or curate's character, and the condition of the church and parish, even sometimes transcribing inscriptions on silver. In St David's bishops were sent rural deans' visitation reports to brief them before they undertook a visitation. Bishop Drummond's letter of appointment to rural deans in 1749 shows he had the highest expectation of the diligence of rural deans in inspecting parishes, and required them to 'give a true report so that he might admonish or praise' the incumbent.[44]

As we have seen some bishops compiled a *notitia* recording and analysing the information gathered at visitations. Robert Drummond at St Asaph in 1749 compiled an outstandingly detailed survey of the diocese from the visitation questionnaire returns, with detailed comments on the state of repair of the church, the parsonage, the terrier (land register), the books, the parish registers, the prayer desk and the pulpit, to assist him in his primary visitations. He also confirmed, on twenty-one different occasions during his visitation over four weeks in August and September 1749, a total of 5,489 candidates.[45] In the 1770s Shute Barrington, as bishop of Llandaff, compiled a digest of the visitation returns.[46] The standard and detail of visitations of the Welsh dioceses seems at least as high as in the best of the English dioceses, and the use of rural deans was unusual.[47]

The normal means of monitoring the conduct of clergy and disciplining the refractory was by means of the diocesan consistory courts. Bishops usually intervened personally only in unusual circumstances. The limited evidence suggests that bishops, even when absent in London, were kept well informed of events in their dioceses. William Lloyd at St Asaph, predictably, kept a very close eye on his clergy. Bishop Wynne of Bangor acted against an incumbent reported to him by a rural dean for celebrating clandestine marriages.[48] Bishop Ottley complained to his registrar in May 1714 of

> a great disorder of late wch I wonder you did not tell me of. Mr [Griffith] Jones of Llandilo Abercowen's going about

> preaching on weekdays, sometimes in churches and sometimes in churchyards and sometimes on the mountains to several hundreds of auditors and at Llanwenog had the Church doors broken open for him the first Thursday in April. I see it is high time to repair to my diocese.[49]

Later, in October 1714, Sir John Philipps reported to the SPCK that Griffith Jones of Laugharne

> has lately undergone a sort of Tryal before the Bp of St David's at Carmarthen where several of the Clergy appear'd against him, whose principal accusation was his Neglecting his own Cure and intruding himself into the churches of other Ministers without their leave, the contrary whereof was manifestly prov'd viz that he never preach'd in any other place without being invited by ye Incumbent, Curate, or some of ye best inhabitants of the Parish. That he had indeed preach'd twice or thrice without ye walls of ye Church, the reason of which was because the church was not large enough to contain ye hearers which sometimes amounted to 3 or 4,000 people. That his defence was so clear and satisfying that the Bishop declar'd he was willing Mr Jones shd preach anywhere, having an invitation from the Minister of ye place.[50]

Bishop Claggett of St David's acted on the many complaints he received alleging William Williams's neglect of his curacy at Merthyr and declined to ordain him priest.

Bishops of Welsh dioceses varied considerably in the amount of patronage they possessed. Bishops of Llandaff had patronage of only three livings in the diocese, apart from the twelve prebendal stalls in the cathedral, which varied in value from £40 to 13*s*. 4*d*. a year. Generally bishops appointed members of their family and friends to the better-endowed stalls, and local clergy to the less well endowed stalls.[51] In Bangor in 1778 the bishop had seventy-eight out of 116 livings[52] making him the second most powerful episcopal patron in the Established Church, second only to the archbishop of Canterbury.[53] The bishop of St David's too had considerably more patronage than most bishops, 102 livings, comprising a third of the livings in the diocese. However, they were concentrated in Cardiganshire and Pembrokeshire, the poorest part of the diocese.[54] Bishops

Womack and Ottley normally appointed Welsh-speakers to livings in their gift.[55] In St Asaph Bishop Lloyd was careful only to appoint Welsh-speaking clergy to Welsh-speaking parishes. John Wynne normally only appointed incumbents from the diocese to stalls in St Asaph cathedral.[56]

Otherwise patronage was in the hands of lay people. In Glamorgan lay magnates presented incumbents to two-thirds of the livings: Lord Mansell had eleven livings, Lord Windsor eight, six other members of the county gentry had between two and a half and seven and a half livings. No one else had more than two. Lord Mansell kept in close touch with his livings and with other people's use of patronage. In Llandaff diocese lay patrons often presented relatives to their best livings. Chaplains, who were usually recruited from among close relatives, families who had served the family well in some professional capacity, or had first-rate recommendations for their learning and virtue, were often presented to the local parish, and were in a good position to receive other livings in their master's gift, and meet other potential patrons.[57] Otherwise patrons largely drew on local men for appointments, sons of Glamorgan and sons of Monmouthshire in those counties respectively. Local gentry tended to appoint graduates to the parish in which they lived, and in any case graduates tended to receive the better-endowed livings. Lay patrons also tended to appoint people of similar ecclesiastical and political views to themselves.[58] In St David's the Crown had seventy-eight livings, and lay patrons 111.[59]

The Welsh dioceses have the only instances during our period of bishops of the Established Church being disciplined, both in the period immediately after the Revolution of 1688: Thomas Watson, bishop of St David's 1687–99, and Edward Jones, bishop of St Asaph 1692–1703.[60] Watson was appointed under James II, and supported his policies. After William III's succession he was accused of using Roman Catholic ritual, not praying for William and Mary, extorting money for collations, ordinations and institutions, tearing up tenants' leases and forcing them to pay for new leases. The chancellor of the diocese, Robert Lucy, the son of Watson's predecessor but three, whom Watson attempted to remove, rallied the clergy of the diocese against him. Lucy petitioned Archbishop

Tillotson to order an inquiry, and Tillotson appointed a commission to visit the diocese, and suspended Watson. Tillotson was satisfied there was evidence against Watson and determined to proceed against him, but died. His successor, Tenison, cited Watson to appear before him in his Court of Audience at Lambeth. Watson at every stage contested the jurisdiction of the archbishop's court, but the House of Lords and the courts consistently supported the archbishop's jurisdiction, and eventually in August 1699 Tenison decreed a sentence of deprivation, and, after a further series of appeals, in November 1704 the House of Lords ejected Watson from the temporalities of the see. Carpenter's view is that Watson had behaved in a manner liable to create suspicion, and was unworthy of his office. He concluded that technically Watson may have committed simony, but that the case was not clearly proven, and had been fuelled by his attempts to reform the cathedral chapter, enforce residence by clergy and raise the best income possible from the episcopal estates. His robust, obstinate and completely tactless manner, his Jacobite sympathies, and his unwillingness to accommodate himself to William III's claim to the throne and the Revolution Settlement did not help his case.

Edward Jones, bishop of St Asaph from 1692 was accused of giving men without 'Learning or Degrees' the best preferment in the diocese. There were also claims of corruption, oppressive treatment, and neglect of the welfare of the diocese. In 1697 thirty-eight of the most prominent beneficed clergy in the diocese laid a complaint under thirty-four heads against him to Archbishop Tenison. Tenison suspended him, ordered a metropolitical visitation of the diocese and cited Jones to his Court of Audience in June 1700. The accusations were found proven and he was sentenced to six months' suspension. When Tenison refused to restore him to office at the end of the suspension, he formally confessed his guilt of simony and neglect of his duties, and was restored to office. He used his subsequent visitation in 1702 to upbraid the clergy for breaching their oaths of canonical obedience in their behaviour towards him.

The sharpest criticism brought against the bishops during this period is that, apart from those who were Welsh, they lacked interest and concern for the nation to whom they ministered. Among post-Restoration bishops, William Thomas

(1678–83) and John Lloyd (1686–7) of St David's; Robert Morgan (1666–73)[61] and Humphrey Humphreys (1689–1702) of Bangor; and William Lloyd (1680–92), who learned Welsh on his appointment to be able to use Welsh to preach and administer the sacraments and confirm,[62] John Evans (1702–16) and John Wynne (1714–27) of St Asaph were Welsh-speakers.[63] George Griffiths (1660–7) of St Asaph played a significant part in translating the Prayer Book into Welsh.[64] Lloyd of St Asaph lobbied Archbishop Tillotson and Mary II that his successor should speak Welsh.[65] Although Richard Smallbroke of St David's (1724–31) was reputed to have learned a smattering of Welsh, and John Harris of Llandaff (1729–39) was Welsh-born and Richard Trevor, appointed to St David's in 1744, was of a Denbighshire gentry family, after John Wynne's translation to Bath and Wells in 1727 there was no Welsh-speaking bishop in Wales until 1870.

The lack of Welsh-speaking bishops was resented by contemporaries. In 1703 an anonymous correspondent asked Archbishop Tenison to only recommend Welshmen for Welsh sees, claiming:

> When we had bishops that could preach in Welsh, and did take pains to instruct the people, the generality of the people did keep the unity of the church, it may be as well as any part of the nation. But now of late there has been another course to make choice of perfect strangers to our country and language.[66]

Tenison recognized the need to nominate Welshmen to Welsh sees. In 1701 he had written to Archbishop Sharp of York, 'We had scarce any other choice for [Bangor] required a perfect Welshman . . .'[67] George Hooper was reluctant to accept St Asaph in 1703 because of his ignorance of Welsh.[68] Contemporary Englishmen agreed. Bishops Hough of Worcester and White Kennett of Peterborough thought the appointment of Welsh bishops to Bangor would be 'much more welcome to the people and undoubtedly more useful'.[69] Why Welsh-speaking or Welsh-born candidates were not appointed to Welsh dioceses is not clear. Until 1745 it might have been feared that Welsh clergy, with suspect Jacobite sympathies, might ally with

Welsh Jacobite gentry to support a Stuart rebellion. But thereafter there was no shortage of able Oxford-educated clergy of Welsh origins. Nor is there evidence of any anti-Welsh bias among ministers. At the least, lack of Welsh isolated bishops from the great majority of clergy whose first language was Welsh, and from laity whose only language was Welsh.

There is little evidence of hostility to the Welsh language by the bishops. The Act of Uniformity of 1662 had enjoined the bishops of Welsh sees and of Hereford to see that a Welsh translation of the Prayer Book was prepared. This was published in 1664. In 1700 Humphrey Humphrey of Bangor, a leading figure in contemporary Welsh antiquarianism and literature, was reported to be funding, along with his clergy, the printing of a newly translated Welsh Prayer Book, and proposed sending copies to the Welsh congregations in Pennsylvania.[70] In 1706 the bishops of St Asaph, Bangor and Hereford agreed to subscribe to, and secure subscriptions for, a duodecimo edition of the Prayer Book in Welsh. Bishop Fleetwood of St Asaph in 1710 criticized clergy for preaching in English when gentry families were present in church. Archdeacon Tenison of Carmarthen in his visitation in 1710 noted that introducing Welsh sermons into parishes attracted people from dissenting meeting houses, and that introducing services in English could provoke people to attend a meeting house.[71] Bishop Philip Bisse of St David's was one of the few bishops recorded as opposing translations into Welsh, when in 1711 he was reported to the SPCK as objecting to the translation of Robert Nelson's *Feasts and Fasts* 'from an opinion that the publicity of ye Book in Welsh will obstruct the English Tongue which he will endeavour to propagate by erecting Charity Schools'. In 1714, it was reported to the SPCK that the four bishops of Welsh dioceses (Bisse having now departed to Hereford) had promised to promote printing the Welsh Bible and Prayer Book, and recommend it to their clergy.[72]

In the predominantly Welsh-speaking diocese of St David's Bishop Ottley was encouraged by his nephew to appoint a Welsh-speaking precentor to the cathedral,[73] and his successor, Richard Smallbroke, encouraged the SPCK to produce a Welsh translation of the Book of Homilies, and proposed an English translation of 'a Collection of Hymns in Welch . . .' very much esteem'd for the Vein of Piety and good Sense in them', 'made and published by Mr Pritchard, formerly Vicar of Landovery'.[74] He objected to Moses Williams's proposal for a folio Welsh Bible bound in calf, to sell at 10*s*. 6*d*, only because he wanted a simpler, cheaper edition, to sell at 2*s*. 2*d*.[75] Bishop Claggett distributed a Welsh translation of Edmund Gibson's *Pastoral Letter* on Methodism.[76] In St Asaph, which was also predominantly Welsh-speaking, it was alleged that at a dinner for clergy and prominent lay people Bishop Drummond had said it would be beneficial if the Welsh language were completely uprooted, and his successor, Thomas Newcome, was also claimed to be anti-Welsh.[77]

The embittered Evan Evans, in an essay of 1764–5, blamed all the Church's weaknesses on oppressive foreigners who allegedly cared little for the souls of the people and were motivated by pecuniary considerations. He claimed: 'There are now only clergy unfamiliar with the language, taking possession of the best places in every Diocese, while the native Welsh serve under them for a trifle.' However, there is no evidence that bishops extensively appointed non-Welsh-speaking clergy to Welsh-speaking parishes in their gift. Following the case brought in the Court of Arches by a group of parishioners against Thomas Bowles, rector of Trefdraeth and Llangwyfan on Anglesey in 1770, on the grounds that he was incapable of ministering in Welsh in a Welsh-speaking parish, the dean declared that according to canon and statute and Article 24 Welsh-speaking incumbents should be appointed to Welsh-speaking parishes, and that ignorance of Welsh was sufficient grounds for a bishop to refuse to institute a priest presented to him.[78] There is little evidence of churchwardens criticizing clergy for not using Welsh, and considerable evidence that most bishops of Welsh dioceses recognized the importance of promoting worship, preaching and teaching in the 'language understanded of the people'. If there were criticisms of an incumbent's lack of competence in Welsh, bishops had little legal capacity to resolve the problem. They could only request the incumbent to appoint a Welsh-speaking curate. In the unlikely event that a bishop had an English-speaking parish in his patronage available to offer such an incumbent, he could not be forced to accept it.

As we have seen, all the bishops were actively involved with the major 'ginger group' for the development of pastoral ministry in the Church, the SPCK. They supported the SPCK in promoting the new translation of the Bible into Welsh, and the establishment of diocesan libraries in each Welsh diocese. It may be no coincidence that, as we will see, the other major agency for the improvement of the condition of the clergy, Queen Anne's Bounty, seems to have acted to the greater benefit of Welsh dioceses than English dioceses. The bishops of Welsh sees may not have neglected the interests of their dioceses during their long spells in London, and may have had close links with the London Welsh community.

The bishops also took an interest in the Welsh diaspora in the North American colonies. There were claimed to be 6,000 Welsh-speakers in Pennsylvania and other colonies.[79] In 1714 the bishops of the Welsh dioceses, in appealing for funds for a new Welsh Bible, noted the substantial need among Welsh-speakers in North America. They were keen to recruit Welsh-speaking clergy to work in the Welsh-speaking settlements in Pennsylvania and West Virginia, especially among the Quakers and Baptists who had migrated from Wales to Pennsylvania in the 1680s. Welsh clergy also went to work in the West Indian islands. At least thirty-seven went to North America between 1701 and 1735. Some went to key posts: Henry Harris, of Monmouthshire and a fellow of Jesus, was appointed by the SPG as lecturer at King's College, Boston, in 1708, and in 1719 Emmanuel Jones of Anglesey was reported teaching at William and Mary College.[80]

Consistory Courts

Each diocese had a consistory court, presided over by the chancellor of the diocese, or a surrogate in his place, with a registrar and proctors. The courts handled ecclesiastical matters, including testamentary matters, moral cases relating to sexual conduct, and defamation, as well as church attendance, discipline of the clergy and upkeep of the parish church, and non-payment of tithe and church rates.

Usually courts sat locally – in St Asaph in each deanery. The diary of Henry Prescott, registrar of the diocese of St Asaph from 1712, shows him moving from deanery to deanery, carrying out the court's business in local centres such as Wrexham and Oswestry.[81] To cope with the vast distances in the diocese of St David's the court sat in each archdeaconry, at Brecon, Carmarthen and St David's, and in the archdeaconry of Cardigan it was peripatetic, sitting chiefly at Penboyr, Cardigan and Lampeter, and occasionally at Llanrhystud, Trefilan, St Dogmaels and Cilrhedyn. There were two registrars for the diocese, one at Brecon and another, for the western archdeaconries, at Carmarthen. In 1723 an office was opened at Haverfordwest for the archdeaconries of St David's and Cardigan, but as there proved to be insufficient business, the court ceased to sit there and cases were heard at Carmarthen.[82] The dispersed courts in St David's attracted criticism: some deputies were alleged to have been irregular in attendance and negligent, and there were complaints against Charles Morgan, the registrar at Carmarthen.[83]

Court days began with morning prayer in the parish church, or the cathedral if the sitting was in the cathedral city. In St Asaph, at least, Prescott frequently commented, as on 21 May 1712, there was 'a Court of few, about 7 Causes'.[84] As registrar, Prescott examined the witnesses for both sides. In a difficult case of a contested will at Newtown in May 1715, the day began at 9 a.m. and business continued until 9 p.m., with a break for dinner, for two days, and the third day they adjourned to Sir Vaughan Price's house to examine Lady Price, one of the witnesses. The next day the court adjourned to Tregynon, and then to Mr Balney's house at Gregynog, where two more witnesses were examined that day and six the next, and the following day they adjourned to Berriew, where three more witnesses were examined at the vicarage.[85] Prescott undertook the circuit three or four times a year. Going on circuit also enabled court officials to visit churches where faculties had been applied for to alter a church, and to hear any objections. On 6 September 1717 Prescott noted that he visited Henllan to 'see the place for an intended Gallery in the West end and hear some slight objection against it'.[86]

It is not clear in what language the business of the courts was conducted. As there is no evidence of complaints, it seems likely that business was in Welsh, although Prescott does not seem to have spoken or understood the language, and no reference is made to translating witnesses' testimony for his benefit.[87] Evidence of allegations of defamation was certainly given in Welsh.

The task of the consistory courts was to achieve reconciliation between the parties and God and one another.[88] The registrar's job was to attempt to discover the truth, and to reconcile aggrieved and disputing parties. On 30 April 1712 at Oswestry Prescott noted: 'After dinner I make an end of the Controversy btwixt the 2 late Curates and the Churchwardens of St Martin's', and on 1 May in a case 'betwixt Mr Clapham, vicar of Kinnerley and one Pain, Steward to Smith the Impropriator', which involved 'Clamor, passion and reflexion', he noted: 'I endeavour to compose both with some success.' The punishment of the courts, even public penance, was intended to enact an act of reconciliation between an offender and God, and the local community with whom the penitent had been in the wrong.

The courts' business was varied. Between 1686 and 1688 in St Asaph there were 73 cases of unlawful marriage, 59 of not paying church rate, 49 of fornication, 38 for having a bastard, 25 of the church being out of repair, 14 of misbehaving in church, 16 of not going to church, and small numbers of other cases. The books are missing for the years 1710–58, but between 1758 and 1762 there were 47 cases of defamation, 15 of non-payment of tithe, 3 of disputes over seats, and only 1 or 2 cases of 10 other offences. After 1760 an increasing number of defendants in defamation cases failed to appear in court and were excommunicated.[89] Tables 4.1, 2, 3 and 4 illustrate the range of cases in the other Welsh dioceses. In the case of St David's, the survival of papers from the archdeaconries of St David's and Cardigan is too fragmentary to permit a comparison. When it is remembered that the cases have been listed by decade, it is clear that even when numbers seem large, the figures represent only a few cases in an average year, for example an average of only seven tithe cases or eighteen cases of fornication in the busiest of years. The pattern of cases in courts in Welsh dioceses appears similar to that in English dioceses.[90]

Table 4.1 Diocese of St David's: cases before the consistory court in the archdeaconry of Brecon, 1662–1759[91]

	Tithe	Seats in church	Church rate	Defamation	Fornication	Bastardy	Attacking clergy	Clandestine marriage	Misbehaviour in church
1662–9	24	7	3	13	1	2	1		
1670–9	9	1		5		2		2	1
1680–9	10	1	2	7	3	2		3	1
1690–9	16	6	3	4	6	6	3	7	3
1700–9	57	4	3	30	6	45	2	11	3
1710–19	20	2	6	21	5	23	3	13	4
1720–9	47	11	8	63		50	4	19	12
1730–9	47	11	1	105	1	29	2	7	14
1740–9	43	8	2	39	1	10	1	4	4
1750–9	40	4		49	2				

Table 4.2 Diocese of St David's: cases before the consistory court in the archdeaconry of Carmarthen, 1664–1759[92]

	Tithe	Seats in church	Church rate	Defamation	Fornication	Bastardy	Clandestine marriage	Misbehaviour in church	Non-attendance at church
1664–9	1	1					2		
1670–9	2			2					
1680–9	28	4	5	41	1	16	7	8	11
1690–2			2	6					
1706–9		1		6		1			
1710–19	2	1		3		1			
1720–9	3	1	3	8		4	1		1
1730–9	9	4	3	27					
1740–9		1	9	29		1		1	
1750–9	16		6	32	1	2	1	5	

Table 4.3 Cases before the consistory court in the diocese of Llandaff, 1710–59[93]

	Tithe	Seats in church	Church rate	Defamation	Fornication	Clandestine marriage	Misbehaviour in church	Adultery
1710–19	36	5	5	88	1		1	1
1720–9	76	2	12	125	2	2	2	2
1730–9	70	9	7	162	8		3	
1740–9	63		2	77		2	2	
1750–9	29	5	4	53	2		8	

Table 4.4 Cases before the consistory court in the diocese of Bangor, 1734–59[94]

	Tithe	Seats in church	Church rate	Defamation	Fornication	Clandestine marriage	Misbehaviour in church	Adultery	Bastardy
1734–9	1			3	10				
1740–9	2	1	9	7	7	2	2		3
1750–9	1		2	5	182		2	34	

The courts depended on the willingness of churchwardens to present offenders to the courts, or of individuals to come into court themselves, especially for defamation cases, and so were reliant on the good will and consent of the population for their business. This may account for their relative inactivity against dissenters in the aftermath of the Restoration.

5
The Welsh Clergy

Clergy Incomes

In parts of Wales at the Reformation, the suppression of religious houses, and alienation to lay people of tithes with which they had been endowed in return for providing priests for parishes, had practically disendowed the Church. In the two northern dioceses 43 per cent of livings were impropriated to lay people or appropriated to an ecclesiastical body, and in the southern dioceses 53 per cent.[1] In the early eighteenth century the poverty of the Welsh clergy was a commonplace assumption. Arthur Bedford of Bristol, writing to John Chamberlayne, the first secretary of the SPCK, in 1699 lamented 'the contempt of the Clergy occasion'd by the small Provision for them'.[2] Erasmus Saunders, writing about the diocese of St David's a decade later refers to clergy as 'Abject' figures, of 'despicable Appearance', 'who are deny'd for their Service and Labour such reasonable Encouragements as are necessary for Subsistence, and mocked with Salaries so very scanty: as a Plowman or an Hostler, or one of their generous Patron's Footmen wou'd probably disclaim to accept of'. He pointed out that poverty tempted clergy to be 'irregular in conduct' and rendered them 'Contemptible'.[3] John Macky, a well-travelled Whig writer, alleged in 1722 that the clergy in Wales relied on funeral offerings and kept ale-houses to make ends meet.[4] However, there never seems to have been a shortage of recruits for ordination.

It is a mistake to generalize about Wales as a whole. Bishop Drummond of St Asaph reported after his primary visitation in 1753 that he found the diocese 'In general much better than was imagined by strangers. The provision for the clergy not so small but that they might live with credit and comfort.'[5]

However Bishop Sherlock noted on his translation to Salisbury in 1743 he had left 'many worthy clergy but meanly provided'.[6] In the diocese of Llandaff, the average net income of a clergyman was barely two-thirds of his counterpart in north Wales.[7] The poverty of the clergy was real in the south. The incumbents of Llandegfeth, of Llanfair Cilgedin and Coychurch who died in 1683, 1724 and 1737 respectively, were all insolvent at their deaths.[8] Clergy widows could be left very badly off. In 1734 William Bulkeley on Anglesey noted: 'walked today to Cemaes . . . spent 6d for ale at Mrs Jones's house ye late Viccar's Widow', and in 1755: 'Gave a Guinea to an old Gentle-woman, a clergyman's widow distressed with poverty.'[9] John Lloyd, curate of Narberth, reported to Bishop Trevor in October 1744 that Samuel Morris, late incumbent of Llangan in Carmarthenshire, 'hath left a widow in deplorable circumstances so extremely poor that if she be not admitted to have a subsistence of that fund whereof Clergymen's widows are partakers, she must inevitably be relieved by the parish; she has not the value of 40s in the world.'[10] Generally clergy were best off in the dioceses of Bangor and St Asaph (Table 5.1) but even within the vast diocese of St David's there were significant variations between archdeaconries (Table 5.2). In Llandaff diocese forty-two of the 180 livings (24 per cent) were donatives, with perpetual curates, whose stipend was paid by the impropriator. Bishop Tyler's commission of inquiry in 1718 'to Inform ourselves of ye true and clear and improv'd yearly value of every Benefice' shows that the curate of St John the Baptist in Llantrisant was paid by voluntary subscription. Guy estimated that generally impropriators paid between a quarter and a third of the tithe income to perpetual curates.[11] In Carmarthen archdeaconry in St David's the variation was much greater. At Llanddowror, valued at £40 in 1710, the perpetual curate received £9.7*s*., at Llansteffan, valued at £300, the perpetual curate was paid £10 a year, and at Llangain, valued at £80 a year, the perpetual curate was paid £6. Clerical appropriators were not necessarily more generous than lay impropriators. In Llandaff at Penterry the appropriator paid the perpetual curate £2 a year in 1718, and the prebendary of Warthacwm in Llandaff Cathedral was supposed to pay £4 a year to the perpetual curate of Llandevaud, but in 1718 was

Table 5.1 Values of livings of northern dioceses compared with those of St David's

	Less than £10	£10–20	£21–30	£31–40	£41–50	£51–60	£61–70	£71–80	£81–90	£91–100	£101+
St Asaph, 1705–1715[12]	3	14	20	22	26	15	17	20	3	2	16
Bangor, 1756[13]				12	4	10	10	13	3	8	23
Bangor, 1778[14]		4	1	4	2	5	6	3	3	8	54
St David's in the first half of the eighteenth century[15]	63	101	64	45	33						

Table 5.2 Value of livings in the diocese of St David's in the first half of the eighteenth century

Archdeaconry	No. of returns	Less than–£10	£10–19	£20–9	£30–9	£40–9	£50+
St David's	87	18	35	17	5	10	2
Carmarthen	82	12	25	13	16	9	7
Cardigan	80	20	23	20	8	4	5
Brecon	93	13	18	14	16	10	22

reported to be six years in arrears. Not all impropriators were irresponsible. Thomas Jones of Llandeilo in Radnorshire who leased the tithes of the parish noted in 1717 that it was 'my care as well as my duty to provide for the parishioners of the said parish such a curate as may discharge himself to their satisfaction'.[16] Impropriators had an interest in appointing a satisfactory incumbent so that parishioners would not resent paying tithes.

Not surprisingly, in very few perpetual curacies and donatives was there a parsonage house. In 1771 only four perpetual curates in Llandaff resided in their parishes. The poverty of perpetual curacies meant that their incumbents were usually pluralists, to which legally there was no bar, as perpetual curacies were not regarded as benefices with cure of souls.[17] All perpetual curates in Llandaff held other livings, and fourteen employed a curate to care for one of their parishes, who himself had other parishes to care for. All parishes that were perpetual curacies had small populations, although in the second half of the eighteenth century a few had growing populations – Margam with 229 families in 1763, Bedwellty with 350 and Newchurch with 150.[18]

Even in the two northern dioceses, where average incomes were higher, there were some very poor livings. At Betws-y-Coed, in the diocese of Bangor, John Jones, who in 1749 signed himself 'Your Lordship's most Humble, most Obedient but most discouraged humble Servant', had served the forty families in the parish for thirty-five years, and reported that he was also master of Llanrwst school, in Denbighshire, and claimed his income was 'the small Pittance of £3. 14*s*. 4*d*. a year'.[19]

The Welsh dioceses were not unique in having a high proportion of parishes with small endowments and low incomes. In 1712, Lincolnshire had 64 per cent and Bedfordshire 47 per cent of livings with incomes of less than £50 a year;[20] in 1707 the Craven deanery in west Yorkshire had 68 per cent of benefices estimated at less than £50 a year;[21] and the four deaneries on the Cumbrian coast, had 83.5 per cent of rectories, vicarages and chapelries with incomes of less than £50 a year, and 46 per cent with incomes of less than £10 a year.[22] Even a southern diocese like Chichester in 1724 had 53 per cent of benefices with incomes of £50 a year or less.[23]

St Asaph in 1705–15, with 59 per cent with incomes of less than £50 a year, was comparable with many English dioceses, but St David's, with all its livings below £50 a year in the first half of the eighteenth century, was extremely poor compared with even the remotest and poorest areas of English dioceses with what are generally reckoned to be the poorest incomes.

It was not always easy to ascertain the actual income of a living. The source of vicars' and rectors' income was glebe land, either from letting or cultivating it, and tithes.[24] Both sources linked incumbents closely with the local economy, and their incomes fluctuated in line with their parishioners' incomes. The fluctuations could be considerable, at Llanfechell on Anglesey from £111. 9*s.* 8*d.* in 1742 down to £87. 15*s.* 4*d.* in 1756. At Llanfechell in mid-century the tithes, with the exception of one farm, were paid in kind, and the rector sold the produce of the great tithes in the different districts of the parish by auction, and the purchaser paid an agent to collect the tithes in kind.[25] In the deaneries of Penllyn and Edeirnion in Merioneth in the 1730s tithes were also mostly paid in kind.[26]

It is difficult to evaluate the evidence for disputes over the payment of tithe, for the survival of court records varies, and in the southern dioceses, where there is surviving evidence of fairly numerous disputes in the consistory courts (Table 5.3), many disputes may have involved lay tithe owners in impropriated livings rather than clergy. Eryn White has suggested that protests arose when people felt they had been unfairly assessed for payments, rather than as a matter of principle.[27]

Probably, as in England, most clergy with glebe farmed at least part of it themselves to provide basic foodstuffs. Some may have farmed in a large way. William Morris reported:

> Mr Evans [rector of Llanfechell on Anglesey] is a parson that lives in the middle of the island [at Treban nine miles from Llanfechell] and, as he is a considerable farmer and an agent for some gentlemen, frequents most fairs and publick meetings and is acquainted with all the gentry and clergy in the county.[28]

Table 5.3 Tithe disputes coming before consistory courts, 1664–1759

	1664–9	1671–9	1680–9	1690–9	1700–9	1710–19	1720–9	1730–9	1740–9	1750–9
Archdeaconry of Brecon[29]	24	9	10	16	57	20	47	47	43	40
Archdeaconry of Carmarthen[30]	1	2	28			2	3	9		16
Diocese of Llandaff[31]						36	76	70	63	29
Diocese Bangor[32]								1	2	2

Parsonage houses usually had associated farm buildings, as at St Andrews Major in Llandaff diocese, where it was noted:

> The Granary has part of the floor of earth and lime. There are two barns one to the northward or north east of the House, joining the Churchyard, thatched. The other to the eastward of the House . . . thatched. The House and Barns stand in a large Foldyard, . . . Behind the lesser Barn is a rickyard, adjoining to that a small piece of garden ground. The glebe consists of fifty acres.[33]

Augmentation of Incomes

The four Welsh dioceses were significant beneficiaries of augmentations by Queen Anne's Bounty, which from 1714 awarded grants, by lot, to benefices with incomes of less than £35 a year, increased to £50 in 1718, from money received from the taxes of First Fruits and Tithes paid by bishops and those clergy with benefice incomes of over £50 a year.[34] The Bounty had been established as part of the programme of reforming and improving pastoral ministry in the Established Church. After further legislation in 1715 the Bounty could also augment donatives and perpetual curacies, which was highly beneficial for the dioceses of St David's and Llandaff. Between 1721 and 1780, 372 Welsh parishes and chapelries received 664 augmentations amounting to a total value of £132,800. Grants were of £200, with which to purchase agricultural land, the income from the rent of which augmented the incumbent's income. As many as 168 parishes and chapelries received two augmentations during the course of the period, fifty received three augmentations, and one received four augmentations. This amounted to a considerable re-endowment of Welsh parishes. The majority of grants went to the two poorest dioceses, 225 to parishes and chapelries in St David's and seventy-three in Llandaff, while in the two northern dioceses thirty-two parishes and chapelries in St Asaph and forty-two in Bangor received augmentations. A higher proportion of Welsh parishes received augmentions than English parishes. The diocese of Chester, which was reckoned to have a very large number of poor livings and chapelries, with 526 parishes and chapelries received 331 augmentations, and Norfolk where about 60 per cent of livings were valued at less than £50 a year and about 12 per cent at less than £20 a year, received 126 augmentations by 1806.[35]

The Governors of the Bounty might match benefactions of £200 from private benefactors with a grant of £200. Welsh parishes, however, received proportionately fewer private benefactions than English parishes. Fifty-seven parishes and chapelries in Wales received such benefactions – 16 in St Asaph, 7 in Bangor, 41 in St David's and 13 in Llandaff. Of the benefactors 7 for St Asaph were women, and 4 clergy, 1 in Bangor was a woman and 2 clergy; in St David's, where until the passing of the Mortmain Act in 1735 there were more augmentations as a result of benefactions than by lot, 5 were women; and in Llandaff, 10 were women and 3 were clergy.[36] Augmentations in Wales appear to have been made to the poorest livings, especially perpetual curacies and chapelries with very small, if any, endowments.[37] In St David's, the archdeaconry of Brecon received significantly more augmentations than the other archdeaconries, probably because it had more chapelries, although in general the livings in that archdeaconry were better endowed than in the other archdeaconries. Most of the benefactions were by clergy, the chancellor of the diocese, for example, making five benefactions between 1723 and 1753.[38] A further piece of legislation, initiated by the Welsh bishops in 1714 'for taking away mortuaries within the Dioceses of Bangor, Llandaff, St Asaph and St David's', absolved incumbents in Welsh dioceses from paying mortuary fees to their respective bishops, which also modestly improved their financial positions.

Generally the value of benefice incomes in Welsh parishes improved during the course of the eighteenth century, as in most English parishes. The salary of the perpetual curate of Llandevaud in Llandaff diocese increased from £4 in 1718 by 150 per cent to £10 in 1771, although it was still only the equivalent of the wages of a 'tolerably expert husbandman' in the area.[39] In the more prosperous livings of the diocese of Bangor, in Caernarfonshire, in the late 1670s the average income of twenty-six livings was £48. 16*s*. 10*d*.; in 1756 it was

£84. 12*s*. 3*d*., and in 1778 £117. The increase in the value of the livings seems to have been a result of the development of the county's agriculture and increase in demand for agricultural foodstuffs, which pushed up prices.[40]

Curates

Assistant curates, as opposed to perpetual curates, who, as we have seen, were actually incumbents, were thought to be particularly poverty-stricken and irresponsible. In the 1680s Lawrence Womack, bishop of St David's, inveighed against non-resident incumbents who 'place illiterate curates for scandalous stipends' in their livings. In 1721 William Wotton complained to Archbishop Wake of 'a parcel of strolling curates in south Wales, and some such there also in north Wales, who for a crown or at most for a guinea would marry anyone under a hedge'.[41] The anticlerical William Bulkeley, whose comments should probably be viewed with scepticism, complained in 1737 of the immorality and hypocrisy of Robert Pugh, curate of Llanbadrig on Anglesey, and alleged that Owen Bulkeley, curate of Llanddeusant was 'six years ago but a common labourer', whom at the behest of an MP, under pressure from an incumbent whose vote he wished to secure, Bishop Herring had ordained without any educational requirements.[42]

The term 'curate' included both someone newly ordained serving an apprenticeship to an incumbent, and an experienced priest in charge of a parish because the incumbent was non-resident or incapacitated from undertaking duty because of infirmity or age. Examination of the visitation returns for the diocese of Llandaff in 1763 highlights the confusion there might be over the term 'curate': only thirteen 'curates' in Glamorgan did not also hold a benefice, and twelve in Monmouthshire, of whom only four appear never to have become incumbents.[43] Most curates, serving parishes on behalf of non-resident incumbents, were incumbents of neighbouring parishes, augmenting their incomes and fulfilling their energies by looking after a neighbour's parish. Curates, like perpetual curates, not having a cure of souls, were not inhibited by canon or statute law from holding a benefice or another curacy. Few curates subsisted only on the salary for a single curacy. If this is borne in mind, curates' stipends do not seem so low. If a curate was incumbent or curate of a neighbouring small parish on a stipend or salary of between £15 and £30 a year, and had a house of residence in one of the parishes and some glebe to cultivate, he would not have been so badly off. In St Asaph in 1749 three curates were paid in the range £10 to £14, six in the range £15 to £20, thirty-three in the range £20 to £24, three in the range £25 to £29, one was paid in the range £30 to £34 and one £50.[44] In Llandaff in 1763 the average stipend for a curate was £16 a year, and the highest was £30 a year.[45] As the eighteenth century progressed curates' salaries increased. In Caernarfonshire in 1778 the highest curates' salary was £40 a year.[46] In Wales, as in England, there is little real evidence of an oppressed underclass of clergy in the form of unbeneficed 'curates'.[47] There is little distinction between incumbents and curates at any level. In Caernarfonshire, in 1775 at least, more than half the curates were graduates.[48]

Diocesan authorities from time to time intervened to ensure adequate salaries for curates. In 1724 the chancellor of St Asaph ordered Thomas Wilkin the rector of Llansannan to pay his curate £20 a year to serve the parish, he being incapable of doing it himself owing to illness. The chancellor also ordered the sum to be sequestered from the tithes if it was not paid.[49] Curates could and did appeal to bishops against arbitrary notice of dismissal by incumbents, and bishops would look into their cases and take their part against the incumbent, especially if the curate was supported by the congregation.[50]

Pluralism and Non-residence

In Llandaff the *Notitia Episcopatum* of 1665 showed little pluralism among clergy, and Bishop Beaw's visitation of 1703 suggests that most parishes were served by the incumbent, whether resident or not.[51] Erasmus Saunders's claim that 'there are some churches that are totally neglected, and that very rarely have any Service perform'd in them' seems an overstatement,[52] but there was increasing incidence of pluralism in the two southern dioceses during the period. Bishop Clavering's visitation of Llandaff in 1726 shows more parishes in the care of curates for absentee incumbents, and incumbents serving as curates of neighbouring parishes.[53] In the deanery of Ultra Aeron in Cardiganshire in the diocese of St David's in 1733 there were 14 incumbents in twenty-four parishes, of whom 4 had a single parish, 6 had two incumbencies, 3 had three, and 1 had four, all of which he served himself. He lived at Llangeitho and began his Sunday duties three miles from home at Nantcwnlle with Morning Prayer at 8 a.m., returned to Llangeitho for Morning Prayer at 10 a.m., went on to Llanbadarn Odwyn for Morning Prayer at noon, and in the afternoon had a return journey of ten miles to Llanddewi Brefi for Evening Prayer at 4 p.m. The next week he began at Llanbadarn at 8 a.m., proceeding to Llangeitho at 10 a.m., Nantcwnlle at midday and Llanddewi at 4 p.m., preaching at each on alternate Sundays.[54] In St Asaph, by contrast, in 1733 eighty-five out of 116 parishes had resident incumbents, of whom a significant number occupied their own houses.[55] In Bangor in 1749 sixty-four incumbents were resident, out of 114 returns.[56]

The reason for holding four parishes in plurality in Ultra Aeron was financial. The total income amounted to £46. 13*s*. 4*d*. In fact throughout the diocese of St David's it was not unusual for one man to serve three parishes.[57] Unusually in Gower deanery in 1755 all the clergy resided in one of their parishes, and no curate served more than two parishes, usually adjacent to each other.[58] In 1763 in the diocese of Llandaff, of 145 parishes which provided answers to the bishop's inquiries, thirty-four parishes had resident incumbents and thirty-nine had resident curates. John Guy has pointed out that most clergy served parishes local to where they lived, and that modest pluralism ensured clergy an income of *c*.£100 a year. Non-residence and pluralism was not necessarily a symptom of idleness.[59] In Bangor, however, incumbents of more valuable livings tended to hold two such livings rather than those of small value,[60] and in Llandaff it is notable that, of the few parishes in the gift of the bishop, Shute Barrington presented the more valuable benefices to non-resident clergy.[61]

Another factor contributing to the incidence of non-residence and pluralism, in addition to low levels of incomes of parishes, was the condition or absence of parsonage houses. Even in one diocese there could be a contrasting picture. In 1717 in St David's diocese Brecon deanery had seventeen benefices; fourteen of these had parsonage houses, of which only two were noted as out of repair, with eleven resident incumbents and two resident curates. In sixteen parishes of Builth deanery only two had parsonage houses, and Sub Aeron had thirty-two livings and eleven houses.[62] In St David's diocese, as a whole, in 1733 in 160 livings 100 had parsonage houses, of which fifty-seven had resident incumbents and another twelve resident curates. Of the sixty livings without a parsonage house, only seven had a resident incumbent, and nine a resident curate.[63] Even where there was a parsonage house it might not be considered habitable, as in Ultra Aeron where only five of the nine parsonage houses in the twenty-four parishes were reckoned as habitable.[64] In Llandaff in 1763 the most commonly stated reason for non-residence was the lack or inadequacy of a parsonage house.[65] In 1749 Bishop Pearce of Bangor's visitation returns show there too there were few parsonage houses, but most incumbents rented or bought houses in their parishes.[66] Presumably with better-endowed benefices they could afford to do that. In Llandaff diocese thirty-two benefices did not have a parsonage house, or it was considered unsuitable.[67]

However, large numbers of clergy, who were technically non-resident through not living in the parsonage house, lived nearby or in their parishes. This was the case in Llandaff,[68] and non-resident incumbents who did not live sufficiently close to do duty themselves employed a curate, who, as we have noted, might be incumbent of a neighbouring parish; otherwise a curate was often resident in the parish.[69] Guy has noted a tendency for local incumbents to cluster in nearby towns. Three local incumbents lived in Abergavenny and two in Usk.[70] Even incumbents who lived a long way from their parish might be in regular touch, and reside for part of the year. Dr Pardo, principal of Jesus College Oxford, was clearly in close touch with his Welsh parishes.[71] John Carne of Nash, who was curate of Llanmaes from 1762 and of Llysworny from 1765, was also rector of Plumtree in Nottinghamshire and spent part of every year in each parish.[72]

The 1745 visitation of St David's shows a sharp drop in the number of resident clergy, and in Llandaff pluralism and non-residence increased from the mid-eighteenth century, perhaps because of a decline in agriculture and poor harvests.[73] In the second half of the eighteenth century there may have been a loss of Welsh clergy to England. In the diocese of London 1.1 per cent of the clergy before 1720 were of Welsh origin, 5.5 per cent between 1721 and 1760, and 6.1 per cent between 1761 and 1800,[74] and there was a steady increase in the number of Welsh names amongst Hampshire clergy in the course of the eighteenth century.[75]

Non-residence does not seem to have been regarded as unacceptable, although some bishops monitored it. Bishop Beaw of Llandaff, in his last visitation, noted clergy who were legally exempt from residence, or who held benefices in plurality under licence.[76] Most bishops were, in any case, themselves pluralists. In 'An Account of the Persons Presented for Non-residence' in the archdeaconry of Brecon in 1720 only two names appear, but the deputy registrar added a note: 'there were no more presented, tho' I know of several others who do not', and added the names of another twelve.[77] Often clergy failed to mention to bishops that they held a living in another diocese. Evangelical clergy appear to have had no qualms about non-residence. John Richards, presented to Coity by Lady Charlotte Edwin in 1758, also held Wooton and Newcastle.[78] In 1770 Richards's evangelical successor, Thomas Davies, reported to the bishop of Llandaff at his visitation that he was out of the parish for about half the year on 'Business' in England, and on extended visits to Trefecca and other Methodist centres.[79] In the diocese of St Asaph, Bishop Lisle included from 1747 a clause in deeds of institution stating, 'you will reside on the said [Vicarage] unless your absence shall be dispensed with by your Diocesan.'[80]

Few complaints survive from parishioners about non-residence of their clergy. The only examples that have come to light are against Methodists. The parishioners of Llanwrtyd complained about William Williams of Pantycelyn's absences from his curacy in the early 1740s, and the bishop refused to ordain him priest.[81] There were complaints from Coity to Bishop Barrington about Thomas Davies's absences. It was objected that the services at the parish church were conducted 'without due reverence and solemnity' by a 'variety of persons whose religious principles render them obnoxious to the inhabitants'. Davies responded by attributing the complaints to their 'disaffected and turbulent spirit', and pointed out that there was no parsonage house, and he had asked David Jones of Llangan (another Evangelical) to look after the parish.[82]

Clerical Education

Most clergy serving in Wales were Welsh, but there was little interchange between north and south Wales. In south Wales there was significant migration of clergy between counties. The majority of the clergy in Glamorgan were not born in the county but came from other south Wales counties.[83]

In 1710 in St Asaph 61 per cent of the clergy, and in 1726 in Llandaff 63 per cent were graduates, but in 1714 in St David's only 32 per cent of the clergy were.[84] There was a high proportion of graduates among the clergy in Bangor.[85] This distinctive pattern continued for the rest of the century.

Oxford was the most convenient university to attend from Wales, and Jesus was the college predominantly attended by Welshmen. It was virtually a Welsh enclave. In 1700 all twenty-seven freshmen, and in 1710 all thirty-two were Welsh. Recruitment was broad-based in terms of class: between 1690 and 1732 the college contributed the largest number of any college who matriculated as sons of plebeians or *pauperes pueri*, many of whom did not stay to take a degree, and this may account for a proportion of the non-graduate clergy in Wales. Servitorships at Jesus were allegedly much in demand in the early eighteenth century. The Welsh gentry often sent their sons to Jesus, rather than to grander colleges; for example Sir Watkin Williams Wynn chose Jesus rather than Christ Church.[86] Nine bishops of Welsh sees during our period had been at Jesus, as had the majority of the graduate clergy in Glamorgan.[87]

Non-graduate clergy were not peculiar to south Wales. In Chester diocese there also was a high proportion of non-graduate clergy.[88] Welsh non-graduate clergy were educated at grammar schools, of which there were fourteen in St David's diocese in 1665. They had a classical curriculum, ensuring their pupils' competence in Latin and Greek to read the New Testament and the Fathers in their original languages, as well as standard works of theology, many of which were in Latin, as well as competence in English. They, like graduates with only a bachelor's degree, needed to study theology and deepen their 'piety and virtue' and carefully reflect on the clerical office, to equip themselves for ordination. Henry Owen, chaplain to Shute Barrington, bishop of Llandaff, published *Directions for Young Students in Divinity*, which originated in advice and reading lists issued to ordination candidates.[89]

Detailed evidence does not survive about the examination of ordination candidates in the Welsh dioceses, However, as we have seen, bishops took great care in checking candidates' papers to ensure they were properly examined, and some were referred and advised to try again, and some rejected.[90]

Bishop Bull encouraged his clergy to 'ply your studies, give your selves to reading, and chiefly of the holy Scriptures and the writings of learned men'.[91] Probate inventories of clergy show that all clergy owned books. They were a feature of the most threadbare inventories of the least well-to-do clergy. The most prosperous and well-educated clergy had the most books. Geraint Jenkins has suggested their bookshelves were as well stocked as their means would allow, and has pointed out that the range of their reading material testifies to cultivated tastes.[92] Eryn White has pointed out that printed subscription lists bound in with books during the period include names of large numbers of clergy.[93]

Clergy were prominent among Welsh authors during this period, especially those writing in Welsh. Thirty-six authors of Welsh books in the period 1660–1740 can be identified as clergy. Clergy contributed significantly to Welsh scholarship during the period. Most respondents to Edward Lluyd's requests for material for Welsh parishes for the 1695 revised edition of *Britannia* were clergy.[94] Humphrey Humphreys was a member of the circle of antiquarians and historians including

Thomas Baker, White Kennet, Edmund Gibson and Thomas Tanner. He had a keen interest in Welsh literature, collected Welsh manuscripts, and was respected as a patron of bards and prose writers. At Bangor he encouraged a small group of antiquarians to study the history of the cathedral.[95] Later in Bangor diocese, Henry Rowlands, rector of Llanidan in Anglesey, in *Mona Antiqua Restaurata*, of 1723, wrote about the ancient history of Anglesey, arguing for the Hebrew origins of the Welsh language.[96] Hugh Davies, rector of Llandegfan, and then of Aber, wrote *The Botany of Anglesey*, and Nicholas Owen, rector of Mellteyrn, published *British Remains: or a Collection of Antiquities relating to Britain* in 1777.[97] In the 1730s a flourishing school of historians based on the chapter at Llandaff Cathedral was studying the ecclesiastical and parochial antiquities of Glamorgan. Thomas Davies, James Harris and Francis Davies investigated the parishes of the diocese, their dedications and feast days, and communicated the fruits of their studies to friends in antiquarian circles at Oxford. In the diocese of St Asaph in 1730 John Wynne, rural dean of Penllyn and Edeirnion, reporting on his visitation, discussed the etymology of the place names in the deaneries.[98] Welsh clergy produced some of the finest works of Welsh literature. Rhys Prichard, vicar of Llandovery, died in 1644, but his lively and memorable verses explaining Christian doctrine to the unlettered were only published in the 1660s. Theophilus Evans, vicar of Llangammarch and Llanfaes in Breconshire, published *Drych y Prif Oesoedd* in 1716, with a second edition in 1740, which was claimed to be 'the most widely read history book in Welsh in the eighteenth century'.[99] David Lewis, vicar of Cadoxton juxta Neath, in *Flores Poetarum Britannicorum* in 1710 sought to collect the best works of Welsh poets throughout the ages. Evan Evans was a scrupulous scholar of early Welsh poetry manuscripts, and the main exponent of Welsh Celticism, but had a miserable ecclesiastical career, moving round to escape his debts.[100] Goronwy Owen, despite a very brief clerical career in Wales as curate of Llanfair Mathafarn Eithaf, and curacies near and in Oswestry, before a succession of other curacies in England and then in Virginia, had an enormous influence on Welsh poetry throughout the nineteenth century. The outstanding lexicographical work of the eighteenth century, *An English–Welsh Dictionary*, published in instalments between 1770 and 1783, was by James Walters, rector of Llandough. Eryn White has pointed out that some of the most brilliant and productive Welsh scholars of the age were clergy, who also endeavoured to provide appropriate religious literature for their parishioners.[101]

Pastoral Ministry

George Bull, bishop of St David's 1705–10, in his guidance for ordination candidates and visitation charge to his clergy, identified five tasks for the clergy: 'reading divine service, or the prayers of the Church', preaching, catechizing, administering the sacraments of baptism and the Lord's Supper, and visiting the sick. He emphasized exemplary conduct as essential for a priest, and frequency in private prayer. He pointed out that clergy required wisdom to know what and how to preach, in leading their own lives, in choice of friends, in managing their family and knowing their flock. Bull reminded them of their accountability for the souls committed to their charge, and that the 'chief and most indispensable requisites are these two; a passionate desire to save souls, and an unwearied diligence in the pursuit of the noble design'.[102]

During the late seventeenth and early eighteenth centuries there was a movement among leading bishops, clergy and lay people, encouraged by successive archbishops of Canterbury, to make further reforms in pastoral ministry in the parishes. We have seen examples of this in relation to bishops' diocesan administration and the augmentation of benefice incomes by Queen Anne's Bounty. Other aspects were the publication of handbooks for clergy, mostly written by reforming bishops, such as Bull of St David's, and the establishment of the SPCK and SPG, which established information networks across dioceses, as well as useful publications. Most bishops of Welsh dioceses were closely involved in these activities.

Clerical Meetings

An initiative encouraged by bishops to improve pastoral ministry in the late seventeenth century was regular meetings of clergy, usually on a deanery basis. In 1699 Archbishop Tenison issued a circular to the bishops asking them to promote such meetings in their dioceses. Some Welsh bishops, like Beaw of Llandaff and Watson of St David's, were suspicious of and hostile to such meetings, fearing they might take on the character of 'associations' and lead to prophesyings, a feature of seventeenth-century Puritanism. However, Humphreys and subsequently Evans of Bangor, Beveridge and subsequently Jones of St Asaph, and Bull of St David's and Tyler of Llandaff all encouraged them. Correspondents of the SPCK regularly refer to such meetings. In December 1699 Robert Wynne, rector of Llanddeiniolen, near Bangor, reported that Humphreys had 'given a strict charge to his clergy to meet frequently' by deaneries 'and make it their constant endeavour to stir up each other to strict and conscientious discharge of the Ministerial Functions'. He divided Anglesey into three divisions and required clergy to meet monthly, and to send minutes of meetings to him. The surviving minutes of the March, April and June 1700 meetings show them resolving 'to take all possible care of their own livings that they may be standing patterns and examples to their respective flocks'.[103]

In January 1700 it was reported that the clergy of the deaneries of Bodelwyddan, Pool and Wrexham in the diocese of St Asaph had met and agreed to meet monthly. In June 1700 it was reported from Llantrisant in Glamorgan that the clergy there hoped to meet fortnightly. From Carmarthenshire there was the more muted response

> that some of the prime clergy are cautious about Associations . . . till the bishop is appointed. That some are so dispersed that they have few Meetings unless accidentally and some promise to do their Duty without entering into any Society, and those that have entered themselves to meet once a month or Six Weeks

In August 1700 a society of clergy and gentry in Pembrokeshire was reported. In 1710 William Davies, rector of Llanwrin in Montgomeryshire, reported a society of clergy and gentlemen 'who meet once a month to excite each other in the Prosecution of good designs'.[104] A fruit of clerical societies in some areas, as we will see, was charity schools, for example in Wrexham and Denbigh.[105] Evidence for societies mostly disappears after the early years of the eighteenth century, and it is unclear whether they continued meeting or not.

The vast geographical size of many Welsh parishes, divided up into chapelries, militated against the ideal of personal pastoral care envisaged by Bull. Non-residence also limited pastoral availability. Edward Tenison, archdeacon of Carmarthen in Bull's own diocese, in a visitation during the vacancy of the see in 1710, noted that at Llanycrwys near Lampeter the curate lived ten miles away, and burials were neglected because of his unavailability, and that this had driven parishioners into a new Presbyterian meeting house in the parish.[106] Erasmus Saunders, also writing about St David's just after Bull's time, regretted that pluralism meant that clergy arrived breathless, and hastened from place to place, services were hurried, and sometimes either early or late; there was little time, he claimed, for sermons, or to visit the sick, give instruction or admonish wrongdoers.[107]

Preaching

Bull emphasized the need to preach sermons congregations would understand. He advised clergy to buy and study sermons, recommending Tillotson's. He noted that preaching requires 'the knowledge and understanding of the holy scriptures, and, in order thereunto, some skill in the learned languages and other parts of human knowledge; it requires good judgement and discretion.' To those incapable of preaching, he recommended reading a homily from *The Book of Homilies* or a chapter or section from *The Whole Duty of Man*.[108] William Wynne of Lasynys in Merioneth was at least one cleric who had a large collection of published sermons as a resource for preaching.[109]

If William Bulkeley of Llanfechell is typical, the Welsh gentry loved listening to sermons. He always recorded texts of sermons in his diary. He expected sermons to be about fifteen minutes, and complained when one overran to seventeen minutes. He also complained about the rector's occasional practice of preaching a sermon in two parts, or if a sermon was repeated, and frequently complained that he could not understand a sermon. The rector, Richard Bulkeley, seems to have written his sermons out in full. The squire once noted that the rector had forgotten his sermon book and needed to go home to collect it. Robert Morgan of Llanddyfnan and then Ross also wrote out his sermons in full, in English and Welsh intermixed, and allowed his curate to use his sermons.[110] Tact in preaching, as Bull had advised, could be pastorally effective; it was noted of the curate of Llanuwchllyn in Merioneth that dissenters in the parish had been reconciled by his 'lack of zeal and skill in argument' and not criticizing them from the pulpit.[111]

Catechizing

Providing catechetical instruction, especially for the young, was another feature of the movement for pastoral renewal in the late seventeenth and early eighteenth centuries. Bishop Lloyd of St Asaph in 1680 urged his clergy to catechise children and young people every Sunday afternoon. In 1704 Bishop Beveridge of St Asaph alleged that catechizing had been generally neglected or 'slightly performed' for 'many years together', and pointed out that getting children to repeat the Prayer Book Catechism by rote 'signifies very little unless they understand what they say', and that achieving this was 'one of the hardest duties belonging to the ministerial office'. He published his *Church Catechism Explained for the Use of the Diocese of St Asaph* for his clergy, providing a few pages of explanation of the questions and answers in the Catechism, and then a comprehension test. If children showed they had not understood the explanation, he advised catechists to explain again, otherwise to move on to the next question.[112] It was translated into Welsh by Thomas Williams, rector of Denbigh, and published in 1708.

Most catechisms translated into Welsh under the auspices of the SPCK were for the use of householders and schoolmasters, who were expected to provide the basic groundwork of catechetical teaching.[113] A prime purpose of charity schools was to teach children the Catechism. John Jones, dean of Bangor, specified in his bequest in 1727 of £100 to each of the five schools he founded that children be taught the Catechism in Welsh.[114] Explaining the Catechism in Welsh and then learning to read with the Bible was also at the heart of Griffith Jones's educational method used in the circulating schools.[115]

Visitation returns show that by the 1730s most clergy catechized in church on Sundays in Lent after the second lesson at Evening Prayer, which continued as the norm for the rest of our period. Catechizing in church on Sundays was a public means of testing and publicizing the results of detailed work done in schools and at home by parents. James Harris introduced catechetical lectures for adults in the chapels in the extensive parish of Llantrisant in Glamorgan.[116]

Distribution of Books and Pamphlets

A further weapon in the clerical armoury to promote education was the distribution of tracts and books. Thomas Gouge's Welsh Trust in the 1670s noted 'there are very few Divinity Books in the Welsh Language' and no Welsh Bibles, and proposed, 'to contribute towards the Printing of some Pious Treatises in the Welsh Language, to be freely given away to poor Persons and Families there; so especially towards the Printing of the Welsh Bible in Octavo . . .' In the winter of 1674–5 the trust bought and distributed thirty-two bibles and 479 New Testaments in Welsh, 'which were all that could be had in Wales or London', 500 copies of *The Whole Duty of Man* in Welsh, and 2,500 copies of Lewis Bayley's *The Practice of Piety* 'with some hundreds of other treatises translated into Welsh to be given to poor People in Wales'. In 1678 the trustees 'with the encouragement given by the Lord Mayor and the Court of Aldermen and other charitable persons in and about the City of London did set upon the printing of some thousands of such books in the Welsh Language'. Eight thousand Bibles were printed, with the Prayer Book 'and the Singing Psalms' and the Apocrypha bound in. Books were distributed in parishes in all thirteen Welsh counties.[117] Bibles were sold for 4*s.* 2*d.* each, but were given free with devotional books in Welsh to people who could read the language.

Large numbers of devotional books were translated into Welsh, including Allestree's *The Whole Duty of Man* (in 1672), à Kempis's *De Imitatione Christi* (in 1684), Bunyan's *Pilgrim's Progress* (in 1688), and *The Christian Monitor* (in 1689). Large numbers of pamphlets, aimed at yeomen and husbandmen and their families were also translated. The first Welsh hymn books were published in 1703 and 1705, and books of carols were also published.[118] Books needed to be cheap to be widely read. Pamphlets usually sold at ½*d.* each.

Four of the five founders of the London-based SPCK, which, with Queen Anne's Bounty, was one of the significant agencies for the reform of pastoral ministry in the Established Church, especially through its publishing activities, had strong Welsh connections: Sir Humphrey Mackworth, whom we have already noted, Thomas Bray, who was of Welsh descent and educated at Oswestry grammar school, Sergeant Hook, who had been chief justice of Caernarfon, and Colonel Colchester, who was patron of several Radnorshire and Breconshire schools. A leading magnate of south Wales, Sir John Philipps, was an early member. Eight of the first twelve letters received by the committee were from Welsh correspondents.[119] The activities and networks of the Welsh Trust probably set a precedent for the SPCK and Wales. John Evans, formerly chaplain to the East India Company station at St George in India, and subsequently bishop of Bangor, was elected a committee member in July 1699, and appears to have taken charge for Wales, receiving reports from Welsh correspondents, including John Pember for Pembrokeshire, John Vaughan for Carmarthenshire, James Harris for Glamorgan, Herbert Pye for Monmouthshire, Humphrey Jordan for Breconshire and Radnorshire, Dean Jones for Anglesey and Caernarfonshire, and John Price for Denbighshire and Flintshire. Later Evans chaired the committee to provide libraries in each Welsh diocese. He was also active on the committee of SPG, and was charged by Bishop Compton of London to recruit Welsh clergy for Pennsylvania.[120] John Tyler, bishop of Llandaff from 1706, was also a great supporter of the SPCK, and encouraged their 'Welsh policy'. The SPCK office in London, especially when Henry Newman was secretary, provided a clearing house for the interests and needs of Welsh correspondents in all matters.[121]

The society supplied books to Welsh charity schools at cost price, and seems to have had a special rate for providing books and pamphlets to Welsh members.[122] Erasmus Saunders thought the SPCK did some good in the diocese of St David's, but feared it was 'very insufficient to answer our Necessities, or to reform Disorders, so spreading and establish'd as they are here'.[123]

Through the society Welsh members were in touch with the European Evangelical Revival. Sir John Philipps corresponded with Auguste Francke to elicit practical information on the cost of maintaining orphans in Halle, and with Swiss rational orthodox theologians.[124] He and other Welsh correspondents were active in the 1720s in raising money for an Arabic translation of the New Testament proposed by the SPCK, and in the 1730s raised money for the persecuted Salzburger Protestants.[125]

The society was responsible for printing at least 50,000 Bibles in Welsh between 1718 and 1752, and in 1757 ordered another 15,000 Welsh Bibles and 5,000 New Testaments, and in 1768 ordered an edition of 20,000 Bibles with larger print and marginal references, to fund which £2,000 was borrowed, and recovered from subscribers.[126] There seems little evidence to support the claims of Geraint Jenkins and W. R. Ward that the SPCK saw providing literature in Welsh as a short-term expedient until charity schools were successful in teaching English.[127]

The SPCK, perhaps spurred on by suspicion of Quaker and Independent Welsh publishing initiatives, also sponsored Welsh translations of books. In February 1700 John Evans was asked to produce 'a List of such Welch books as are proper to be sent to Correspondents in Wales' and 'That Dr Evans be desir'd to find a fitt person who may translate into Welch'

Josiah Woodward's pamphlets. The subsequent list consisted largely of books previously distributed by the Welsh Trust. New editions of pamphlets were planned and new translations commissioned.[128]

In the correspondence between the secretary and local correspondents there are frequent references to the dispatch and receipt of packets of books, usually small devotional books, collections of prayers or tracts for distribution to parishioners. Packets of books seem to have been sent annually to correspondents. Bishop Tyler of Llandaff in 1706 offered to distribute tracts translated into Welsh at his confirmations. In 1709 it was reported that Archdeacon Tenison had funded printing Thomas Williams of Denbigh's Welsh translation of Dr Assheton's *Treatise of the Sacrament*. Robert Wynne, of Gresford in Denbighshire, reported 'That to encourage the late Edition of the Welsh Comm: Prayer he had lately taken 100 of them and dispersed them among the poor'. In 1712 John Price of Wrexham reported 'That he did not send for little books as the Society might expect, because he has the conveniency of having them at Shrewsbury at a Cheap rate'. The establishment of a printing press at Shrewsbury was of great benefit for distributing literature in Wales. Initially the secretary of the SPCK, Henry Newman, had bought in copies of the Welsh translation of the Bible to meet orders from Welsh correspondents but, as we have noted, the society commissioned at least 60,000 copies of Welsh Bibles by 1768. The SPCK poured out Welsh Prayer Books, alphabet books, catechisms and devotional works, also providing, as we will see, large numbers of Welsh books for Griffith Jones's schools.[129]

Until at least the 1780s clergy continued to order large numbers of books directly from the SPCK, including Bibles, and dozens of tracts to distribute among parishioners. Joshua Thomas of Penpont, Breconshire, in 1749 reported his parishioners' impatience because of the delay in the arrival of Welsh Bibles. In 1752 James Brooke of Noyadd Llannarth, Cardiganshire, ordered 400 Bibles and other literature, and in 1753 Joshua Thomas ordered another 400 Bibles.[130] William Wynn, writing to Richard Morris in September 1753, reported being told on a visit to the SPCK's office that 'the Society expects every Corresponding Member sh'd distinguish not only each

Diocese, but each Parish and even each Family wherein they propose to distribute [Welsh Bibles]', because of the great demand for them.[131]

Societies for the Reformation of Manners

A further aspect of the reform of pastoral ministry in the late seventeenth century, especially in towns, was the establishment of societies for the reformation of manners, to act as vigilante groups to monitor and report such matters as Sunday trading, gambling and sexual irregularities. There is evidence of such societies in Caernarfonshire, Carmarthenshire and Pembrokeshire.[132] Bishop Humphrey Humphreys commended them to the clergy of the diocese of Bangor in 1699.[133] There is no evidence about how long the societies survived and what they contributed to the mission of the Church, or how they related to the consistory courts. In England there is little evidence for their activities outside London and Bristol, and the London societies ceased to publish reports of prosecutions sponsored by the societies in 1738.[134]

Religious societies

Societies for reformation of manners were only one example of numerous networks of zealous lay people, usually with clerical support and oversight, in late seventeenth- and early eighteenth-century England and Wales who gathered to encourage good works and devotion. Religious societies, in which men, especially young men, associated for prayer, Bible study, and to review their spiritual lives and join together in charitable projects, like the support of charity schools to teach poor children to read the Bible and Prayer Book and to learn and understand the Catechism, were significant features of most towns.[135] Clergy of the Established Church enthusiastically advocated such societies, as instruments for deepening the devotional lives of men. Josiah Woodward's *An Account of the Rise and Progress of the Religious Societies in the City of London*[136] was one of the SPCK's most frequently distributed pamphlets and provided a model constitution and rules for a society. It was a text that seems to have influenced Howell Harris in developing his societies in the 1730s, which suggests that, though there is little surviving evidence for religious societies in Welsh parishes, they featured in Welsh parish life, and that their members may have been among the key members of early Methodist societies.

Clergy as Magistrates

From the 1730s clergy were appointed in relatively large numbers as magistrates. Glamorgan had six clerical magistrates in 1743, and thirty-seven in 1793. Clergy made up 20 per cent of new magistrates appointed in Pembrokeshire between 1728 and 1788. The first clerical magistrate was appointed in Merioneth in 1726; by 1776 there were twenty-four, out of 100 magistrates. In most Welsh counties by the 1790s clergy represented between a quarter and a third of the names on the commission for the peace, and a far higher proportion of active magistrates.[137] This was a parallel pattern to what was happening in England.[138]

Supervision of the Clergy

Inevitably official reports about clergy tend to dwell on what was wrong, and what needed improvement. The report to Bishop Hare of St Asaph by John Wynne, rural dean of Penllyn and Edeirnion, for example, on the condition of parishes in his deanery after his visitation in 1730, dwells on the sins of omission and commission of his neighbours, making depressing reading. However, twenty years later, Bishop Drummond reported to the Duke of Newcastle after his primary visitation of St Asaph in 1753 that he found its state 'in general much better than was imagined by strangers . . . the body of the clergy, though not learned men, were good and able parish priests.'[139]

Supervision of clergy was by means of the visitation process, when churchwardens were required to report anything amiss with the conduct of their incumbent. Lay people could always complain directly to the bishop, or bring a complaint before the consistory court. Despite rumours and innuendo,[140] few cases were brought against clergy in consistory courts. In 1705 the churchwardens of Cyffig in the archdeaconry of Carmarthen presented the curate for adultery and 'frequenting houses of ill-fame and fathering a bastard sworn to him', but such cases were rare.[141] In the archdeaconry of Brecon there were occasional presentments of clergy for neglecting their duty – 3 between 1692 and 1699, 2 between 1700 and 1709, 3 between 1710 and 1719, 4 between 1720 and 1729, 2 between 1730 and 1739 and 1 between 1740 and 1749. In the archdeaconry of Carmarthen there were similar numbers – 1 between 1680 and 1689, 2 between 1720 and 1729, 5 between 1740 and 1749, and 3 between 1750 and 1759.[142] In Llandaff consistory court between 1722 and 1754 there were 21 cases against clergy, 12 for allegations of neglect of duty, 5 involving accusations of drunkenness, 1 involving adultery, 1 accusation of attempted rape, 1 for persisting in conducting services after having been suspended by the bishop, 1 for officiating without a licence and 1 for forging a baptism certificate in order to be ordained.[143] There is no surviving evidence from the court papers of other dioceses.

Comments during the course of visitations suggest that this is not the whole story. Archdeacon Tenison, in visiting Carmarthen archdeaconry in 1710, noted pastoral neglect at Llanycrwys near Lampeter, where the non-resident curate had neglected burials, accusations of drunkenness against the clergy at Llandyssilio and Trelech, and allegations of conducting clandestine marriages by the incumbent of Llansteffan.[144] The rural dean of Penllyn and Edeirnion during his visitation of the deanery in 1730 described the rector of Llandderfel, Robert Edwards, as 'a wretch and a monster', negligent, extravagant, drunken and suspected of sexual immorality, arson and attempted murder. The church was also claimed to be in poor order.[145] The curate of Bedwas, Glamorgan, admitted paternity of a bastard child by a distant relative who had been a servant in his house, and was deprived.[146] It is difficult to know whether credence should be given to the comment of Elizabeth Baker in 1781 in the Dolgellau area about 'the excessive drinking that their [Welsh] Clergy are in general addicted to – which is one reason the Methodists yearly increase'.[147]

As we have noted, bishops preferred to deal with as many matters of clerical discipline as possible themselves, or by their chancellors, in private.[148] They were keen to avoid the expense and scandal of consistory court cases against clergy.

6
The State of the Parishes

The State of Religion in Wales

Parish churches were the hub of communal life; as we have seen, dissent was a small movement in Wales for most of this period. The Church was central to people's lives. Most clergy were local men, who spoke the language of their parishioners. There was a real revival in the Established Church in Wales in the late seventeenth century and the first half of the eighteenth century. The Scriptures and liturgy were available in the vernacular, and considerable energy was put into translating catechetical and devotional material and providing instruction in the basic tenets of the Christian faith in Welsh. In spite of criticizing the administration and lack of resources in the Welsh Church, Erasmus Saunders provided a glowing picture of the engagement of people in the poorest of the Welsh dioceses, St David's, in the life of the Established Church. He suggested: 'an extraordinary Disposition to Religion . . . prevails among the People of the Country', noting:

> They don't think it too much when neither ways nor weather are inviting, over cold and bleak Hills to travel three or four miles or more, on foot, to attend the Publick Service: sometimes as many more to hear a Sermon, and many times for several Hours together in their damp and cold Churches to wait the coming of their Minister, who by Occasional Duties in his other Curacies, or by other Accidents may be oblig'd to disappoint them, and to be often variable in his Hours of Prayer.
>
> Then also to supply in some measure the want of a regular Publick Service there are many, even of the common People, who gladly make the best use of what little Knowledge they

> have gain'd, and take the Pains privately, by Reading or Discourse to instruct one another in their Houses, and it is not uncommon to see Servants and Shepherds, as they have an opportunity, strive to do these good Offices to educate another. It is by this Means that most or all of them do attain the knowledge of reading and writing in their native Language.
>
> . . . to make their private Instructions more agreeable and effectual, as they are naturally addicted to Poetry, so some of the more skilful and knowing among them frequently compose a kind of Divine Hymns or Songs which they call Halsingod or Carolion which generally consist either of the Doctrinal or Historical parts of Scripture, or of the Lives and worthy Acts of some, eminent Saints.[1]

The fruit of this may be seen in Edward Tenison, archdeacon of Carmarthen's, estimate, after his visitation in 1710, that there were 760 poor people in twenty-nine parishes in the archdeaconry who were able to read.[2]

Edward Samuel, in his introduction to *The Truth of the Christian Religion*, in 1716 said: 'God be thanked, the light of the Gospel shines as bright in Wales as in any other country, there are more religious and useful books published, there is more and probably better preaching than at any time these last thousand years.'[3] There was, however, a tendency to look on the dark side. Dissenters (in England) charged bishops and clergy in Wales with negligence, ignorance and indifference; some correspondents of the SPCK believed these criticisms, and repeated them in letters and reports. Arthur Bedford, the SPCK's Bristol correspondent, in 1701 complained of 'great Ignorance and Atheism in Wales'.[4] Erasmus Saunders also dwelt on the 'the growing Irreligion, the Ignorance and Profaneness' in south-west Wales, and lamented: 'Ah, poor *desolate* and forsaken Church.'[5] Saunders's criticisms were intended as an appeal to those who could direct new resources to improve the position of the Church in south-west Wales. John Loveday, visiting Breconshire in 1730, recorded their guide claiming 'the generality of the Clergy . . . [were] a drunken set of People. Drawn through the University (this was his expression) with small improvement in anything but

Debauchery.'[6] Evan Evans in an essay of 1764–5 attributed the Church's weaknesses to oppressive foreigners, who cared little for the souls of the people, were motivated largely by pecuniary considerations and received the best livings.[7] There was at least latent anticlericalism among the gentry. William Bulkeley, while devoted to the Church, ranted in his diary about the 'knavish' principles of the clergy and their 'Priestly craft and cant'.[8]

William Williams of Pantycelyn, the hymn-writer, claimed in an elegy to Howell Harris, the initiator of the Welsh Revival, that before 1735 'Wales had lain in a state of torpor, having no priest, preacher or bishop sufficiently enlightened or concerned to improve the plight of the poor and ignorant',[9] and Luke Tyerman, the biographer of John Wesley, claimed that in 1736 'In the pulpits of parish churches [in Wales] the name of Christ was hardly ever uttered'.[10] They included dissenters as well as the Established Church in their condemnation. This view, as we have seen, does not do justice to episcopal administration, or the Welsh clergy, nor, as we will see, to the state of Welsh parishes.

Church Buildings

Visitations prompted clergy and churchwardens to maintain churches in good repair. Humphrey Humphreys of Bangor wrote special injunctions to the Anglesey clergy to care for their church buildings and adjured them to make a solemn resolution 'That we will endeavour to excite our Wardens and parishioners to repair and adorn their respective Churches as becomes places dedicated to the worship of the most high God'.[11] Many country churches were in poor condition, probably reflecting the poverty of many rural parishes, lacking the means to fund major repairs, as the same defects were often cited at successive visitations. In 1672 in the archdeaconry of Carmarthen twenty parishes were presented for church windows being out of repair, eighteen for defective bells, eleven for defective roofs. The numbers were about the same in 1705 and 1750.[12] Between 1686 and 1688 twenty-five parishes were presented for their church being out of repair, and fifty-nine individuals were presented for not paying church rate.[13] In 1733 in twenty-four parishes of the deanery of Ultra Aeron in Cardiganshire only three churches were reckoned in good condition, only three had communion rails and three even lacked communion vessels, but all had Welsh Bibles and Prayer Books.[14] Seven out of eleven churches in the deanery of Penllyn and Edeirnion in Merionneth in 1730 seem to have been in poor condition.[15]

There is little evidence of people refusing to pay church rates for church repairs, unless they thought they were expected to pay more than their fair share. Communities were often much involved in providing and laying rushes for the floors of the aisles and under the benches and pews, and on the window sills, as at Llanfechell on Anglesey, where rushes were changed six times a year.[16]

Major work was done to some churches. Cardigan parish church was rebuilt in 1702–3, and there are many reports during Bishop Ottley of St David's time of churches under repair.[17] At Caerleon 'the church here was new pewed, paved, whitewashed, etc in 1725.'[18] At Llanfechell on Anglesey in 1734 the chancel roof was extensively repaired, unfortunately at the expense of removing the medieval tester 'with Monstrous figures upon it' from over the altar, and in 1749 the squire, William Bulkeley, gave a 'New Purple Table Cloth with a silk fringe about it for the Communion Table'.[19] In Llandaff the archdeacon and chapter of the cathedral seem to have regularly spent money on the maintenance of chancels of churches in their gift.[20] In St Asaph diocese the Faculty Book from 1713 to 1769 records 2 faculties for new organs, 2 for new pulpits, 15 for galleries, and 80 for pews.[21]

Cathedral fabrics were not neglected. At St David's the chapter had by 1715 spent £1,500 repairing damage done to roofs, glass in the windows and the organ during the Civil War and Interregnum. The interior was painted in 1710, and between 1726 and 1736 another £500 was spent on the fabric.[22] At St Asaph, between 1660 and 1670 *c.*£500 was spent on repairing the cathedral; later Bishop Wynne raised £600 from the clergy and gentry and contributed himself for repairs to the cathedral after storm damage in 1715.[23] At Llandaff, the ruined cathedral was rebuilt by John Wood of

Bath from 1734.[24] At Bangor, Dean John Jones left £100 to the cathedral for an altarpiece and an altar cloth.[25]

Liturgy

Bishops expected that there should be Morning and Evening Prayer in every parish every Sunday, with a sermon at least at one of the services. Bishop Bull required that services should be 'read audibly, distinctly and reverently', and recommended a 'decent interval' between the first and second service on a Sunday.[26] Services could be very long. On Easter Day 1734 William Bulkeley at Llanfechell on Anglesey noted that the service, at which there were 170 communicants, lasted from 9 a.m. until a quarter to 12; on 26 December 1736 he noted that including the sermon, the administration of Holy Communion, and the reading of an Act of Parliament the service lasted until 1.45 p.m.; and on 30 April 1738 he noted that the Sunday service also included two burials, a christening and the churching of a woman.[27] Bishop Bull had recommended that baptism should be 'on the Lord's day in a full congregation of Christian people'.[28] Compared with England, especially southern England, Wales has a very high proportion of parishes with two Sunday services, except for Llandaff diocese, which is much closer to the English pattern (Table 6.1).

Whether 'holy day' meant major holy days, such as Christmas, Epiphany and Ascension Day or on every day for which the Prayer Book provides a special collect, epistle and gospel is unclear. By the 1770s attendance at weekday services seems to have been negligible. In 1776 the rector of Llanrûg in Caernarfonshire noted that 'Divine Service is due upon every Festival' but 'a Congregation is seldom assembled', and at Botwnnog, the incumbent noted: 'Divine Service is never performed on Weekdays, seldom on Holidays for want of a Congregation, Except Christmas, Ascension and the Epiphany.'[29]

Table 6.1 Frequency of services on Sundays and 'holy days', 1733–78

	Twice on Sunday	Once on Sunday	On 'holy days'
Diocese of St Asaph 1733	110	2	74
Diocese of St Asaph 1749	120	5	77
Diocese of Bangor 1749	114	43	100
Diocese of Bangor 1778	93	23	
Archdeaconry of Cardigan Ultra Aeron Deanery 1755	3	10	
Archdeaconry of St David's 1755	1	14	
Archdeaconry of Carmarthen 1755	55	21	
Archdeaconry of Brecon 1755	7	9	
Diocese of Llandaff 1763	31	105	

Table 6.2 Frequency of celebration of Holy Communion, 1773–78

	Once a month	Four times a year	Three times a year
Diocese of St Asaph 1733	80	15	
Diocese of St Asaph 1749	74	15	
Diocese of Bangor 1749	46	52 (26 six times p.a.)	
Diocese of Bangor 1778	41	22 (27 six times p.a.)	
Archdeaconry of Cardigan Ultra Aeron Deanery 1755	8	3	
Archdeaconry of St David's 1755	4	5	
Archdeaconry of Carmarthen 1755	55	14	
Archdeaconry of Brecon 1755	12	2	
Diocese of Llandaff 1763	23	51	53

Wales also has a much higher frequency of celebrations of Holy Communion than in England, except, again, in Llandaff (Table 6.2). Monthly celebrations of Holy Communion were general in towns and larger parishes.[30] In Llandaff in 1763 communicant numbers at Easter in towns seem only to have been a small proportion of the population – at Gelligaer forty communicants from about 700 families, at Eglwysilan forty-two out of 300 families and at Merthyr Tydfil ten or twelve from 140 families. However in rural parishes there is a striking correlation between numbers of families and numbers of communicants. In some cases the figures are identical. At Llangwm there were ten families and ten communicants.[31] In the northern dioceses numbers of communicants in many parishes significantly exceeded the numbers of families (Table 6.3).

Table 6.3 Numbers of communicants compared with numbers of families in some parishes in the dioceses of St Asaph and Bangor in 1733 and 1749 respectively

	Number of families in parish	Number of Easter communicants
Diocese of St Asaph	52	100
	200	300
	150	200
	55	140
	34	120
Diocese of Bangor	100	240
	50	140
	125	300
	20	50
	35	80
	200	350

These are suspiciously round figures, but they presumably roughly reflect the numbers of families and number of communicants, in proportion. When at Easter 1734 William Bulkeley at Llanfechell on Anglesey noted there were only 170 communicants, from about ninety families, he added that a 'great Mortality' had destroyed almost half the parish within the previous seven or eight years.[32] In 1778 the clergy at Bodfean, Ceidio, Denio and Penllech in Caernarfonshire, reported that the number of Easter communicants and the number of regular churchgoers was identical, but this seems to have been exceptional.[33]

There were varieties of practice in celebrating Holy Communion. At Llanfechell the rector, Richard Bulkeley, was criticized by the squire for leaning 'much towards Popery' as 'a rigid observer of superstitious ceremonies and several that were not required by the Rubrick, and particularly in consecrating the Bread and Wine at the Sacrament he used to lift them up and shew them to the people and speak with an Emphasis This is my Body, etc'.[34] At Llangar, where there was a dispute about a pew within the altar rails the rural dean inquired 'what method the former rectors . . . had observ'd in administering the sacrament, whether the minister was wont ordinarily to give it at the table, or to go round the church'. In Llansanffraid, St Asaph, where Holy Communion was only celebrated once a year, the church was described as in poor condition, with a 'tattered worn out chalice having a hole or 2 actually patched up with brown paper'.[35] Bishop Bull reminded clergy of their duty not to administer holy communion to 'persons known to be vicious and scandalous' and required clergy to 'rebuke people of their faults'.[36]

Occasional references suggest that in north Wales there were generally good congregations on Sundays, and people behaved well in church, even remaining quiet for three or four minutes when the rector discovered he had forgotten his sermon, and went home to fetch it. References to a 'great congregation' at Llanfechell by William Bulkeley, are far more frequent than a 'thin congregation'. When the congregation was 'thin' it was usually noted as being on account of 'wakes' in a neighbouring parish. He even recorded 'a large congregation' when there was no sermon.[37] In Caernarfonshire in 1778 it has been estimated that the regular Sunday attendance was about half the numbers of Easter communicants.[38]

It is difficult to know whether there is truth in Erasmus Saunders's claim, probably relating to south Wales and the diocese of St David's, that 'some churches are totally neglected, and very rarely if at all have any Service perform'd in them', of which he noted eight, and that there were 'several where we are but rarely to meet with Preaching, Catechising or Administration of Holy Communion' and that in others prayers were read only once a month.[39] David Howell has claimed that in the archdeaconry of Carmarthen in 1775 Sunday services were scantily attended, with very few parishes having Sunday congregations of more that forty, and most fewer that twenty.[40]

Occasionally there were disturbances in church resulting in consistory court cases for misbehaviour in church – 1 in Llandaff between 1710 and 1719, 12 between 1720 and 1729, 3 between 1730 and 1739, 2 between 1740 and 1749 and 8 between 1750 and 1759, and in Bangor 2 between 1740 and 1749, and 2 between 1750 and 1759. Such small numbers are insignificant compared with the numbers of parishes in these two dioceses and the timescales.

Table 6.4 The language in which services were conducted, 1749–78

	Welsh	English	English and Welsh
Diocese of St Asaph in 1749	54	18	37
Diocese of Bangor in 1749	111	3	7
Diocese of Bangor in 1778	110	1	6
Archdeaconry of Cardigan Ultra Aeron Deanery 1755	11	0	0

As we have seen, most of Wales was Welsh-speaking, and in Welsh-speaking areas Welsh was the language of worship (Table 6.4). However, clergy faced difficulties in bilingual areas, or areas where there was change. English was gaining ground in Radnorshire, and in Monmouthshire, and in the coalfields of Flintshire, and in parts of Montgomeryshire, from where John Catlyn of Kerry reported to SPCK in 1715:

> in that part of the Country the English Tongue prevails so much that Welch is but little regarded. That the Welch Books sent him by the Society would stick upon his hands, did he not take care to disperse them into Radnorshire and the upper parts of Montgomeryshire.[41]

In the industrializing areas of Glamorgan, for example around Merthyr Tydfil and in most towns, English was gaining ground. John Loveday noted in 1729 that in Cardiff 'they have not had a Welsh Service in the memory of Man: not one in a hundred there understanding more of Welsh than is sufficient to go to market with', while at Newport, Monmouthshire, 'Several.. understand Welsh so that once in two months or thereabouts the Minister changes with some Welshman who reads prayers and preaches in Welsh which pleases the Inhabitants who do not like their having an English Minister.'[42] Eryn White has suggested that in bilingual areas it was not uncommon for the officiating minister to take a straw poll of English- and Welsh-speakers at the beginning of the service, and then determine which language or mixture of languages to use.[43]

In areas where both Welsh and English were spoken in St Asaph diocese, considerable efforts were made to accommodate both. At St Asaph in 1749 daily services in the cathedral were in English while Sunday and holy day services in the parish church were in Welsh. At Halkyn the morning service was in Welsh as far as the second lesson, and then in English as far as the Communion, which was in Welsh, with an English sermon one week and one in Welsh the next. At Caerwys and Bodfari the second lesson and the Litany were in English, and once a month the sermon was in English. At Mold morning service alternated between English and Welsh, but the second lesson was always in Welsh, and Sunday Evening Prayer and weekday services were always in English. At Queenshope Morning Prayer was in English, with the second lesson in Welsh, and the Holy Communion in Welsh, with Welsh and English sermons alternately, and Evening Prayer was in English with the second lesson in Welsh. At Wrexham Welsh and English was used in alternate weeks, and the first lesson was always in English and the second lesson in Welsh. At Mwynglawdd Sunday Evening Prayer was in English 'for which there is a Subscription by ye Miners'. At Ruabon the Sunday services were partly in Welsh and partly in English, depending on who was there. However, if the sermon was in Welsh, catechizing was in English and vice versa. In Pool and Cedewain deaneries in Montgomeryshire in most parishes there were complex combinations of Welsh and English, although in three parishes only English was used. At Berriew 'Some of the Parishioners complain that they have not for some time Welsh Duty', at Bettws 'More Welsh duty is required', and at Llanllwchaiarn, where there was only a Welsh sermon once a quarter, the incumbent noted: 'Complaints are much yt Welsh Duty is not performed every third Sunday or at least once in the month.'[44]

Rural deans' reports illustrate discontent by Welsh-speakers and the difficulty of achieving acceptable compromises. At Holywell the rural dean reported there was dissatisfaction that more Welsh was not used, and there was not a fixed Sunday for the Welsh sermon. He 'recommended that Mr Price to have the Service every other Sunday in Welsh for that then his Welsh parishioners would be better pleased, and probably the English parishioners'. Increasing use of English was resisted, as at Northorp where the rural dean reported:

> Welsh and English alternately every other Sunday, the Welsh Inhabitants loudly exclaim against this Method as an Innovation being always used to the greater part of the Services in Welsh every Sunday till Mr Brereton was collated to this living and to have Welsh Sermons than what they have at present.[45]

Communal celebrations

Wales had a number of distinctive communal religious seasonal customs. On Anglesey at Christmas William Bulkeley noted *Plygain*:

> The old Popish superstitious custom of celebrating the birth of Christ by performing Divine Service before Day by Candlelight is still used here, as it is in most parts of the Country, the first morning service begins here betwixt 5 and 6 of the clock, the Parson preached.

In 1737 he noted 'a prodigious number of people'. At Easter in the 1730s the schoolchildren collected eggs in the previous week. On Easter Monday the rector communicated the sick in their houses after Morning Prayer. Then the vestry meeting was held, followed by sports and Evening Prayer. On Easter Tuesday the squire and the rector attended a football match with a neighbouring parish. In 1734 Bulkeley noted that 400 or 500 people came to watch the match which lasted three or four hours. Afterwards he and the rector and the parish gentry drank ale with the players 'after which we went home having finished Easter Holyday innocently and merrily'. At Whitsun the sports included football and cockfighting (in 1734 Bulkeley's opponent in a cockfight was the parson of Llantrisant) and interludes, all of which were attended by the rector. Interludes, which became prominent from the late seventeenth century, were simple dramatic performances, usually depicting a few biblical or allegorical characters.[46]

Each parish celebrated its patron saint's day, with a wake or *mabsant* beginning with a service in church, and games of fives or tennis, cockfighting, bear-baiting and usually some fighting between young men, and music and dancing, and much eating and drinking, usually in the churchyard. At Holyhead the alleged bones of the saint were carried through the town on the three Sundays of the wakes weeks.[47] The offerings at St Beuno's shrine at Clynnog were so considerable that no church rate was necessary. In Cardiganshire the alleged petrified bones of St David's oxen were kept in Llanddewi Brefi church, and the alleged brain pan of St Teilo was used by devotees of his well at Llandeilo.[48] There were also pilgrimages to holy wells. Clergy played an active part in these activities, and their presence may have been a moderating influence.

In the middle years of the eighteenth century wakes seem to have begun to decline. At Llanfechell in 1736 the service was transferred to the nearest Sunday. At Holyhead the dancing and water-carrying associated with the *mabsant* were 'suppressed by a pious curate . . . about 1745'. Athletics, boat and horse races were substituted. Suggett has pointed out that Browne Willis's correspondents referred to *mabsant* as a recent institution, and suggests they are a post-Restoration innovation, not a pre-Reformation survival, spreading from towns to the countryside, and were popular because they provided an identity for parishes to differentiate them from their neighbours.[49] William Bulkeley and William Morris regarded wakes as occasions for immorality and idleness. Dissenters also disapproved of them, and Howell Harris and William Williams of Pantycelyn were highly critical of *mabsants*, and discouraged their society members from attending them. However, despite Methodist opposition, they survived into the nineteenth century.

Distinctive popular religious practices were associated with funerals. Family, friends and neighbours gathered at the deceased's house the night before the funeral, on arrival kneeling before the body and saying the Lord's Prayer. As dusk fell, Evening Prayer was said by the priest, and psalms and carols were sung during the night. The priest said the Lord's Prayer before the body was carried from the house, and at every crossroads passed, where the bier was put down, and finally when the churchyard was entered. Sometimes a bell was rung in front of the procession and psalms sung. Evening Prayer was said before the Burial of the Dead. Afterwards members of the congregation placed an offering for the priest on the altar or the altar rail.[50] Geraint Jenkins has suggested that there was also much recourse to witches, astrologers and cunning men in eighteenth-century Wales,[51] and David Howell has alleged that there was 'a coherent structure of folk beliefs, an alternative belief system which co-existed with orthodox Christian belief'.[52]

Music

Music was a distinctive characteristic of the Established Church in Wales. *Halsyngod* and *carolau* which set to music the doctrine of the Church, history, parts of the Bible, the acts of saints and examples of piety and virtue were a central part of popular devotional life in the Welsh Church. Verse and music were easily committed to memory. *Halsyngod* composed by clergy and men of letters, were usually drenched in scriptural references. Erasmus Saunders commented:

> It is not to be expressed what a particular Delight and Pleasure the young People take to get these Hymns by heart and to sing them with a great deal of Emulation of excelling each other, and this is a Religious Exercise that are us'd to as well at home . . . as upon some Publick Occasion: such as at their Wakes, and solemn Festivals and Funerals and very frequently in their Churches in the Winter Season, between All Saints and Candlemass: at which Times before and after Divine Service, upon Sunday and Holydays eight or ten will commonly divide themselves to four or five of a side, and so forming themselves, as it were, into an imitation of our Cathedral or Collegiate choirs, one part first begins, and then by way of Alternate Response, the other repeats the same Stanza.[53]

Manuscript copies of *halsyngod* increased in the period 1661–77, and then declined, and revived after 1690, and declined again towards the middle of the eighteenth century, perhaps being superseded by Methodist hymns. Welsh ballads, which began to be printed from 1699 following the introduction of printing at Shrewsbury, and were particularly popular in north Wales, had strong scriptural references.[54] *Plygain*, consisting of scriptural carols sung early on Christmas morning, and throughout the Christmas season in churches, to popular tunes, but not intended for congregational participation, were popular in north Wales. Wassail songs were sung at houses at Christmas, New Year, Twelfth Night, Candlemas and May Day, and at weddings. New songs were regularly composed for these occasions.[55]

Singing the psalms at Morning and Evening Prayer seems to have been a popular innovation in the early eighteenth century. In 1718 John Harris at Llantrisant reported: 'That by singing Psalms in the Morning and Evening Service they have a greater Number of People at Church than they had before'.[56] 'Singing Psalms' were bound in with the edition of the Bible published by the SPCK in 1718.[57] There was also enthusiasm for singing church services, as there was in England.[58] At Newtown, Montgomeryshire, the incumbent reported in 1733: 'Prayers are constantly read and chaunted on all Holy Days (and an Anthem sung) likewise on Wednesday and Friday thro' ye Year. On all Festivals relating to our Blessed Saviour full Choir Service is perform'd.'[59] In 1738 Edward Owen of Penrhos on Anglesey reported 'Our singing goes on pretty well having . . . upward of forty scholars we have learn'd two or three psalms, ye magnificat and an anthem, and ye Litany.'[60]

Music in church attracted charitable donations and bequests. In 1734 Sir John Price gave an organ and an endowment 'to settle a competent stipend on an Organist and his successor Organists there for the time being and for ever'. It was noted that he 'had been at the expense and trouble [of] Instructing Several men, women and Children to Sing and chant the Psalms and Hymns and Anthems in the Laudable manner used in the Cathedrals and Collegiate Churches of this Kingdom'.[61] In Caernarfonshire in 1743 Griffith Humphreys, a Pwllheli gentleman, left an annuity of 20*s*. a year for life 'to the two most artful persons and best psalm singers for Salms on Sunday in the Church of Denio, as shall be judged and approved to be the most capable and best singers by my

Executor'. In 1744 Griffith Jones of Llannor bequeathed £40 to the 'greatest objects of charity' in that parish

> as shall excel in singing of Psalms by notes toward the more decent and continual melody in publick worship of God [as] a small encouragement to such people as shall be devoutly inclined to the worship of God in the Church of Llannor in the way of the Church of England.[62]

Teaching children to sing the psalms was a part of the charity schools' curriculum, and a way of demonstrating the achievements of masters and children to attract contributions to finance the schools. Schoolmasters were employed to teach congregations to sing. In 1738 William Bulkeley on Anglesey noted: 'Nicholas Oughton that teaches the people of Llanerchymedd to sing Psalms came to this Church today with fifteen of his Scholars to sing, that we of this parish might have tryall of his singing (being about to employ him to teach here).'[63]

Howell Harris's first initiative in exhorting in late 1736 was in the company of John Games, a music teacher, whom he accompanied on his peripatetic teaching for six months or so, until they fell out.[64] Music, especially hymns, became central to the Welsh Evangelical Revival, providing a medium for the expression of the whole gamut of religious experience from doubt to assurance, including thanksgiving, supplication and instruction. The first collection of hymns in Welsh, *Pasc y Christion*, had been published in 1703 by Thomas Baddy, a Presbyterian minister in Denbigh,[65] and from 1740 small collections of hymns for the use of Methodist societies were published along with tracts. Gradually hymns replaced psalms in Methodist meetings. William Williams of Pantycelyn introduced new metrical forms in his 800 or so Welsh hymns, and developed the hymns to emphasize spiritual experience and personal salvation, making Christ the object of a believer's affections, using imagery from the Song of Songs, and extensive other biblical allusions.[66] Williams and many others drew on the folksong tradition, included refrains and dialogues and developed an oral folk tradition, often using familiar tunes.[67]

Libraries

Access to books to stimulate the preaching and pastoral ministry of the clergy and the deepening of the faith of the literate laity was a key aspect of the late seventeenth-century reform of pastoral ministry. One way of meeting this, for poor clergy unable to afford to buy books, was to provide parochial, deanery or diocesan lending libraries. Wales, as one of the poorest regions of the kingdom, was specially targeted for the provision of libraries.

In the 1690s Thomas Bray himself raised funds to provide small parochial libraries for six poor Welsh parishes. Between 1703 and 1711, and again in the 1760s libraries for Wales were a main concern for the SPCK.[68] From 1703 Sir Humphrey Mackworth agitated for the establishment of a special committee for the provision of libraries for Wales. It was initiated in 1705, with Mackworth and Sir John Philipps among the members, along with Mr Stokes, rector of St Alphege London Wall and archdeacon of St Albans, and Henry Hoare, the banker. Stokes drew up 'Proposals for Erecting Lending Libraries in Wales', of which 250 copies were ordered to be printed. This attracted considerable English support and contributions of money and books. It was agreed to lay the proposals before the Welsh bishops and the bishop of Worcester. They gained support in Wales, and it was reported that 'several Gentlemen at Carmarthen at the last Quarter Sessions did subscribe 40s a piece . . . and that they intend to make application throughout the county'. There was some debate about whether the libraries should be open to parishioners as well as clergy. When the 'Deed of Trust for Settling Parochial Libraries in Wales; and also the Form of the Covenant to be Entered into by the Rectors of Parishes and their Successors' came before the SPCK committee in 1708, it was recommended that the libraries should not be restricted to clergy.

Carmarthen, Bangor, Cardiff and Denbigh were proposed as locations for the libraries, but after discussion Cowbridge and St Asaph were substituted for Cardiff and Denbigh, as better centres for the dioceses of Llandaff and St Asaph. Books were provided from donations and SPCK stock, although some were criticized as worthless. The process of dispatching and setting up diocesan libraries was slow. In 1708 Edward Meyricke gave two houses in Carmarthen for the schoolmaster and the library, John Vaughan proposed names of trustees, and the bishops of Bangor, Llandaff, Hereford and Worcester signed the deed for the library. The collection was dispatched in four boxes by carrier to Alderman Bachelor in Bristol, who forwarded it to John Vaughan in Carmarthen on board the *Phillis* of Carmarthen. The mayor, council and burgesses of Carmarthen thanked the society for 'their Ecellt Benefaction', but in 1712 it was still not unpacked, and the bishop of St David's was asked to intervene. Later in 1708 the catalogue of books for the Bangor library was chosen, and in June 1710 it was reported that the books for Bangor had been sent to the Castle and Falcon in Aldersgate to be sent to Chester 'pursuant to a Direction from the Lord Bishop of Bangor'. In 1710 the bishop of Llandaff recommended the names of twenty-five gentlemen as trustees for the library at Cowbridge, and the books were dispatched by wagon to Bristol, and thence by water to Aberthaw and onward by wagon to Cowbridge. In November 1711 it was reported that the library for St Asaph was ready packed, and that £194. 17*s*. 1*d*. had been spent on the four libraries.[69]

The deed of the Cowbridge library throws light on its intended use. Clergy and schoolmasters living within ten miles of the town, trustees and anyone giving 10*s*. in cash or books to the library might borrow books. Borrowers were required to pay a deposit, and sign a form undertaking to return the book by a specified date, when the deposit would be repaid. If the book was damaged the deposit would be forfeit. The library was open from 10 until 12 on market days. The trustees were required to inspect it annually and check the stock against the catalogue, to keep an acquisitions book and minute book, and to report to the bishop on the condition of the library. The trustees were less than diligent. Their first meeting was in 1714, six years after the library was dispatched, when they agreed to set up presses for the books in the room over the vestry in Cowbridge Church, and appointed the schoolmaster as librarian. Occasional meetings were held until 1725, after which no meeting was recorded until 1764. The stock was strong on the Fathers and seventeenth-century divines, on Aquinas and Reformation authors, and had numerous volumes of sermons and SPCK tracts. In 1736 a 'Book Society' was set up in association with the library, and between then and 1745 about 150 books were added to the library.[70]

At least ten parochial libraries were also provided for Welsh parishes, with an endowment of less than £30 a year, by the SPCK between 1707 and 1715. A deposit of £5 was required before a library was dispatched, which could not have been easy for incumbents of such parishes to raise. Use of them was restricted to incumbents.[71] A major problem with parochial libraries was their upkeep. This was highlighted in a letter in March 1730 from Thomas Jeans of New Town Hall, Montgomeryshire, about 'the State of Parochial Libraries in Wales' which he noted were needed in many places, but pointed out: 'unless there can be found a Method to make the Parish Officers accountable for the Books, they will be (generally speaking) lost at the Death of every Incumbent', for 'Clergymen's Executors are not always of that Integrity as is to be wished'.[72] In St Asaph diocese rural deans checked libraries during their routine inspection of parishes.[73] From 1757 the Associates of Dr Bray, established after Bray's death in 1730, focused on the needs of Wales and north Lancashire and provided a further forty-five libraries for poor Welsh parishes until 1768, when they ceased to found new libraries.

Schools

A central part of the programme for forwarding the reform of the pastoral ministry of the Established Church was providing instruction for children in the faith of the church by means of the Prayer Book Catechism, and teaching them to read, so that they could read the Bible and the Prayer Book for themselves. The motivation for instruction in reading was not a desire to educate children (and adults), but to save them.

Under the Protectorate sixty-three schools were established in Welsh market towns to teach the three Rs in English.[74] Thomas Gouge, the ejected minister of St Sepulchre's Southwark, and author of a number of popular devotional books, visited Wales in 1671–2. Subsequently, together with a number of leading Anglicans, including John Tillotson, Simon Patrick,

Edward Stillingfleet and Edward Fowler, and leading dissenters, including Richard Baxter, William Baker, Matthew Pool and Thomas Firmin, he established the London-based Welsh Trust. The trust deed, in addition to publishing tracts, proposed

> to raise and maintain several Schools for teaching the poorest of the Welsh Children to read English, and the Boys to learn to Write and Cast Accounts; whereby they will be enabled to read our English Bibles and Treatises, to be more serviceable to their Country, and to be more comfortable in the world.

They agreed to contribute subscriptions 'providing that this charitable and pious work be ordered and managed by Dr Tillotson Dean of Canterbury' and twenty others whose names were subscribed. Subscriptions were received from 'the quality in and about London' and bishops and clergy. From Wales a number of influential landowners, some of whom had been commissioners under the Protectorate, subscribed, including Edward Harley, Edward Mansell, Thomas Mostyn, Trevor Williams, John Awbrey, Henry Owen and Sir Erasmus Philipps.

Between Michaelmas 1674 and Michaelmas 1675 it was reported that in eighty-six of the 'chief towns and parishes' in Wales 1,162 children were 'put to school to read English and the boys to learn to write and to cast Accounts' over and above 'the 200 put to School the last year by the Charity of others before the Trust began'. It also was noted:

> Which Pious and charitable undertaking hath already provoked divers of the Landlords and Inhabitants of Several Towns and Parishes in Wales to put 863 of the poorest Welsh Children to School upon their own account. So that 2225 in all are already put to school.

Some schools were funded by Gouge, some from the Welsh Trust and some by towns (Table 6.5). They were generally administered by the incumbent and churchwardens of the parish.[75] Probably because of their use of English, schools were mostly in English-speaking areas, and towns.

Table 6.5 Schools reported to the Welsh Trust in 1675 and 1678

	1675	1678		1675	1678
Carmarthenshire	11	6	Radnorshire	3	3
Pembrokeshire	12	14	Caernarfonshire	4	4
Glamorganshire	16	16	Denbighshire	8	5
Breconshire	2	1	Flintshire	7	4
Monmouthshire	12	11	Anglesey	1	
Cardiganshire	7	1	Montgomeryshire		6

After Gouge's death in 1681 the trust ceased to function. There were differences of views among the subscribers about the schools. Stephen Hughes, the ejected incumbent of Meidrim, Carmarthenshire, objected to English as the medium of education; Bishops Lucy of St David's and Lloyd of Bangor were hostile to Gouge as a dissenter, and the withdrawal of Charles II's indulgence to dissenters in 1681 soured the relationship between dissenters and the Established Church. Eryn White has pointed out that thirty of the charity schools subsequently established under the auspices of the SPCK were in places where previously there had been schools under the auspices of the Welsh Trust.[76]

There was renewed interest in establishing schools to teach poor children to read and learn the catechism in the early years of the eighteenth century amidst general concerns about the 'great Ignorance and Atheism in Wales',[77] and fears that the Welsh would be prey to popery, superstition and magic. An important focus for this activity was the SPCK, with its strong Welsh links. One of the society's prime objects was disseminating information about establishing schools for poor children, and providing books for the schools.[78] The society's Welsh correspondents were encouraged to support initiatives for schools and to visit them and report once or twice a year on their progress to the SPCK committee. The London Welsh supported the schools, along with English subscribers, including Sir John Thorold, who was subsequently a supporter of John Wesley, Sir Francis Gosling, Stephen Hales and London bankers and physicians.[79]

The SPCK provided background information and encouragement, but the establishment of schools was down to local initiatives. Dean Jones of Bangor set up his first charity school in Bangor in 1699, and in 1700 reported that he had set up 'several schools for poor children in these parts'; James Harris, the vicar of Llantrisant, a prebendary of Llandaff and principal of Jesus College, Oxford, set up two schools at Llantrisant in Glamorgan in 1699, and schools were set up at Llwydiarth in Montgomeryshire in 1700 by the curate, and at Wrexham in 1701 by John Price, the vicar, and Margaret Jeffreys, Anne Williams and Lady Dorothy Jeffreys.[80]

Bishop Bull of St David's issued a circular letter to his clergy exhorting them to establish schools in their parishes. Clergy were significant founders of charity schools, securing funding from voluntary contributions by groups of lay people and collections taken in church at the celebration of Holy Communion. Leading lay people were also important. The outstanding example was Sir John Philipps of Picton Castle who supported twenty-two schools in Pembrokeshire, providing all the funding, including clothes and food for the children. John Vaughan of Derllys called together the freeholders of his lordship, and with their support set up a school. Sir Humphrey Mackworth persuaded the Company of Mines Adventurers, of which he was deputy governor, to establish a school at Neath for miners' children and to provide a chaplain at the Esgair Hir mines in Cardiganshire to read prayers daily and preach, and to teach the children of miners and workmen the Catechism. John Price, vicar of Wrexham, reported in 1706 that 'the gentry are giving much support for schools'. Women were significant patrons of schools. Mrs Edward Vaughan endowed schools at Llanfihangel and Llanfyllin with £1,200. Over thirty schools were founded by women between 1699 and 1740.[81]

There was always a risk that, when schools were only supported by one benefactor, after the benefactor's death the funding would cease, as happened when Sir John Philipps died in 1737 and left no endowment for his schools. John Jones, dean of Bangor, however, left bequests of £10 to the schools at Bangor, Llanllechid, Aber, Gyffin, Llanfihangel Ysceifiog with Llanffinan, Pentraeth with Llanddyfnan, and £50 to Rhoscolyn with Llanfair-yn-Neubwll and Llanfihangel-yn-Nhowyn, Llanfihangel-y-Traethau with Llandecwyn, Llandegfan and Beaumaris.[82]

The schools were held during the day, in evenings or on Saturdays. Some schools also provided for teaching adults. Day schools were usually from 7 to 11 in the morning and 1 to 5 in the afternoon in summer and from 8 to 11 and 1 to 4 in the winter.[83] Some masters were licensed by the bishop, as at Abergele charity school in Denbighshire, 'to teach the rudiments of the English tongue, and the art of Writing and Arithmetic and to expound and instruct the children . . . in the Catechism of the Church of England'.[84]

Dean Jones specified that poor children in the schools he endowed should be taught to 'read Welsh perfectly' and that the Bible, the Prayer Book and Catechism were to be taught in Welsh, and writing and arithmetic, if possible, although at Beaumaris and Bangor, which were on the road to Holyhead and the route to Ireland, Welsh was not compulsory.[85] John Price of Wrexham, Robert Gwynne of Gresford and Thomas Wise of Denbigh promoted teaching in Welsh as the language best understood by parents.[86] Probably most schools in north Wales used Welsh. There is no mention of the use of Welsh in schools in south Wales, except at Swansea, where Thomas Collins in 1710, was '. . . of the Opinion the People in Wales ought not to be Indulg'd with Welch Translations which already too much Abound in a Language that keeps Men in ignorance of many things touching their Religion and Civil Life'.[87]

The SPCK recommended that schoolmasters be paid £4 or £5 a year, and that they should be aged over twenty-five, communicants and 'of sober life and conversation'. In November 1708 Sir John Philipps proposed recruiting charity schoolmasters from members of the London religious societies, who should gain experience of teaching in the London charity schools. There is no evidence that this happened, although elsewhere, as at Norwich, charity school trustees recruited masters trained in London.

How successful the schools were is unclear. There are many references to parental apathy. Dean Jones reported to the SPCK in December 1699 that 'their poverty is so great that they cannot allow themselves to learn. Ignorance and Unconcernedness are the reigning diseases.' It was reported in 1708 that Sir John Philipps 'found it difficult to persuade Parents to send their Children and keep them there, their own want of Education making them stupid as to every consideration of ye advantage of it in their Children'. In 1715 John Pendre of Prendergast, Pembrokeshire, reported that 'Puncheston School fell because ye Master could not prevail upon parents to send their children to be taught there'.[88] In 1716 Dean Jones further reported that numbers in his schools were small, 'for it was difficult to keep the children at school regularly for they had to beg victuals from door to door'.[89]

In the diocese of St Asaph it has been claimed the poor took advantage of the schools.[90] The rural dean of Rhos reported, in response to Bishop Hare's request for information about schools in 1729, that there were twelve schools in 25 parishes in his deanery, of which six were charity schools. In the deanery of Penllyn and Edeirnion the rural dean reported 4 schools in eleven parishes, of which 3 were charity schools.[91] About sixty-eight schools were set up in St Asaph diocese between 1700 and 1738.[92] By 1740 there were ninety-six schools in Wales founded under the auspices of SPCK, and another sixty-one charity schools.[93]

After 1715, fewer charity schools were established, twenty-eight being established between 1716 and 1740 compared with sixty-eight between 1699 and 1715.[94] After the Hanoverian succession, London charity schools were suspected of infiltration by Jacobite influences, and London and Welsh benefactors may have hesitated further to increase suspicions of Jacobite influences in Wales.[95] Local factors may have militated against the success of charity schools. The poverty of the poor, as Dean Jones pointed out, meant that they could not afford to spare their children from working. The scattered nature of Welsh rural parishes meant that children had to walk long distances to schools. Language was probably not an issue as it is clear that schools in which Welsh was the medium of teaching were common.

Dissenters established a number of schools for the poor. Dr David Williams of Wrexham bequeathed money to establish dissenting schools in Denbigh, Caernarfon, Montgomery, Llanuwchllyn, Newmarket, Pwllheli, Llanbrynmair and Wrexham. Elementary schools were attached to some dissenting academies, as at Carmarthen.[96]

Griffith Jones of Llanddowror, who was presented to the living by his brother-in-law, Sir John Philipps, and who, as we have noted, was investigated by Bishop Ottley in 1714 for preaching in other people's parishes, translated or wrote over thirty Welsh books, mostly catechisms and devotional books, and became a corresponding member of the SPCK in 1713. He was much concerned about the 'ignorance of the poorer sort', saw education as the first stage of evangelism, and developed the idea of charity schools to provide a sparer, more focused educational approach.[97] He and Philipps had visited Scotland in 1718, and may have derived the idea of 'circulating' schools from Scottish 'ambulatory schools', one of which they saw in Dumfriesshire. Sir Humphrey Mackworth had also in 1719 proposed using itinerant schoolmasters. In September 1731 Jones sought the SPCK's support for a Welsh-language school at Llanddowror, and there developed the concept of a 'circulating school'. It was 'for all Comers to learn to read and be supplied with Books and taught gratis'. He requested from the SPCK '40 or 50 of the small volume of ye Welch Bible, upon the usual terms, that they favour their members with, and other Books' for which Sir John Philipps paid. Jones was next in touch with the SPCK in September 1736, ordering '500 Welsh psalters bound with the Welsh Alphabet'; in October he ordered '100 Church Catechisms in Welsh and 500 Welsh Bibles'; in November '4000 of the little Tract to persuade ignorant people to read, etc'; and in January 1737 he ordered 1,000 Bibles and commented: 'the Welch Schools increase beyond their ability to manage.'[98] In May 1737 Dr Pardo, the principal of Jesus College, Oxford, agreed to pay for binding 500 Welsh Prayer Books and 500 Welsh bibles for Jones's schools.

The aim of Jones's schools was to teach poor people and children the Catechism in order to save them from 'the general Corruption, Curse, and Guilt of the human race', and to save individuals and the nation from judgement, which was experienced in crime, cattle plague, the sword, famine, earthquakes and shipwrecks. He cited the examples of St Mark, who he claimed had set up a catechetical school in Alexandria, and Origen, teaching at Caesarea, and Cyril, at Jerusalem.[99] Jones's aim was to 'train up Disciples to our blessed Redeemer'. He noted that 'several of the Welch scholars have even taught their own Parents to read the Word of God' and persuaded them to say the prayers they had learned at school, and grace before and after meals. He was clear that rote learning was not enough. Pupils must understand the Catechism.[100]

Lessons were in Welsh and pupils were

> Instructed daily in the Principles and Duties of Religion out of the Church Catechism and the Explanation of it for Four or Five and sometimes for Six Months or longer, as those who desire to learn have Need of them, and at such Times of the Year as the Poor can best spare from their Labours to attend them.[101]

Masters moved on when, after four to six months, pupils had learned the Catechism and were able to read the Bible, sing the Psalms and pray. Teaching writing was forbidden. Jones claimed that within six or seven weeks reading Welsh could be taught. The schools varied in size from nine pupils to over seventy, most having between thirty and forty pupils. In 1737 Jones reported to the SPCK:

> the Adult People, Men and Women make up two-thirds of the Scholars, and most of the Masters instruct for three or four hours in the evening after school time, about twice or thrice as many as they had in their schools by day, who could not attend at other time.

It was, Jones pointed out, cheaper to teach in Welsh, because people did not have first to learn a foreign language. Once they were literate in Welsh they could more easily learn English. Teaching in Welsh would protect the poor Welsh from 'Atheism, Deism, Infidelity, Arianism, Popery, lewd Plays, immodest Romances and Love Intrigues', all of which were available in English. In 1739 the SPCK committee 'desired [Mr Jones] to signify what care is taken to instruct the Children of the Welsh Schools in the English Language'.[102] Although no reply is recorded, the 'Accounts' of the schools, in 1749 noted: 'Some English Charity Schools are included, set up of late for the Poor that do not understand Welch'.[103]

Jones carefully selected young men to train for 'some weeks' as teachers, renting cottages at Llanddowror as a hostel for them. By 1738 he had about fifty trained teachers. As time went on, he recruited former students as teachers. They were also required to instruct children in worship and morality.

Strict economy was exercised. Parishes where a school was held were required to contribute the offertory collected at a celebration of the Holy Communion towards the costs of their school. Teachers were paid £2 a quarter.[104] Overheads were minimal, apart from paying teachers. No buildings were required, for teaching was in the parish church, or a house or barn. People were expected to bring their own candles for evening classes. Jones reckoned he could teach six children or poor people to read at the cost of £1.

However, fund-raising was necessary, which Jones sought to do through his reports published as *Welch Piety*, recording the progress of the schools, and appealing for charitable donations from the rich and pious. In the report for 1747–8 he listed Sir John Thorold, the Revd Dr Hales, of Teddington, the Revd James Sparrow of Bath, Dr Hadley of Donington, Berkshire and Francis Gosling, banker, of London, as people to whom donations might be sent, and noted that 'the Donations of the last year did hardly answer the Expence'.[105] In 1758 he listed another five English agents for collecting funds, including Slingsby Bethel, MP for the City of London, and six Welsh clergy. Jones was a highly professional organizer and fund-raiser. In his latter years, suffering poor health, he spent much time in Bath, where he enlisted the support and contributions of influential people for his schools. He established a Corresponding Society in which he enrolled supporters, who were invited to join in intercessions for his work, make financial contributions, prepare for setting up schools, and inspect schools taking place in their locality. The SPCK contributed no direct funds, but provided vast numbers of Welsh Bibles, psalters, catechisms and small books for use in the schools, at cost price. They also sought subscriptions for this work from their network, and the SPCK secretaries, Henry Newman and Thomas Broughton, worked hard to promote the Welsh schools and provide books for them. Jones regularly expressed thanks for this help.

The scheme depended on the support of parish clergy, to make available their churches for teaching, and to announce the commencement of the schools. Jones provided the method and the plan of action, but local support and encouragement were essential. He sent out the teachers, and they reported back to him, and he paid them, but incumbents were responsible for their local management and for inspecting the schools. Initially there was some hesitation by incumbents to receive schoolmasters sent by the incumbent of another parish, but they were quickly won over by the effect of the schools on their parishes. Inevitably, some teachers were criticized by some clergy as ignorant and insubordinate, and were suspected of undermining their authority and alienating people from the church. Jones indicated that he wished to receive criticisms, noting in his 1747–8 report that any criticisms should be 'particularised in Writing' so that the fault might be corrected, and pointing out that 'The care and conduct of School masters is always submitted to parish ministers'.[106]

Jones's 1757–8 report included 'Testimonials Relating to the Masters and Scholars of the Schools' which quoted extracts from thirty-two letters from clergy and gentry, all glowing with praise. Clergy noted that children now joined in the responses at church and had learned morning and evening prayers and graces to say at home. Watkin Watkin, 'gentleman' of Llandysiliogogo, Cardiganshire reported: 'When the Parents and other Labourers, and indeed many Farmers, saw the Children so well instructed in the Principles of the Christian Religion, then they, who were of riper years, flocked there by Night . . . desiring with great Concern to be likewise instructed.'[107]

In the early 1740s the numbers of schools declined, and it was suspected that some masters were Methodist exhorters, and that schools were a Methodist undercover movement. In north Wales masters were attacked as Methodists. William Bulkeley of Llanfechell on Anglesey claimed in 1748 that 'The Clergy are generally all against these itinerant Schools and do all they can to depreciate them calling them the Nurseries of the Methodists'.[108] In 1752 John Evans, rector of Eglwys Gymyn, linked the schools with Methodism in his scathing attack, *Some Account of the Welsh Charity Schools: and of the Rise and Progress of Methodism in Wales through the Means of*

Them. However after 1745 numbers recovered, as shown in Tables 6.6 and 6.7. By 1773 some 276,434 children and adults had been taught over thirty-six years, the total population of Wales at the time being estimated at about 480,000.

Table 6.6 Numbers of Welsh circulating schools, 1737–73[109]

Year	No. of schools	No. of scholars
1737	37	2,400
1738	71	3,981
1739	71	3,989
1740	150	8,765
1741	128	7,995
1742	89	5,123
1743	75	4,881
1744	74	4,253
1745	120	5,843
1746	116	5,635
1747	110	5,633
1748	136	6,223
1749	142	6,543
1750	130	6,244
1751	129	5,669
1752	130	5,724
1753	134	5,118
1754	149	6,018
1755	163	7,015
1756	172	7,063
1757	220	9,037
1758	218	9,834
1759	206	8,369
1760	215	8,607
1761	210	8,023
1762	225	9,616
1763	279	11,770
1764	195	9,453

Year	No. of schools	No. of scholars
1765	189	9,029
1766	219	10,986
1767	190	8,422
1768	148	7,149
1769	173	8,637
1770	159	9,042
1771	181	9,844
1772	219	12,044
1773	242	13,205
Total since 1737	5,844	276,434

Table 6.7 Location of Welsh circulating schools in 1748, 1758 and 1773

County	1748	1758	1773
Anglesey	13	21	14
Breconshire	3	6	16
Cardiganshire	4	15	48
Carmarthenshire	34	68	50
Caernarfonshire	5	31	17
Denbighshire	11	10	7
Flintshire		2	4
Glamorganshire	22	26	18
Merioneth	2	10	10
Monmouthshire		6	30 (26 English schools)
Montgomeryshire	7	5	4
Pembrokeshire	21	18	25
Radnorshire	2		

After Jones's death in 1761 Bridget Bevan, widow of Arthur Bevan, MP for Carmarthen, niece of Sir John Philipps and heiress of John Vaughan of Derllys, who had been the SPCK's correspondent in Carmarthen, took responsibility for managing the schools. She demonstrated considerable business acumen and organizational skills, and, as Table 6.6 shows, the schools prospered and increased, in numbers and size. The number of schools teaching in English increased, and at least three schoolmistresses were appointed. After her death in 1779, her niece, Lady Elizabeth Stepney, and nephew, Rear Admiral William Lloyd, took possession of the £10,000 she had left of her and Griffith Jones's money to continue the schools. The other two trustees took the case to the Court of Chancery but the case was not resolved or the funds recovered until 1804.

Jones was on close terms with George Whitefield, the Countess of Huntingdon, Howell Harris and Daniel Rowland. Harris and Rowland looked to Llanddowror as their spiritual home, and to Jones and the schools as agents of spiritual regeneration. Harris advocated holding schools wherever his societies were 'settled' and urged the use of Griffith Jones's *Catechism*.[110] Although Jones dissociated himself publicly from the Methodist movement he cannot be dissociated from the Welsh Revival. The two movements had much in common: the ability to read Welsh and a knowledge of the Catechism were preconditions for the spread of Methodist societies; and the method of teaching in the evening schools, with prayers and psalm-singing, was not dissimilar from the practice of Methodist societies.

7
Methodism in Wales

Methodism in Wales was an outcome of the pastoral revival of the Established Church, a revival which had emphasized the basic education of the laity by the parish clergy, so that they could read the Bible and knew the Catechism, and the formation of religious societies of devout lay people for self-examination, Bible reading, prayer and thanksgiving, and using hymns. Howell Harris, the son of a carpenter, was the most influential early leader of Welsh Methodism. He was nourished on Anglican classics of spirituality, such as Lewis Bayly's *Practice of Piety* and *The Whole Duty of Man* and was converted when hearing Griffith Jones preach on Palm Sunday 1735. He believed he had a direct commission from God, and immediately began visiting the sick, exhorting people and holding devotional meetings.[1]

Griffith Jones of Llanddowror is the key figure in the origins of Welsh Methodism. He was never a Methodist, and was critical of the movement, but was responsible for the conversion experiences of the two early leaders, not only Howell Harris, but Daniel Rowland. His early, but abandoned, practice of itinerant preaching in the second decade of the century may have provided a model for Harris and Rowland. They learned their preaching style from him; he provided Harris in particular with a link with the wider world of Evangelical awakening; and his importation of Welsh Bibles via the SPCK provided the raw material for the revival. His circulating schools provided many recruits for Methodist societies. However, Jones disapproved of Harris for continuing to preach after being refused ordination by Bishop Squire of St David's, and thought both Harris and Rowland harsh and conceited, and made defective by their enthusiasm in 'common sense, common manners, veracity and common honesty'. From May 1741 he was estranged from them.[2]

Despite being refused ordination Harris continued itinerant preaching and establishing societies. He continued to regard himself as an Anglican, and remained a frequent communicant at his parish church, and refused, as a layman, to baptize.[3] Daniel Rowland was curate to his father at Llangeitho. After his conversion he became known as 'the angry cleric' because of his rigorous chastisement of sinners, but, influenced by a neighbouring dissenting minister, Philip Pugh, Rowland began to place greater emphasis on salvation through Christ's redemption. He began to preach in other parishes, but only after asking the incumbent's permission to use the church, and he too began to establish societies of his converts in the vicinity of Llangeitho. Because of his parochial responsibilities, he did not undertake long preaching journeys.[4]

The societies established by Rowland and Harris were intended to consolidate converts' experiences of conversion, to provide for self-examination, for testing their conversions, for overcoming the temptations of the world and for cultivating love of neighbour.[5] Harris and Rowland regarded the societies as part of the Established Church, not a separate denomination. In general they found a degree of sympathy and tolerance from many parish clergy, although some were hostile. Methodist leaders generally disliked the designation 'Methodist'. Eryn White has pointed out that they resisted using both Anglican and dissenting terminology; 'exhorting' rather than 'preaching' in 'society houses' when they had them rather than 'meeting houses'.[6] There was little initially to distinguish them from parish religious societies, except their emotion and energy, the itinerancy of their leaders and exhorters, most of whom were laymen, and the inclusion of women in the societies. Methodist societies attracted the sort of people who had joined religious societies, and may have taken over parish societies.

Welsh Methodism is a distinctively Welsh phenomenon, pre-dating the English revival and relatively little influenced from England, and the Wesleys in particular. Unlike English Wesleyan Methodism, its theology is Calvinistic, though Welsh Methodists differed from dissenters in engaging with their experience of conversion and emotions, rather than with reason, and their polity became largely Presbyterian. There were links through Howell Harris with the wider Evangelical awakening in continental Europe and especially North America. George Whitefield, the English Calvinistic Methodist leader, was an important link in the 1730s and 1740s with the Evangelical Revival in New England, writing to Howell Harris about what he saw there. The publication of Jonathan Edwards's works in England strongly influenced Howell Harris and Daniel Rowland. Edwards gave them a vocabulary to explore and explain their own experiences.[7]

Welsh Methodism's Calvinism also owed something to the experimental seventeenth-century Calvinism of Vavasor Powell, whom Howell Harris claimed as an inspiration.[8] Harris and Rowland may also have been influenced by Calvinism through contacts with Particular Baptists.[9] In addition William Williams of Pantycelyn's father was an Independent, and Williams had attended a dissenting academy either at Llyn-llwyd near Hay or at Talgarth.[10]

In the early days of the Revival there was some cooperation between Harris and some Baptists, but he disliked their exclusivism and what he regarded as the 'dryness' of their preaching, and fell out with them over suspicions of Baptist attempts to proselytize among his members.[11] He was initially welcomed at Independent meeting houses, but was suspected of not respecting the independence of local congregations.[12] In 1739 Harris spoke enthusiastically of David Williams, a Presbyterian minister in Cardiff, and of a dissenting minister in Montgomeryshire, who were 'field preaching'.

However, on a pragmatic level he was clear that to join with the dissenters would have been to ally his societies with a marginal group in Welsh society, and thus isolate them from the majority of the population.[13] There were, however, secessions from Methodists to dissent; the society at Defynnog in Breconshire seceded in 1742 and the society at Groes-wen in Glamorgan, having insisted on a communion service in their society house in 1745 and having requested the ordination of their exhorters, broke away to form an Independent congregation. Harris pointed out that societies were 'little branches' of the Church not a church. In 1747 he visited Anglesey to try to dissuade the few societies there from seceding.[14]

Howell Harris and Daniel Rowland saw themselves leading a renewal movement within the Established Church; spiritually renewing it rather than constitutionally reforming it; and supplementing it in large parishes where the church was geographically remote, or where a parish priest was thought to have lost, or never established, his grip. Methodism was probably initially successful because of its sense of novelty, in providing an alternative to traditional forms of piety. It attracted the young, and gave a sense of specialness and exclusivity, and grounds for disregarding the rest of the world.

Welsh Methodism was, in its origins, a south Wales phenomenon. Harris, and later William Williams of Pantycelyn, worked in Breconshire, Radnorshire and Montgomeryshire, and Rowland in Cardiganshire and Carmarthenshire. The English-speaking areas of Glamorgan and Pembrokeshire were more receptive to John Wesley's brand of Methodism. All made forays into the north, but with little initial success. Welsh Methodism was protean in character, including an attitude of mind, emotion in preaching and extempore prayer. It was a fluid and amorphous movement, and grew fitfully. Outside the counties of south Wales, the early harvest was small. No distinctive Methodist organization was established in north Wales until Thomas Charles settled in Bala in 1784.[15] No one leader achieved the authoritarian hold John Wesley established over Methodism in England.

Some clergy were enthusiastic about Methodism. At Jesus College, Oxford, there were sympathizers with John Wesley's holy club.[16] Harris told Whitefield in 1739: 'There are two or three young curates here [Monmouthshire] who are well-wishers to religion.'[17] Some Glamorgan clergy invited Harris to preach in the 1730s.[18] When he created an organizational framework for his societies Harris chose clergy as the leaders, usually as moderators of the quarterly associations.[19] At the quarterly meeting at Llangeitho in 1783 Thomas Charles noted about twenty clergymen, along with between sixty and eighty exhorters.[20] Identification with Methodism, however, often meant prolonged absence from their parishes.[21]

Despite their adherence to the Established Church Methodists could be highly critical of it and assertive of their own rightness. Harris accused the clergy of indifference, and denounced those who did not respond to him as 'carnal and evildoers'.[22] He credulously believed hair-raising stories about clergy, for example that the incumbent of Haverfordwest had allegedly sired and slaughtered a substantial number of illegitimate children and buried them in the parsonage garden.[23] Lewis Morris from Llanfair ym Muallt in Breconshire alleged in 1747 that he had heard Harris say: 'God had never been before in Llanfair.' Morris regarded Harris's hearers as 'drunk with religion'.[24]

A great strength of early Welsh Methodism was Harris's organizational skills.[25] The societies were a means of holding converts together, keeping alive the first enthusiasm, sustaining it with instruction and maintaining order among the converts. It is unclear whether Harris modelled his societies on Josiah Woodward's *Account of the Rise and Progress of the Religious Societies in the City of London and of their Endeavours for the Reformation of Manners*,[26] but there are close similarities with Harris's practice. In 1737 he petitioned the bishop for permission to establish a society, but receiving no response, he began forming societies in earnest.[27] By mid-1738 six or so societies had been established, by the end of that year Harris claimed there were sixteen societies in Glamorgan, Breconshire, Monmouthshire and Carmarthenshire, and by the end of February 1739 he claimed there were twenty-seven societies. Rowland, lacking Harris's organizational skills, saw himself as a preacher rather than a founder of societies, but Howell Davies founded at least fifty-four societies in Pembrokeshire between 1740 and 1750. Societies were also founded by exhorters of existing societies.

Some of the societies in parts of Cardiganshire and Carmarthenshire met in chapels-of-ease, for example at Ystradffin, Capel Ifan and Capel Llandyfan. In the later 1740s some societies began to acquire 'society houses', for example at Groes-wen near Caerphilly, in Glamorgan, and at Cames in Cil-y-cwm in 1747 and Llansawel, Carmarthenshire, in 1749.[28] By 1750 they had eight houses. They were financed from collections. Acquisiton of a house gave a society a degree of permanency and stability. Although Harris and Rowland did not wish them to be registered as meeting houses, possession of a house could lead to demands by members and exhorters, as at Groes-wen, that Holy Communion be celebrated there.[29]

From time to time a society acquired a dissenting meeting house, as at Llwynpiod, when they took over an Independent meeting house in 1760 after the founder died. At Cynwyl Gaeo in Carmarthenshire some Independents seceded to the Methodists.[30] In north Wales, in Caernarfonshire, on his first visit to Llŷn in 1742 Harris visited the strongholds of dissent and seems to have attracted members to his own societies.[31] Occasional comments by clergy in the 1749 visitation returns also suggest that Methodism had brought some dissenters into the Established Church. During the 1750s, however, there were many more secessions to dissent.

Most early societies met in farmhouses, which may indicate the social position of the local leadership. Membership in general seems to have been drawn from the middling sort, from the social strata from which religious societies in towns had recruited. In rural areas, where societies previously had been uncommon, they recruited farmers and craftsmen; the sort of people who had benefited from the circulating schools. This was the upwardly mobile background of Harris himself. George Whitefield noted in 1739 that the forty or fifty people who came to hear him at Cwmiou from Pontypool were on horseback. Among the 43 exhorters and superintendents up to 1750, of whom the occupations of 23 can be identified, 5 were farmers, 5 schoolmasters, 3 carpenters, 2 blacksmiths, 2 butchers, and 1 farm labourer, weaver, chandler, physician, maltster, bookbinder and clockmaker respectively.[32] Some gentry joined societies: in Caernarfonshire John Williams of Bryntirion, Mrs Robbins of Penrhyn, Penmorfa, Mrs Lowry Wynne of Porthdinllaen and Mrs Sydney Griffith of Cefnamwlch.[33] There were also aristocratic sympathizers. Griffith Jones was part of the network of the Phillipps of Picton Castle. The Countess of Huntingdon took an interest in Harris, and eventually located her training college at Trefeca. She influenced Lady Charlotte Edwin to present clergy sympathetic to the Revival to her husband's seven livings, including Llangan, Coychurch and Coity in the Vale of Glamorgan. The Thomases of Wenvoe presented Methodist clergy to their livings, and Robert Jones of

Fonmon Castle, with whom John Wesley stayed on his occasional visits to south Wales, presented an incumbent of Wesleyan sympathies. Marmaduke Gwynne of Garth, Breconshire, whose daughter married Charles Wesley, was also a Methodist sympathizer.[34]

Women, as William Williams of Pantycelyn noted in his elegies, played an important part in early Methodism.[35] Harris at an early stage was encouraged by women such as Mrs Mary Parry of Llangasty Talyllyn and Mrs Philips of Llanfihangel Talyllyn.[36] A significant number of Harris's correspondents were women. While men occupied the official and administrative roles, women outnumbered men in the membership and were a significant part of sustaining the Revival's information network, notably through contributions to religious magazines, like *The Weekly History*. Women seem to have been more prepared to talk about their inner spiritual experiences and discuss their doubts and anxieties.[37] Although seating at meetings for women and men was rigidly separated, membership of societies gave women an opportunity to contribute to discussions with men. Widows played an important part in offering hospitality to exhorters. Membership took women out of the domestic and work routine, and offered them friendship and support outside the family and traditional community networks, and opportunities for organizing and managing. Naivety among the male leaders could lead to difficulties in relationships. Harris was attracted to a thirty-five-year-old widow, Elizabeth James, but Whitefield proposed first, and though Harris claimed she preferred him, he believed God had chosen her for 'brother Whitefield' and stood back. Five days after the wedding Harris, on the rebound, proposed to Anne Williams, whom he did not marry for two and a half years.[38]

As we have noted, the circulating schools initiated by Griffith Jones created the precondition for the development of the Methodist Revival in Wales. Mary Clement has demonstrated the close identity between places where circulating schools had been set up by 1740 and the location of Methodist societies.[39] Griffith Jones was unhappy about these claims, although in 1737 he had employed Harris as a superintendent of schools. He claimed:

> I little thought that any would have the front enough to say that teaching the Poor to read would make them Dissenters . . . No weapons can be employed properly or successfully against the whims of some who pass under the name Methodists than the Bible and the Welsh Schools.

He also complained of the 'wilfull and very foolish dishonesty of Mr Daniel Rowland in employing Schoolmasters contrary to the written rules', and thought some of the Methodist leaders

> defective in Common Sense, common Manners, and veracity or common honesty: and indulge a very arrogant, proud, railing and slandering Temper, such has been their behaviour towards everybody who in the gentlest Manner have talked with them about their very gross Absurdities which can never pass for Religion with any but the grossly ignorant.[40]

In 1741 Jones dismissed some masters for exhorting. In 1743 twelve Caernarfonshire clergy complained to him that his masters were speaking at night in Methodist meetings and accusing the clergy of not preaching the Gospel.[41]

The leaders of the Revival were young men. Harris, Rowland and Williams were twenty-two, twenty-one and nineteen respectively when they had their conversion experience. Of the forty-three exhorters and superintendents who served up to 1750 whose ages are known, the average age on joining a society was twenty-three.[42] Sermons by emotional young men had a great appeal. Women flocked to hear them. Members too were mostly in their twenties, women usually outnumbering men. The women were mostly unmarried. It is not surprising that the 'flesh was a problem for early Methodists'. There were strict rules to protect members from the temptations thereof. Marriage within societies was encouraged, providing permission from the society was granted. There were frequent expulsions for 'marrying out'.[43]

The exhorters were the 'NCOs' of the movement. 'Private' exhorters preached in two or three societies, and 'public' exhorters preached in a group of societies. Each society had a steward, who was often a private exhorter, who looked after the money and poor members, kept the register and led the singing. Stewards came to have spiritual oversight of societies. From 1744 societies were expected to have catechizers. Private exhorters might be moved from one society to another if they lacked ability to exhort frequently in the same society. Societies varied in size. Llangeitho had 100 members; Ruthin in Glamorgan had 4 members. The average was between 10 and 30. Numbers do not necessarily reflect the local population. The remote village of Llansawel had 51 members in 1751, while the Carmarthen society never had more than 12 before 1750. There were few societies in towns. Some societies grew rapidly, some remained static, some declined rapidly. Disputes, especially over doctrine, could lead to the decline of a society. Often family groups joined, but sometimes individual joiners suffered persecution from their families. Harris planned to divide societies into bands of married men and married women and single men and single women, but most societies were too small for such subdivision.

Membership was by application, supported by testimony from existing members about the applicant's life, disposition and conduct. Evidence of conversion was considered, at the next meeting the candidate was cross-examined, and at the following one required to make a public declaration of intention and commitment. There was then a public cross-examination, and a declaration of assent to the Thirty-nine Articles. After promising to assent to the procedures of the society a candidate was admitted 'on trial' for some months before being accepted into full membership. Many were refused membership.

Societies met once or twice a week, frequency being influenced by geography and working patterns. They seldom met on Sundays or during church service times. Meetings lasted for two or three hours or longer, and occasionally all night. Whatever was the majority language was used. They began with a hymn, the first official hymn book being produced in 1742. Harris arranged for singers to visit societies and teach tunes to members, usually English tunes. Hymns had a catechetical function. There were then extempore prayers for an hour or so, in which up to twelve people might take part, to which members added 'Amen' or 'Alleluia'. From the mid-1740s directions for prayer were sent round. An exhortation followed, or a letter, especially from Harris, might be read. Testimony-giving by each member was a central feature, relating personal spiritual experience, confessing sins, giving praise for sins forgiven. Societies gave members an experience that enabled them to voice deeply held emotions, and to express themselves in imaginative metaphorical styles based on Scripture and frequently reflected in the hymns they sang.[44]

Members were encouraged to read the Bible at home and to learn Griffith Jones's *Catechism*. They were under strict discipline, and subjected to frequent strict spiritual examination. Absence from a meeting and church on Sundays required explanation, otherwise expulsion ensued. Members were disciplined for 'evil thoughts', 'loose words', 'carnal laughter' and especially for causing disputes in the society. They were expected to be honest in their business dealings. They were expelled for drunkenness, dancing, 'sins of the flesh' and marrying 'out', and criticized for going to wakes. There were many expulsions. The effect of such discipline was to form a sober band of people who shared a sense of corporate responsibility and provided strong spiritual, personal and charitable support for one another.

This style and discipline suggests why converts might regard themselves as 'particular' and 'special' and why they developed an exclusivity, using their own style of speech, identifying themselves with the early Church, on a crusade against sin, the world and the devil.[45] It also explains why other people found them difficult, and how membership could divide families.

Superintendents supervised societies over a wide area, and were usually promoted from among the public exhorters. As we have seen, they were men of the middling sort, sometimes quite comfortably off. If they had financial difficulties it may well have been because of the amount of time they gave to the societies rather than to their own affairs. They needed to be good organizers, and away from home a lot.

From 1737 Harris and Rowland had met regularly, thus creating an identifiable 'movement'. In 1740 Whitefield's *Letter . . . to the Religious Societies lately set on foot in England and Wales* was translated into Welsh, and encouraged the idea of forming an 'association' of societies. Harris began to work out a form of governance for the societies, and in October

1740 a meeting was held of all the Revival leaders. Harris's frequent absences in London made it important to have an organization that would work in his absence, and it was agreed that the associations should meet monthly, the first monthly meeting being held in February 1741. This agreed rules to regulate the movement and laid down fundamental principles and a broadly Calvinist theology. The rules were adopted at an association meeting in January 1742, and set the framework for Welsh Methodism for the next generation. From 1743 minutes were kept of these meetings. The association members comprised the clergy, that is, Rowland, William Williams, Howell Davies, David Jenkins, John Powell, curate of Aberystruth, Monmouthshire and later rector of Llanmartin, Thomas Lewis, curate of Merthyr Cynog and vicar of Llanddew, and Harris, and the public exhorters. There was an annual association, a quarterly association and a monthly association. Major decisions were made at the quarterly association. The chief officer was the moderator, Whitefield, when he was present. Monthly associations were held locally, and chaired by clergy or, in their absence, by superintendents. Monthly associations received detailed reports from each private exhorter of a society.

Harris and Whitefield intended one association for England and Wales, which was why Harris wanted Whitefield to be moderator. Other Welsh Methodist leaders were less interested in the wider development of Methodism, and did not attend association meetings outside Wales. The association therefore effectively existed for Wales alone. It was highly autocratic, societies were not consulted, and association meetings did not really debate. The system worked well while the leaders agreed among themselves.

Although Welsh Methodism was predominantly Welsh-speaking, nurtured on the Welsh Bible, and conceived and bred in Wales, most members had little self-conscious awareness of it as a Welsh movement. However, the literature that emerged from it, especially hymns, was a potent force for the future of Welsh religion and culture.

Harris in particular, as we have noted, encouraged awareness of the broader Evangelical Revival, so that members might see themselves as part of an international movement. Through

Griffith Jones, Harris knew of the SPCK's links with Halle and the German Pietists. He established close contacts with, and was strongly influenced by, the Moravians with their strong international network, whom he first encountered in 1739, and who had a base in Pembrokeshire, at Haverfordwest, where their first bishop in Britain, John Gambold, was a schoolmaster in 1743–4. Perhaps the most important contribution Moravians made to Welsh Calvinistic Methodism, as to the Wesleyan Methodist tradition, was encouragement of congregational hymn-singing.[46] Harris was also in touch with James Erskine in Scotland. He distributed various London-based revivalist magazines in Wales, to keep the revival communities in touch with one another. Harris's letters show that he was remarkably well informed about European revivalism, and, as we have seen, about Jonathan Edwards's Revival in North America. As a close associate of Whitefield, Harris spent much time in London and was in close touch with the Wesleys. He had contacts with Isaac Watts and Philip Doddridge, the leading dissenters, and knew of the English Evangelicals – Walker of Truro, Berridge of Everton, Romaine and Haweis – and visited Henry Venn in Huddersfield. Through Whitefield, during its first phase Welsh Methodism was linked with a figure of international importance. They read about him in revivalist magazines like *The Weekly History*, and themselves wrote letters to magazines describing the Revival in Wales.[47] Daniel Rowland, however, had less interest in the wider issues of Revival and was especially hostile towards the Moravians' theology.

Methodism did, however, arouse popular hostility, partly, as we have seen, because people did not know what to make of it. Members of societies were not dissenters, but they behaved like dissenters, and their relationship with the Established Church was ambiguous. Their leaders claimed to be loyal churchmen, but they and the exhorters harshly criticized the clergy and could give an impression of spiritual superiority. This could infuriate people, and aroused a 'laddishness', never far below the surface among eighteenth-century men. When Whitefield preached in the town hall in Cardiff in March 1739 'a great man of the town got a dead fox and set his hounds to hunt him round the hall, and others threw stones on the tiles over our dear brother's head. But all this only animated him and the hearers more.'[48] People suspected them of the Puritanism that had so disrupted life in the Church and society in the previous century, and of establishing conventicles.

The authorities were puzzled how to react to apparent disturbances of Church order and the peace. In January 1740 Harris was arrested by a magistrate in Pontypool, under the Riot Act, for open-air preaching. Pressure was brought to bear on the government by leading London dissenters, and the charge was withdrawn. Harris believed that this was a divine sign to continue itinerating.[49] He was also suspected, against the background of the war against Spain, of being a Spanish spy. Crowds could be violent. In October 1740 William Seward, Whitefield's business manager, when preaching at Cusop near Hay, was struck by a stone from the crowd and died as a result.[50] William Evans was mobbed at Newtown, Montgomeryshire, in February 1744, and was knocked unconscious.[51] Satires in the form of 'interludes' alleged that Methodists were prone to sexual irregularity and broke up families, which were not surprising accusations if young men and women attended all-night meetings which were thought to compete with loyalty to family and community.

There is little evidence that Methodists were persecuted or badly treated by clergy. In Cardiganshire they seem to have been regarded as an organic part of the Church.[52] Clergy seem not to have known quite what to make of them. The incumbent of Caerdeon noted on his visitation return to Bishop Pearce of Bangor in 1749: 'Several Itinerant Methodist Preachers as Weavers, Taylors, and such vulgar Fellows often pour some fulsome Stuff among these people but so far as I know no one of them is a proffesed Methodist.'[53] In north Wales, where Methodist 'teachers' are identified as south Wales men, the few Methodists were mostly identified as churchgoers, as at Holyhead, where the incumbent noted: 'There are about six Methodists in this parish, but their behaviour is much mended of late, and they all attend ye Church constantly.' However, in St David's the diocesan authorities were clearly cautious and kept a record of leading Methodist suspects. A list from the 1740s notes:

Methodists
Daniel Rowland Llangeitho Cardiganshire
Griffith Jones Carmarthenshire
Howell Harris a layman
Howell Davies Curate to Mr Bateman Pembrokeshire
William Williams assistant to Daniel Rowland, ordained deacon by Bishop Claggett
David Thomas An Incourager of Methodists and suffers Preaching in his School

Brecknockshire
Roderick Gwynn of Garth an Encourager of Wm Williams
Griffith Gwyning[54]

Griffith Jones would have been annoyed to know that his name was on such a list.

In spite of the clear organizational structure established in the early 1740s, Harris and Rowland never really got on. They were both self-willed. Harris was severe and humourless. He was controlling, and Whitefield alleged he had a 'desire for power'. He stressed his precedence, felt insecure in the presence of clergy and claimed a divine commission to order the societies. He could be overbearing and dictatorial. Association meetings were disastrous if both Harris and Rowland were present. Harris's preaching was long-winded and emotional, and he did not take care over his use of language. Rowland believed Harris had elevated his own authority above Scripture. He also suspected him of Moravianism because he, consciously or unconsciously, adopted some Moravian language and imagery. In the second half of the 1740s it was suspected that Moravians were trying to subvert Methodist society members, and especially Harris himself.[55]

After 1745, the Revival was thought to be waning, and Harris set out to 'purify' and enforce order on the societies, but he alienated many society members and exhorters. He responded by excluding, as disruptive influences, those who disagreed with him. His lengthy visits to London to supervise Whitefield's Tabernacle and his resulting absences were also much disliked. By mid-1748 Harris was increasingly isolated.

Later that year he met Madam Sydney Griffith of Cefnamwlch, who had been converted, along with her husband, in 1746. Subsequently she visited Trefeca, they met again in north Wales, and she proposed travelling with him, which, he became convinced, was God's will. During their time spent together he felt renewed by her presence, and regarded her as a prophetess. Although he claimed that their relationship was spiritual, Anne Harris was hostile to it, and did not want Madam Griffith at Trefeca.[56] Rowland and Williams never alleged sexual misconduct on Harris's part, but they believed his behaviour was open to misunderstanding, his doctrine anomalous and his treatment of society members harsh. In June 1750 they gave notice of separating from him. It would seem that Harris was suffering a prolonged mental breakdown. He spent much of 1751 travelling round explaining to societies that the separation had been instigated by Rowland. By the end of the year, however, he realized that the exhorters were deserting him, and retired to Trefeca and established a 'family', probably modelled on the Moravian colony at Fulbeck in Yorkshire, over which he envisaged Madam Griffith and himself presiding. When Madam Griffith died in 1752 Harris collapsed and virtually disappeared from the scene of Welsh Methodism until 1763. His enthusiasm, conviction and heroic organizational skills, involving travelling on average 6,000 miles a year, preaching three, four, even five times a day, had largely created Welsh Methodism. His irrational, wilful and domineering behaviour almost destroyed it. However, without Harris's energy and organizing skills there would have been no second Revival in 1762

In Glamorgan after 1750 some societies seceded into Independency, their exhorters were ordained by their fellow members, and society houses were registered as meeting houses. The rest accepted Rowland's leadership.[57] Rowland consolidated his position as leader of the societies in Carmarthenshire and Cardiganshire; he had Whitefield's support and the funds, but lacked the organizational ability to steer the movement forward. However, Harris's organizational structure survived, and responsibility for managing the societies passed to William Williams of Pantycelyn. Brought up in Cefnarthen Independent

Church, he was converted by Harris in 1737, became a communicant in the Established Church and was ordained deacon as curate of Llanwrtyd and Llanddewi Abergwesyn in Breconshire. Accused of absenting himself from his parishes and neglecting the services, in 1743 he was refused ordination as a priest. However, his mother had left him comfortably off with a small but prosperous estate, and he could afford to live independently. From 1743 he supervised the Cardiganshire and Carmarthenshire societies, and undertook regular preaching tours, visiting north Wales in 1742, 1744 and 1748. He had the good sense and good temper that Harris lacked, and ensured that the movement continued and remained within the Established Church.[58]

In 1762 a new Revival began, inspired by Williams's hymns and Rowland's preaching, significantly, at Llangeitho, Rowland's own parish. His preaching had always had a dramatic impact on his hearers. Harris had noted in 1743 that it was 'very common for scores to fall down by the power of the word' when listening to Rowland. It was also reported that people were thrown into agitation, and capered and embraced, shouted, cried and laughed, and that women pulled off each other's caps.[59] The 1762 Revival manifested itself in 'shaking and leaping [and] groaning and loud talking, as well as loud singing, repeating the same line or stanza over and over thirty or forty times . . . [jumping] until they were quite exhausted, so as often to be obliged to fall down on the floor'. Perhaps as a result of the revival, Bishop Squire in 1763 deprived Rowland of his curacy at Llangeitho, when he declined to give an undertaking that he would limit his itinerant preaching. However, his parishioners built a chapel for his use and Llangeitho remained a centre for Methodism. John Wesley was highly critical of the external bodily expressions of the Revival, regarding them as the work of Satan. The Revival lasted two or three years, and was followed by further Revivals, at Cae-bach in 1769, and in parts of Glamorgan and Monmouthshire between 1778 and 1782, and 1785 and 1787.[60]

During the 1750s Williams had devoted more of his time to reading, studying and writing, and was able to interpret the pastoral and spiritual needs of the converts from the new awakening, binding the Revival into scriptural evidence and

Christian tradition, and justifying the claims of extraordinary experience and emotion.[61] In May 1763 Rowland, Williams and other clerical leaders invited Harris to join them again, and he returned to preaching, but not to a dominant role in the movement. He went on preaching tours in Glamorgan in 'his chaise with two horses' with 'God is my peace' painted on the sides. Vast crowds came to hear him preach, but he was still suspected of Moravianism.

As late as the 1770s many clergy in Llandaff diocese did not classify Methodists as dissenters, and sometimes did not mention them at all in the bishop's visitation returns, even in places like Llangan where they were numerous, presumably because they were regarded as loyal Church people.[62] Laity, however, did not necessarily welcome an incumbent with Methodist tendencies. The mayor, churchwardens, council and burgesses of Tenby in 1777 presented the rector, William Edwards, in the consistory court for preaching extempore and for his harsh and unintelligible sermons. In his defence he pointed out that he had introduced a monthly celebration of Holy Communion, and services on Wednesdays and Fridays. The court and bishop, however, were out of sympathy with him, and he was suspended for three years.[63] From the 1770s, although some clergy continued to support the movement, more society houses were built, and pressure increased from exhorters for the sacrament to be celebrated in them.

The strength of Methodism lay in rural communities, where the resources of the Church were thinly stretched, but even in south Wales Methodist exhorters' ministrations only touched a minority of the population. Methodist penetration of north Wales was slow, despite Harris's and Williams's periodic preaching tours, and was regarded with suspicion. In Bangor diocese in 1742 Richard Jenkinson of Llanidloes was presented in the consistory court for preaching in improper places without a licence, and in 1743 several unnamed persons of Llanidloes were presented for keeping unlawful meetings in houses. A similar charge was made against Robert Ellis of Llanberis and in 1747 against persons of Llangian, Mellteyrn and Llanengan.[64] Although there were reported to be five societies on Anglesey in 1748, the numbers of Methodists noted by clergy in visitation returns declined between 1749 and 1776.[65] One of the difficulties was language. The Welsh dialect spoken in south Wales was not easily understood by north Walians. In visitation returns the few references by clergy always note that preachers are south Wales men. There is evidence of exhorters from the south being attacked by mobs at Bala, Dolgellau and Wrexham. In Caernarfonshire although three society houses were built in the 1750s the majority of the population reacted with hostility to Harris and his exhorters. Methodism seems to have taken root in parishes where there had been circulating schools, and where there had been a tradition of dissent, but these were few.[66] A further reason for the lack of success of Methodism in the north may have been the greater number of resident clergy.

Although John Wesley made fifty-three journeys to Wales, eighteen of which were en route to Ireland, his brand of Methodism had little impact on Wales, although he had some success in Breconshire and Radnorshire, where Sally, daughter of Marmaduke Gwynne, whom Howell Harris had converted, married Charles Wesley in 1749. Initially, between 1739 and 1742, his visits were at the invitation of Howell Harris. Language as much as doctrine separated Wesleyan and Welsh Calvinistic Methodism. John Wesley made no attempt to intervene in the division between Howell Harris and Daniel Rowland in the 1750s. Otherwise the few Wesleyan societies in Wales were along the coach road through Carmarthenshire to south Pembrokeshire. In 1758 Wesley established a circuit in Glamorgan, where he had a friend and ally in Robert Jones of Fonmon Castle, with whom he stayed when visiting south Wales. There were at times societies in Cardiff, Llantrisant and Llanwynno. In 1761 he sent a preacher, Thomas Taylor, to south Wales, where he established several societies on the Gower, and in Pembrokeshire, but then withdrew. By the time Wesley visited Glamorgan and Pembrokeshire in 1763 only one society survived. In 1772 Brecon, where there was a Wesleyan society, was listed as head of a circuit, and there was also a society in Hay. Wesley's only significant success was a group in Swansea, who seceded from the Calvinistic Methodist society, and by 1789 had acquired a meeting house.[67] John Wesley never really established any contact with Daniel Rowland and William Williams.

Before 1780 the influence of Methodism on Welsh life was limited. Its greatest influence was on some of the pious middling sort, where it promoted piety and moral values, and encouraged a serious attitude to life, but also a degree of morbidity and self-righteousness. However, the revivalism pioneered by Howell Harris and Daniel Rowland had already, as we have seen, had an impact on the dissenting tradition in Wales, and would determine the direction of much of the religious life of Wales in the ensuing century. After 1762 William Williams of Pantycelyn's prose and poetry largely formed the Welsh Methodist mind and imagination, and gave Welsh culture a new direction. His hymns provided a language for prayer and worship not only for Welsh Calvinistic Methodists but for future Christians of all denominations.

Notes to Part II

3. The Restoration Church

1. *Mercurius Publicus*, 27 (28 June–5 July 1660), 417–18, quoted in I. M. Green, *The Re-establishment of the Church of England 1660–1663* (Oxford, 1978), p. 10.
2. Jenkins, *History of Modern Wales*, p. 129.
3. R. Hutton, *The Restoration: A Political and Religious History of England and Wales 1658–1667* (Oxford, 1985), pp. 99, 126, 147.
4. G. M. Griffiths, 'The restoration in St Asaph: the episcopate of Bishop George Griffiths 1660–1666', *JHSCW*, 13 (1963), 28–9.
5. Jenkins, *History of Modern Wales*, pp. 134–43.
6. Green, *Re-establishment of the Church of England*, pp. 95, 102, 184, 255.
7. Jenkins, *Protestant Dissenters in Wales*, p. 43, and R. Tudur Jones, *Congregationalism in Wales*, ed. Robert Pope (Cardiff, 2004), pp. 52–3.
8. NLW, SA/MB/15 Collations and Institutions 1631–43, 1660–8.
9. Griffiths, 'Restoration in St Asaph', 21–2.
10. Arthur Ivor Pryce, *The Diocese of Bangor during Three Centuries* (Cardiff, 1929), p. xxxiii.
11. John R. Guy, 'The significance of indigenous clergy in the Welsh Church at the Restoration', *SCH*, 18 (1982), 335–43.

[12] Quoted in John Spurr, *The Restoration Church of England 1646–1689* (New Haven and London, 1991), p. 199.
[13] Jenkins, *History of Modern Wales*, p. 141.
[14] Walter T. Morgan, 'The prosecution of Nonconformists in the consistory courts of St David's 1661–1688', *JHSCW*, 12 (1962), 28–54.
[15] A. Tindal Hart, *William Lloyd: Bishop, Politician, Author and Prophet 1627–1717* (London, 1952), pp. 41–8, and Tudur Jones, *Congregationalism in Wales*, p. 65.
[16] Hutton, *The Restoration,* pp. 129, 160.
[17] See David Russell Barnes, *People of Seion: Patterns of Nonconformity in Cardiganshire and Carmarthenshire in the Century before the Religious Census of 1851* (Llandysul, 1995), p. 14.
[18] Morgan, 'Prosecution of Nonconformists', 50.
[19] Glanmor Williams, 'The dissenters in Glamorgan 1660–*c*1760', in *Glamorgan County History IV*, p. 471.
[20] Griffiths, 'Restoration in St Asaph', 30–1.
[21] Hutton, *The Restoration*, p. 231.
[22] David Howell, *The Rural Poor in Eighteenth Century Wales* (Cardiff, 2000), p. 137.
[23] *John Loveday of Caversham 1711–1789: The Life and Times of an Eighteenth Century Onlooker*, ed. Sarah Markham (Wilton, 1984), pp. 62, 122.
[24] J. H. Overton, *The Nonjurors* (London, 1902), pp. 483–7.
[25] Peter D. G. Thomas, 'Jacobitism in Wales', *WHR*, 1 (1962), 279–300, and Craig D. Wood, 'The Welsh response to the Glorious Revolution of 1688', *JWRH*, n.s. 1 (2001), 15–33.
[26] See Jenkins, *Foundations of Modern Wales*, pp. 91, 111, 125; Vivianne Barrie-Curien, *Clergé et pastorale en Angleterre au XVIIIe siècle: le diocèse de Londres* (Paris, 1992), p. 378; and E. D. Evans, 'John Evans, bishop of Bangor 1702–1716', *Transactions of the Honourable Society of Cymmrodorion*, n.s. 7 (2000), 53.
[27] *Correspondence and Minutes of the SPCK relating to Wales 1699–1740*, ed. Mary Clement (Cardiff, 1952), pp. 57, 184, 283.
[28] Jenkins, *Foundations of Modern Wales*, pp. 120–3.
[29] M. G. Jones, *The Charity School Movement* (Cambridge, 1938), pp. 282–4.
[30] Williams, 'Dissenters in Glamorgan', p. 483.
[31] David Ceri Jones, 'Welsh Methodism and the international

Evangelical Revival 1735–1750' (unpublished Ph.D. thesis, University of Wales, Aberystwyth, 2001), 27, 116, 256 ff.

32 For a discussion of the historiography of dissent in Wales see Jenkins, *Protestant Dissenters in Wales*, pp. 3ff.

33 *The Compton Census of 1676*, pp. xxxvii, xli, xliii, lxxix.

34 D. R. L. Jones, 'Fame and Obscurity: Samuel Jones of Brynllywarch', *JWRH*, 1 (1993), 56.

35 E. Calamy, *The Account of the Ministers . . .. Ejected after the Restoration in 1660* (1713), II, p. 718, quoted in R. Tudur Jones, 'The Older Dissent of Swansea and Brecon', in *Links with the Past: Swansea and Brecon Historical Essays*, ed. Owain W. Jones and David Walker (Llandybïe, 1974), p. 119.

36 W. T. Morgan, 'Cases of subtraction of church rate before the consistory court of St David's', *JHSCW*, 9 (1959), 88.

37 John R. Guy, 'Riding against the clock: the visitations of Edward Tenison in Carmarthen and Ossory in the early eighteenth century', in *Contrasts and Comparisons: Studies in Irish and Welsh History*, ed. John R. Guy and W. G. Neely (Llandysul, 1999), pp. 59, 61.

38 Jenkins, *Protestant Dissenters in Wales*, p. 52.

39 *The Compton Census* , pp. 452, 475, 491, 512.

40 Jenkins, *Protestant Dissenters in Wales*, pp. 59–60.

41 Watts, *The Dissenters from the Reformation to the French Revolution*, p. 510.

42 Jones, 'Older dissent of Swansea and Brecon', pp. 122–3, 125.

43 James K. Salter, 'Isaac Maddox and the Dioceses of St Asaph and Worcester 1736–1759' (unpublished M.A. thesis, University of Birmingham, 1962), 35–7.

44 *The Diocese of Llandaff in 1763: The Primary Visitation of Bishop Ewer*, ed John Guy, South Wales Record Society, 3 (1991), 175–6.

45 Jones, *Congregationalism in Wales*, pp. 70–3.

46 Watts, *The Dissenters*, p. 510.

47 NLW, B/QA/2 Bishops Visitation Queries and Answers 1749.

48 Jones, 'Older dissent of Swansea and Brecon', pp. 130–1. The 'Church Book' of the Independent Church at Llangyfelach in Glamorgan dating from about 1700 gives a glimpse of the life of an Independent church.

49 Jones, *Congregationalism in Wales*, pp. 89–92.

50 Ibid., pp. 102–7.

51 Ibid., pp. 111–23.

52 Ibid., pp. 97–9, and Geraint H. Jenkins, *Literature, Religion and Society in Wales 1660–1730* (Cardiff, 1978), p. 216.

[53] Watts, *The Dissenters*, p. 519.

[54] D. Densil James Morgan, 'The development of the Baptist movement in Wales between 1714 and 1815 with particular reference to the Evangelical Revival' (unpublished D.Phil. thesis, University of Oxford, 1986), 93.

[55] Ibid., 2.

[56] Salter, 'Isaac Maddox and the dioceses of St Asaph and Worcester', 39–40.

[57] NLW, SA/MB/19, The State of the Diocese of St Asaph 1749.

[58] NLW, B/QA/2, Bishops' Visitation Queries and Answers 1749.

[59] Emmanuel, 'Dissent in the counties of Glamorgan and Monmouth', *loc. cit.*

[60] Guildhall Library, MS 3083/1, Minutes of the Committee of Dissenting Deputies.

[61] See Christine Trevett, 'William Erbery and his daughter Dorcas: dissenter and resurrected radical', *JWRH*, 4 (1996), 32–3, for examples of services being disturbed by Quakers.

[62] G. F. Nuttall, *The Welsh Saints 1640–1660*, pp. 56–67.

[63] *Correspondence and Records of the S. P. G. Relating to Wales, 1701–1750*, ed. Mary Clement (Cardiff, 1973), pp. 5–7.

[64] Geraint Jenkins, 'Quaker and anti-Quaker literature in Welsh from the Restoration to Methodism', *WHR*, 7 (1974–5), 403–26.

[65] Pryce, *Diocese of Bangor during Three Centuries*, p. 1, and NLW B/QA/2.

[66] Salter, 'Isaac Maddox and the dioceses of St Asaph and Worcester', 39.

[67] Jenkins, *Protestant Dissent in Wales*, pp. 30 ff., and for the development of Baptist churches before 1660 see T. M. Bassett, *The Welsh Baptists* (Swansea, 1997), pp. 14–32, and B. R. White, 'John Miles and the structures of the Calvinistic Baptist mission to south Wales 1649–1660', in *Welsh Baptist Studies*, ed. Mansel John (Llandysul, 1976), pp. 35–70.

[68] White, 'John Miles', pp. 56, 57, 59, 65.

[69] B. G. Owens, 'Rhydwilym Church 1668–1689', in *Welsh Baptist Studies*, pp. 93–104.

[70] Bassett, *Welsh Baptists*, pp. 48–51.

[71] Watts, *The Dissenters*, p. 510.

[72] NLW B/QA/2.

[73] Bassett, *Welsh Baptists*, pp. 92–105

[74] This section owes much to Morgan, 'Development of the Baptist movement', chs 1–5.

[75] *The Compton Census of 1676*, pp. 452, 475, 491, 512.

[76] Philip Jenkins, 'Church, nation and language: the Welsh Church 1660–1800', in *The National Church in Local Perspective: The Church of England and the Regions*, ed. Jeremy Gregory and Jeffrey S. Chamberlain (Woodbridge, 2003), p. 270.
[77] Ed. W. J. Smith (Cardiff, 1968).
[78] Michael R. Lewis, 'The pilgrimage to St Michael's Mount: Catholic continuity in Wales', *JWEH*, 8 (1991), 51–4.
[79] E. T. Davies, 'The Popish Plot in Monmouthshire', *JHSCW*, 25 (1976), 32–43.
[80] Philip Jenkins, 'A Welsh Lancashire: Monmouthshire Catholics in the Eighteenth Century', *Recusant History*, 15 (1979–81), 183.
[81] John Guy, 'The Anglican patronage of Monmouthshire recusants in the seventeenth and eighteenth centuries: some examples', *Recusant History*, 15 (1979–81), 452–4.
[82] T. G. Holt, SJ, 'Jesuits in Montgomeryshire 1670–1785', *JWRH*, 1 (1993), 66–73.
[83] Williams, 'Dissenters in Glamorgan', p. 475.
[84] Philip Jenkins, 'Old and new Catholics: the Carne family of Glamorgan', *Recusant History*, 17 (1984–5), 362–73.
[85] Jenkins, 'A Welsh Lancashire', 181.
[86] John Glyn Parry, 'Stability and change in mid-eighteenth century Caernarfonshire' (unpublished MA thesis, University of Wales, Bangor, 1978), 347.
[87] Dom Aidan Bellenger, 'Seeking a bishop: Roman Catholic episcopacy in Wales from the Reformation to Queen Victoria', *JWRH*, 4 (1996), 53–5.
[88] Daniel G. Mullins, 'Catholicism in Wales in the eighteenth century', *JWEH*, 2 (1985), 1–5.
[89] Jenkins, 'A Welsh Lancashire', 183–4.
[90] Eryn M. White, 'Popular schooling and the Welsh language', in *The Welsh Language before the Industrial Revolution*, ed. Geraint H. Jenkins (Cardiff, 1997), p. 317.

4. Episcopal Administration

[1] Edward Carpenter, *Thomas Sherlock 1678–1761, Bishop of Bangor 1728, of Salisbury 1734, of London 1748* (London, 1936), p. 128, quoting Gooch MSS.
[2] NLW, SA/MB/17.
[3] NLW, SD/BR/4.
[4] NLW, LL/SB/4, 5 and 6.
[5] NLW, B/BR/3 and 4.

[6] See, for example Arthur Warne, *Clergy and Society in Eighteenth Century Devon* (Newton Abbot, 1969), pp. 23–30.
[7] Clement, *Correspondence and Minutes of the SPCK*, pp. 11–12.
[8] Bristol, estimated at £450 a year, Oxford at £500, Rochester at £600 and Gloucester at £900 in 1762, were on a par with or even poorer than the Welsh dioceses.
[9] D. T. Hirschberg, 'Episcopal incomes and expenses 1660–1760', in *Princes and Paupers in the English Church 1500–1800,* ed. Rosemary O'Day and Felicity Heal (Leicester, 1981), p. 213.
[10] Hart, *William Lloyd*, p. 40.
[11] William M. Marshall, *George Hooper 1640–1727, Bishop of Bath and Wells* (Milborne Port, 1976), pp. 90, 97.
[12] Hart, *William Lloyd*, p. 71.
[13] Walter T. Morgan, 'Two cases concerning dilapidations to property in the diocese of St David's', *NLWJ*, 7 (1951–2), pp. 151–4.
[14] William Gibson, 'The finances of the diocese of St David's in the eighteenth century: the reforms of Bishop Charles Moss 1761–1773', *JWEH*, 3 (1986), 50.
[15] Carpenter, *Thomas Sherlock*, p. 128
[16] Edward Carpenter, *Thomas Tenison, Archbishop of Canterbury: His Life and Times* (London, 1948), p. 236.
[17] Gibson, 'Finances of the diocese of St David's', 54–9.
[18] Bickham Swell-Escott, 'William Beaw: a Cavalier bishop', *WHR*, 1 (1963), 405.
[19] *The Diary of Henry Prescott, LL.B., Deputy Registrar of Chester Diocese*, 2, ed. John Addy and Peter McNiven, Record Society of Lancashire and Cheshire, 132 (1994), pp. 461–2.
[20] *John Loveday of Caversham*, p. 128.
[21] Clement, *Correspondence and Minutes of the SPCK*, pp. 11–12.
[22] Leslie W. Barnard, 'Bishop Bull of St David's: scholar and defender of the faith', *JWEH*, 9 (1992), 40.
[23] Norman Sykes, *Church and State in England in the XVIIIth Century* (Cambridge, 1934), p. 64.
[24] Ibid., pp. 357–8, quoting BL. Add MSS 32702, f. 13, 35590, f. 7, 32717, f. 528 and 32926, f. 328.
[25] John Richard Guy, 'An investigation into the pattern and nature of patronage, plurality and non-residence in the old diocese of Llandaff between 1660 and the beginning of the nineteenth century' (unpublished Ph.D. thesis, University of Wales, Lampeter, 1983), 145.
[26] For a discussion of patronage see Stephen Taylor, 'Church and state in England in the mid-eighteenth century: the Newcastle

years 1742–1762' (unpublished Ph.D. thesis, University of Cambridge, 1985).

27 Gilbert Wright, 'Humphrey Humphreys, bishop of Bangor and Hereford 1648–1712', *Anglesey Antiquarian Society and Field Club* (1949), 67.

28 Barnard, 'Bishop Bull', 37 ff.

29 William Gibson, 'A Welsh bishop: John Wynne of St Asaph 1714–1727', *JWEH*, 1 (1984), 29.

30 See Sydney R. Thomas, 'The diocese of St David's in the eighteenth century: the working of the diocese in a period of criticism' (unpublished MA thesis, University of Wales, Swansea, 1983), 62–7, 155–68, and NLW SD/Misc/1279.

31 Hart, *William Lloyd*, p. 64.

32 Spurr, *Restoration Church of England*, p. 180.

33 Hart, *William Lloyd*, pp. 55–9.

34 NLW, SA/MB/57.

35 E. G. Wright, 'Bishop Humphrey Humphreys (1648–1712): a study of the literary and antiquarian movements in Wales in the XVIIth and XVIIIth centuries' (unpublished MA thesis, University of Liverpool, 1948), 19; Clement, *Correspondence and Minutes of the SPCK*, p. 2; and Evans, *Religion and Politics in Mid-eighteenth Century Anglesey*, p. 47.

36 J. V. Davies, 'The diocese of St David's during the first half of the eighteenth century' (unpublished MA thesis, University of Wales, Aberystwyth, 1936), 17–18.

37 Barnard, 'Bishop Bull', 50, and Thomas, 'Diocese of St David's in the eighteenth century', 95–7.

38 John Guy, 'Perpetual curacies in eighteenth century south Wales', *SCH*, 16 (1979), 327.

39 For detailed information about the visitation process, and its practice in the Established Church in the seventeenth and eighteenth centuries see Arthur Burns, *The Diocesan Revival in the Church of England c1800–1870* (Oxford, 1999), pp. 23–7.

40 *Diary of Henry Prescott*, p. 24, and Gibson, 'A Welsh bishop', 29–41.

41 NLW, SA/QA/1.

42 Sykes, *Church and State in England in the XVIIIth Century*, pp. 145–6, quoting BL Add MSS 35590, f. 342.

43 Davies, 'The diocese of St David's', 135.

44 See NLW, SA/RD/1, following, Rural Deans Reports, and NLW SD/Misc/1340 for the deaneries of Melmith, Elvall, Brecon and Hay.

45 NLW, SA/MB/19 and SA/V/1. For an account of Drummond's

administrative and visitorial activities in St Asaph, and subsequently as archbishop of York, see Judith A. Jago, *Aspects of the Georgian Church: Visitation Studies of the Diocese of York 1761–1776* (Cranberry NJ, 1997), pp. 56–86.

[46] Guy, 'Investigation into the pattern and nature of patronage', 142.

[47] For the fitful use of the office of rural dean in English dioceses see Burns, *Diocesan Revival in the Church of England,* pp. 75–8.

[48] Gibson, 'A Welsh bishop', 37.

[49] NLW, Ottley Papers no. 1627.

[50] Clement, *Correspondence and Minutes of the SPCK*, p. 72.

[51] Guy, 'Investigation into the pattern and nature of patronage', 152–243, 797–800.

[52] NLW, B/Misc Vols/1 The Benefices within the Diocese of Bangor . . . 1778.

[53] Jeremy Gregory, *Restoration, Reformation and Reform 1660–1832: Archbishops of Canterbury and their Diocese* (Oxford, 2000), p. 37.

[54] Davies, 'The diocese of St David's', 52.

[55] Ibid., 1 ff., 39.

[56] Gibson, 'A Welsh bishop', 34.

[57] Philip Jenkins, 'Church patronage and clerical politics in eighteenth century Glamorgan', *Morgannwg*, 28 (1984), 32–47.

[58] Guy, 'An investigation into the pattern and nature of patronage', 797–800.

[59] Davies, 'The diocese of St David's', 52.

[60] For a detailed account of both cases see Carpenter, *Thomas Tenison*, pp. 205–47, and for the case against Jones, Owain W. Jones, 'The case against Bishop Jones of St Asaph', *JHSCW*, 14 (1964), 58–65.

[61] Pryce, *Diocese of Bangor*, p. xxxviii.

[62] Erasmus Saunders, *A View of the State of Religion in the Diocese of St David's about the Beginning of the Eighteenth Century, 1721* (Cardiff, 1949), p. 38.

[63] Wright, 'Humphrey Humphreys', 61–76 and Evans, 'John Evans', 51.

[64] D. R. Thomas, *A History of the Diocese of St Asaph* (London, 1874), p. 111.

[65] Hart, *William Lloyd*, p. 85 and Swell-Escott, 'William Beauw', 408.

[66] Jenkins, *Literature, Religion and Society*, p. 8 quoting LPL MS 930 f. 33.

[67] Carpenter, *Thomas Tenison*, p. 247.
[68] Marshall, *George Hooper*, p. 90.
[69] Jenkins, *Literature, Religion and Society*, p. 9.
[70] Clement, *Correspondence of the SPCK*, p. 5, and *Correspondence and Records of SPG*, p. 20.
[71] Eryn M. White, 'The Established Church, dissent and the Welsh language *c*.1660–1811', in *The Welsh Language before the Industrial Revolution*, ed. Geraint H. Jenkins (Cardiff, 1997), p. 244.
[72] Clement, *Correspondence and Minutes of the SPCK*, pp. 256, 278.
[73] NLW, Ottley Correspondence Letter 1551.
[74] Clement, *Correspondence and Minutes of the SPCK*, pp. 42, 158, 291.
[75] White, 'The Established Church, dissent and the Welsh language', 238.
[76] Davies, 'The Diocese of St David's', 47.
[77] White, 'The Established Church, dissent and the Welsh language', 238–9.
[78] Geraint H. Jenkins, '"Horrid unintelligible jargon": the case of Dr Thomas Bowles', *WHR*, 15 (1991), 509–11.
[79] Clement, *Correspondence and Records of the SPG*, p. 13.
[80] Clement, *Correspondence and Minutes of the SPCK*, pp. 104, 165, and *Correspondence and Records of SPG*, pp. 5–15. For a list of Welsh clergy working in the colonies 1675–1740 see Mary Clement, *The SPCK and Wales 1699–1740* (London, 1954), pp. 178–90.
[81] Until either diocesan reorganization in the 1840s or disestablishment in 1920 a number of parishes in the dioceses of St David's and St Asaph were in England, including Oswestry, which like Shrewsbury was a centre for the borders. Some Welsh parishes were, and remain, in the English dioceses of Hereford or Lichfield.
[82] Walter J. Morgan, 'The consistory courts in the diocese of St David's 1660–1858', 1, *JHSCW*, 7 (1957), 7.
[83] Davies, 'The diocese of St David's', 140.
[84] *Diary of Henry Prescott*, p. 358.
[85] Ibid., pp. 440–1. The cause papers are lost, so no details of the case are known.
[86] Ibid., p. 592.
[87] J. Gwynfor Jones, 'The Welsh language in local government: J.P.s and the Courts of Quarter Sessions 1536–1800', in *The Welsh Language before the Industrial Revolution*, pp. 199–204,

suggests that this was the case in cases before Quarter Sessions and Petty Sessions.

88 For a discussion of the role of the courts see W. M. Jacob, 'In love and charity with your neighbours . . .: ecclesiastical courts and Justices of the Peace in England in the eighteenth Ccentury', *SCH*, 40 (2004), 203–17.

89 NLW, SA/CB/15, 19 Consistory Court Act Books 1686–88 and 1758–62.

90 W. M. Jacob, *Lay People and Religion in the Early Eighteenth Century* (Cambridge, 1996), pp. 135–54.

91 NLW, Schedule of Church in Wales Records Diocese of St David's, vol. 5.

92 NLW, Schedule of Church in Wales Records Diocese of St David's, vol. 7.

93 NLW, Schedule of Church in Wales Records Diocese of Llandaff, vol. 5.

94 NLW, Schedule of Church in Wales Records Diocese of Bangor, vol. 4.

5. The Welsh Clergy

1 Jenkins, 'Church, nation and language', 268.

2 *Correspondence and Minutes of the SPCK,* p. 249.

3 Saunders, *A View of the State of Religion in the Diocese of St David's*, pp. 27, 29.

4 John Macky, *A Journey through England in Familiar Letters from a Friend to a Friend Abroad*, 2 vols (1722), II, pp. 145–6, quoted in M. F. Snape, 'Poverty and the northern clergy in the eighteenth century', *Northern History*, 36 (2000), 83.

5 Sykes, *Church and State in the XVIIIth Century*, p. 274, quoting Bishop Drummond to the Duke of Newcastle, 27 July 1753, BL Add MSS 32732, f. 371.

6 Carpenter, *Thomas Sherlock*, p. 130, quoting *Gentleman's Magazine* (1790), 293.

7 Jenkins, 'Church, nation and language', 268

8 Guy, 'An investigation into the pattern and nature of patronage', 709.

9 Evans, *Religion and Politics in Mid-eighteenth Century Anglesey*, p. 88.

10 Quoted in Thomas, 'Diocese of St David's in the eighteenth century', 249.

11 Guy, 'Perpetual curacies in eighteenth century south Wales', 327.

12 NLW, SA/MB/57 *Notitia* of Bishop Fleetwood 1708–1715.
13 NLW, B/Misc Vols/5 Value of Dignities and Livings 1756.
14 NLW, B/Misc Vols/1 The Benefices within the Diocese of Bangor together with the Names of the Several Incumbents and Patrons to which is added the present Improved Value of the Several Livings . . . by Richard Burn, Secretary 1778.
15 Davies, 'Diocese of St David's during the first half of the eighteenth century', 78
16 Thomas, 'Diocese of St David's in the eighteenth century', 242.
17 See Guy, 'An investigation', 672.
18 For perpetual curacies in the diocese of Llandaff see Guy, 'Perpetual curacies in eighteenth century south Wales', 330.
19 NLW, B/QA/2 Bishops Visitation Queries and Answers 1749.
20 *Speculum Dioceseos Lincolniensis 1705–1723*, ed. R. E. G. Cole, Lincoln Record Society, 4 (1912), and *Episcopal Visitations in Bedfordshire 1706–1720*, ed. Patricia Bell, Bedfordshire Historical Record Society, 81 (2002).
21 Philip Rycroft, 'Church, chapel and community in Craven 1764–1851' (unpublished D.Phil. thesis, University of Oxford, 1988), 54.
22 Eric J. Evans, 'The Anglican clergy of northern England', in *Britain in the First Age of Party 1680–1750: Essays presented to Geoffrey Holmes*, ed. Clyve Jones (London, 1987), pp. 225–7.
23 *Chichester Diocesan Surveys 1686–1724*, ed. Wyn K. Ford, Sussex Record Society, 78 (1994).
24 For an account of tithe see Jacob, *Lay People and Religion in the Early Eighteenth Century*, pp. 36–9.
25 Evans, *Religion and Politics in Mid-eighteenth Century Anglesey*, p. 168.
26 *A Report of the Deanery of Penllyn and Edeirnion by the Revd John Wynne, 1730*, ed. G. M. Griffiths, Merioneth Miscellany 1, Merioneth Historical and Record Society (1955), pp. 13, 26, 29.
27 Eryn M. White, '"A poor benighted Church"? Church and society in mid-eighteenth century Wales', in *From Medieval to Modern Wales: Historical Essays in Honour of Kenneth O. Morgan and Ralph A. Griffiths*, ed. R. R. Davies and Geraint H. Jenkins (Cardiff, 2004), p. 139.
28 Evans, *Religion and Politics in Mid-eighteenth Century Anglesey*, p. 81.
29 NLW, Schedule of Church in Wales Records Diocese of St David's Vol. 5, SD/CCB(G) Consistory Court Papers General Archdeaconry of Brecon.

[30] NLW, Schedule of Church in Wales Records Diocese of St David's Vol. 10, SD/CCC(G) Consistory Court Papers General Archdeaconry of Carmarthen.

[31] NLW, Schedule of Church in Wales Records Diocese of Llandaff Vol. 5, LL/CCC(G) Consistory Court Papers General of the Diocese of Llandaff.

[32] NLW, Schedule of Church in Wales Records Diocese of Bangor Vol, 4, B/CC/G Consistory Court Papers General of the Diocese of Bangor.

[33] Quoted in Guy, 'An investigation', 436.

[34] For an account of Queen Anne's Bounty see Ian Green, 'The first five years of Queen Anne's Bounty', in *Princes and Paupers in the English Church 1500–1800*, ed. Rosemary O'Day and Felicity Heal (Leicester, 1981).

[35] W. M. Jacob, 'Church and society in Norfolk 1700–1800', in *The National Church in Local Perspective*, p. 191.

[36] In Norfolk, 47 people (28 laymen and 19 clergy) gave benefactions of £200. See Jacob, 'Church and society in Norfolk', 184.

[37] See Christopher Hodgson, *An Account of the Augmentation of Small Livings by the Governors of Queen Anne's Bounty*, (1826).

[38] For a detailed discussion of the impact of Queen Anne's Bounty on the diocese of St David's see Davies, 'The diocese of St David's', 78–98.

[39] Guy, 'Perpetual curacies in eighteenth century south Wales', 328.

[40] Parry, 'Stability and change in mid-eighteenth century Caernarfonshire', 138, 303.

[41] Jenkins, *Literature, Religion and Society in Wales 1660–1730*, p. 5.

[42] Evans, *Religion and Politics in Mid-eighteenth Century Anglesey*, pp. 88–9.

[43] *The Diocese of Llandaff in 1763*, pp. 185–8.

[44] NLW, SA/MB/19 The State of the Diocese of St Asaph 1749.

[45] *The Diocese of Llandaff in 1763*.

[46] Parry, 'Stability and change in mid-eighteenth century Caernarfonshire', 303.

[47] For a similar pattern of incumbents in Norfolk serving neighbouring parishes for non-resident incumbents, who were usually serving a curacy elsewhere, see Jacob, 'Church and society in Norfolk', 193–4.

[48] Parry, 'Stability and change in mid-eighteenth century Caernarfonshire', 313.
[49] NLW, SA/FB Faculty Book 1713–1769.
[50] Thomas, 'Diocese of St David's in the eighteenth century', pp. 223–4.
[51] Guy, 'An investigation', 770, 803.
[52] Saunders, *A View of the State of Religion in the Diocese of St David's*, p. 23.
[53] Guy, 'An investigation', 772.
[54] E. D. Jones, 'Some aspects of the history of the Church in north Cardiganshire in the eighteenth century', *JHSCW* (1953), pp. 102–3.
[55] NLW, SA/QA/1 Bishop's Visitation Queries and Answers 1733.
[56] NLW, B/QA/2 Bishop's Visitation Queries and Answers 1749.
[57] Davies, 'The diocese of St David's', 63.
[58] E. T. Davies, 'The Church of England and schools 1662–1774', *Glamorgan County History*, IV (1974), p. 447.
[59] *The Diocese of Llandaff in 1763*, p. 181, and Guy, 'An investigation', 275.
[60] Pryce, *The Diocese of Bangor during Three Centuries*, p. lxxv.
[61] Guy, 'An investigation', 172
[62] Davies, 'Diocese of St David's', 58, 127.
[63] Ibid., 58–9.
[64] Jones, 'Some aspects of the history of the Church in north Cardiganshire', 104.
[65] *The Diocese of Llandaff in 1763*; Guy, 'An investigation', 711.
[66] Pryce, *The Diocese of Bangor during Three Centuries*, p. lxii.
[67] *Diocese of Llandaff in 1763*.
[68] Ibid., p. 185.
[69] Ibid., pp. 183–4.
[70] Guy 'An investigation', 756.
[71] Clement, *Correspondence and Minutes of the SPCK*, p. 158.
[72] John Guy, 'The Revd John Carne of Nash', *JHSCW*, 23 (1973), 56–70.
[73] Davies, 'Diocese of St David's', 59; Guy, 'An investigation', 803.
[74] Barrie-Curien, *Clergé et pastorale en Angleterre*, p. 378.
[75] *Parson and Parish in Eighteenth-Century Hampshire: Replies to Bishop's Visitations*, ed. W. R. Ward, Hampshire Record Series, 13 (1995), p. xxvii.
[76] Guy, 'An investigation', 658
[77] Davies, 'Diocese of St David's', 55.
[78] Guy, 'An investigation', 536.

[79] R. W. D. Fenn, 'Thomas Davies, rector of Coity 1769–1819', *JHSCW*, 13 (1963), 42.
[80] NLW, SA/MB/18 Register of Institutions 1726.
[81] Glyn Tegai Hughes, *Williams Pantycelyn* (Cardiff, 1983), p. 3.
[82] Fenn, 'Thomas Davies, rector of Coity', 42–4.
[83] Davies, 'The Church of England and schools 1667–1774', 440.
[84] Jenkins, *Literature, Religion and Society*, p. 213.
[85] Pryce, *The Diocese of Bangor during Three Centuries*, p. xxxviii.
[86] G. V. Bennett, 'University, Church and society 1688–1714', in *The History of the University of Oxford, Vol. V: The Eighteenth Century*, ed. L. S. Sutherland and L. G. Mitchell (Oxford, 1986), pp. 381, 384.
[87] Davies, 'The Church of England and schools 1667–1774', 440.
[88] Michael Snape, *The Church in an Industrialising Society* (Woodbridge, 2003), p. 169.
[89] Henry Owen, *Directions for Young Students in Divinity*, 2nd edn (1773).
[90] Thomas, 'The diocese of St David's in the eighteenth century', pp. 155–68.
[91] 'The principal parts and branches of the pastoral office with rules and directions for the due performance of each of them; in a charge to the clergy of the diocese of St David's', in *The Clergyman's Instructor: or A Collection of Tracts on the Ministerial Duties*, 5th edn (Oxford, 1843), pp. 300–1.
[92] Jenkins, *Literature, Religion and Society*, pp. 279–81.
[93] White, 'The Established Church, dissent and the Welsh language', 248.
[94] Philip Jenkins, 'The Anglican Church and the unity of Britain 1560–1714', in *Conquest and Union: Fashioning a British State 1485–1725*, ed. Steven G. Ellis and Sarah Barber (London, 1995), p. 127.
[95] Wright, 'Bishop Humphrey Humphreys', 86–112.
[96] Geraint H. Jenkins, 'Historical writing in the eighteenth century', in *A Guide to Welsh Literature c1700–1800*, ed. Branwen Jarvis (Cardiff, 2000), pp. 27–32.
[97] Pryce, *Diocese of Bangor,* p. lxvi.
[98] *A Report of the Deanery of Penllyn and Edeirnion.*
[99] E. Wyn James, '"The new birth of a people": Welsh language and identity and the Welsh Methodists c1740–1820', in *Religion and National Identity: Wales and Scotland c1700–1800*, ed. Robert Pope (Cardiff, 2001), p. 23.
[100] Ffion Llywelyn Jenkins, 'Celticism and pre-Romanticism: Evan

Evans', in *A Guide to Welsh Literature*, ed. Branwen Jarvis (Cardiff, 2000), p. 17.

101 White, 'Established Church, dissent and the Welsh language', p. 248.

102 'A companion for the candidates for holy orders; or the great importance and principal duties of the priestly office by the Rt Revd Father in God, George Bull, D.D., late lord bishop of St David's', in *The Clergyman's Instructor*, p. 290.

103 Wright, 'Humphrey Humphreys', p. 65.

104 Clement, *Correspondence and Minutes of the SPCK*, pp. 2–5, 7–9, 29.

105 W. T. Havard, 'Educational and religious movements in the diocese of St Asaph in the eighteenth century', *NLWJ*, 4 (1945–6), pp. 36–7.

106 Guy, 'Riding against the clock', 62.

107 Saunders, *A View of the State of Religion in the Diocese of St David's*, pp. 25–6.

108 *The Clergyman's Instructor*, pp. 279, 295–6.

109 Susan C. Passmore, 'The Rev William Wynne of Lasynys: an eighteenth century Merioneth cleric', *Journal of the Merioneth Historical and Record Society*, 12 (1994–7), 256.

110 Evans, *Religion and Politics in Mid-eighteenth Century Anglesey*, pp. 72–7.

111 *A Report of the Deanery of Penllyn and Edeirnion*, p. 9.

112 See Ian Green, *The Christian's ABC: Catechisms and Catechising in England c1530–1740* (Oxford, 1996), pp. 132, 264.

113 Jenkins, *Literature, Religion and Society*, p. 81.

114 Pryce, *Diocese of Bangor*, p. xlv.

115 Glanmor Williams, 'Griffith Jones Llanddowror (1683–1761)', in *Pioneers of Welsh Education* (Swansea, 1964), p. 15.

116 Clement, *Correspondence and Minutes of the SPCK*, p. 4.

117 M. G. Jones, 'Two accounts of the Welsh Trust 1675 and 1678', *Bulletin of the Board of Celtic Studies*, 9 (1939), pp. 71–80.

118 For a much fuller account of devotional and religious prose and verse see Jenkins, *Literature, Religion and Society*, pp. 113–61.

119 Clement, *The SPCK and Wales 1699–1740*, p. xiv

120 Evans, 'John Evans, Bishop of Bangor 1702–1716', p. 49.

121 Clement, *The SPCK and Wales*, p. 76.

122 Clement, *The SPCK and Wales*, p. 25; *Correspondence and Minutes of the SPCK*, p. 163.

123 Saunders *A View of the State of Religion in the Diocese of St David's*, p. 3.

[124] See W. R. Ward, *The Protestant Evangelical Awakening* (Cambridge, 1992), p. 308.
[125] Clement, *Correspondence and Minutes of the SPCK*, pp. 222, 234.
[126] White, 'Popular schooling and the Welsh language', p. 324; W. K. Lowther Clarke, *A History of the SPCK* (London, 1959), p. 104.
[127] Jenkins, *Literature, Religion and Society in Wales*, p. 37; Ward, *The Protestant Evangelical Awakening*, p. 319.
[128] See Clement, *History of the SPCK in Wales*, pp. 26 ff. and for a list of books translated into Welsh and distributed by the SPCK, p. 166.
[129] Clarke, *A History of the SPCK*, pp. 103–4.
[130] Mary Clement, 'A calendar of Welsh letters to the SPCK 1745–1783', *NLWJ*, 10 (1957), 1–7.
[131] *Additional Letters of the Morrises of Anglesey 1735–1786*, ed. and trans. Hugh Owen (1947), p. 247.
[132] Jenkins, *Literature, Religion and Society in Wales 1660–1730*, p.108; Clement, *Correspondence and Minutes of the SPCK*, p. 8.
[133] Wright, 'Humphrey Humphreys', 64.
[134] For an account of societies for the reformation of manners in England see Jacob, *Lay People and Religion in the Early Eighteenth Century*, pp. 125–35.
[135] See Ibid., pp. 77–92; F. W. B. Bullock, *Voluntary Religious Societies 1520–1799* (St Leonard's–on-Sea, 1963), pp. 128–203.
[136] First published in 1699 and in its fifth edition in 1724.
[137] Jenkins, 'Church, nation and language', p. 281.
[138] See Jacob, ' "... In love and charity with your neighbours" 205–17.
[139] Sykes, *Church and State in England in the XVIIIth Century*, p. 274, quoting BL Add MSS 32732, f. 371.
[140] For example by Howell Harris, about the incumbent of Haverfordwest, see p. 169.
[141] NLW, SD/CPD/23 Archdeaconry of Carmarthen Churchwardens' Presentments.
[142] NLW, Schedule of Church in Wales Records Diocese of St David's Vols 5 and 7.
[143] NLW, Schedule of Church in Wales Records, Diocese of Llandaff Vol. 5.
[144] John Guy, 'Riding against the clock', 62–4.
[145] *A Report of the Deanery of Penllyn and Edeirnion*, p. 25.
[146] Guy, 'An Investigation', 784

[147] Howell, *The Rural Poor in Eighteenth Century Wales*, p. 151.
[148] W. M. Jacob, 'Supervising the pastors: supervision and discipline of the clergy in Norfolk in the eighteenth century', *The Pastor Bonus, Dutch Review of Church History*, 83 (2003), 296–308.

6. The State of the Parishes

[1] Saunders, *View of the State of Religion*, pp. 32–3.
[2] Jenkins, *Literature, Religion and Society in Wales*, p. 298.
[3] Quoted in Clement, *The SPCK and Wales 1699–1740*, p. 55.
[4] *Correspondence and Minutes of the SPCK*, p. 250.
[5] Saunders, *View of the State of Religion*, pp. 19–20.
[6] *John Loveday of Caversham*, p. 56.
[7] Quoted in White, 'The Established Church, dissent and the Welsh language', 239, 241
[8] Evans, *Religion and Politics in Mid-eighteenth Century Wales*, p. 100.
[9] Quoted in Jenkins, *Protestant Dissenters in Wales*, p. 2.
[10] Luke Tyerman, *The Life of John Wesley* (London, 1870), I, p. 220.
[11] Evans, *Religion and Politics in Mid-eighteenth Century Anglesey*, p. 85.
[12] NLW, SD/CPD/25 and SD/CPD/30, Archdeaconry of Carmarthen Churchwardens' Presentments
[13] NLW, SA/CB/15 Consistory Court Act Book 1686–8.
[14] Jones, 'Some aspects of the history of the Church in north Cardiganshire', 104.
[15] *Report of the Deanery of Penllyn and Edeirnion, passim.*
[16] 'The diary of William Bulkeley of Brynddu, Anglesey', *Anglesey Antiquarian Society and Field Club Transactions* (1931), 86.
[17] Davies, 'The diocese of St David's during the first half of the eighteenth century', 108–11, 116.
[18] *John Loveday of Caversham*, p. 45.
[19] Evans, *Religion and Politics in Mid-eighteenth Century Anglesey*, pp. 9–16.
[20] Guy, 'An investigation', 375–6.
[21] NLW, SA/FB, Faculty Book 1713–69.
[22] Wyn Evans, 'St David's Cathedral: the forgotten centuries', *JWEH*, 3 (1986), 83–6.
[23] Griffiths, 'Restoration in St Asaph', 17; Gibson, 'A Welsh bishop for a Welsh diocese', 36.
[24] Donald Buttress, 'Llandaff Cathedral in the eighteenth and nineteenth centuries', *JHSCW*, 16 (1966), 61.

[25] E. Gilbert Wright, 'Dean John Jones 1650–1727', *Anglesey Antiquarian Society and Field Club Transactions* (1952), 41.
[26] *The Clergyman's Instructor*, p. 294.
[27] Evans, *Religion and Politics in Mid-eighteenth Century Anglesey*, pp. 21–2.
[28] *The Clergyman's Instructor*, p. 297.
[29] Parry, 'Stability and change in mid-eighteenth century Caernarfonshire', 316.
[30] *Diocese of Llandaff in 1763*, p. 193.
[31] Ibid., pp. 195–6.
[32] Evans, *Religion and Politics in Mid-eighteenth Century Anglesey*, pp. 17–18.
[33] Parry, 'Stability and change in mid-eighteenth century Caernarfonshire', 316.
[34] Evans, *Religion and Politics in Mid-eighteenth Century Anglesey*, p. 69.
[35] *Report of the Deanery of Penllyn and Edeirnion*, pp. 31 and 40.
[36] *The Clergyman's Instructor*, pp. 298–9.
[37] 'The diary of William Bulkeley of Brynddu', 56, 69, 77.
[38] Parry, 'Stability and change in mid-eighteenth century Caernarfonshire', 316.
[39] Saunders, *A View of the State of Religion*, pp. 23–4.
[40] Howell, *The Rural Poor in Eighteenth Century Wales*, p. 150.
[41] Clement, *Correspondence and Minutes of the SPCK*, p. 77.
[42] *John Loveday of Caversham*, p. 43.
[43] White, 'A poor benighted Church?', 131.
[44] NLW, SA/MB/19 The State of the Diocese of St Asaph 1749 compiled by Robert Drummond, Bishop 1748–61.
[45] NLW, SA/RD/26 Rural Dean's Inspections 1749.
[46] Evans, *Religion and Politics in Mid-eighteenth Century Anglesey*, pp. 28–39, and 'The diary of William Bulkeley of Brynddu', 29, 43.
[47] *Morris Letters*, I, p. 296
[48] Richard Suggett, 'Festivals and social structure in early modern Wales', *Past & Present*, 152 (1996), 79–112.
[49] Ibid., 92, 98.
[50] *The British Magazine*, 5 (1835), reprinted in *Religion and Society in England and Wales 1689–1800*, ed. William Gibson (Leicester, 1998), pp. 141–2, and Evans, *Religion and Politics in Mid-eighteenth Century Anglesey*, p. 52.
[51] Geraint H. Jenkins, 'Popular beliefs in Wales from the Restoration to Methodism', *Bulletin of the Board of Celtic Studies*, 27 (1976–8), 446.

[52] Howell, *The Rural Poor in Eighteenth Century Wales*, p. 154.
[53] Saunders, *A View of the Present State of Religion*, p. 33.
[54] Jenkins, *Literature, Religion and Society 1660–1730*, pp. 154–61.
[55] Rhiannon Ifans, 'Folk poetry and diversions', in *A Guide to Welsh Literature c1700–1800*, pp. 187–90.
[56] Clement, *Correspondence and Minutes of the SPCK*, p. 96.
[57] Ibid., p. 285.
[58] For which see Jacob, *Lay People and Religion in the Early Eighteenth Century*, pp. 218–21, and Nicholas Temperley, *The Music of the English Parish Church, I* (Cambridge, 1978), chs 5 and 6.
[59] NLW, SA/QA/1 Bishop's Visitation Queries and Answers 1733.
[60] E. Gwynn Jones, 'Correspondence of the Owens of Penrhos 1712–1742', *Anglesey Antiquarian Society and Field Club* (1954), 67.
[61] NLW, SA/FB, Faculty Book 1713–69.
[62] Parry, 'Stability and change in mid-eighteenth century Caernarfonshire', 315–16.
[63] Evans, *Religion and Politics in Mid-eighteenth Century Anglesey*, p. 24.
[64] W. G. Hughes-Edwards, 'The development and organisation of the Methodist societies in Wales 1735–1750' (unpublished MA thesis, University of Wales, Bangor, 1966), 72–3.
[65] Jenkins, *Literature, Religion and Society 1660–1730*, p. 149.
[66] Kathryn Jenkins, 'Williams Pantycelyn', in *A Guide to Welsh Literature c1700–1800*, p. 273, and Hughes, *Williams Pantycelyn*, pp. 77–116.
[67] Brynley F. Roberts, 'The literature of the "Great Awakening"', in *A Guide to Welsh Literature c1700–1800*, p. 282.
[68] For an account of the movement for the provision of parochial libraries in England and Wales see W. M. Jacob, 'Parochial libraries 1680–1760', in *The Cambridge History of Libraries in Britain, II* (Cambridge, 2006).
[69] Clement, *Correspondence and Minutes of the SPCK*, pp. 14–18, 38–9, 257 ff.
[70] Ewart Lewis, 'The Cowbridge diocesan library 1711–1848', *JHSCW*, 4 (1954), 38–41, and 7 (1957), 80–2. There were similar rules for the Bangor library. See Clarke, *A History of the SPCK*, p. 80. For the catalogue of the St Asaph Library as augmented by various benefactors, see NLW SA/MB/10.
[71] For details of the parishes to which libraries were dispatched by Bray and the SPCK, see *Directory of the Parochial Libraries of*

the Church of England and the Church in Wales, revised edn, ed. Michael Perkins (London, 2004), pp. 410–37.

[72] Clement, *Correspondence and Minutes of SPCK*, p. 157.

[73] Havard, 'Educational and religious movements in the diocese of St Asaph', 44.

[74] Jenkins, *Protestant Dissenters in Wales*, p. 19.

[75] Jones, 'Two accounts of the Welsh Trust 1675 and 1678', 71–80, and Jones, *The Charity School Movement*, pp. 281–8.

[76] White, 'Popular schooling and the Welsh language', 320

[77] Arthur Bedford, rector of the Temple Church in Bristol, to John Chamberlayne, secretary of the SPCK, 8 January 1701, in Clement, *Correspondence and Minutes of the SPCK*, p. 10.

[78] For a brief account of the SPCK's role in relation to charity schools in England see Jacob, *Lay People and Religion in the Early Eighteenth Century*, pp. 162–72.

[79] Ward, *The Protestant Evangelical Awakening*, p. 320; Jones, *The Charity School Movement*, p. 302; Clements, *Correspondence and Minutes of the SPCK*, p. 184; and Geraint Jenkins, 'An old and much honoured soldier', *WHR*, 11 (1982–3), 461.

[80] Clement, *SPCK and Wales*, Appendices 2A and B.

[81] Clement, *SPCK and Wales*, pp. 11–13, 58, and for a list of women benefactors of schools see pp. 160–1; Jones, *Charity School Movement*, pp. 290 ff.; and Havard, 'Educational and religious movements in the diocese of St Asaph', 37–9.

[82] Wright, 'Dean Jones 1650–1727', 40–1.

[83] Clement, *SPCK and Wales*, pp. 4, 9.

[84] Clarke, *A History of the SPCK*, p. 57.

[85] NLW, SA/MB/18.

[86] Clement, *SPCK and Wales*, p. 10.

[87] Clement, *Correspondence and Minutes of the SPCK*, p. 34.

[88] Ibid., pp. 2, 23, 82.

[89] Clarke, *History of the SPCK*, p. 57.

[90] Havard, 'Educational and religious movements in St Asaph', 39

[91] G. M. Griffiths, 'Education in the diocese of St Asaph 1729–30', *NLWJ*, 6 (1949–50), 394–5.

[92] Havard, 'Educational and religious movements in St Asaph', 37.

[93] Clement, *SPCK and Wales*, p. 160. For a complete list of charity schools founded in Wales 1699–1740, including dates, patrons and schoolmasters and their salaries, see ibid., pp. 102–55.

[94] Ibid., p. 159.

[95] See Jacob, *Lay People and Religion*, p. 171, and above p. 70.

[96] Clement, *SPCK and Wales*, p. 19.

1. Rûg Chapel, Merioneth, built in 1637

2. Caebach Chapel, Llandrindod Wells, Radnorshire, built in 1715

3. Capel Newydd, Nanhoron, Caernarfonshire, built in 1769

4. Ynyscynhaearn Church, Caernarfonshire, rebuilt in 1830–2

5. Llanddoged Church, Denbighshire, rebuilt in 1838–9

10. Llandyfrydog Church, Anglesey, restored in 1862

11. Llandysilio Church, Montgomeryshire, rebuilt in 1867–8

12. Llandaff Cathedral in 1898

97 The best sources of information about the circulating schools are Clement, *SPCK and Wales*, pp. 21–5; Jones, *The Charity School Movement*, pp. 297–313; Glanmor Williams, 'Griffith Jones Llanddowror (1683–1761)', in *Pioneers of Welsh Education*; and Jenkins, 'An old and much honoured soldier'.

98 Clement, *Correspondence and Minutes of the SPCK*, pp. 163, 175.

99 [Griffith Jones], *Welch Piety: or A Further Account of the Circulating Welch Charity Schools from Michaelmas 1747 to Michaelmas 1748 In a Letter to a Friend* (1749), pp. 6, 10, 11.

100 [Griffith Jones], *Welch Piety: or A Further Account of the Circulating Welch Charity Schools from Michaelmas 1757 to Michaelmas 1758, to which are annexed Testimonials Relating to the Masters and Scholars of the said Schools: In a Letter to a Friend* (1758), pp. 5, 7, 12.

101 [Jones], *Welch Piety* (1749), p. 20.

102 Clement, *Correspondence and Minutes of the SPCK*, p. 314.

103 [Jones], *Welch Piety* (1749), p. 5.

104 NLW, B/QA/2.

105 [Jones], *Welch Piety* (1749), pp. iv, 4.

106 [Jones], *Welch Piety* (1749), p. 18.

107 [Jones], *Welch Piety* (1758), p. 31.

108 Evans, *Religion and Politics in Mid-eighteenth Century Anglesey*, p. 108.

109 [Jones], *Welch Piety* (1749), *Welch Piety* (1758) and *Welch Piety, or A Further Account of the Circulating Welch Charity Schools from Michaelmas 1772 to Michaelmas 1773, being Testimonials Relating to the Masters and Scholars of the said Schools together with a list, shewing the Place where each School was kept and the Number of the Scholars Taught therein* (1773).

110 M. H. Jones, *The Trevecka Letters* (Caernarfon, 1932), Introduction, p. 80.

7. *Methodism in Wales*

1 Geraint Tudur, *Howell Harris: From Conversion to Separation 1735–1750* (Cardiff, 2000), pp. 16–23.

2 Eifon Evans, *Daniel Rowland and the Great Evangelical Awakening in Wales* (Edinburgh, 1985), pp. 139–41.

3 Geoffrey E. Nuttall, *Howell Harris 1714–1773: The Last Enthusiast* (Cardiff, 1965), p. 43.

[4] Evans, *Daniel Rowland and the Great Evangelical Awakening*, pp. 29, 49, 64.
[5] Derec Llwyd Morgan, *The Great Awakening in Wales*, translated by Dyfnallt Morgan (London, 1988), pp. 163 ff.
[6] Eryn M. White, '"The people called Methodists": early Welsh Methodism – the question of identity', *JWRH*, n.s. 1 (2001), 2.
[7] See Jones, 'Welsh Methodism and the international Evangelical Revival', 280 ff.
[8] R. Tudur Jones, 'The sufferings of Vavasor Powell', in *Welsh Baptist Studies*, p. 89.
[9] As suggested by Watts, *The Dissenters*, p. 399.
[10] Hughes, *Williams Pantycelyn*, pp. 2–3.
[11] Morgan, 'The development of the Baptist movement in Wales', 109–33.
[12] Jones, *Congregationalism in Wales*, pp. 111–13.
[13] For a full discussion of Harris and the Established Church see Tudur, *Howell Harris*, pp. 96–118.
[14] Watts, *The Dissenters*, pp. 446–51.
[15] Jenkins, *The Foundations of Modern Wales*, p. 347.
[16] R. W. Greaves, 'Religion in the University 1715–1800', in *The History of the University of Oxford, Vol. V. The Eighteenth Century,* ed. L. S. Sutherland and L. G. Mitchell (Oxford, 1986), p. 443.
[17] Graham C. G. Thomas, 'George Whitefield and friends: the correspondence of some early Methodists', *NLWJ*, 27 (1991–2), 75.
[18] Gomer Morgan Roberts, 'Calvinistic Methodism in Glamorgan 1737–1773', in *Glamorgan County History, IV*, p. 500.
[19] Hughes-Edwards, 'The development and organisation of the Methodist societies in Wales', 264–8.
[20] Morgan, *The Great Awakening in Wales*, p. 66.
[21] See R. W. D. Fenn, 'Thomas Davies rector of Coity 1769–1819', *JHSCW*, 13 (1963), 41–70.
[22] Tudur, *Howell Harris*, pp. 20–3.
[23] White, 'Poor benighted Church'?, 127 quoting NLW Calvinistic Methodist Archives, Diaries of Howell Harris, 54, 13 March 1740.
[24] *Additional Letters of the Morrises of Anglesey 1735–1786*, ed. and trans. Hugh Owen, Honourable Society of Cymmrodorion, 49, pt 1 (1947), p. 188.
[25] An excellent account of the societies is provided by Hughes-Edwards, 'The development and organisation of the Methodist societies'. This section is largely dependent on that account.

26 4th edn, 1712.
27 Tudur, *Howell Harris*, pp. 63 ff.
28 Barnes, *People of Seion*, p. 72.
29 Hughes-Edwards, 'The development and organisation of the Methodist societies', 108–23.
30 Barnes, *People of Seion*, p. 78.
31 Parry, 'Stability and change in mid-eighteenth century Caernarfonshire', 321.
32 Hughes-Edwards, 'The development and organisation of the Methodist societies', 131.
33 Parry, 'Stability and change in mid-eighteenth century Caernarfonshire', 337.
34 Jenkins, 'Church patronage and clerical politics in eighteenth century Glamorgan', 47.
35 Kathryn Jenkins, 'Williams Pantycelyn', in *A Guide to Welsh Literature c1700–1800*, p. 272.
36 Hughes-Edwards, 'The development and organisation of the Methodist societies', 71.
37 Jones, 'Welsh Methodism and the international Evangelical Revival', 230–43
38 For Anne Harris see Geraint Tudur, '"The king's daughter": a reassessment of Anne Williams of Trefecca', *JWRH*, 7, 1999, 55–75.
39 Clement, *SPCK and Wales*, p. 100.
40 Parry, 'Stability and change in mid-eighteenth century Caernarfonshire', 333, quoting *Welch Piety, I*, pp. 3, 53; and Gomer M. Roberts, 'Griffith Jones's opinions of the Methodists', *Journal of the Calvinistic Methodist Society*, 34 (1950), 55.
41 Williams, 'Griffith Jones Llanddowror', 21.
42 Hughes-Edwards, 'The development and organisation of the Methodist societies', 136.
43 Eryn Mant White, '"The world, the flesh and the devil" and the early Methodist societies of south west Wales', *Transactions of the Honourable Society of Cymmrodorion*, n.s. 3 (1997), 49–50.
44 See Brynley F. Roberts, 'The literature of the "Great Awakening"', in *Guide to Welsh Literature c1700–1800.*
45 White, 'The world, the flesh and the devil', 46–7.
46 Hughes, *Williams Pantycelyn*, p. 77.
47 For a detailed account of the Welsh Revival in its international context see Jones, 'Welsh Methodism and the international Evangelical Revival', 280–337. This has now been published as

'A Glorious Work in the World': Welsh Methodism and the International Evangelical Revival (Cardiff, 2004).

[48] Thomas, 'George Whitefield and friends', 176.

[49] Tudur, *Howell Harris*, pp. 59–60.

[50] Richard W. Evans, 'The relations of George Whitefield and Howell Harris', *Church History*, 30 (1961), 181.

[51] Hughes-Edwards, 'The development and organisation of the Methodist societies', p. 138.

[52] Geraint H. Jenkins, 'The Established Church and dissent in eighteenth-century Cardiganshire', in *Cardiganshire County History, III* (Cardiff, 1998), pp. 453–77.

[53] NLW, B/QA/2 Bishops Visitation Queries and Answers 1749.

[54] NLW, SD/Misc/1279 Names for Orders.

[55] Evans, *Daniel Rowland and the Great Evangelical Awakening*, p. 279.

[56] Tudur, 'The king's daughter', 65–74.

[57] Roberts, 'Calvinistic Methodism in Glamorgan', 520–4.

[58] The evidence for Welsh Methodism in the 1750s is slight because for the earlier period the main source is Harris's massive archive of letters and diaries, but Rowland's papers appear to have been lost by the Countess of Huntingdon to whom they were passed on his death.

[59] Quoted in Watts, *The Dissenters*, p. 411, and Jenkins, 'The Established Church and dissent in eighteenth-century Cardiganshire', 462.

[60] Morgan, *The Great Awakening in Wales*, p. 16.

[61] Hughes, *Williams Pantycelyn*, pp. 53 ff.

[62] Roberts, 'Calvinistic Methodism in Glamorgan', 577–8.

[63] Thomas, 'Diocese of St David's in the eighteenth century', 267–8.

[64] Pryce, *The Diocese of Bangor during Three Centuries*, p. xlviii.

[65] Evans, *Religion and Politics in Mid-eighteenth Century Anglesey*, pp. 106–7.

[66] Parry, 'Stability and change in mid-eighteenth century Caernarfonshire', 323–37.

[67] A. H. Williams, 'John Wesley and the archdeaconry of Brecon', in *Links with the Past: Swansea and Brecon Historical Essays*, ed. Owain W. Jones and David Walker (Llandybïe, 1974), pp. 154–9; Roberts, 'Calvinistic Methodism in Glamorgan', 518; A. H. Williams, *John Wesley in Wales 1739–90* (Cardiff, 1971).

Part III

1780–1850

8

Calvinistic Methodism: Growth and Separation

By the last quarter of the eighteenth century Calvinistic Methodism had made a major impact on the dioceses of Llandaff and St David's, but had still to make a comparable impact on the dioceses of Bangor and St Asaph. These new developments resulted from the passing of the leadership of Calvinistic Methodism from Daniel Rowland to Thomas Charles. Rowland remained active until shortly before his death in 1790. He still travelled to preaching engagements and drew vast crowds to his monthly communion services in the chapel he had built at Llangeitho, where he had ministered following the withdrawal of his licence to the curacy of Llangeitho by Bishop Squire of St David's in 1763. As late as 1789 he was involved in the Evangelical Revival that took place in the Llanwrtyd area of Breconshire.[1] Charles had been born at Llanfihangel Abercywyn (Carmarthenshire) in 1755 and educated at the Nonconformist academy in Carmarthen where he joined a Society of Calvinistic Methodists. He first heard Rowland preach in 1773 and was deeply affected. After three years at Jesus College, Oxford, he was ordained deacon by the bishop of Oxford in 1778, and priest in 1780, serving a series of curacies in Somerset. He returned to Wales in 1783 to marry Sally Jones of Bala. He was briefly curate of Llanymawddwy (Merioneth), but was given notice because of his Calvinistic Methodist sympathies in 1784. He never held any further preferment after that date but settled in Bala, living on his wife's income from the shop she had inherited, and devoting himself fully to the Calvinistic Methodist cause.[2] The first Evangelical Revival had occurred in Bala in 1781 and there was a further one, led by Charles, in 1791. In 1795 there were major conversions to Calvinistic Methodism, mostly 'effecting children and young people', in north Caernarfonshire.[3] This was the beginning of the movement which by the early nineteenth century had made north-west Wales an even stronger bastion of Calvinistic Methodism than those areas of south Wales in which the movement had started.[4]

The Established Church in Wales was extremely divided in its attitude to Calvinistic Methodism. Whereas in England there was relatively little clerical support for Wesleyan Methodism or the Countess of Huntingdon's Connexion, in Wales the leadership of Calvinistic Methodism was very firmly in the hands of people who had been ordained to the Anglican ministry and who, even if they no longer held preferment within the Established Church, still regarded themselves as clergy of that establishment. In the Vale of Glamorgan the Calvinistic Methodists had the full support of several Anglican incumbents: David Jones at Llangan (1767–1810), Edward Davies at Coychurch (1768–1821) and Thomas Davies at Coity (1769–1819). Jones had been responsible for the erection of Salem Chapel at Pencoed in 1775.[5] Some bishops, like Watson of Llandaff (1782–1816), were tolerant of Calvinistic Methodism; others like Horsley of St David's (1788–93) and St Asaph (1802–6) were less so, and it was Horsley who refused to institute Simon Lloyd to the perpetual curacy of Llanuwchllyn (Merioneth) in 1803 because of his support for the Calvinistic Methodists.[6] Horsley's view was that 'the crime and folly of the Methodists consists, not so much in heterodoxy, as in fanaticism; not in perverse doctrine, but rather in a disorderly zeal for the propagation of the Truth'.[7] However, as one critic of Horsley pointed out, there was some inconsistency in attacking Methodists for preaching doctrines such as that of justification by faith when Horsley had defended such doctrines in his own publications: 'If Dr Horsley should zealously and faithfully preach this doctrine himself, and . . . actually promote others who do the same, I have no doubt but he would soon obtain some such title as that of the *Methodistical Bishop*.'[8]

In his final Charge as Bishop of St Asaph Horsley conceded that the majority of Methodists were 'pious, well-meaning people, and none of them as far as I can understand, Dissenters in doctrine from the Established Church' but they were 'unremitting in their attempts to alienate the minds of the Laity from their proper pastors, the regular Clergy . . . This schismatical spirit, and this desire of promoting schism, I take to be their principal crime, and a heavy crime it is indeed.' Horsley urged his clergy not to attack the Methodists directly:

> From controversy in your sermons, upon what are called the Calvinistic points, I would by all means advise you to abstain . . . Lay down the doctrine categorically without dispute about it, taking care to stick close to the Bible, the Thirty-Nine Articles, and the Homilies.

The clergy would, in Horsley's view, best secure the support of their parishioners, and minimize the efforts of the Methodist preachers, by 'the soundness of your own doctrine and the innocency of your own lives'.[9] In Anglesey, evidence from the 1801 visitation returns shows a considerable division among the island clergy in their attitude to Calvinistic Methodism. Whereas the rector of Llanallgo had allowed the Methodists to hold a voluntary Sunday school in his church, the curate of Amlwch stated: 'I am thoroughly convinced it [Methodism] is used as a cloak to hide every vice which can disgrace the Christian character', and the rector of Llanddeusant opined that the Methodist chapel in his parish was attended by 'people of low rank and mean capacities . . . The Preachers I am informed are of the lowest Order of the People such as Shoemakers, Smiths &c, &c; it is said that Clergymen regularly ordained come there sometimes from South Wales to preach.'[10] In 1791 Brecon magistrates fined Thomas Bowen twenty pounds for preaching at an unlicensed meeting, the evidence against him having been presented by a local clergyman.[11] However, at Newport (Pembrokeshire) the incumbent in 1799 permitted the building of a Methodist chapel in the churchyard, described in the property deeds as 'a Meeting House erected by divers well disposed persons . . . for hearing the Divine Worship according to the doctrinal Articles and Homilies of the now Established Church of England'. What became known as the Church Chapel was later used as a Sunday school, but retained its original tiered seating until about 1970; in 1987 it was converted to serve as a parish hall.[12] There were also cases of Sunday schools being held by

Methodists in other Pembrokeshire churches, for example in 1804 at Brawdy and Hayscastle.[13]

One of the strongest episcopal attacks on the Calvinistic Methodists was contained in the 1808 Charge of Bishop Randolph of Bangor. For Randolph the real problem with Methodism was that it was a dissenting movement operating within the Established Church: the Methodists

> shelter themselves under the wing of the Church whenever they can; they covet our orders, if attainable; they solicit and purchase by their friends the patronage of our livings . . . they attend our Church . . . they teach our Catechism, but at the same time seek to introduce another of their own . . . they stand convicted, in a manner, by their own confession, of the most direct and plainest schism.

The success of Methodism 'is founded on the depreciation of moral conduct and the exaltation of enthusiasm, or imaginary conversion', which Randolph condemned as wholly unscriptural. However, he added: 'it is with particular satisfaction . . . that I have reason to believe that hardly a single established Clergyman in this Diocese is tainted with the prevailing enthusiasm, as many are in other parts.'

Randolph believed that the Established Church had facilitated the growth of Methodism through its failure to make adequate provision for the education of the laity. He regarded as complacent clergy who reported on the existence of dissenting schools within their parishes,

> without seeing how much it was incumbent on themselves to take similar measures, not only in order to provide for the children being duly instructed, but to prevent them from being perverted . . . I should think that the meanest peasant who can read his Bible might easily be shewn either the corruption of Popery, or the vanity of modern enthusiasm.

He urged his clergy to improve on the 'scanty' provision of Church schools in the diocese of Bangor, and to establish schools in which children were taught the Church catechism and to read the Bible.[14]

Whereas in England the appeal of Wesleyan Methodism or the Countess of Huntingdon's Connexion was geographically patchy, and indeed very limited in many parts of southern England,[15] it was only in areas along the border with England, such as the districts surrounding Chepstow, Knighton and Monmouth, that Calvinistic Methodism failed to make a significant impact in Wales. By the religious census of 1851 Calvinistic Methodists were the dominant religious group in much of mid- and north-west Wales, and the Established Church, from which the Calvinistic Methodists had separated, correspondingly weak.[16] In the late nineteenth and early twentieth centuries both Anglicans and Nonconformists were agreed that this was because the religious establishment in Wales had been weakened by internal corruption and lethargy as well as a process of Anglicization, but these assumptions have been greatly undermined by recent research and other reasons have to be found for the success of Calvinistic Methodism in Wales. Theologically Calvinistic Methodism shared almost identical beliefs and practices with the Countess of Huntingdon's Connexion in England, though the elaborate preparations for communion 'which sometimes involved several days of preaching' have been seen as 'reminiscent of the sacramental meetings of Scottish and Irish Presbyterians'.[17] Michael Watts sees three main reasons for the continued appeal of Calvinistic Methodism in Wales in the late eighteenth and early nineteenth centuries. The first was the revival of the circulating schools first established by Griffith Jones of Llanddowror, the management of which had been taken over after his death in 1761 by Mrs Bridget Bevan of Laugharne. When Mrs Bevan herself died, her will, which had provided for their continued endowment, was challenged by one of her executors and the schools were forced to close, though the charity had become operational again by the early years of the nineteenth century. They were in the interim revived by Thomas Charles of Bala in 1785, and by 1794 he was employing twenty teachers across five counties. Many of the converts in the Revivals at Bala in 1791 and Caernarfonshire in 1793, as well as those in some of the later Revivals, had attended these circulating schools. The second reason was the geographical arrangement of many parishes in which the parish church was situated at a considerable distance from the main centres of population. This was the case both at Nevern (Pembrokeshire), a parish with a population of 1,642 in 1851, spread over 22 square miles, but in which only nineteen dwellings were located within a quarter of a mile of the parish church; and at Llanddeiniolen (Caernarfonshire), where the parish church was 'well placed as regards the old agricultural population', but where the much larger population working in the newer slate quarries 'lies at a distance from the church of from three to five miles'. By 1851 Nevern had six and Llanddeiniolen thirteen dissenting chapels, with much larger attendances than those at the respective parish churches. The third reason was the emotional preaching which clearly had an enormous appeal to the Welsh temperament; some preachers, like John Elias and Robert Roberts in north Wales, 'preached in tears' or with 'alternating passages of calm and outbursts of exclamation'. The fact that this preaching was almost invariably in Welsh and designed to appeal to illiterates was a bonus, and indeed so much valued that the Caernarfonshire monthly meeting refused to allow John Elias to go to Manchester for six months to improve his education and to learn English.[18]

Even though some of the leaders of Welsh Calvinistic Methodism had been denied ecclesiastical preferment by bishops hostile to Methodism, or had witnessed other examples of, perhaps understandable, prejudice from an Established Church reluctant to embrace Evangelical enthusiasm, they were nevertheless determined to remain within it. It was only the eventual recognition that there were not enough sympathetic clergy within the Established Church to celebrate communion services for the growing number of Calvinistic Methodist congregations, most of whom had by then built their own chapels, that persuaded Thomas Charles to agree to the ordination of some lay preachers so that they could celebrate Holy Communion. He had, however, been under pressure to do so for some time. A letter to Charles from Thomas Jones of Denbigh dated 4 January 1810 expressed some of the tension that existed within the associations:

> It is indeed matter of grief to me (as to many others) that you was not present at Ruthin Association, and still more so to

> think of your being absent on account of our proceeding respecting the Sacraments . . . The Scriptures appear to me as clear and positive in commanding the use of *both* sacraments in the Church of Christ, also plainly in favour of the celebration of the Lord's supper more frequently, if not more statedly, than is practised amongst us . . . I observe that baptism is not administered amongst us . . . [yet] in several of our Societies there are many people who are very unwilling to have their children baptised in the Church of England, and by her ministers. This unwillingness, as well as the number of people inclined to it, seems to be continually increasing; and as to communicating in the Church of England, there are but very few of our people who are so inclined . . . several seek the ordinance from Dissenting Ministers though with a mind unwilling through more than one consideration . . . compelling any of our members to seek for either of the sacraments from without the pale of our connection is a thing we ought not to be guilty of, as being contrary to the word of God and to the universal customs of the Churches of God, in every age and country.[19]

The writer stated that, though he had the greatest respect and reverence for Charles, he thought his views were misguided and ought to change. Faced with this sort of pressure Charles reluctantly agreed to accept that his position was untenable, with the result that the first ordinations took place in 1811 with nine preachers ordained for north Wales and thirteen for south Wales at separate association meetings in Bala and Llandeilo.[20] The independent church adopted a presbyterian system of government. At the bottom of the structure were the private societies which were responsible for arranging the services in each chapel as well as admitting and disciplining members. The preachers and elders of these private societies were members of the presbyteries or monthly meetings which comprised all those chapels within a specific geographical area. The monthly meeting had oversight of all the private societies within its area and ensured that their affairs were properly conducted 'in accordance with the word of God and the rules of the Connexion'. The meetings of the Quarterly Association also comprised representative preachers and elders and met twice every three months, once in north and once in south

Wales. The association had 'authority to decide all matters pertaining to the Connexion everywhere', and its meetings were the occasion at which 'those who have been chosen to be ordained shall be approved and receive authority to administer the ordinances of Baptism and the Lord's Supper'. Under the rules of the Connexion 'no ordained preacher shall consider himself the minister of one church more than another but that all may administer . . . the sacraments in every Church . . . as their own convenience and the demand of the churches may determine'. It was, however, expected that, though ministers were ordained to serve the Connexion as a whole, they would 'take more particular care of the church of which they are members and the neighbouring churches'.[21]

The schism between the Calvinistic Methodists and the Established Church which resulted from the ordinations of 1811 did not lead to an immediate breakdown between the two bodies, despite the strengthening of opposition from many clergy. In Cardiganshire, John Williams of Lledrod continued to support the Methodists, but his colleague, Hugh Lloyd of Llangeitho, who had been friendly before 1811, did not; even so the Llangeitho Methodists refused to host association meetings at their chapel so as not to offend Lloyd. Some Methodist congregations were turned out of chapels in which the trust deeds laid down that they could only be used by those conforming to the doctrines and practices of the Established Church. Previously sympathetic Anglican clergy, like William Jones at St Dogmael's (Pembrokeshire) and John Davies at Cynwyl Elfed and Abernant (Carmarthenshire), refused to have anything to do with the Methodists after 1811.[22] Some Anglican landlords continued to use the threat of eviction, as they had during the eighteenth century, to prevent their tenants from attending Calvinist Methodist services, or refused permission for chapels to be built on their estates.[23] Even so, unwillingness to separate themselves completely from the Established Church remained strong. Before 1811 only seven Calvinistic Methodist chapels in Cardiganshire had been registered as dissenting meeting houses; in the parish of Llangwyryfon the congregation of the Tabor chapel did not 'cease to attend the Anglican church after their morning service' until 1869.[24] An interesting illustration of how the schism seems not to have affected the relations between Calvinistic Methodists and the Established Church in the short term can be seen at Llanidloes (Montgomeryshire) in 1813. A letter from a local farmer to Thomas Charles on 5 May of that year stated:

> We have it in contemplation to form a Bible Association here, we have spoke to several concerning it, and they seem all very wishful of having it. The Revd John Davies our clergyman has promised to be to us all the assistance that lays in his power, to attend the Committee's meetings and to be a subscriber &c. We have been told by Mr Hugh Jones that you promised (at the Aberystwyth Association) to be present at our Meeting, which we were very glad to learn.

The writer referred in the same letter in the warmest terms, to a series of Calvinistic Methodist preachings over three days in Llanidloes at which

> There was hardly a person in town but did attend the meetings constantly, and there was a solemn appearance to be seen in the whole congregation . . . In the publick houses before the meetings there was the greatest economy, and when the service time was up all immediately attended.[25]

The fact that the incumbent of Llanidloes was prepared, whatever private reservations he might have had, to work with Calvinistic Methodists in setting up a local society to study the Scriptures casts a very different light on the nature of the Calvinistic Methodist schism from the Established Church from that given in the older histories, whether written by Anglicans or Nonconformists, and suggests that a detailed new study of this topic, using the considerable quantity of local evidence that has survived, would make a major contribution to a better understanding of this important event in Welsh religious history.

One serious impact of the Calvinistic Methodist schism was that on Evangelicalism within the Established Church. It was not simply that those clergy who had supported the Methodists had to choose between loyalty to the establishment or secession, but that Evangelicals who remained within the Established Church were viewed with even greater suspicion by those bishops hostile to Evangelicalism. All those clergy beneficed in 1811, who had previously supported the Methodists, remained within the Established Church; a number of curates and some unbeneficed clergy, such as Thomas Charles and Simon Lloyd, were among the seceders. Although bishops, such as Burgess of St David's and Cleaver of St Asaph, were still prepared to ordain Evangelicals, others, such as Marsh of Llandaff, were not. Burgess's successor at St David's, J. B. Jenkinson, condemned Evangelical practices such as extempore prayer in his 1828 Charge, and Bethell of Bangor was also very hostile. A few Evangelicals even managed to maintain loose connections with the Calvinistic Methodists. Richard Bassett, rector of the Glamorganshire parishes of Eglwys Brewis (from 1832) and Colwinston (from 1843) continued to attend 'Methodist societies and associations . . . and even remained a trustee of some of their chapels' until his death in 1852. An important nucleus of Evangelical clergy survived in the diocese of St David's, where they tended to dominate some of the clerical associations which Bishop Burgess had established, and it was from these roots that a new group of Evangelicals began to grow after 1820. The distribution of Evangelical clergy in Wales by 1845 can be plotted by those parishes that were in that year supporting the Evangelical Church Pastoral Aid Society. There were 29 of these in the diocese of St David's and 33 in that of Llandaff, but only 4 altogether in those of Bangor and St Asaph, in which the significantly greater patronage of the High Church Hackney Phalanx bishops, Bethell and Carey, had clearly stifled the preferment of Evangelical clergy.[26] Even in the diocese of St David's Bishop Jenkinson, who had succeeded Burgess in 1825, did his best to restrict the growth of Evangelicalism by breaking up the clerical societies established by his predecessor. Archdeacon Beynon of Cardigan, writing to Jenkinson on 21 October of that year noted: 'since your Lordship came to the Diocese we have heard no more of the "Clerical Meetings", alias itinerant preachings, and it is probable we shall hear no more of them, as they will of course conclude they do not meet with your Lordship's approbation.'[27]

One of the most distinguished members of the younger group of Evangelical clergy was the future bishop of St Asaph,

Joshua Hughes. Hughes had been a protégé of David Griffiths, the pro-Methodist vicar of Nevern (Pembrokeshire) 1783–1834, and was presented to the united benefice of Llandingad and Llanfair-ar-y-Bryn (Carmarthenshire) in 1846. George Borrow was present at a weekday evening service conducted by Hughes in 1854 and the element of continuity with an earlier Calvinistic Methodism is unmistakable:

> The sermon which was *extempore* was delivered with great earnestness . . . when he had finished a man in a neighbouring pew got up and spoke about his own unworthiness . . . his sins of commission and omission, and dwelling particularly on his uncharitableness and the malicious pleasure which he took in the misfortunes of his neighbours. When the man had concluded the clergyman again spoke, making observations on what he had heard and hoping that the rest would be visited with the same contrite spirit as their friend.[28]

By contrast there were far fewer manifestations of Tractarianism in south Wales, despite the brief early experiment at Llangorwen, where a new church was consecrated in 1841.[29] Bishop Bethell of Bangor ordained a number of Tractarian clergy, some of whom later became ritualists, but the impact of the Oxford Movement on Wales was generally very limited before the last quarter of the nineteenth century.[30]

It was not just the Established Church which was transformed by Calvinistic Methodism. It also had a significant effect on the older branches of Protestant dissent in Wales, which were reactivated by the Evangelical Revival. Between 1800 and 1851, 136 dissenting chapels were built in Cardiganshire compared with 3 new Anglican places of worship. Of these 54 were built by the Calvinistic Methodists, 16 by Baptists and 10 by Unitarians.[31] A similar pattern could be observed throughout other parts of Wales. By 1851 the Independents were strongest in mid- and south-west Wales and the Baptists in south-east Wales.[32] Among the Independents the period between 1800 and 1840 was seen 'as the golden age of preaching'. Many of these preachers were, like those of the Calvinistic Methodists, itinerant and not all were of good character. The Independents were also making significant contributions to the mission field by the early nineteenth century.[33]

They also began to develop formal associations of their chapels. Assemblies were held for north, south-east and south-west Wales, and below them were Quarterly Meetings, usually held for all the chapels in a particular county. Some Independents felt that the development of such formal structures threatened the 'independence' of individual ministers and congregations and this could be a source of conflict. Most ministers and congregations, however, saw the advantages of cooperation, particularly when it could be used for fund-raising and for helping to clear the debts that many chapels were burdened with.[34] The Welsh Independents were also strengthened by a number of local Revivals, of which the most significant were those in west Wales in 1828 and north Wales in 1839.[35]

The Welsh Baptists were both influenced and divided by Calvinistic Methodism. Some Baptists welcomed a greater degree of emotionalism and spontaneity in their services, but others were concerned that such developments threatened theological orthodoxy.[36] Like the Independents they endeavoured to silence theological dispute by channelling their energies into missionary work. A particular initiative of the Welsh Baptists was the launching of a mission to Roman Catholic Brittany in 1821. It had relatively little success, and the first permanent chapel, with an average attendance of some 30–40 at the Breton morning service and about 100 at the French evening service, was not opened until January 1846.[37] Both the Baptists and the Independents were, like the Calvinistic Methodists, especially active in the development of Sunday schools.[38] A major increase in the number of Baptists in Wales took place from the last quarter of the eighteenth century. There were significant surges in membership in 1789 (603 baptized), 1795 (822) and 1807 (1368). The total number of Baptist congregations in south Wales increased from 35 in 1790 to 81 by 1815, with an estimated number of nearly 10,000 converts.[39] Wesleyan Methodism, by contrast, made relatively little impact in most parts of Wales. It was considerably weakened in north-west Wales by the secession of *Y Wesle Bach* in 1831. This secession was caused by the demand of some ministers that they should be paid salaries at a time when most Nonconformist ministers in Wales had secular jobs. This was particularly true of the Calvinistic Methodists: John Jones, minister at Blaenannerch (Cardiganshire), was an agricultural worker; Daniel Davies at Aberporth (Cardiganshire) was a lime-burner, John Jones at Talysarn (Caernarfonshire) was a quarry worker and his wife kept a shop. Many Baptist ministers were shopkeepers, their ministries depending on the success of their businesses. By 1826 Christmas Evans, pastor at Caerphilly (Glamorgan) was, exceptionally, paid £40 a year by his congregation, who also provided him with a house and a field for his horse. However, in Anglesey in 1792, he had had a salary of only £17 a year and 'a bare, cold, tumbledown cottage', in return for preaching in two chapels and seven or eight private houses; 'in addition he published pamphlets on current affairs and religious books which he advertised from the pulpit and sold to his congregations after the service.'[40]

As in England, many Nonconformists objected to paying the compulsory church rates in addition to the costs of maintaining their own chapels and ministers.[41] In 1832 a rate was levied in Aberystwyth to pay for a second Anglican church in the town. The Nonconformists argued that the existing church was 'large enough to contain many more than are in the habit of attending it', and many refused to pay. The churchwardens decided to distrain upon their goods, including those of John Matthews, a Calvinistic Methodist draper.[42] In 1837, after disputes over Church rates, dissenting parishioners at Llanelli and Llannon (Carmarthenshire) elected Nonconformists as churchwardens, but this action backfired when the vicar of Llanelli, Ebenezer Morris, took legal action against his wardens, an Independent and a Unitarian, 'for failing to fulfil their duties', an action that resulted in their imprisonment.[43] A question about the payment of parish clerks included in Bishop Connop Thirlwall's visitation queries in 1842 revealed that in at least a tenth of the parishes in the archdeaconry of Carmarthen no rates were being levied as a result of Nonconformist opposition to them.[44] These disputes did nothing to increase the popularity of the Established Church or reduce that of Nonconformity. By the religious census of 1851 there were only five out of 48 registration districts in Wales in which the Established Church could attract more than a fifth of the population to attend its services, and they were all areas in which English either already was, or was becoming, the dominant language: Brecknock, Chepstow, Monmouth, Montgomery and Pembroke. By contrast there were eighteen registration districts, including not just substantial parts of north-west Wales, but also areas of south-east Wales where Welsh was not the dominant language, in which fewer than a tenth of the inhabitants attended services in the Established Church.[45] The damage that had been done to the Established Church by the Calvinistic Methodist schism of 1811, and the contemporary growth of the older branches of Protestant dissent in Wales, had clearly been enormous, and it is difficult to see how it could have been avoided. As Thomas Charles's biographer has pointed out, 'the Methodist fathers ignored the discipline of the Bishops from the first, and the Bishops and the clergy retaliated handsomely by persecutions, inhibitions, and the withholding of preferments'.[46] Whilst the second part of this quotation clearly requires some modification, in the light of recent research, it would be difficult to challenge the accuracy of the first part.

9
A Reforming Episcopate

The fact that between 1727 and 1870 no Welshman held an episcopal see in Wales has encouraged the image of the Welsh Church as both an Anglicized, and an Anglicizing, institution. This chapter will suggest that this image of the Welsh Church is a fiction, though it will not disregard some of the significant problems which undoubtedly reduced the effectiveness of the Welsh Church in this period. The diocesan geography was a major one. The diocese of Llandaff covered a relatively compact area of south-east Wales but it was the part of the principality in which the population trebled in the first half of the nineteenth century; in 1835 it had 192 benefices, a population of 184,000, and a net episcopal income of £1,043 per annum, the lowest of any diocese in England or Wales. Bangor and St Asaph were also of manageable size, though each diocese included peculiars belonging to the other; in 1835 Bangor had 124 benefices, a population of 153,000, and a net episcopal income of £3,938 per annum, and St Asaph a population of 197,000, 131 benefices and a net episcopal income of £6,082 per annum. By contrast, the diocese of St David's covered the whole of five counties and portions of a further three with a total population of 373,000 and 407 benefices, yet the annual income of the bishop was only £2,915.[1] It was, therefore, a potentially unattractive offer of preferment to those anxious to secure a bishopric. It might have been thought, therefore, that when diocesan reorganization first began to be considered in the 1830s, the priority would have been to reduce the size of St David's diocese, but this was not the case. An initial proposal to unite the sees of Bristol and Llandaff, opposed by the bishop of the latter, was abandoned in favour of a union between Bristol and Gloucester. The proposed union of the dioceses of Bangor and St Asaph was not opposed by either bishop, but there was strong opposition from some clergy and laity; in 1846 a bill to retain both dioceses passed its second reading in the House of Lords and the proposal was abandoned.[2] The impetus for this bill had come from the clergy of the diocese of St Asaph who, at a meeting held on 19 October 1842, requested Bishop Carey to nominate a committee to consider the best means of preventing the proposed union with Bangor. Carey, somewhat reluctantly one suspects, agreed to the demand and indeed had a meeting with the home secretary, who promised that the Cabinet would review the proposal. The committee produced a number of printed statements pointing out the defects of the proposed union and secured the support of the Earl of Powis to put their case in the House of Lords. As a tribute to his persuasiveness and the energy that he had put into the task, a Powis Testimonial Fund was established for 'the institution of exhibitions at Oxford or Cambridge for candidates for Holy Orders, tenable by natives of Wales, who . . . are acquainted with the Welsh language'. By 13 March 1848 a total of £5,125. 17*s*. 6*d*. had been contributed to this fund.[3] The two dioceses were, however, substantially reorganized so that the peculiars within them were eliminated and they covered the north-eastern and north-western counties of Wales respectively. There were also minor adjustments to the boundaries of the dioceses of Llandaff and St David's, with the Herefordshire parishes in both dioceses being transferred to that of Hereford (see Figures 9.1 and 9.2).[4]

One peculiarity of the Welsh Church before the 1840s was the suspension of most archidiaconal powers. The archdeacons did not hold courts, enforce decisions, institute churchwardens or make parochial visitations. In the diocese of St Asaph the single archdeaconry had been combined with the bishopric, and in that of Bangor, two out of three archdeaconries – those of Anglesey and Bangor, but not that of Merioneth – had been similarly combined. The archdeacon of Llandaff acted as head of the cathedral chapter but carried out no other functions. The diocese of St David's had four archdeacons, all of whom were members of the cathedral chapter and who were frequently influential figures in the diocese, but no specific functions were attached to the office. Inspections of church fabrics were

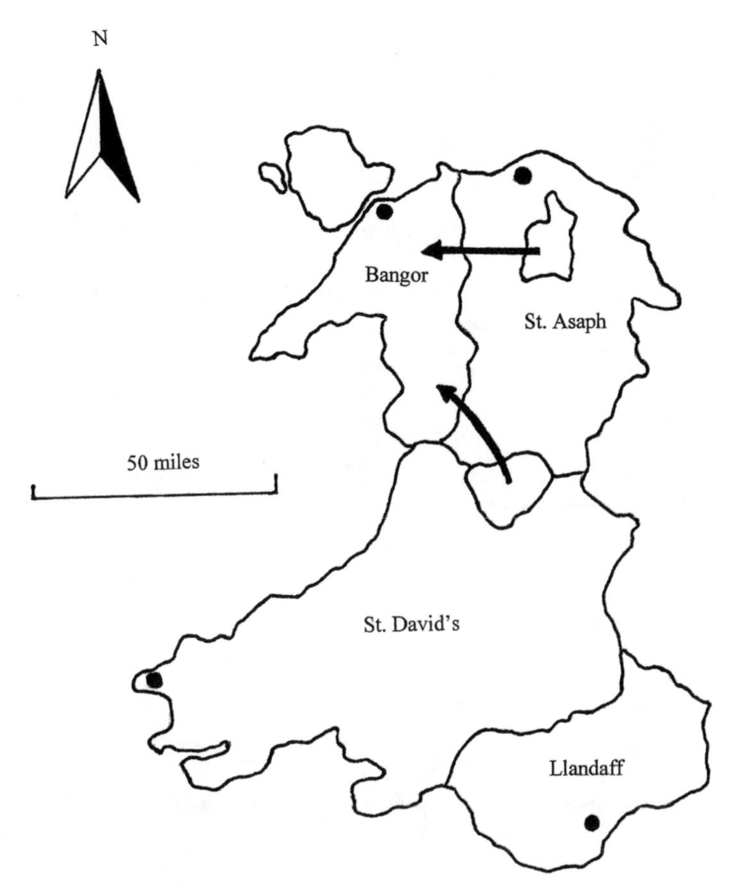

Fig. 9.1 – Welsh dioceses before reorganization in 1846

carried out, as they were in the diocese of St Asaph, by the rural deans who, unlike in most English dioceses, had survived in every Welsh diocese apart from Llandaff, where the office was restored by Bishop Marsh (1816–19). The anomalies relating to the Welsh archdeaconries were resolved in 1843–4 when separate deans were appointed for the cathedrals at Llandaff and St David's, the precentor of the latter having previously been head of the chapter, and the archdeaconries of Anglesey, Bangor and St Asaph separated from their respective bishoprics. Most Welsh bishops exercised considerable patronage in

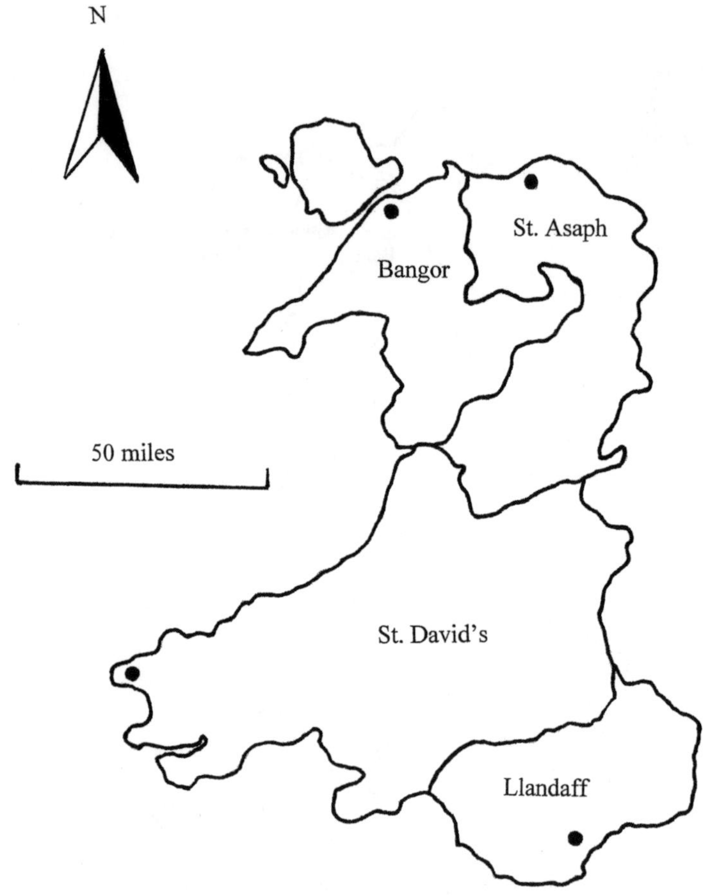

Fig. 9.2 – Welsh dioceses after reorganization in 1846

relation to the benefices in their dioceses: 121 (92.4 per cent) at St Asaph, 76 (61.3 per cent) at Bangor, 97 (23.8 per cent) at St David's; the exception was Llandaff where the bishop was patron of only seven benefices (3.6 per cent) in the diocese.[5] For the remainder of this chapter we will look individually at the four Welsh dioceses and the role of their respective bishops in the promotion of ecclesiastical reform during the late eighteenth and early nineteenth centuries. It is, however, important to note that three bishops in this period held more than one

Welsh diocese: John Warren, St David's 1779–83 and Bangor 1783–1800; Samuel Horsley, St David's 1788–93 and St Asaph 1802–6, holding the English diocese of Rochester in the intervening period; William Cleaver, Bangor 1800–6 and St Asaph 1806–15. The dioceses of Bangor and St Asaph, as the richest Welsh bishoprics, were in this period always filled by translation, normally from poorer English sees, whereas the much poorer dioceses of Llandaff and St David's were sees to which existing bishops were never appointed in this period; the appointees were, however, with the exceptions of Richard Watson and Edward Copleston at Llandaff, and Lord George Murray and J. B. Jenkinson at St David's, translated, often after a relatively short interval, to more important English, Irish or Welsh bishoprics.

Diocese of Bangor

The diocese is one of the best documented in Wales, with a range of visitation returns covering most of the period between the mid-eighteenth and early nineteenth centuries, and with the result that it has attracted some attention from local historians. The three longest episcopates were those of John Warren (1783–1800), H. W. Majendie (1809–30) and Christopher Bethell (1830–59). William Cleaver (1800–6) appears to have had less impact on the diocese than he did as bishop of St Asaph between 1806 and 1815, where he was noted as an opponent of pluralism and a supporter of church restoration and the foundation of both day and Sunday schools.[6] He had combined the bishopric of Bangor with the principalship of Brasenose College, Oxford, where he was resident, but resigned the office on his translation to St Asaph.[7] There is, however, clear evidence that, when occasion demanded, Cleaver was a strict disciplinarian at Bangor. In 1805 he refused to permit 'a change in the time of service' at Llandudno requested by the curate, who also served the church of Llandrillo-yn-Rhos. He was, however, prepared to sanction an early service at Llandrillo 'if they will be satisfied there with early Prayers so that you may begin your duties at Llandudno between 11 and 12 o'clock'.[8] At Dolgellau the parishioners had petitioned the rural dean of Ardudwy and Ystumaner in 1801 that the 8 a.m. service should be dispensed with as the rector lived two miles away, there being no glebe house. There were also services at 11 a.m. and 3 p.m. on Sundays, and 'every week' on Tuesdays, Fridays and Saturdays. Cleaver sanctioned the discontinuation of the early Sunday service but requested that a copy of his authorization be entered into the vestry book.[9] The weekday services on Friday mornings and Saturday evenings were still in existence in 1832.[10] John Randolph was translated from Oxford to Bangor to succeed Cleaver in 1807, but within two years had been translated from Bangor to London. His 1808 Charge, as we have seen, dealt primarily with the dangers posed by the growth of Methodism, but also condemned 'wilful non-residence', of which 'there are few instances' in the diocese, and stated that he would sanction non-residence only where the circumstances justified it. Warren, Majendie and Bethell have all been seen as reforming bishops, and at least one contemporary clearly had a high opinion of Cleaver and Randolph as well, since he noted 'that the diocese has in no respect been carelessly treated by the appointment of unknown or inefficient characters'.[11]

Warren resided in the diocese for at least part of each year for most of his episcopate, spending between five and six months there in 1792. He appointed only graduates to benefices within his gift; this included appointments for three of his nephews, one being made chancellor of the diocese in 1791, a second being appointed dean in 1793 and a third being collated to the prebend of Llanfair in 1797 (a prebend he held until his death in 1845). The younger John Warren, who was only twenty-six or twenty-seven when he succeeded to the deanery, had been involved in a brawl at university during which he was wounded in the forehead with a sword. However, he appears to have been an exemplary dean, one who 'performed all his clerical duties with great correctness and propriety ... respected by all around him'. As a member of the cathedral chapter, by virtue of holding the archdeaconries of Anglesey and Bangor in addition to the bishopric, Bishop Warren strongly influenced the chapter's decision in 1787 to convert the one cathedral sermon on Sundays, alternately in English and Welsh, into two sermons, one in English and one in

Welsh at the services in that language. There were four Sunday services in the cathedral. In the early nineteenth century the English services were at 11 a.m. and 5 p.m., and the Welsh ones at 7 a.m. and 3.15 p.m. By the middle of the century they were mostly a little later, with Morning Prayer in Welsh at 9.15 a.m. and English at 11.30 a.m., and Evening Prayer in English at 4.15 p.m. and Welsh at 6 p.m. The more elaborate music was reserved for the English services; the Welsh services had originally had no music, but simple settings were in use by the mid-nineteenth century. There were also services in the cathedral on Wednesdays and Fridays. Warren also made substantial improvements to the bishop's palace at Bangor and insisted that the parishioners at Amlwch should spend more than the £800 they had allocated for the rebuilding of their parish church; as a result a building begun in 1792 was not completed until 1800 and the total cost was £2,500.[12] Warren's 1784 Charge had concentrated on 'the duties of the parochial clergy'. He emphasized 'the well reading of the Common-Prayer', the importance of preaching and catechizing, and the 'Duty incumbent on the Parochial Clergy . . . of Visiting the Sick'. Ministers needed to be of 'sober and unblemished life . . . It is not sufficient for a Preacher of Righteousness to avoid open and scandalous Sins; but he ought to be an example to others in all those excellent virtues.' Like Randolph after him, Warren was keen to enforce clerical residence, pointing out that licences for non-residence were 'not granted, as a favour to any person, but . . . can . . . only be justified, when the Service of the church, or of the state, makes it reasonable'.[13]

Majendie was, as a bishop, in a very similar mould to Warren. He resigned his prebend at St Paul's Cathedral, London, on his translation from Chester to Bangor, and resided in his new diocese for two-thirds of each year between May and January or February. He had a good reputation as a preacher and was 'essentially a pastoral rather than a political bishop'.[14] He used his Charges and the visitation process to initiate an extensive programme of diocesan reform. This resulted in the repair of churches, the establishment of day and Sunday schools, and an attempt, largely unsuccessful, to establish two Sunday services in as many parishes as possible.

Recent research on Majendie[15] has shown that he was something of a pioneer in using the visitation process as a means of really getting to know his diocese and rooting out abuses where he had the power to do so. Among the documents surviving in the archives of the diocese of Bangor is an abstract compiled by Majendie himself 'of Matters observable, as resulting from an examination of the answers to the Queries proposed to the Clergy of the Diocese preparatory to the Primary Visitation, placed under the head of each Parish, in Alphabetical order in each County'.[16] This included, in many cases, a note of matters which the bishop intended to raise with the clergy concerned either during the visitation or at a later date. Although there is no surviving evidence of such documentation having been compiled at subsequent visitations, it almost certainly was, since Majendie also used his 1814 and 1817 Charges to record in some detail the progress that had been made in matters in which he had a specific interest, such as the regular maintenance and repair of church buildings, and to lay down markers for matters which he intended to address in the future.

Majendie's interest in education clearly had an impact in some parts of the diocese of Bangor, especially within the archdeaconry of Merioneth. Mary Parry, in her will dated 9 June 1817, left £1,000 to the rector and churchwardens of Llanbedr to teach poor children, 'boys and girls in equal numbers'. This bequest was used to build a school with two classrooms, one for boys and one for girls, accommodation for a master and a mistress, and to provide annual salaries of £28 for the former and £16 for the latter. Poor children, selected by the rector and churchwardens, were taught free of charge English reading, writing and accounts. Other children were charged fees and could be taken from parishes other than Llanbedr. A similar bequest had been used in 1810 to establish a school for the parishes of Llanenddwyn and Llanddwywe, at which children were taught to read both English and Welsh. By 1837 there were in Merioneth schools at Dolgellau, with 32 pupils including 14 paying scholars; Llandanwg, with 12 poor children of both sexes; Llanegryn, with 67 children; and Tywyn, with 21 children plus paying pupils.[17] Schools at Bala and Corwen, in the eastern part of the county, had been noted by Bishop Cleaver of St Asaph in 1807.[18]

Majendie presented his future son-in-law, J. H. Cotton, son of the dean of Chester and previously a young curate in his former diocese, to the living of Derwen (Denbighshire) in 1809; in 1810 he moved to become vicar of Bangor and precentor of the cathedral, adding to this preferment the livings of Llandyfrydog and Llanfihangel Tre'r Beirdd (Anglesey) from 1814 to 1821, the rectory of Llanllechid (Caernarfonshire) from 1821, and later the livings of Gyffin (Caernarfonshire) and Llanfihangel Ysgeifiog with Llanffinan (Anglesey). He retained these livings after his appointment to the deanery of Bangor, in succession to Dean Warren, in 1838. He was Majendie's right-hand man in his diocesan programme of ecclesiastical reform. Bishop and son-in-law were instrumental in promoting a major restoration of Bangor Cathedral, begun in 1824. The nave was separated from the choir and transepts by a screen placed one bay west of the crossing. The western part of the nave was fitted up for Welsh services with a pulpit and reading desk positioned on opposite sides of the railed altar, placed against the screen and covered with a crimson carpet and cushions at each end. The choir, transepts and east end of the nave were fitted up for English services and incorporated another altar and pulpit and the bishop's throne. The choir was stalled and the transepts pewed. This restoration cost £5,300.[19]

Diocese of Llandaff

Compared with Bangor, Llandaff is a rather poorly documented diocese, with large gaps in the visitation records and an almost complete dearth of episcopal correspondence. It is, however, the best researched of the Welsh dioceses and has attracted the attention of several postgraduates seeking topics for theses. It also had, in Richard Watson and Edward Copleston, two of the longest-serving Welsh diocesans of the late eighteenth and early nineteenth centuries. An older generation of historians saw Watson as a blatant careerist, who was non-resident in his diocese and held several other preferments at the same time, including the Regius Professorship of Divinity at Cambridge. Recent writers have viewed him in a different light and seen him as diligent in his episcopal duties, despite his non-residence, and a committed proponent of ecclesiastical reform.[20] He favoured the equalization of episcopal incomes and patronage in order to reduce the desire for translation from one diocese to another, and the redistribution of cathedral endowments to provide better incomes for the parochial clergy and a reduction in the number of pluralities. He pointed out that his own pluralism was made necessary by the poverty of his bishopric and that his total preferment was never worth more than £2,000 per annum. He carried out nine full visitations of his diocese between his consecration in 1782 and his death in 1816. He also confirmed regularly, both at the traditional centres at Abergavenny, Caerleon, Cowbridge and Llandaff, and occasionally also at Chepstow, Neath and Usk. In 1809 he confirmed for the first time at Merthyr Tydfil since

> this place had become, from a small village, a great town containing ten or twelve thousand inhabitants . . . [it was] my duty not only to go to confirm the young people there, but to preach to those who were grown up, that I might, if possible, leave among the inhabitants a good impression in favour of the teachers in the Established Church, when compared to those of the sectarian congregations into which the people were divided.[21]

He required his beneficed clergy to reside, wherever this could be achieved, and that each church should have two Sunday services and services on holy days. In his 1802 Charge Watson urged the clergy to read widely and to take seriously their responsibilities for any school established in their parishes, especially in ensuring the appointment of 'diligent, virtuous, and pious' schoolmasters.[22] He also insisted that the clergy should dress properly.

> A peculiar sort of apparel distinguishes the clergy from the laity. It is not unusual to see young clergymen, who seem desirous of abolishing this peculiarity . . . A clerical habit produces a degree of respect, which would not otherwise be paid to him, to the poorest curate in the kingdom.[23]

He was not, however, averse to a degree of nepotism, appointing both his son and his nephew to prebendal stalls in Llandaff Cathedral. The latter held three cathedral prebends in 1800, together with the well-endowed perpetual curacy of St Bride's Wentlooge.[24]

An attempt to regulate the pluralism of the cathedral chapter was made in 1803, when

> in future every [chapter] living that becomes vacant shall be offered to the Lord Bishop, then to the archdeacon, Chancellor and Precentor, and then to the nine prebendaries according to the seniority of their admission . . . Provided always that no member shall retain two livings in the gift of this chapter till every junior member has refused to serve.[25]

Watson's attempts to enforce clerical residence seem to have been very unsuccessful, with only thirty-two out of 192 livings having resident incumbents in 1810.[26] Nevertheless much of this non-residence was caused by the non-existence or poor condition of parsonage houses, and 'Watson deserves recognition, for not only did he realise that the church was in need of reform, he was one of the first to present a constructive programme' for such reform.[27] Even his own non-residence in the diocese could be blamed on the fact that the bishop of Llandaff had no official residence and had to find his own accommodation. When Bishop Sumner was translated from Llandaff to Winchester in 1827 he wrote to his successor-designate, Edward Copleston, on 7 December of that year: 'I am desired by the landlord of the house I lately rented in Monmouthshire to ask you whether you will be desirous of tenanting it. It is well situated for the Diocese, of convenient size, and thoroughly furnished – the rent £200 a year.'[28] Copleston took on the lease of this house, at Llansantffraid near Abergavenny, moving in 1835 to Llandough Castle and, towards the end of his episcopate, to Hardwick House, Chepstow.[29]

Watson's successor, Herbert Marsh (1816–19), encouraged the establishment of parochial schools and support for the Society for the Promotion of Christian Knowledge in its work of distributing bibles and prayer books.[30] Despite his short stay in the diocese, caused by his speedy translation to the see of Peterborough, Marsh's episcopate was considered a great success. Archbishop Howley of Canterbury, writing to Bishop Copleston on 8 November 1828, expressed his

> pleasure to find that you are satisfied with the state of your Diocese. The present Bishop of Peterborough put things into a good train there, and the two succeeding Bishops [Van Mildert and Sumner] have I conceive omitted no opportunity of forwarding the progress of improvement, which I have no doubt will continue to advance under your direction.[31]

However, despite Marsh's reforms, there was still much to do. William Van Mildert (1819–26) found at his primary visitation of 1821 a cathedral without choristers, singing men or organist, and no houses for the prebendaries or vicars choral; only a third of parochial livings with glebe houses; only one in five churches 'in decent and respectable condition'; and in Merthyr Tydfil, then the largest town in the diocese, church accommodation for only 900 out of a population of 18,000. The impact on him was such that, after his translation to the see of Durham, he sent an annual gift of £100 at Christmas to be distributed in his former diocese.[32]

Van Mildert's successor, C. R. Sumner (1826–7), spent only twenty months in the diocese before his translation to Winchester, but had clearly developed a good sense of what needed to be done and did not hesitate to advise Copleston accordingly, in two letters of 7 and 10 December 1827:

> I have ordered my publisher to send you a copy of what proves to be my parting as well as primary charge to a body of clergy whom I hope you will allow me some opportunity of recommending to you in a more particular manner. I can promise you from them great affection and great respect, and from many, great piety; and I trust in these qualities you will overlook the want of some of the learning which you will have been accustomed to meet in their brethren of your own [Oriel] College, and of the university [of Oxford] . . . you will find the Honble W. B. Knight, Chancellor of the Church and Diocese of Llandaff an invaluable assistant. He is a man of very considerable talent . . . intimately acquainted with the

> character of every clergyman under your superintendence . . . He was appointed Chaplain by Bishop Marsh, originally; and has since been successively employed in the same capacity by Bishop Van Mildert and myself . . . He is a perfect master of the Welsh language, in which it is in most cases necessary that the Candidates for Orders should be examined, in addition to the usual routine.[33]

Copleston was to rely as heavily on Knight as his predecessors had done. Knight died in 1845,[34] Copleston four years later.

The real problem for the diocese of Llandaff in the early nineteenth century was the enormous increase in its population, though this increase was largely confined to a small number of valley parishes. The person who had to cope with this problem was Copleston. The general view of the diocese's older historians has been that Copleston, unlike his successor, Alfred Ollivant, was simply not equal to the task, but this judgement is almost certainly unfair, since Copleston was trying to address problems which he did not have the resources to resolve. It was the bishops appointed after 1840 – the new generation headed by Thirlwall at St David's (1840), Short at St Asaph (1846) and Ollivant at Llandaff (1849) – that reaped the full benefits of the legislative reforms of the 1830s. Copleston, like his immediate predecessor, at least enjoyed a more secure income than earlier bishops of Llandaff after it was decreed that the bishop should also hold the deanery of St Paul's, the duties of which could be easily combined with his visits to London on parliamentary business. Between 1801 and 1841 the population of the diocese of Llandaff increased from 95,549 to 259,852 and was estimated to be in excess of 300,000 at the time of Copleston's death. Although Copleston still left enormous problems for his successors, the statistics for his episcopate, as shown in Table 9.1, are really quite impressive. He preferred to visit parishes unannounced, 'which I take to be much more useful than formal ones', and sometimes visited as many as eight churches a day, all on horseback. He encouraged the establishment of a Diocesan Church Building Society and subscribed £100 annually to its funds. In the last decade of his episcopate a total of more than £22,000 was spent on church building and restoration in the diocese and

Table 9.1 Increase in the number of glebe houses, resident clergy, churches with two Sunday services, Sunday schools and day schools in the diocese of Llandaff between 1827 and 1850

	1827	1850
Glebe houses	100	153
Resident clergy	97	162
Churches with 2 Sunday services	26	100
Sunday schools	66	228
Day schools	39	176

many new churches were erected. At Bedwellty, by the end of Copleston's episcopate, three churches and six clergy had replaced the 'single church and clergyman' that he had inherited; at Newport, in the same period, two churches and five clergy had replaced 'a single church and clergyman'.[35] The recent edition of Copleston's surviving correspondence held in the archive room of Llandaff Cathedral confirms that Copleston's administration of his diocese was both efficient and meticulous, and the editor, Roger Brown, has done much in his preface to rescue Copleston from the negative press he has received in the past, pointing out, in particular, that for the last ten years of his life he was battling against increasing ill health 'which left him prostrate for days on end'.[36]

One area in which Copleston was later criticized was his alleged failure to give adequate priority to the improvement of Llandaff Cathedral. This had become ruinous by the early eighteenth century, and a modest classical structure in which to hold the cathedral services had been built within its ruins. Copleston took the view that providing for the pastoral needs of the parishes was a greater priority than restoring the cathedral to its pre-Reformation size. In a letter to the new dean, Bruce Knight, on 29 March 1845, he wrote:

> We shall thus improve the exterior of the fabric as viewed by approaching it, and we shall fit up in a handsome style the interior of the choir for divine service, which is all that is ever likely to be used, and which I certainly long to see assume a

> characteristic form . . . As soon as ever our parish churches are put in a decent condition, i.e. not only restored but improved in true architectural style, becoming the houses of God – with dignity and elegance proportionate to the importance of the parish in which they stand, we may think of renewing the vast pile in its full dimensions.[37]

Reluctance to spend money on the cathedral had been noted in 1838 when the two vicars-choral informed the chapter of 'the complaint of the Inhabitants . . . respecting the inconvenience they feel on account of the cold state of the cathedral that many are prevented, especially during the winter months, from that regular attendance on the Service there, which they would otherwise feel inclined to give'. The vicars-choral recognized that 'the times are inauspicious for entering largely into expensive alterations' but hoped that the chapter might 'give them permission to solicit the aid of such of the Inhabitants as would be willing to come forward to contribute' towards more modest alterations to the internal arrangements.[38]

Despite the strenuous efforts of Copleston and his predecessors, progress towards an improvement of church accommodation and religious provision by the Established Church was painfully slow in some of the valley parishes. At Llantrisant the monthly communion services of the 1760s had been reduced to quarterly ones by the first decade of the nineteenth century. Tonyrefail had no communion services at all in the 1780s and 1790s.[39] In the Rhondda Valley the church at Ystradyfodwg was ruinous by 1842 and had to be rebuilt. A new church was opened at Glyntaff in 1838, but church accommodation in the ecclesiastical districts of Glyntaff, Llanwynno and Ystradyfodwg still only made provision for 1,382 out of a total population of 12,523. By contrast the seventeen Nonconformist chapels in the three districts provided accommodation for 4,463. The clerical stipends remained low: £166. 15*s*. 0*d*. at Glyntaff, £118. 14*s*. 0*d*. at Ystradyfodwg, and £102. 10*s*. 0*d*. at Llanwynno, where the non-resident incumbent also served the Monmouthshire curacy of Llantilio Pertholey until 1850. Anglican attendances were deplorable: only 10 at Ystradyfodwg and 56, with between 6 and 8 Easter communicants, at Llanwynno; although the three Sunday services at Glyntaff were estimated to have attracted a total congregation of 493 there were still only twelve Easter communicants.[40]

Diocese of St Asaph

The comparative wealth of this diocese meant that it was normally filled by translation from another see, and some bishops had held two bishoprics before that of St Asaph; of the early nineteenth century bishops, Samuel Horsley (1802–6) was 69 on his translation to the see, William Cleaver (1806–15) 64, John Luxmoore (1815–30) 59 and William Carey (1830–46) 60. None were therefore in the prime of life though there is no evidence that the diocese was slackly administered. The level of episcopal nepotism was, however, high even by contemporary standards. Between 1774 and 1854 the deanery of St Asaph and chancellorship of the diocese was filled by W. D. Shipley, son of Bishop Jonathan Shipley (1769–88), and C. S. Luxmoore, son of Bishop Luxmoore, both of whom held other benefices in the diocese. Luxmoore also collated another son to the prebend of Meifod in 1826 and to other benefices in the diocese. Bishop Lewis Bagot (1790–1802) collated his brother, beneficed in Staffordshire, to the prebend of Faenol in 1796, and Bishop Cleaver his son to the same prebend in 1809; he held this prebend and other benefices in the diocese until his death in 1854. Cleaver collated another son, who also held the rectories of Corwen (Merioneth) and Newtown (Montgomeryshire), to the fourth cursal stall in St Asaph cathedral in 1815. Bishop Horsley collated his son to the prebend of Llanfair (second portion) in 1803, and he also held the vicarages of Chirk and Gresford (Denbighshire) and the rectory of Castle Caereinion (Montgomeryshire). An analysis of the membership of the cathedral chapter of St Asaph in the late eighteenth and early nineteenth centuries shows that, excluding the appointments made by bishops of their relations, the vast majority of cathedral preferments, twenty-five out of thirty-two, went to clergy beneficed in the diocese, many of whom bore Welsh surnames; only seven were non-resident career pluralists beneficed in England.[41] A similar situation prevailed at St David's cathedral. Of the twenty members of the chapter in 1833 all but five were clergymen holding benefices in the diocese of St David's, or, in one case, no other preferment, and thirteen had Welsh surnames. Five members of the cathedral chapter were also prebendaries of the collegiate church at Brecon. Here a third of the twenty-one prebendaries held benefices in England and just over half had Welsh surnames.[42] The monopoly that Englishmen enjoyed in relation to episcopal appointments was certainly not replicated among the senior ranks of the other clergy in Wales.

One of the matters of greatest concern to Bishop Horsley was the question of unlicensed curates. In the Charge delivered shortly before his death in 1806, and published posthumously, he expressed serious concern at the number of these in the diocese and stated that it was 'a very high offence against ecclesiastical discipline; the continuance of which I think it necessary to declare, I shall not endure'. Each curate was ordered to appear before his rural dean 'and to exhibit to the said Rural Dean his letters of orders, a testimonium signed by three clergymen of his godly life and conversation, and his nomination to the cure by the incumbent of the living'. Licences would then be issued to all those whose papers were in order and no other person would be allowed to act as a curate in the diocese. Any unlicensed curate would be proceeded against in the ecclesiastical courts. If any non-resident incumbent refused to nominate a curate the bishop would exercise his powers to do so. No licence would be considered valid unless it specified the stipend to be paid to the curate, but Horsley was content to allow incumbents and curates to agree a mutually acceptable stipend between themselves.[43]

A survey of the diocese of St Asaph carried out in 1807 provides perhaps the best snapshot of the condition of any of the Welsh dioceses in the early nineteenth century.[44] The diocese comprised a total of thirteen rural deaneries, varying in size from one parish (Queenhope) to twenty-six parishes (Rhos). The smaller deaneries were grouped together so that the total number of rural deans was 8 rather than 13, and 6 of these had Welsh surnames. All were incumbents of parishes in the deaneries of which they were rural deans. The extent of pluralism and non-residence in the diocese was high. Partly this was a result of no fewer than thirteen benefices, excluding sinecure rectories, being attached to the bishopric or offices in the cathedral. The bishop, who was also the archdeacon, held no fewer than five of these and the dean held three. There were also, as Table 9.2 shows, many cases of clergy holding two benefices in the diocese, serving one personally and employing a curate in the other. Some of these benefices were adjacent to, and some at a considerable distance from, one another. It is, however, important to note that all had curates and that most curates had a reasonable stipend. In cases where this had been considered too low, as at Guilsfield, it was recorded that this was to be raised.

Table 9.2 Examples of pluralism in the diocese of St Asaph in 1807 showing parishes in which incumbents were resident and non-resident and the stipends paid to curates in the latter

Parish where resident	Parish where non-resident	Curate's stipend
Aberhafesp	Berriew	Not stated
Betws-yn-Rhos	Llanddulas	£50 + surplice fees
Castle Caereinion	Hirnant	£50
Cemmaes	Llanbrynmair	£52 10*s*. + house
Erbistock	Chirk	£75
Flint	Llanerfyl	£50 + surplice fees + house
Llanfyllin	Llangadfan	£50
Llanfynydd	Llansannan	£52 10*s*. + house
Meifod	Guilsfield	£40 including fees, to be increased to £60
Tywyn (Bangor diocese)	Mallwyd	£60 + house

There were a number of cases of one clergyman serving two adjacent parishes and in one case this figure rose to three, the perpetual curate of Eglwys-yn-Rhos acting as curate to the non-resident incumbents of Llangystennin and Llansantffraid Glan Conwy. The diocese comprised 119 parishes and chapelries, excluding those in Shropshire. In cases where the language of the services was recorded, fifty-nine churches had all their services in Welsh and eleven, mostly close to the English border, in English. Twelve churches had both English and Welsh services, the invariable rule being that if Morning Prayer was read in English then Evening Prayer was read in Welsh, the reverse being the case on alternate Sundays. At Gwaunysgor there were services on the mornings of most holy days, and at Llanrwst 'a Lecture was founded by Mr Maurice Wynne . . . on every Tues (being their Market Day) except Holy Days with a salary of £20 a year for the Lecturer who reads likewise the Prayers of the Day.' At Nercwys there was a benefaction for ten sermons or lectures each year. It was also noted that in this church

> the Com^{n} Table is in the Body of the Chancell and a seat for the Fam of Hendre is erected in ye place where it ought to stand by one Mr Wynne (an ancestor of the Fam) decd who removed it thence into the place where it now stands and (as it is said) obtained a Faculty from the Ecclal Court for that purpose.

Provision for education was generally good. Thirty-nine parishes had schools, there were two at Denbigh and three at Llanfyllin. At Ruabon '18 Boys are taught to read English, 6 of them are cloathed and maintained and are taught to write and arithmetic if found capable.' Four parishes had parochial libraries, that at Eglwys-yn-Rhos having been 'given by the Soc for promoting Christian Knowledge – several of the Books are missing.' At Llanuwchllyn there was 'A Presb Sch for teaching poor children to read and write endowed with £8 a year by one Williams a Dissenting Minister decd about the year 1730'. Sixty-three parishes had benefactions that provided money for the poor, 7 to provide bread, 4 to provide clothing, and 1 (Llanfyllin) to provide fuel. Nine parishes had endowed almshouses. To supplement more institutional provision, eight parishes had benefactions to teach children to read and, less often, to write, and one (Llanrhaeadr-ym-Mochnant) to provide apprenticeships. Two parishes also had benefactions for the repair of the church.

Although provision for education was already good, compared with that in some other dioceses, Bishop Cleaver was keen to increase it and was a strong supporter of the National

Society for Education established in 1811. Some of his clergy were less enthusiastic. In reply to a circular letter from the bishop in 1812, the rector of Machynlleth thought it would require a good deal of persuasion to prevent the dissenters, 'so numerous in this part of Wales', from objecting to the establishment of a National School in the town.[45] At Mold it was suggested that any 'effectual plan adopted in this neighbourhood for carrying into execution the designs of the National Society' should be achieved by expanding the existing school, but that the present master would support such a development.[46] Bishop Cleaver's successor, John Luxmoore, gave a greater priority to the establishment of Sunday schools and, in a series of undated additions to Cleaver's 'State of the Diocese', noted those parishes that established them. He also noted when Sunday schools had been established by either the Calvinistic or the Wesleyan Methodists, and that there were far more of those than Sunday schools associated with the Established Church.[47] When Thomas Vowler Short became bishop of St Asaph in 1846 there were some parishes in the diocese in which pastoral provision was still unsatisfactory. At Llanfynydd (Flintshire) a new church had been built and ecclesiastical district assigned in 1843, and a new schoolroom built in 1845, but 'there is no house attached to the incumbency, neither is there one in the whole District for a Clergyman to lodge. The want of a House near the Church and School is very severely felt.'[48] The endowment of the benefice, at £80 per annum, was also considered inadequate. Another poorly endowed benefice was Llanllugan (Montgomeryshire), with an annual income of only £86. Here the non-resident incumbent did not understand Welsh, spoken by all his parishioners, and the curate of an adjoining parish was paid £30 each year to conduct the services. The congregation seldom exceeded ten or twelve and the sacrament had not been administered for the last two years as there were no communicants.[49] Inquiries by the bishop elicited the response that 'Dissent is so strong in this Parish that it is difficult to muster a congregation. The church has been formerly well attended, but has been in late years almost deserted; there having been often only the Minister and Clerk.' A day school was held in church, but the parishioners objected to the use of the church catechism and most children were baptized by dissenting ministers. There was a Baptist chapel near the church where the minister preached against infant baptism. The dissenters had tried to set up a British School in the parish but had failed. A National School was clearly much needed, but there were no funds for this or even for repairs to the church, which was in poor condition. The curate, who also served Llanfair Caereinion, did so without a licence, for which he craved the bishop's pardon. He was 'now in the 68th year of my age . . . I dread the thought of destitution.'[50] Here was a real-life version of the clerical hero of Trollope's *Last Chronicle of Barset*, Josiah Crawley, perpetual curate of Hogglestock.

There were, however, other parishes in the diocese in which much progress was made during the early nineteenth century. At Welshpool, where William Clive (1795–1883)[51] was vicar from 1819, a new parsonage house was built and church accommodation was increased by 300 free sittings in 1825–6 by adding two new galleries. In 1839–44 a new place of worship, Christ Church, was erected as a chapel-of-ease at a cost of £6,000, £5,000 of which was raised by subscription. Clive himself gave £200 and the font, Dean Luxmoore of St Asaph paid for the paving of the chancel and the Clive family of Powis Castle gave £700. National Schools for boys and girls were established in 1821 and a public dispensary opened in 1827. Clive also founded a clerical association for clergy in the vicinity of Welshpool.[52] In the parish of Llandrinio the chapelry of Penrhos was made a separate incumbency in 1841. The single Sunday service at twelve noon in 1780 had become two services, at 10.30 a.m. and 3.30 p.m. by 1845. The old chapel-of-ease was replaced by a new parish church at a cost of £1,070, with the Diocesan Church Building Society and the Incorporated Church Building Society contributing £150 and £100 respectively. The incumbents of the neighbouring parishes agreed to a reduction of their incomes from tithes to create an annual stipend of £131 for the new incumbent, and in 1850 a parsonage house was completed at a cost of £1,006.[53] Charles Luxmoore, vicar of Guilsfield, was noted as 'an exemplary parson, who was resident in his parish and performed double duty there each Sunday'. In 1823 he rebuilt the vicarage at a cost of £1,874 with some assistance from Queen Anne's Bounty. There was also double duty at Manafon on Sundays and festivals, the services alternating between Welsh and English. The rectory, built in 1795 at a cost of £286. 5*s*. 10*d*., was partly rebuilt in 1849.[54]

Diocese of St David's

As is the case with the diocese of Bangor, that of St David's is also well documented and has been the subject of some detailed research in recent years. Its bishops included two of the most notable ecclesiastical reformers of the late eighteenth and early nineteenth centuries, Samuel Horsley (1788–93) and Thomas Burgess (1803–25). Horsley personally examined his ordination candidates, maintained a strict discipline over clerical appointments, issued instructions for the proper observance of holy days and encouraged the holding of monthly celebrations of Holy Communion.[55] Burgess was a major innovator. In 1804 he established a 'Society for Promoting Christian Knowledge and Church Union in the Diocese of St David's' with five primary objectives: to distribute bibles, prayer books and religious tracts, in both English and Welsh; to establish libraries for the use of the clergy; to enable ordinands to obtain a decent education; to establish schools for the education of the poor; and to promote the setting up of Sunday schools. He also encouraged his rural deans to form clerical societies in their deaneries 'to organize Sunday schools, to promote theological study, and to support each other in their clerical work', in essence precursors of the ruridecanal conference established in some English dioceses before 1850.[56] Both Horsley and Burgess were strong disciplinarians, taking action against clergy at Gwenddwr and Llanfihangel Nant Bran (Breconshire) for neglect of duty. The churchwardens, overseers and principal inhabitants of Gwenddwr petitioned Bishop Horsley in 1789, claiming that the accusations of neglect against their curate were unjust. His failure to conduct one Sunday service was because he thought someone else was conducting it for him, but the person who had agreed to substitute for him had forgotten that it was the same day that he was to take possession of the vicarage of Glascwm (Radnorshire). He had failed to conduct a wedding because the couple to be married kept changing their minds about the date. He did not reside in the parish because he could not find lodgings that he could afford and was therefore obliged 'to reside in his father's house at Llanwrtyd' about seven or eight miles away. The petitioners noted that his stipend was only £15 per annum and asked 'who can support himself with lodging, meat, cloathes and many other necessaries &c. suiting and becoming a Clergyman with so little a sum?'[57] The curate at Llanfihangel Nant Bran offered a similar defence to Bishop Burgess in 1824 on a charge of failing to read the Sunday service there: the 'Vicar of Merthyr Cynog faithfully promised to do the duty at Llanfihangel for me at the appointed hour but I understand afterwards that he did not attend til seven in the Evening.'[58]

Burgess's most important legacy to the Welsh Church was, however, the establishment of St David's College at Lampeter. Whereas the dioceses of Bangor and St Asaph experienced little difficulty in attracting graduate clergy, there were problems in those of Llandaff and St David's, especially the latter. This problem was caused by the wide disparity between the northern and southern dioceses in respect of benefice incomes. In 1829–31 these averaged £271 in the diocese of St Asaph and £252 in that of Bangor, compared with £177 in the diocese of Llandaff and £137 in that of St David's. In St David's diocese the average curate's stipend was as low as £55 per annum. Out of 762 men ordained in the diocese in the late eighteenth century only 45 were graduates; 37 had matriculated at a university without taking a degree; 680 had never attended a university.[59] The paucity of grammar schools within the diocese had meant that local men seeking ordination had been mostly educated by private schoolmasters, many of whom were dissenting ministers, or at one of the dissenting academies. Even some of the senior clergy were non-graduates. Thomas Beynon, archdeacon of Cardigan 1814–33, was educated at the dissenting academy at Carmarthen and ordained to the curacy of Cathedine (Breconshire) in 1768. He acted as estate agent to the Vaughans of Golden Grove, who secured his preferment to the Carmarthenshire livings of Llanfihangel Aberbythych, Llanfihangel Cilfargen and Llandyfeisant (1770–1833), Llanedi (1782–6) and Penboyr (1784–1833); he was also rural dean of Emlyn and, from 1796, prebendary of

Brecon, financing the rebuilding of churches in his parishes, contributing to the foundation of the college at Lampeter, and acting as patron of antiquarian societies and eisteddfodau.[60] Bishop Horsley insisted that in future all candidates for ordination must have been to a 'reputable public school' and provided them with lists of books on which he would 'examine the candidates for Orders, and in which I shall expect to find them expert'. Unfortunately the chief result of this policy was a drop in the number of ordinands, from 25 a year in the period 1750–87 to 6 in the period 1788–1800, rising to 8 in the period 1801–25. Burgess stipulated that he would only ordain non-graduates who had studied divinity at one of nine licensed grammar schools in the diocese: Brecon, Cardigan, Carmarthen, Haverfordwest, Lampeter, Rhayader, St David's, Whitton (Radnorshire) and Ystrad Meurig (Cardiganshire).[61] The bishops of Llandaff made similar use of the grammar schools at Cowbridge and Usk.[62]

Burgess first announced his intention of founding a college for the training of ordinands in 1804, and by the end of the year over £1,000 had been raised. By 1806 he had decided that the college would be established at Llanddewibrefi (Cardiganshire), and in 1809 W. J. Rees, rector of Cascob (Radnorshire), was invited to become the first principal. However, progress was slow. By 1820 only £13,000 had been collected and the offer of a site in Lampeter, a few miles further south, persuaded Burgess to locate the college there. The foundation stone was laid in 1822 and the first students were admitted in 1827. The total cost was £22,000 of which £5,000 was contributed by Lord Liverpool's government, and the patronage of six benefices was transferred to the new college to provide an income for the staff, who were to hold these benefices whilst carrying out their teaching duties. By that time Rees was considered too old to become the first principal, but his twenty-two-year-old nephew Rice Rees was appointed the first Professor of Welsh. Llewelyn Lewellin became the first principal and Professor of Greek and Theology, later becoming also vicar of Lampeter as well as prebendary and dean of St David's, and holding all these offices in plurality until his death in 1878. The future bishop of Llandaff, Alfred Ollivant, as vice-principal and Professor of Hebrew and Theology, was the third academic member of staff. A Professor of Latin was appointed in 1839. sixty-four students were admitted in the first year, of whom all except two came from St David's diocese; 59 had previously attended grammar schools in the diocese and 36 were the sons of farmers. Despite the fact that Bishop Jenkinson had made it clear in his 1828 Charge that 'the Principality of Wales can now boast an establishment which offers to the students many of the peculiar advantages of the academic discipline', and

> conceiving it to be my duty to encourage, by every means in my power, an institution so well adapted to place the Church in this Diocese on a more respectable footing . . . I shall in future look exclusively to St David's College, and to our Universities for a supply of candidates

for ordination, the number of admissions in subsequent years was much lower, varying from a high of thirty-one in 1838 to a low of eight in 1850.[63]

Although the bishops were English, most of the other influential clergy in the diocese of St David's during the late eighteenth and early nineteenth centuries were Welsh. They included Thomas Beynon, noted above, and two other archdeacons of Cardigan, Thomas Vincent and John Williams, and three archdeacons of Carmarthen: Benjamin Millingchamp, H. T. Payne and Richard Venables. Vincent, a member of a Welsh landed family, was archdeacon of Cardigan from 1770 until his death in 1798. Williams was the son of the headmaster of Ystrad Meurig grammar school. He became vicar of Lampeter in 1820 and would have been (rather than Llewelyn Lewellin) the first principal of the college there had he not in 1824 accepted the rectorship of Edinburgh Academy. Despite this preferment he retained the vicarage of Lampeter until 1833, when he became archdeacon of Cardigan. He moved back to Wales in 1847 to become the first warden of Llandovery College, resigning this post and his archdeaconry on the grounds of ill health in 1853. Benjamin Millingchamp was also educated at Ystrad Meurig grammar school, serving as a chaplain to the navy and in India before settling at Plas Llangoedmor (Cardiganshire) in 1798; he was briefly archdeacon of Carmarthen in 1827–9, and his collection of oriental manuscripts is now in the National Library of Wales.[64] His successor, H. T. Payne, was the son of the rector of Llangattock (Breconshire) and educated at Worcester and Balliol Colleges, Oxford. He was ordained to the curacy of Llanelli (Breconshire) in 1784 and instituted to the rectory of Llanbedr Ystrad Yw and Patricio (Breconshire) in 1793. From 1799 he was also vicar of Defynnog (Breconshire) and prebendary of St David's Cathedral. Payne was one of the leading antiquaries in the diocese and a patron of eisteddfodau, his achievements being recognized by his brief tenure of the archdeaconry of Carmarthen in 1829–32.[65] Richard Venables, archdeacon of Carmarthen 1832–58, was another member of a Welsh landed family, vicar of Nantmel (Radnorshire) and chairman of Radnorshire quarter sessions for twenty-five years.[66]

The vacancy in the see of St David's in 1840 was the first occasion on which there was considerable agitation for the appointment of a Welsh-born and Welsh-speaking bishop, though there were no very obvious candidates.[67] The new bishop, Connop Thirlwall, recognising the sensitivity of his appointment, learned Welsh sufficiently well to be able to preach in the language, though his proficiency was later exaggerated. Thirlwall has been seen as the first of the 'modern' bishops in Wales, joined at St Asaph by T. V. Short in 1846 and at Llandaff by Alfred Ollivant in 1849, and contrasted somewhat unfairly with his contemporaries at the time of his appointment. Whilst he was undoubtedly an energetic bishop, overseeing the building of fifteen new churches and the restoration of forty others during the first decade of his long episcopate, his cold intellectualism made it difficult for him to relate to his clergy. He did, however, insist on Welsh-speaking clergy being appointed to Welsh-speaking parishes, and argued strongly for bilingual education at a time when some were seeking to promote the use of English over that of Welsh. He also set up a fund for the augmentation of the many poor livings in the diocese, contributing annually the surplus from his own income. His contempt for many of his own clergy, however, remains the stuff of legend; they included two of his archdeacons, Richard Davies of Brecon and John Williams of Cardigan.[68] These were the men who had attempted to block, and certainly succeeded in delaying, Llewelyn Lewellin's installation as precentor of St David's in 1840.[69] Davies was described at the time as 'somewhat more than eccentric, I might almost say deranged' for his failure to deal with important administrative matters when he was the canon in residence.[70] Williams finally confirmed Thirlwall's low opinion of him by unsuccessfully canvassing for the vacant bishopric of Llandaff in 1849.[71] Thirlwall's attitudes were reflected in the nature of his visitation Charges; whereas those of many bishops tended to deal with practical issues relating specifically to the diocese, and problems that had been highlighted by the replies to the visitation queries, Thirlwall's were highly academic in tone and concentrated heavily on giving his opinion on matters of contemporary politics and theological debate. His 1845 Charge did, however, draw attention to the large number of parishes in the diocese which had abandoned 'the practice of collecting at the offertory', a practice he wished to see restored.[72]

A particularly valuable snapshot of one corner of the diocese of St David's is provided by the manuscript of 'A Parochial Visitation of the Deanery of the Third Part of Brecon . . . by Henry Thomas Payne, Rural Dean of that District', which covers the years 1785–7.[73] This substantial volume includes detailed descriptions of the topography and antiquities of the parishes in the rural deanery as well as comments on the fabrics of the churches and parsonage houses, the church services, parochial charities and other matters. At Llanelli

> the Floor was very slovenly, uneven and Ill-paved, the seats irregular and crowding upon the Isles; the Reading Desk shabbily patch'd up with Old Ends of rough Boards had more the appearance of a Toll Gatherer's Stall, in a small Market Town, than what ought to be, the Principal Seat in the Temple of God, and besides was so encroached upon, by a Neighbouring Pew, as to leave very scanty Room for the officiating Clergyman; and the Roof for the most part unceiled, and wholly out of repair.[74]

At Llangatwg 'the communion table is an old crazy Piece of Furniture, which ought to give place to a new one; the carpet of Blue Cloth, which covers it is new, but rather too scanty.'[75] At

Crickhowell, though 'the Body of the Church is decently ciel'd and paved and the seating tolerably regular . . . the Surplice is a very wretched one, and the Books of Service, both in Welsh and English, are very much out of repair.'[76] At Llangynidr some improvements had been made between Payne's visits in 1785 and 1787:

> At my first Visitation . . . the inside of the Church wore a very indecent Appearance; every corner almost being crowded with rubbish, and the Windows very foul, and in many places broken. This matter has since (though very imperfectly) been remedied. The Church Wardens still promise a further attendance to it.[77]

There were 'filthy heaps of rubbish crowded into every corner' at Llanfihangel Cwmdu,[78] and at Llanywern 'the Communion Table is very poor, and is cover'd with a shabby old carpet of blue cloth';[79] at Llanhamlach 'the South Isle is neither ciel'd nor paved and does not appear to have been ever used', but an application to demolish it had been refused.[80] By contrast the church at Talgarth 'is far more decently kept, and in better repair, than any other within the Deanery. It is well ceiled, seated and paved . . . The Communion Table is provided with a Handsome Carpet';[81] and at Llandyfaelog Tre'r Graig the church was 'neatly ceiled and decently paved and seated, the Reading Desk and Pulpit together with the Communion Table are ornamented with handsome cushions and coverlids of crimson Damask'.[82]

The condition of some parsonage houses also left a lot to be desired. At Llanbedr Ystrad Yw it 'consists of only one small Room, with a closet',[83] at Llanfihangel Talyllyn it was 'a wretched Cottage',[84] and at Llangynidr it was 'tolerably roomy but inconvenient . . . The present Rector upon his coming upon the Living, found the whole of the Premises in shamefully dilapidated State but he assures me that it is his intention to put the whole into decent tenantable condition with all convenient speed.'[85] However, at Talgarth the vicarage was 'small but in good habitable repair',[86] at Llanfilo the rectory was 'decent and habitable',[87] and at Llanhamlach it was 'roomy, but . . . it seems to be in habitable repair'.[88]

Church services, even in this eastern part of the diocese, were still mostly in Welsh though, compared with the parishes in the archdeaconries of Cardigan and Carmarthen, there were very few celebrations of Holy Communion. Four, or sometimes three, times a year was the norm even in an urban parish like Crickhowell. At Talgarth there were quarterly communion services 'at the publick Charge of the Parish: but at the Desire of the Family of Trevecka, and at their private expence, on the first Sunday in every Month'.[89] At Llangatwg 'the services on Saints Days can not be kept up, so regularly as the Rubric directs, owing to the Backwardness of the country people, in quitting their Rural Occupations for the sake of Religion'. There was only a quarterly communion service, but two celebrations on Easter Sunday 'early in the morning in Welsh . . . and again at Eleven o'clock, in English'. The traditional service of *Plygain*, early on Christmas Day, had been discontinued by the present rector 'as Devotion seemed to have the last share in the Business and many Irregularities were committed by the Young People assembled together'.[90] The *Plygain* service was, however, still observed at Crickhowell, Llanbedr Ystrad Yw and Llangynidr.[91] There was at this date little challenge from dissent. Even at Crickhowell 'there are no establish'd Dissenting Meeting Houses of any Denomination in this Parish, but I am inform'd that Methodistical Societies occasionally meet in some private houses.'[92] There was also a fear that, though there was no meeting house in the parish of Llanfilo, 'it is to be feared that its proximity to Trevecka has mislead [*sic*] several of the inhabitants' into support for the Calvinistic Methodists.[93]

One of the most noticeable features of the state of religion in Payne's rural deanery is the lack of parochial charities. Even in an important market town like Crickhowell, 'there are no public schools, hospitals, or other Donations, either to the Poor, or for other Uses'.[94] At Llanelli

> a little Day School is occasionally open'd by permission of the Rector, where reading is taught by an Old Person for a livelihood; some few Benefactions have been given by well disposed Persons, for Charitable Purposes; on a Painted Board in the chancel is recorded the following account of a

> Benefaction given for the preaching of six Welsh Sermons annually on catechetical subjects.[95]

At Llangatwg 'the parish clerk, by permission, teaches a little Twopenny School for the poor children',[96] and at Llanbedr Ystrad Yw there was a benefaction of £5 per annum for the education of poor girls 'who are to be instructed in Reading, Writing and sewing Plainwork', and one of £2. 10*s*. 0*d*. for the same purpose in the chapelry of Patricio. A further sum of £1. 10*s*. 0*d*. was

> to be laid out in the Purchase of Books, vizt a Bible, a Book of Common Prayer, and the Whole Duty of Man, to be given to each of the Girls educated in the above school at the age of Fifteen provided she shall then be capable of Reading.

If no books were required in a particular year this sum was to be distributed 'among such Poor Aged Widows, as receive no Relief from the Parish'.[97] At a slightly later date a group of parishes in this rural deanery, in the patronage of the Duke of Beaufort, manifested a particularly glaring example of non-resident pluralism. The parishes of Crickhowell, Llanelli, Llanfihangel Cwmdu, Llangatwg and Llangenni were all held by the fifth duke's son, Lord George Henry Somerset, who combined them with the incumbency of Tormarton (Gloucestershire) and a prebend at Bristol Cathedral. His combined emoluments were £2,818 per annum out of which he paid curates' stipends of £356. It was particularly unfortunate that some of these parishes were ones in which there was a rapidly expanding population and where, in the case of Llangatwg, the parish church was five miles distant from the main centre of population and separated from it by 'a large and extensive tract of mountain and wild uninhabited country'.[98] Another example of high-handed patronage occurred at Llanywern. In a letter dated 25 January 1814 Thomas Lewis described himself as 'the oldest curate in the deanery of Brecon, aged 78 years'. For fifty-three years he had served the neighbouring parishes of Llanfihangel Talyllyn, at a stipend of £30 per annum, and Llanywern, where the annual stipend was £25. He was now being deprived of the latter curacy by the non-resident incumbent, and appealed to Bishop Burgess to overrule this decision as it would deprive him of nearly half his income. He stated that he had 'to support myself, my son who is nearly blind, and his two children'.[99] This was at about the same time that Thomas Beynon was reporting to Burgess, in a letter dated 4 January 1813, that 'when I was at Carmarthen last week I was informed that the Rector of Bangor [Teifi] in Cardiganshire had almost drank himself to death, and was not likely to live many months'. This parish, clearly one of the more desirable in the diocese, was described as 'a well-conditioned Rectory of about 200£ *per annum*. There is a Parsonage house and a very good Glebe worth about 70£ a year and the Tythes are about 130£ and annually improving.'[100]

Similar problems to those in south-east Breconshire were manifested, in another part of the vast diocese of St David's, in the Swansea Valley, where there was also a population explosion in the second quarter of the nineteenth century. A new district church was built at Gorseinon in 1839 at the whole cost of J. D. Llewelyn of Penllergaer and it provided some 190 free sittings. In order to provide additional places of worship before new churches could be completed, Bishop Thirlwall authorized the licensing of temporary buildings, as at Clydach where, before the opening of the new district church in 1847, services had been held in the National School.[101] In other parts of the diocese, except Aberystwyth, Carmarthen and Llanelli, where new district churches were built in the 1830s or 1840s, church accommodation was generally adequate, though some were inconveniently situated, as at Llandingad and Llanfair-ar-y-bryn (Carmarthenshire), where both churches were on the outskirts of the market town of Llandovery, well located for that community but remote from many farmsteads and hamlets in the rural parts of both parishes.[102] Before the new district church was built at Aberystwyth the existing parish church could only accommodate 294 people in a parish of 4,128 inhabitants. There were also shortages of schools in some areas. In Cardiganshire schools had been established at Llanfihangel-y-Creuddyn in 1796, Llanrhystud in 1806 and Llanfihangel Gerau'r Glyn in *c*1808. At Aberystwyth and Llanbadarnfawr new schools established in 1813 received grants from the recently formed National Society in 1818. Sixteen National Society schools had been established in the county by 1836 but, in 1847, twenty-two out of sixty-four parishes still had no day school of any sort.[103] The school situation was patchy in Pembrokeshire with schools in seven out of eighteen parishes in the rural deanery of Dungleddy in 1811, but only one in the rural deanery of Castlemartin, and none at all in the rural deaneries of Narberth and Emlyn (the latter including some parishes in the neighbouring counties). Benefactions were left for schools at Amroth, Norton and Roch in the late eighteenth century, and Lord Cawdor paid the salaries of schoolmasters at Stackpole and St Petrox in the early nineteenth century. Positive developments included the introduction of a fortnightly service of preparation for receiving the sacrament at Bletherston and the employment of 'singing masters' to teach psalmody to the congregations at Carew and Gumfreston.[104] Problems with parsonage houses were not infrequent. On 13 February 1824 David Jones, vicar of Castlemartin, petitioned Bishop Burgess for a licence of non-residence on the grounds that his vicarage, 'being a mere Cottage is wholly unfit for residence. He performs the whole duty of the Parish himself and resides at the Parsonage house of Pwllcrochan a few miles distant from his benefice.'[105] The parsonage house at Kerry (Montgomeryshire) was described as 'much decayed . . . and upon the whole dangerous to be inhabited'. A new house was paid for by selling the surplus timber on Kerry glebe valued at £90, and the specification stated that it had to be completed by 1 May 1811.[106] About twenty years earlier the rural dean of Pembroke had painted the most appalling picture of parsonage houses in his deanery and the problems that this caused in relation to residence, though this was to some extent offset by the improved condition of church buildings. In an undated letter to Bishop Horsley he wrote:

> The state of the Churches in my District is now become so decent and in tolerable order, that it is unnecessary for me to trouble your Lordship with particulars; I wish I had as good an account to give of many of the vicarage Houses: that of Nangle stands in the most deplorable condition; next to it

> Mannerbier; St Twinnels, and the Vicarage of Stackpole want thorough repairs. I have made repeated application to the vicars on this subject, to no purpose. I have 22 parishes in my district, six resident clergy only, I believe are at present to be found in the whole . . . Could the number of resident Clergy be encreased, and a better arrangement of curacies if possible be enforced, i.e. that 2 neighbouring Churches should be served by the same officiating Minister; these are the measures which most immediately occur as likely to promote the important ends which engage your Lordship's attention.[107]

An interesting survival, noted by Bishop Thirlwall in 1843, was the practice at Kerry (Montgomeryshire) whereby it was the custom for the sexton 'to perambulate the church during service time, with a bell in his hand, to look carefully into every pew, and whenever he finds anyone dozing to ring the bell'. Thirlwall commented that the danger of being discovered 'is almost always sufficient to keep every one on the alert'.[108]

Two Archdeaconry Case Studies: Anglesey and Carmarthen

These two case studies are based on the extensive surviving visitation records of the dioceses of Bangor and St David's. Three sets of visitation evidence have been examined for the archdeaconry of Anglesey, which was coterminous with the island county, for the years 1801, 1814 and 1837, and four for the archdeaconry of Carmarthen, for the years 1799, 1814, 1828 and 1842;[109] the latter archdeaconry comprised a mix of urban and rural, and some heavily industrialized, parishes in Carmarthenshire (excluding its north-western corner), the Gower deanery in west Glamorgan and south-east Pembrokeshire. Both archdeaconries were predominantly, but not exclusively, Welsh-speaking. A comparison of the evidence from the returns for the respective archdeaconries at about the same time, 1813–14, illustrated in Table 9.3, shows both similarities in respect of Sunday duty and significant differences in relation to clerical residence and the frequency of communion services, despite the presence of reforming bishops in both dioceses over the previous thirty years. As far as the residence of the clergy is concerned, the detailed statistics of which are shown in Tables

9.4 and 9.5, the differences between the two archdeaconries can be accounted for by the fact that, whereas in the archdeaconry of Carmarthen, few clergy served more than two churches, in the archdeaconry of Anglesey the far greater density of churches to population, with many churches being situated within a mile of each other, meant that there were several cases of three, four or even five churches being served by the same clergyman.

Table 9.3 Comparison of visitation evidence for the archdeaconries of Anglesey and Carmarthen in 1813/14

Parishes with	Anglesey 1814 (%)	Carmarthen 1813 (%)
Resident incumbents	7.9	37.2
Resident curates	21.1	23.4
Non-resident clergy	71.0	39.4
Double Sunday duty	10.5	7.4
Single Sunday duty	69.8	88.3
Less than single duty	19.7	4.3
Monthly communion	10.5	73.5
Quarterly communion	80.3	19.1
Less than quarterly communion	9.2	7.4

Table 9.4 Proportion of resident and non-resident clergy in the archdeaconry of Anglesey, 1801–37

Parishes with	1801	1814	1837
Resident incumbents	7	6	12
Resident curates	14	16	17
Non-resident clergy	51	54	47
Total returns	72	76	76

Table 9.5 Proportion of resident and non-resident clergy in the archdeaconry of Carmarthen, 1799–1842

Parishes with	1799	1813	1828	1842
Resident incumbents	38	35	39	52
Resident curates	25	22	23	14
Non-resident clergy	36	37	41	32
Total returns	99	94	103	98

As elsewhere in England and Wales, a common reason for clerical non-residence was the lack of a parsonage house, with clergy being forced to serve their churches from the nearest suitable house that they could acquire. Sometimes this was in one of the parishes they served but it might well be in an adjacent one. The tendency of clergy to congregate in towns, noted in respect of Norfolk in the eighteenth century,[110] was replicated in both archdeaconries, with a number of clergy serving adjacent parishes living in Beaumaris, Carmarthen, Llandeilo, St Clears and Swansea. Some parsonage houses were clearly very inadequate, but the clergy still lived in them. The rector of Trewalchmai and Heneglwys (Anglesey) noted in 1801 that even though 'the Parsonage House is a small cottage thatched with straw' he was 'but seldom abroad'. The one case of scandalous neglect in Anglesey in 1801 was at Rhoscolyn where the rector was 'not to be found and no return made'. As a result the parsonage house had been allowed to fall into a considerable state of disrepair. In 1803 Bishop Cleaver was told that several carpenters had been approached to undertake repairs to the building but that none would do so 'on account of the distance, it being in a remote part of the Island'. The officiating minister, the rector by then being in a poor state of health which had been confirmed by an apothecary's note, was advised to put the house into repair himself, but was promised that the bishop's officials would ensure that he was reimbursed for the expense.[111] A record of the licences for non-residence granted by Bishop Majendie of Bangor in 1812–14 confirmed that fifteen of these had been granted because there was no parsonage house, five on the grounds that the house was currently unfit for residence, and only three on account of the poor health of the incumbent or a member of his family.[112] In 1801 two Anglesey rectors gave ill health as the reason for their non-residence. At Llanfechell and Llanbadrig he had been 'non-resident for several years back on account of constant ill-health in his family'. At Llanrhuddlad the rector stated: 'I reside frequently in the Glebe House, the remainder of my time at Holyhead about 12 miles from hence, where Dr Warren allowed me to go on acc[t] of my health in the year 1795.'

Although reforming bishops were keen to encourage the clergy to perform double rather than single duty, that is two services rather than one each Sunday, the change proved virtually impossible to introduce, especially when clergy were serving two or more churches. Some clergy in Anglesey who had heeded Bishop Majendie's call for double duty told him in 1814 that they had been forced to abandon an afternoon or evening service as they could not get their parishioners to attend both in the morning and later in the day. Thus, as Tables 9.6 and 9.7 show, single duty remained the norm in both archdeaconries throughout the first four decades of the nineteenth century, with even fewer services at a small number of isolated churches in sparsely populated parishes. Nevertheless, where clergy were serving several small neighbouring parishes, they could be extremely busy on a Sunday. In 1801 the clergyman who served the Anglesey parishes of Llechgynfarwy, Rhodogeidio, Llantrisant and Llanfair Gweredog gave a detailed description, with accompanying map, to show the distances he had to travel to conduct services at his four churches. Even though the parsonage house was 'in sufficient repair' he found it more convenient to be non-resident, living instead in a house in the small market town of Llanerchymedd, from which he could most easily reach all his churches. He had a service without a sermon at 8 a.m. once a month at both Rhodogeidio and Llanfair Gweredog, which were, respectively, three-quarters of a mile and one and a half miles from Llanerchymedd. At 9 a.m. he had a service with a sermon every Sunday at Llechgynfarwy, which was 2½ miles from Llanerchymedd, 3 miles from Llanfair Gweredog and 3¼ miles from Rhodogeidio, and at 11 a.m. he had a service with a sermon every Sunday at Llantrisant; this was two miles from Llechgynfarwy with a three-mile journey back to his house in Llanerchymedd. Once a month he had an afternoon service at Rhodygeidio, a 1½-mile round trip from Llanerchymedd, and occasionally afternoon services at Llechgynfarwy, a five-mile round trip, or Llantrisant, a six-mile round trip. Every Sunday he travelled at least 7½ miles and on some he might travel up to 12 miles in the morning and a further 6 miles in the afternoon. Apart from the towns and a few of the large villages, very few churches had regular weekday services. At Llanbabo (Anglesey) in 1801 it was noted that 'it is not customary to read prayers here on week days, excepting one day in y[e] week during Lent'.

Table 9.6 Frequency of Sunday services in the archdeaconry of Anglesey, 1801–1837

Parishes with	1801	1814	1837
Three Sunday services	1	1	1
Two Sunday services	20	7	6
One Sunday service*	35	53	59
Fortnightly service	12	11	7
Monthly service	4	2	1
No services	0	2	2

* Includes parishes that had two services on some Sundays.

Table 9.7 Frequency of Sunday services in the archdeaconry of Carmarthen, 1799–1842

Parishes with	1799	1813	1828	1842
Four Sunday services	0	0	1	1
Three Sunday services	1	1	0	1
Two Sunday services	10	6	10	17
One Sunday service*	84	83	88	76
Fortnightly service	4	4	4	3

* Includes parishes that had two services on some Sundays.

The tradition of regular catechizing, usually after the second lesson at Evening Prayer, had been abandoned at many churches by the early nineteenth century. The curate of Llandegfan (Anglesey) stated in 1801: 'I have frequently given notice in Church that I wished to catechise the Children. But parents seldom send them, except before Confirmation when I expound it to them.' In the western Anglesey parish of Llanfaethlu, where the rector had similar difficulties in persuading parents to send their children to be catechized, 'the children have been taught their catechism in a Welsh Charity school in this neighbourhood, and have been frequently examined in Church in the presence of the Congregation.' As more and more parishes began to establish Sunday schools, from about 1820, catechizing tended to be transferred from the church service to the Sunday school, and this is noted in several parishes in the archdeaconry of Carmarthen in both 1828 and 1842. Another trend in the early nineteenth century was an increase in the amount of music in the services. Bishop Majendie of Bangor was an advocate of psalmody, and his successor, Christopher Bethell, noted in 1837 those Anglesey churches that had regular singing and those, about a fifth of the total, that had no singing at all. Evangelicals within the Established Church also favoured the introduction of hymns into the service, but many High Church traditionalists were hostile to this innovation as it was not specifically sanctioned in the Book of Common Prayer. The popularity of hymn-singing among the Methodists however, influenced many clergy to abandon their hostility and, in response to a question by Bishop Thirlwall in 1842, it appeared that about a third of the churches in the archdeaconry of Carmarthen were now using hymns in their services.

The most noticeable difference in the service patterns of churches in the archdeaconries of Anglesey and Carmarthen was that in relation to the frequency of communion services. As Tables 9.8 and 9.9 show, whereas in the archdeaconry of Anglesey the English pattern of quarterly communion in the rural parishes, with monthly celebrations in the towns and large villages, was generally observed, in the archdeaconry of Carmarthen monthly celebration was the norm, as it was also in the archdeaconry of Cardigan. The attempt that has been

Table 9.8 Frequency of Holy Communion in the archdeaconry of Anglesey, 1801–37

Parishes with	1801	1814	1837
Monthly communion*	10	8	3
Quarterly communion†	55	61	63
HC on greater festivals	4	3	6
HC at Easter	0	0	2
No Communion	3	4	2

* Includes some parishes that had more than twelve celebrations a year.
† Includes some parishes that had more than four but no more than nine celebrations a year, including several at Easter.

Table 9.9 Frequency of Holy Communion in the archdeaconry of Carmarthen, 1799–1842

Parishes with	1799	1813	1828	1842
Monthly communion*	69	69	76	80
Quarterly communion†	21	18	19	14
HC on greater festivals	5	4	2	0
HC at Easter	1	1	1	0
No Communion	3	2	5	4

* Includes some parishes that had more than twelve celebrations a year.
† Includes some parishes that had more than four but no more than eight celebrations a year.

made to link frequency of communion with the language of the services, with monthly communion being more common in Welsh- than English-speaking parishes,[113] may be an oversimplification. An analysis of the returns for the archdeaconry of Carmarthen shows that it was as much geography as language that produced the difference in the frequency of communion services. Parishes that did not have monthly communion were confined to three specific areas of the archdeaconry: the rural deanery of Gower, which was predominantly English-speaking; north-eastern Carmarthenshire in a triangle bounded by the market towns of Lampeter, Llandeilo and

Llandovery, where all the parishes were Welsh-speaking; and a few parishes in south-west Carmarthenshire in the vicinity of Laugharne and St Clears, some of which were English- and some Welsh-speaking. One point that is worth making is that many parishes, whether they had monthly or quarterly communion, frequently held several celebrations during the Easter period, to ensure that all who wanted to were able to make their communion at the time that the maximum number of communicants had traditionally been recorded. At Tywyn (Merioneth) in the 1830s there were celebrations on Good Friday, Easter Eve, at both 9 a.m. and 11 a.m. on Easter Day, and on the Sunday after Easter.[114] An analysis of the number of communicants, and in the case of the Carmarthen archdeaconry church attendance as well, shows the impact of Calvinistic Methodism, and the growth of older branches of dissent, on the Established Church. In the archdeaconry of Carmarthen, where Methodist activity was well under way by the second half of the eighteenth century, the major decline in congregations and communicants seems to have taken place before 1800. Whereas a few parishes continued to show a further decline after 1800, as many showed an increase in both attendances and communicants in the early nineteenth century, and the vast majority showed little change over a forty-year period. By contrast, in Anglesey, where the impact of Calvinistic Methodism was much later, the decline in the number of communicants over the first three decades of the nineteenth century was, as Table 9.10 shows, quite catastrophic in some parishes. The Carmarthen statistics do call into question the general assumption that, at least in parts of south Wales, the 1851 religious census marks the absolute nadir in the fortunes of the Established Church, and suggest that perhaps this point had been reached half a century earlier.

Bishop Bethell, at his 1837 visitation of Anglesey, made detailed notes on the fabric and furnishings of the churches in the archdeaconry. One of these, at Llanfigael, was so dilapidated that no services were held there, and indeed none had been since 1803. The church was eventually repaired by about 1840 and still retains the furnishings installed at that time.[115] No other churches were in such poor condition, but Llanallgo

Table 9.10 Decline in average numbers of communicants in selected Anglesey parishes, 1801–37

Parish	1801	1814	1837
Bodwrog	40	30	8
Llanbeulan	45	30	8
Llanddanielfab	50	30	16
Llanddona	40	35	19
Llandrygarn	50	45	12
Llanedwen	40	30	28
Llanfachreth	20	14	10
Llanfaelog	55	50	12
Llanfihangel Tynsylwy	16	12	5
Llanfwrog	23	9	8
Llangaffo	30	25	13
Llangeinwen	35	23	11
Llangwyfan	55	12	5
Llansadwrn	18	14	12
Llanynghenedl	30	15	9

Note: Llansadwrn was the only parish with a monthly communion service, and the figures given are those for attendances at these services; there were 120 Easter communicants in 1801 and ninety in 1814; no figure is noted in Bishop Bethell's notebook for 1837.

was in serious need of overall repair, and at Llanfwrog 'the whole interior [was] in a wretched state.' The windows needed mending at Penmon and the roofs were out of repair at Heneglwys, Llanddeusant, Llandrygarn, Llanerchymedd and Llanfairpwllgwyngyll. At Cerrig Ceinwen the floor needed repair. The benches and seats were in poor condition at Aberffraw and Llaneugrad, as were the communion tables at Llanddyfnan and Llanfaes. There was still a school in the church at Llanfachreth. Bethell also noted several churches, including Coedana, Llanbedrgoch, Llanddona, Llandysilio, Llanfair Gweredog, Llanfair Mathafarn Eithaf, Llanfihangel Tynsylwy and Penrhoslligwy, where new carpets were needed for the altar or new hangings for the pulpit and reading desk. Early nineteenth-century bishops seem to have had an eye for detail which few of their later successors were able, or possibly even willing, to emulate, yet it was in the attention to detail that the reform of ecclesiastical institutions was gradually implemented.

Parochial Libraries

Parochial libraries had been established in many parts of England and Wales, as a result of the activities of Dr Thomas Bray and his supporters, during the first quarter of the eighteenth century. In England this activity had largely dropped off by the last quarter of the century and several libraries had become moribund or neglected. In Wales, however, there was a second flurry of activity in the establishment of new, and the augmentation of existing, parochial libraries in the late eighteenth and early nineteenth centuries, particularly in the market towns, as shown in Table 9.11. The library at Cowbridge was established by William Williams 'for the use of the divinity students of that place', namely those being educated at its distinguished grammar school. The libraries established at Holyhead, Kerry and Whitford were designed to be subscription lending libraries, and that at Brecon was turned into one when it was augmented in 1845 by the Brecknock district of the Society for the Promotion of Christian Knowledge. Only two of these libraries still exist in something approaching their original size, that at Dolgellau in the vestry room of the parish church and that from Ystrad Meurig in the library of the University of Wales, Lampeter. A small number of books survive in the National Library of Wales from the former libraries at Abergavenny and Usk, and from the Swansea library in the West Glamorgan Record Office.

Table 9.11 Establishment and augmentation of parochial libraries in Wales, 1780–1850

Parish/town	Date of establishment	Date of augmentation	Number of volumes	Source of benefaction
Abergavenny	1784–5		157	associates of Dr Bray
Beaumaris	1796	1840	357	ditto
Brecon	1834	1845	336	see text
Cardigan		1823	180	Not known
Cowbridge	1827		*c*128	see text
Denbigh	1814	1840	152	associates of Dr Bray
Dolgellau	1796	1840	337	ditto
Haverfordwest	1808		116	ditto
Holyhead	1849		*c*768	see text
Kerry	before 1846		158	see text
Llandeilofawr		1801	307	associates of Thomas Lyttleton
Llangefni	1823		162	associates of Dr Bray
Llangynllo (Rads)	1811		107	ditto
Llanover (Mon)	1829		145	ditto
Llanrwst	1794	1840	338	ditto
Rhayader	1810		120	ditto
Swansea	1793–4		*c*352	ditto
Usk	1828		126	ditto
Whitford (Flints)	before 1840		187	see text
Ystrad Meurig (Cards)	1808–9		133	associates of Dr Bray

Source: M. Perkin, *A Directory of the Parochial Libraries of the Church of England and the Church in Wales* (London, 2004), pp. 410–37.

10
The Welsh Church and the Welsh Language

The charge that the priority of the Welsh bishops in the late eighteenth and early nineteenth centuries was 'to anglicise the Welsh, rather than to "Welshify" the Anglican church' in Wales,[1] was widely accepted in the late nineteenth and early twentieth centuries, not just by Nonconformist critics of the Established Church, but even by many of the Welsh clergy and leading lay figures endeavouring to prevent disestablishment.

> In 1715, with the exception of thirty-five separatists' congregations, the entire people of Wales adhered to the Church. But after that date, for more than a hundred and fifty years, the rulers of the state, in pursuit of worldly policy, sent into Wales chief pastors ignorant of its language and tradition, and aliens in sympathy to the people. During that long period, the followers of the apostles came into Wales, not to accomplish the spiritual work of saving souls, but as Government agents, to destroy the language and quench the national spirit. The fruits of this policy are known to you. The thirty-five meeting houses of 1715 have become, in 1879, nearly three thousand.[2]

Such arguments have been accepted and built upon by more recent Welsh scholars. Those clergy who wanted to promote the Welsh language and Welsh culture had to fight for their beliefs against bishops and higher clergy, the majority of whom 'cared little for the Welsh language and knew next to nothing about the literature and history of Wales'.[3] The inability of the bishops to speak Welsh and the fact that they had been 'selected on the basis of their political loyalty to the government rather than their suitability to serve Wales' created 'an estrangement between the shepherd and his flock'.[4]

Such sentiments take insufficient account of the nature of late eighteenth- and early nineteenth-century episcopacy, in which the political role of the bishop was as significant as his pastoral one, not just in Wales, but in England and Ireland as well, and underestimate the role played by the Welsh clergy, mostly (if not always) actively encouraged by their English-born bishops, many of whom developed some understanding of the Welsh language, in preserving the use of the language when they might easily have done otherwise. As in other Celtic parts of the British Isles, the native language was threatened primarily by economic and social change: the movement of population, the growth of urbanization and commerce, and migration from the rural areas. However, in Wales the continued strength of the native language, in sharp contrast to the severe decline in the use of Irish, Manx or Scottish Gaelic,[5] was also the result of the survival of a substantial printed literature in Welsh, much of it of a devotional character, in addition to the Welsh editions of the Bible and the Book of Common Prayer. Successive generations of bishops in Wales had been determined that, for the benefit of the laity, the services of the Established Church should, in the phrase of the Book of Common Prayer, be in 'such language . . . as they might understand, and have profit by hearing the same', and in the late eighteenth and early nineteenth centuries this was enhanced by a movement led by the Welsh clergy for the promotion of Welsh culture through publications in Welsh, the study of Welsh history and the revival of eisteddfodau.

As far as the provision of services is concerned the evidence is impressive. As Table 10.1 shows, in those parts of Wales which were wholly or predominantly Welsh-speaking, the vast majority of churches had all or most of their services in Welsh. In Anglesey in 1801 all the Sunday services in the island's churches were in Welsh, except in three town churches at Amlwch, Beaumaris and Holyhead. Amlwch had Morning Prayer in Welsh and Evening Prayer in English with Holy Communion four times a year in English and five times in Welsh. Beaumaris had two Sunday services in Welsh and one in English; the language of the three communion services each month was not specified, but by 1837 there was a celebration on the first Sunday of the month in English and on the third

Table 10.1 Language of services in Welsh parish churches, *c*1790–*c*1830

	*c*1790			*c*1810			*c*1830		
County	Welsh (%)	Bilingual (%)	English (%)	Welsh (%)	Bilingual (%)	English (%)	Welsh (%)	Bilingual (%)	English (%)
Anglesey		N/A		97	3	–		N/A	
Breconshire	66	23	11	70	21	9	59	30	11
Caernarfonshire		N/A		95	5	–		N/A	
Cardiganshire		N/A		91	9	–	80	20	–
Carmarthenshire		N/A		79	14	7	64	29	7
Denbighshire	79	14	7	82	12	6		N/A	
Flintshire	52	46	2	58	42	–		N/A	
Glamorgan	54	31	15	51	27	22		N/A	
Merioneth		N/A		100	–	–		N/A	
Monmouthshire	17	24	59	14	18	68		N/A	
Montgomeryshire	52	16	32	47	23	30		N/A	
Pembrokeshire		N/A		30	11	59	30	14	56
Radnorshire	–	4	96	8	–	92	5	–	95

Source: E. M. White, 'The Established Church, dissent and the Welsh language c.1660–1811', in *The Welsh Language before the Industrial Revolution*, ed. G. H. Jenkins (Cardiff, 1997), 270–9.

Sunday in Welsh. Holyhead had services in English rather than Welsh on the third Sunday of the month.[6] In 1845, 51 out of 69 parishes in the archdeaconry of Cardigan had only Welsh services; the remaining 18 had services in both English and Welsh, but some of the former were provided largely for the benefit of non-Welsh-speaking gentry families or English visitors to coastal parishes.[7] In Flintshire the growth of Methodism encouraged the clergy of the Established Church to take 'special care to retain their congregations by ensuring that the language used in church services reflected local needs'. At Trelawnyd in 1809 it was considered safe to use English only once a month as there were only two parishioners who did not understand Welsh, whereas Welsh-speaking parishioners would, if Welsh services were not provided in the parish church, worship in dissenting chapels since 'they do not understand English sufficiently'.[8] Whilst Table 10.1 shows some slippage in the number of parishes with only Welsh services in parts of the diocese of St David's, the comparable growth was in the number of parishes with a mix of Welsh and English services, rather than those with only English services. It is notable that even in border counties like Flintshire, Monmouthshire and Montgomeryshire a significant number of churches had either only Welsh services, or at least some services in Welsh, and that it was only in Radnorshire that almost all services were only in English.

The one diocese that had difficulty finding a sufficiency of Welsh-speaking clergy was Llandaff. When Edward Copleston became bishop in 1828, out of 234 churches in the diocese, 131 only had services in English, 42 only had services in Welsh, and 61 had services in both languages. The largest number of churches with only English services, 104 out of 131, was, not surprisingly, in largely English-speaking Monmouthshire. Lack of Welsh meant that clergy of the Established Church could not compete with Nonconformist ministers in the matter of preaching; as a result the losses to dissent were substantial, particularly in the expanding industrial communities in the south Wales Valleys.[9] Copleston felt that the problem was not just one of a shortage of Welsh-speaking clergy, but a reflection of the fact that, whereas dissenting chapels only had to provide for the linguistic needs of their actual congregations, the parish churches had to meet the linguistic needs of the whole community at a time when the use of Welsh was declining, and that of English increasing, as the main language of communication in south-east Wales. One solution might have been bilingual services, but these were not popular, and there was considerable difficulty in ensuring that every parish with both English- and Welsh-speaking inhabitants had a service in each language every Sunday. In his 1836 Charge Copleston points out that, though he has endeavoured to ensure that the majority of parishes with Welsh-speaking populations had Welsh-speaking clergy,

> the use of Welsh is a much greater bar to the attendance of the English, than that of English to the attendance of the Welsh, for it is seldom that those who have received the most elementary education are ignorant of English – a language in which all the principal concerns of life are transacted.

In 1845 he instituted a detailed inquiry into whether, since there was some disagreement on the matter, it was necessary to ensure the appointment of a Welsh-speaking incumbent to the vacant parish of Llantwit Major (Glamorgan), and he strongly resisted attempts by some lay patrons to appoint non-Welsh-speaking clergy to parishes with a substantial number of Welsh-speaking inhabitants.[10] This was a pragmatic approach to a difficult problem but it is easy to see why Copleston was attacked by some people in Wales, such as Lord and Lady Llanover, for his lack of support for the Welsh language. His views were, on occasion, stated in unduly crude and careless terms, and though he was scrupulous in endeavouring to ensure that people were ministered to in the language of their choice, it is difficult to avoid coming to the conclusion that Copleston saw the use of Welsh as a barrier to the full integration of Wales with England in social and political terms.[11] Indeed it was allegations made against Copleston, who never learned Welsh, and who combined his bishopric with the deanery of St Paul's, London, that were a major motivation of the campaign for the appointment of Welsh-born and Welsh-speaking bishops between 1840 and the appointment of the first bishop to meet these qualifications, Joshua Hughes of St Asaph, in 1870.[12]

The events that had contributed most notably to a revival of Welsh culture and identity had been the establishment of antiquarian societies and the revival of eisteddfodau, and these were both movements in which clergy of the Established Church had not just participated but in many cases taken the leadership. The respective roles of Archdeacons Beynon of Cardigan and Payne of Carmarthen have been noted in the previous chapter. In the diocese of Bangor an early lead was taken by David Ellis, vicar of Criccieth, and P. B. Williams, rector of Llanberis and Llanrug.[13] In that of St Asaph the chief figure was Walter Davies (1761–1849), better known by his bardic name, Gwallter Mechain, taken from his birthplace at Llanfechain (Montgomeryshire). His origins were very humble, and he was apprenticed as a cooper until his academic abilities were recognized and private patrons financed his studies at Oxford. He was ordained in 1795 and from 1807 to 1838 was rector of Manafon (Montgomeryshire). He held Manafon in plurality with Ysbyty Ifan (Denbighshire), where he employed a curate; he was later rector of Llanrhaeadr-ym-Mochnant (Denbighshire), where he died in 1849. He was a model parish priest at Manafon, holding two services, alternately in English and Welsh, on Sundays and festivals.[14] He won his first prizes as a layman at the eisteddfodau held in1789 at Corwen and Bala, these being extremely controversial decisions since he had been informed in advance of the subjects set for the *awdlau*, which were meant to be impromptu compositions. Davies was a regular competitor and frequent winner thereafter and in 1833 was invited by the London-based Cymmrodorion Society to act as co-editor of the works of the fifteenth-century Welsh poet, Lewis Glyn Cothi.[15]

The most concentrated group of clerical patrons of Welsh language and culture was to be found in the diocese of St David's. They included W. J. Rees (1772–1855) of Cascob (Radnorshire), Bishop Burgess's original candidate for the principalship of the college he eventually founded at Lampeter, and John Jenkins (1770–1829) of Kerry (Montgomeryshire), both of whom were friends and correspondents of Walter

Davies; Eliezer Williams (1754–1820), vicar of Lampeter, where he opened a new and much-praised grammar school, from 1805; and the archdeacons, Thomas Beynon and H. T. Payne.[16] In addition to his patronage of Welsh antiquarian and literary studies, Beynon was instrumental in having important religious works translated into Welsh. Writing to Bishop Burgess of St David's on 2 February 1813 Beynon noted that:

> The Revd David Lewis, Vicar of Abernant [Carmarthenshire], has, at my request, translated the Church Catechism . . . into the Welsh Language. He has executed his task in a very superior manner, and I intend having an edition printed for the use of the clergy of the Diocese. If your Lordship should think fit to enjoin the Clergy to a stricter attention to the duty of catechising, they may hereafter be supplied with this useful assistant . . . Mr Lewis's archidiaconal sermons are also very ably composed, both with respect to matter and language. I wish the Society [?for the Promotion of Christain Knowledge] could afford to print them, as they would form a Volume of [out]standing use for the Welsh part of the Diocese.[17]

In 1818 John Jenkins of Kerry, whose bardic name was Ifor Ceri, was instrumental in the founding of 'the Cambrian Society in Dyfed to work for the preservation of Ancient British Literature, poetical, historical, antiquarian, sacred and moral and the encouragement of national music'. Similar societies were established for Gwynedd and Powys in 1819, and for Gwent and Morgannwg in 1821.[18] The Cambrian societies were seen as an Anglican initiative, though they were criticized by some clergy hostile to the promotion of a distinctly Welsh culture; they were also treated at this stage with great suspicion by many dissenting ministers, who saw this revival of interest in Welsh culture and promotion of the Welsh language as an attempt by the Established Church to regain some of the ecclesiastical initiative it had lost to dissent. The rules of the societies, however, stated that 'all dissenters from our Church who are natives of the Principality and are distinguished as authors of creditable works of literature and religion may be Honorary members', and some took advantage of this provision.[19]

The Cambrians' greatest coup was to attract the support of Bishop Burgess of St David's, and it was under his patronage that the first of a series of provincial eisteddfodau was held at Carmarthen in 1819.[20] A year earlier Burgess had presided at the meeting which had laid down the principal objectives of the Cambrian Society in Dyfed; these included making catalogues of all known Welsh manuscripts and collecting copies of every printed book in Welsh, to be kept at the Cymmrodorion library in London. Carmarthen has been seen in retrospect as 'the first of the great modern eisteddfodau';[21] it was the one where the Welsh clergy allied themselves with the Unitarian stonemason, antiquarian and forger of medieval Welsh poetry, Edward Williams, alias Iolo Morganwg, to invent the 'Gorsedd of the Bards of Britain', which thereafter became an essential ingredient of subsequent eisteddfodau, and which has been incorporated into the National Eisteddfod since the launching of this annual event in 1880. At the Caernarfon eisteddfod in 1821 the patrons included Bishop Majendie and Dean Warren of Bangor, the Marquis of Anglesey, Lord Bulkeley and Lord Newborough. A series of eisteddfodau were held at Abergavenny between 1833 and 1854, organized by Thomas Price, vicar of Llanfihangel Cwmdu and Llangattock (Breconshire), who was known by his bardic title of Carnhuanawc, and with the active involvement of those great patrons of Welsh culture and the language, Lord and Lady Llanover. Between 1836 and 1842 Price published, in fourteen parts, his history of Wales from *Earliest Times to the Fall of Llywelyn ap Gruffydd*. He made and played the Welsh harp. He taught himself Breton and assisted with the translation of the Old Testament into that language. At the Abergavenny eisteddfod of 1838 the Breton poet, Count Theodore Hersart de la Villemarqué, was admitted to the Gorsedd of the Bards of Britain, as Bishop Burgess had been nineteen years earlier at Carmarthen.[22]

The clerical domination of the Welsh antiquarian and eisteddfod movement lasted until the notorious Llangollen eisteddfod of 1858, organized by John Williams, 'Ab Ithel', rector of Llanymawddwy (Merioneth) and R. W. Morgan, 'Môr Meirion', perpetual curate of Tregynon (Montgomeryshire). The former had published *The Ecclesiastical Antiquities of the Cymry* in 1844 and translated the latter's *The British*

Kymry, published in English in 1857, into Welsh in time for the eisteddfod. Both combined a moderate Tractarianism with an extreme Welsh nationalism. Williams had collaborated with the more scholarly H. Longueville Jones to co-edit *Archaeologia Cambrensis* and co-found the Cambrian Archaeological Association in 1846–7, but they soon parted company and Williams established the *Cambrian Journal* to promote his own more romantic interpretation of Welsh history. Despite this he was still one of those considered for appointment to the new professorship of Celtic at Oxford. The Llangollen eisteddfod was his final undoing. Williams and several of his relations were awarded prizes, and they denied a prize to the Merthyr apothecary and dissenter, Thomas Stephens, for an essay on the alleged discovery of America by Madoc ap Owain Gwynedd in the twelfth century, because Stephens denied the validity of the legend in which Williams and his co-organizers were strong believers. There were also allegations that the profits of the eisteddfod had gone, not to the Cambrian societies, but into the pockets of the organizers. The Llangollen eisteddfod not only tarnished the reputation of its clerical organizers but it called into question the whole way in which a group of Welsh clergy had dominated and manipulated Welsh antiquarian scholarship over the best part of the previous century. Future eisteddfodau were to be 'non-sectarian, non-political'[23] events. On the Sunday before the Caernarfon eisteddfod in 1862 an interdenominational service was held. An event which until the 1850s had been dominated by the clergy of the Established Church had, by the last quarter of the nineteenth century, become one in which the Nonconformist clergy and laity were playing the dominant role.

So far we have concentrated on what were, generally, the positive attempts by Welsh bishops and clergy to promote the Welsh language and Welsh culture. However, it would be foolish to deny that there were occasions on which both could be contemptuous of their fellow countrymen. Some of this was revealed in the replies of the Welsh clergy to the Commissioners for Education in Wales published in 1847. The English incumbent at Builth Wells described the Welsh as 'very dirty' and 'more deceitful than the English'. The curate of Brecon, also an Englishman, regarded them as similar to the Irish, 'dirty, indolent, bigoted and [curiously] contented'. Even the vicar of Llandeilo, a Welshman, noted that 'unchastity is so prevalent that great numbers are in the family way previous to marriage'.[24] Archdeacon Beynon of Cardigan was extremely critical of what he regarded as the failure of the newly established college at Lampeter to make adequate provision for the teaching of Welsh. Even the redoubtable Rice Rees had to learn to speak Welsh after his appointment as professor of the language, though his later contributions to Welsh historical and literary studies were considerable. Doubts were certainly expressed about Principal Lewellin's proficiency in the language and Beynon regarded the whole programme of study as that of 'an English college'. He had originally given £750 towards the establishment of the college, but now threatened to withdraw an intended bequest, which would have increased the endowment, added books to the library and established a professorship in mathematics and natural philosophy. Although the additional books were given to the library, the remaining parts of the threat seem to have been implemented.[25] When Rice Rees died in 1839, his successor, a relative of the principal's wife, was described as 'totally unfitted' for the post; when he too died there was a vacancy of four years until a Lampeter student of two years' standing was appointed as lecturer in Welsh in 1848. As the college's historian has commented, this cavalier attitude to the teaching of Welsh 'did the College's reputation no good at a time of growing national consciousness in Wales'.[26]

Despite the best intentions of the bishops there were also cases in which non-Welsh-speaking clergy were appointed to Welsh-speaking parishes, though such incidents appear to have been comparatively rare. At Betws Cedewain (Montgomeryshire), where the parishioners had been used to both English and Welsh services, English only was in use from 1795 as the curate spoke no Welsh. In 1820 the churchwardens of Llanbeblig (Caernarfonshire) refused to accept Trevor Hill as their incumbent 'until he had learnt to read the Scriptures in Welsh'. The insistence of the curate of Newmarket (Flintshire) on having Morning Prayer in English on alternate Sundays, even though only two of his 250–300 parishioners understood no Welsh, had by 1809 resulted in many of them attending

'Dissenting meetings on those Sunday mornings when English services were held in their churches'. In 1804 one of the churchwardens of Battle (Breconshire) 'complained that most of the parishioners stayed away from church because so much English was used in the services'.[27] From time to time, however, bishops consented to a change in the language of the services to suit the needs of the inhabitants, even if this led to a reduction in the number of services in Welsh. At Machynlleth in 1800, the bishop permitted an increase in the number of services in English from one to two each month, Morning Prayer on the second Sunday and Evening Prayer on the last Sunday, and required that four of the monthly communion services, on the second Sundays of January, April (except in the case of its being Easter or Low Sunday in which case it should be the Sunday after), July and October, be in English but that services at all other times should be 'in such language as the same have been usually performed and administered heretofore'.[28] In most parishes it was the desires of the inhabitants rather than the wishes of the clergy that determined the language of the services, though the views of the gentry were inclined to carry more weight than those of the other parishioners. Whereas at Llanfair Nant-y-gof (Pembrokeshire) and Pendeulwyn (Glamorgan) this meant services being in English rather than Welsh, at Llandygai (Caernarfonshire) the reverse situation was true. Here the Penrhyn family insisted that services must be in Welsh and 'the English parishioners awarded the curate an additional fee for preaching in their language on alternate Sunday mornings when the Penrhyn family was absent'.[29]

There is no doubt that the views of both nineteenth-century commentators on Welsh affairs and subsequent historians have been unduly harsh in their assessment of the role played by the Established Church in Wales in respect of the Welsh language and Welsh culture. On balance it was a positive one even if, in some of its manifestations, it tended towards flamboyant eccentricity, as in the activities of John Williams, 'Ab Ithel', and R. W. Morgan, 'Môr Meirion'. It was not the unwillingness of the Welsh Church in the late eighteenth and early nineteenth centuries to promote the Welsh language and Welsh culture that contributed to its alienation from the bulk of the Welsh population, but the refusal of the Welsh bishops and clergy to come to terms with what they regarded, with some theological justification, as the dangerous enthusiasm of both Calvinistic and Wesleyan Methodism, which clearly met the spiritual needs of the average Welsh man and woman more effectively than the formality of traditional High Church Anglican worship and preaching.

11
Church Building and Restoration

One of the accusations frequently made against the Established Church in Wales in the late eighteenth and early nineteenth centuries is that many of its buildings were inadequately maintained, and in some cases practically in ruins. This assessment has on the whole been based on a fairly selective analysis of the voluminous contemporary evidence, which has concentrated on the worst cases and chosen to overlook the many examples of church building, rebuilding and restoration in this period. However, as M. L. Clarke pointed out in respect of Anglesey and Caernarfonshire more than forty years ago,[1] a less subjective and more balanced analysis of the evidence tells a very different story, in which the incidences of neglect represent a very small proportion of the known number of church buildings in every Welsh diocese. The most valuable contemporary commentators on Welsh church buildings were Richard Fenton, who visited most parts of Wales between 1804 and 1813; E. H. Hall, whose description of Caernarfonshire dates from 1809–11; and Theophilus Jones, who published his history of Breconshire in two parts in 1805 and 1811.[2] Altogether they provide an extremely comprehensive account of church buildings in the principality in the first decade or so of the nineteenth century, including examples of churches in good, poor or moderate condition as shown in Table 11.1. The most critical of these commentators was Theophilus Jones, yet even he found a reasonable number of churches in good order and there is some evidence that he exaggerated the defects of those that were not, as witness his comments on the church at Merthyr Cynog:

> This church, like most of the other country churches in Breconshire, and I fear in Wales, resembles a large barn, into which something like pens for sheep have been thrown in

> disorderly regularity to rot when they become unfit for use . . . in most of them the windows are broken, the tiles out of repair, so that the rain penetrates and falls upon the heads of those who have a sufficiency of devotion to frequent them on wet days . . . many of them are dark and gloomy . . . and yet with all or many of these defects, the churchwardens annually return that they are in good and sufficient repair![3]

Table 11.1 The condition of Welsh parish churches in the early nineteenth century as recorded by Richard Fenton, E. H. Hall and Theophilus Jones

Churches in	Fenton (%)	Hall (%)	Jones (%)
Good condition	48.0	63.6	17.6
Moderate condition	12.0	4.6	57.4
Poor condition	40.0	31.8	25.0

One of Jones's complaints was that, even when money had been spent on repairing churches, they were allowed to fall once again into a state of disrepair, one example being the church at Llanfihangel Talyllyn:

> within this place were two boards nailed together, with four posts to support them, worth about six-pence for fire wood and for no other purpose; they are covered by a dark woollen cloth, so incrusted with dirt and dust, since the year 1755, when it was bought or given to the church, that it is nearly as hard as the wood it covers and of about equal value. On this the holy communion is administered![4]

Gwenddwr, 'beautiful and adorned by the church wardens in 1790', was once again in a poor condition when Jones visited it in 1801.[5] He noted, however, the very satisfactory rebuilding of Llanhamlach church in 1804, and that, during the summer of 1806, the church at Llangatwg 'was newly ceiled, paved, glazed and seated, so that it now exceeds every other country church in Breconshire in neatness'.[6]

The worst example of a church in poor repair noted by Hall was that at Llandudwen, the condition of which was:

> deplorable. The west end of the roof has fallen in, the south window was totally denuded of glass, and that in the north wall was so encrusted over by a colony of snails that the light was altogether excluded. It was also easy to observe that the pulpit, desk, etc. were roosting places for all sorts of fowl.[7]

At Llanfairfechan

> among other precautions for ensuring decency during divine service, a huge pair of projecting forceps with an iron bite is provided for the seizure of intrusive dogs; but as the application of the engine was usually accompanied by the cries and howling of the patient, the use of it, though once common, has been gradually and generally discontinued.[8]

Fenton found the 'Nave and other parts' of the collegiate church at Brecon 'entirely in ruins . . . The Choir and Chancel, where the Stalls are, in a very little better state', and the church at Ystradffin (Carmarthenshire) 'now fallen down. Service is now performed in a miserable cot.' But Fenton's chief complaint, as with those of other contemporary commentators, is that the interiors of Welsh churches were 'undignified' and 'antiquated', furnished with 'Forms or seats, very heavy and rude' rather than the proper pews more normally found in other parts of the British Isles.[9] They reflected poverty rather than deliberate neglect.

The campaigns of Welsh bishops, such as Burgess at St David's (1803–25), Cleaver at St Asaph (1806–15) and Majendie at Bangor (1809–30), to improve the standards of worship in the churches of their dioceses resulted in extensive programmes of church building and restoration throughout Wales in the first half of the nineteenth century. As Table 11.2 shows, this programme escalated dramatically in the dioceses of both Bangor and St Asaph after 1830.[10] At Aberdaron (Caernarfonshire) it was decided to restore the parish church in 1848 'only seven years after it had been abandoned in favour of a completely new building' described at the time as being of 'atrociously barbarous and even ludicrous design'.[11] This restoration was clearly inspired by the ecclesiological movement of the 1840s though this had made little impact on Wales before 1850.[12] The one exception was the new church at

Table 11.2 Dates of rebuilding or restoration of existing churches and building of new churches in the dioceses of Bangor and St Asaph, 1780–1850

Date of building/rebuilding/restoration	Bangor	St Asaph
1780–1800	1	9
1801–1810	1	2
1811–1820	7	5
1821–1830	10	4
1831–1841	19	20
1841–1850	27	23

Llangorwen (Cardiganshire), completed in 1841 at a cost of £3,000 excluding the fittings.[13] At Llandysilio (Montgomeryshire) the church had been reseated and a new gallery erected in 1833, providing an additional eighty sittings, but by 1843 this was no longer considered sufficient and the incumbent sought permission from Bishop Carey of St Asaph to rebuild the church, keeping the cost down to an estimated £500 by reusing as many materials and furnishings as possible.[14]

Less work has been done on analysing the extent of church building and restoration programmes in the dioceses of Llandaff and St David's than in those of Bangor and St Asaph, but where such investigation has taken place, in Breconshire and Cardiganshire, it has revealed a similar level of activity. In Breconshire the south aisle of Crickhowell Church was rebuilt in 1829 at a cost of £440, and there were major restorations at Llanfihangel Cwmdu in 1830, Llandyfaelogfach in 1831, Garthbrengy in 1833 and Hay-on-Wye in 1834.[15] The rector of Llandyfaelogfach, in his application for funding to the Incorporated Church Building Society, commented: 'I verily believe that the cold damp and uncomfortable state of many of the Churches in the Principality is not the least cause of dissent from the Established Church.'[16]

Another applicant for funding described the church at Llanddeiniol (Cardiganshire) in 1832 'as worse than many an English hovel . . . a most wretched hovel, unworthy of being called a Church'.[17] In the rural deanery of Llanbadarnfawr in the early 1830s no fewer than twelve out of fourteen churches were 'completely rebuilt or otherwise heavily restored on account of the desperately poor state of the fabric'.[18] A report on the churches in the rural deanery of Gower in 1821 showed that out of the twenty-four churches all except that at Ilston, where the chancel was in need of repair, were in good condition. The chancel at Llansamlet had been 'largely rebuilt and the chancel receiving complete repair'; the church at Port Eynon was 'to be painted immediately' and that at Llanmadog was 'receiving improvements by enlarging the windows'.[19] In June 1811 the rural dean of Llandeilo reported that the church at Llanllwni 'is now undergoing a thorough repair' and that 'the floor . . . has been flagged' at Llanegwad. At Llanfynydd 'the Parishioners are repairing the roof and new seating' the nave, 'but the chancel [which was the responsibility of the vicar] is in as bad a state as it possibly can be, and no preparation making for its repair'.[20] A few years later, in 1819, a report by the rural dean of Upper Kemes recorded significant defects in the majority of churches in this rural deanery. Much of the woodwork needed to be painted, decayed or 'worm-eaten' benches to be replaced and roofs to be repaired. At Llantood the situation was so bad that the rural dean recorded that 'the Parishioners promise a new church'. At Moylgrove he had ordered that 'the church [was] not to be converted into a School Room and the Children removed without delay'. The church at Cilgwyn was

> in a ruinous state, and the parishioners in general not inclined to give a shilling toward its repair. The Rural Dean has addressed some of the principal Parishioners on the subject, and has offered to contribute his mite, but he is sorry to say without effect.[21]

In other parts of Pembrokeshire rebuildings or restorations of churches had taken place at Jordanston and Norton in 1797, Capel Colman in *c.*1800, Maenclochog in 1807 and Hayscastle in 1811.[22]

The two main obstacles to the improvement of church building were the expense and liturgical conservatism. At St

David's Bishop Horsley had begun a subscription for the repair of the west front of the cathedral in 1789, and work was completed in 1793 at a total cost of £2,015. 5*s*. 5*d*. The complete repair of the nave followed in 1811.[23] Richard Richardson, who was admitted to the precentorship on 11 June 1816, determined that the restored cathedral deserved a better set of communion plate and altar ornaments, including a pair of candlesticks which cost £93. 16*s*. and a three-volume edition of the Bible, placed on the altar table, which cost a further £88. When Richardson requested each of the prebendaries to subscribe to this purchase, several voiced their objections to such large sums having been spent and stated that they had no recollection of the chapter authorizing the purchase. Certainly it had not been recorded, as had other matters concerning the fabric and furnishings, in the chapter act book. Archdeacon Thomas Beynon, however, stated: 'I entirely approve of what you propose for the Cathedral', and subscribed £10. Several other prebendaries who did subscribe did so under protest, and Richardson was obliged to subscribe £26. 10*s*. himself to make up the deficit.[24] In September1833 the rural dean of North Dewisland was obliged to write to the churchwardens of Llanwnda (Pembrokeshire) instructing them 'to put the Church . . . in good repair and also require the Chancel to be thoroughly repaired, otherwise I shall without delay direct proceedings to be instituted against you as well as others interested in it and who are bound to repair'.[25] The responsibility for the repair of the church at Llanwnda lay, not with an obstructive lay rector, but with the precentor and chapter of St David's.

Similar problems existed in the diocese of Bangor. John Ellis, the curate of Llanddyfnan and Pentraeth (Anglesey), followed up his answers to Bishop Cleaver's visitation queries in 1801 with an explanatory letter:

> In answering the articles enquiring into the state of the Church . . . as there is no black cloth to be put over the Bier in both my Parishes, I answered there was none of course; at Llanddyfnan they defy me . . . I wish, in this case, you would exert your authority and compel their methodistical Heads to do every thing that is right, and it never will be done unless

> they will be wrote to . . . I bought that small convenient Book, called the Book of Office, for the Use of the Parish of Llanddyfnan, they met, and agreed not to pay for it, which is the trifling sum of 3s 6d, which sum I must be out of pocket . . . they are such headstrong people, that I am really rather afraid of them, there will be no harm at all, if you w^{d} have the goodness to write to Pentraeth Wardens, there is no black cloth there and the Roof of the Church is like a sieve, I cannot prevail upon them to repair it.[26]

At Llanwnnog (Montgomeryshire) Cleaver was appealed to in August 1802 to settle a dispute between the two churchwardens which had prevented the roof from being reslated and the incumbent's 'good Intention in repairing the Church in a decent manner'.[27] At Llangoed (Anglesey) in 1818 the church had been completely restored with the exception of the pew belonging to John Thomas of Plasnewydd which it was estimated would only cost the owner 30*s*. or £1 to repair.[28] At Caernarfon, the chapel of St Mary was the responsibility, not of the parish of Llanbeblig, but of the municipal corporation. In 1798 the vicar of Llanbeblig complained to the mayor that 'the Roof, Altar Place, Pulpit, Reading Desk and Pews are in a shameful condition. The Walls perfectly green and every part of the chapel dangerously damp.' Although the corporation obtained an Act of Parliament to rebuild the chapel in 1800 nothing was done for several years. In 1810 £1,000 was raised by public subscription to which the corporation added a gift of £300 and a loan of £1,000 'on mortgage of the Corporation property'. The work was eventually completed in 1814. The church at Llandudno (Caernarfonshire) 'was wrecked in 1839 by a great storm' and not fully repaired until 1855.[29]

The bishops relied heavily on regular inspections by their rural deans to ensure that churches were maintained in good repair, and it was the rural deans who tended to come directly into conflict with difficult clergy and difficult parishioners. The rural dean of Dewisland explained his policy to Bishop Murray of St David's in September 1802:

> The method which, after some experience in the practice of my duty as Rural Dean, I have adopted, is, after making out the Report prior to the Lord Bishop's visitation, to take down

> all the Deficiencies and to send them to the Churchwardens respectively, requiring them to put all such things in order before the Visitation; and, in the subsequent years, to set down such deficiencies only as appear to me to be most prominent, so that by doing a little every year, as Bishop Stuart observed to me, the expence may not be so heavily felt as if it was done at once. And indeed were they to do a little every year, in the course of a few years a great change for the better would take place.

However, even this pragmatic approach had had only limited success. By applying regular pressure 'I have had some things supplied, in several of the Parishes, which were much wanted before' and there were now 'only four Parishes in want of Folio Welsh Common Prayer Books'.[30]

Liturgical conservatism had resulted in many parishes retaining archaic arrangements. St Mary's, Caernarfon, had retained its rood screen until 1782 and one remained in place at Botwnnog (Caernarfonshire) until the rebuilding of the church in 1835.[31] At Clynnog Fawr (Caernarfonshire) the surviving rood loft was used by the singers until the middle of the nineteenth century. At Llanfaglan (Caernarfonshire) the communion table was still placed lengthwise with its short side facing the east wall of the church, an early seventeenth-century Puritan practice, in 1788, and the same arrangement still existed at Llanllyfni (Caernarfonshire) even later.[32] New churches, and major rebuildings or refittings of existing churches, in the early nineteenth century, however, usually followed the prevailing liturgical attitudes of the contemporary Church of England in adopting one of several innovatory methods of arranging the interior so that participation in the services by the laity could be made more effective.[33] One concern was to make the seats more uniform. A plan of the proposed reseating of the church at Clynnog Fawr in 1827 showed the existing pews in red and the new ones in blue. Whilst the former were of varying sizes and had been placed fairly randomly at the east end of the nave and in both transepts, the new pews were almost all of the same size and filled both nave and transepts with empty spaces only at the west end of the nave and adjacent to the doorway in the south transept. All the seating was arranged to face the pulpit and reading desk in the north-west angle of the crossing.[34]

The three most popular liturgical arrangements in Wales in the early nineteenth century were the placing of the pulpit and reading desk on one of the long walls of the nave, or centrally at its east end, or with seating facing it from two or more directions, the T-plan arrangement noted already at Clynnog Fawr. Examples of the long-wall arrangement are shown in surviving plans for Llanbedr Dyffryn Clwyd (Denbighshire) in 1808, Llandyrnog (Denbighshire) in 1815, Llanfihangel Cwmdu (Breconshire) in 1830 and Capel Colman (Pembrokeshire) in 1835. There are also surviving examples at Llanfihangel Helygen (Radnorshire) of 1812, Llanddoged (Denbighshire) of 1838–9 and Llanfigael (Anglesey) of *c*1840, and there are contemporary descriptions of such arrangements at Dolgellau (Merioneth) and Ruthin (Denbighshire). The churches at Llanbedr Dyffryn Clwyd,[35] Capel Colman[36], Llanfihangel Helygen and Llanfigael[37] were or are simple single-cell buildings with the pulpit and reading desk placed in the middle of the seating. Llandyrnog[38] and Llanddoged[39] were double-naved churches with the pulpit and reading desk placed in the middle of the north wall of the north nave and the seating arranged to face them. The church at Llanfihangel Cwmdu had a very broad nave and shallow sanctuary. The pulpit and reading desk were placed in the middle of the south wall of the nave with a gallery 'supported by cast iron pillars' across the whole length of the north wall and approached by staircases at each end.[40] The church at Dolgellau, in the first decade of the nineteenth century, had

> no pews, only Forms of Wood, with the Names of the different proprietors painted on the back . . . half the Seats face the Altar, and the other half face the contrary way, in my opinion producing a very awkward effect, but certainly, by being open, they are more likely to induce those who sit in them to deport themselves more decently than when they are boxed up in high-sided Pews . . . The Pulpit and Reading Desk are very judiciously placed, for hearing and light, in the space between the Windows in the North side, so that there are two Windows on one side and two on the other of the pulpit.[41]

At Ruthin accommodation in the church had been increased in 1810 by the erection of extra galleries so that there were galleries around the east, north and west sides of the north nave and across the west end of the south nave. The seats in the galleries were allocated so that the north gallery accommodated the poor of the parish of Ruthin, the north-east gallery the scholars of Ruthin school, the north-west gallery the tenants of Ruthin Castle estate, and the south-west gallery the organ and singers. The pulpit and reading desk were placed in the middle of the south wall of the south nave and there were box pews in both naves and in the chancel reaching right up to the east end on both sides of the altar.[42]

Although there are no surviving examples in Wales of the central pulpit, placed at the east end of the nave directly in front of the altar, this arrangement was adopted in the new church of St David at Denbigh, erected in 1838–40; and at Newtown (Montgomeryshire), where the old parish church was replaced with a new building, on a new site, at a cost of £5,200, in 1847–9: 'internally three galleries run round its three sides, and the pulpit and desks rise in tiers from the central aisle. The western gallery is occupied by the organ; and the church, which is paved throughout, will seat six hundred.'[43] T-plan arrangements were fairly common in Wales and examples of these survive at Ynyscynhaearn (Caernarfonshire) of 1830–2, Capel Curig (Caernarfonshire) of 1839, and Betws-y-Coed (Caernarfonshire) of 1843.[44] They are also shown in plans of the churches at Llandygai (Caernarfonshire) in 1818, Llantilio Pertholey (Monmouthshire) in 1826 and Llanllyfni (Caernarfonshire) in 1839. The proposed alterations at Llandygai (Figure 11.1) included the erection of an extension at the west end of the nave incorporating a new porch, vestry and staircase to the west gallery.[45] At both Llandygai and Llanllyfni the seating faced the pulpit and reading desk from three directions, in the nave and both transepts, with a few seats at the entrance to the chancel. At Llanllyfni the new arrangement was designed to increase the accommodation in the church to 409: 80 in each transept, 126 in the nave, 18 in the crossing and chancel and 105 (73 in pews and 32 on forms) in a deep west gallery.[46] At Llantilio Pertholey seating faced the pulpit and reading desk, at the south-east end of the nave, from two

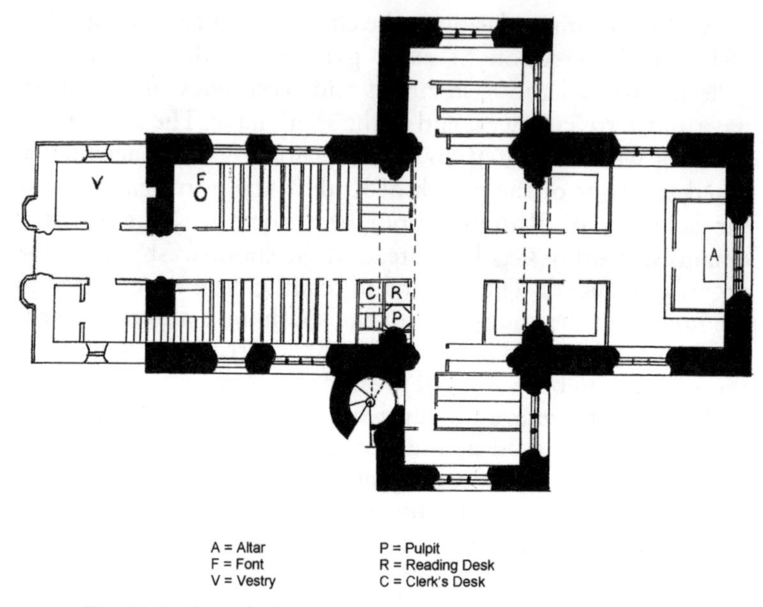

Fig. 11.1 Plan of LLandygai Church, Caernarfonshire, 1818

directions: east in the nave and south in the north transept and very short north aisle.[47] There were also two churches in which the T-plan arrangement was combined with a central pulpit, placed directly in front of the altar, the seating facing it in three directions from the nave and both transepts, shown in the surviving plans of Newport (Pembrokeshire) in 1835[48] and Llanelli (Carmarthenshire) in 1839.[49] An even more unusual version of the T-plan arrangement was that shown in the plan of the church at Grosmont (Monmouthshire) in 1822 (Figure 11.2). Here the church was so large in relation to the population of the parish that the nave was left empty and only the chancel and transepts fitted up for divine service. The seating in the chancel, in which the occupants sat with their backs to the altar, and in the transept, was focused on the pulpit, reading and clerk's desks on the west side of the crossing, the pulpit being placed over the main entrance.[50] This interesting arrangement combines a very similar one extant at Dromard (County Sligo) with the placing of the pulpit over the main entrance as at Teigh (Rutland).[51]

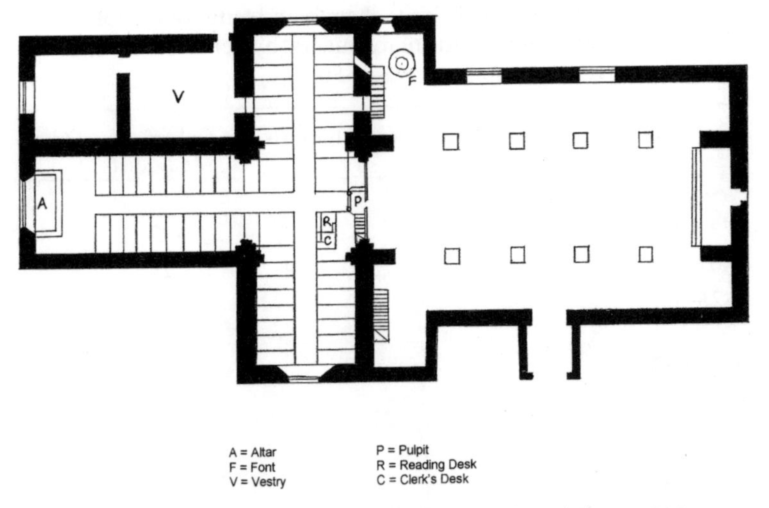

Fig. 11.2 Plan of Grosmont Church, Monmouthshire, 1822

It should be pointed out that, with the exception of the provision of an altar at the east end of the building, these Anglican arrangements of seating in relation to the pulpit and reading desk were very similar to those in Nonconformist chapels of the same period, an enormous number of which were built throughout Wales in the late eighteenth and early nineteenth centuries. A detailed analysis of chapel and Sunday school building dates in Cardiganshire,[52] summarized in Table 11.3, shows the extent of this in one Welsh county and similar patterns of building, rebuilding and enlargement were replicated in most other parts of Wales. Altogether 143 new chapels and Sunday schools were built in the county in this period, and there were almost as many (131) rebuildings and enlargements. The figures show clearly that, although it was the new group of Calvinistic Methodists that built, rebuilt and enlarged the greatest number of chapels and Sunday schools, their growth had a significant impact on the older groups of dissenters, the Independents and the Baptists. The other main dissenting groups in Cardiganshire were the Wesleyan Methodists, mostly in the towns and the larger villages, and the Unitarians, whose strength was in the so-called *smotyn ddu* (black spot) of the Teifi Valley.

Table 11.3 Dates of newly built chapels and Sunday schools, rebuildings and enlargements, by denomination, in Cardiganshire, 1780–1850

Denomination	Independents	Baptists	Calvinistic Methodists	Others
New Buildings				
1780–1800	5	4	17	1
1801–25	14	4	20	16
1826–50	20	12	21	9
Rebuildings/ Enlargements				
1780–1800	1	1	4	1
1801–25	7	3	26	1
1826–50	21	9	36	21
Total schemes	68	33	124	49

All the pre-1800 chapels in Wales were essentially modest buildings, quasi-domestic in character, and normally built for comparatively small amounts of money. One at Three Cocks (Breconshire) was built in 1788 for £240, the gift of Thomas Williams of Brecon, but others were built for much smaller sums, normally well below £200. Such cheap buildings tended to have limited life-spans, so rebuilding or substantial renovation every twenty or thirty years was not uncommon, the dates of rebuilding and renovation frequently being recorded on the plaques erected over chapel entrances.[53] From the early years of the nineteenth century more spectacular buildings were occasionally attempted. The chapel built and financed by William Maddocks MP for his planned new town of Tremadog (Caernarfonshire) in 1810 was 'a classical temple placed in the rugged landscape of the north: Athens and Rome had come to Caernarfonshire.'[54] The increased wealth of Nonconformist congregations in the later nineteenth century, and the desire to adopt designs featuring the pulpit platform, resulted in the majority of these earlier chapels being either completely rebuilt or substantially reordered internally, so that the number of surviving early Nonconformist interiors in Wales is now rather smaller than the total number of pre-1850 Anglican interiors. The few that do survive mostly have their pulpits placed centrally on the long wall; these include Capel Newydd at Nanhoron (Caernarfonshire) of 1769, Yr Hen Bethel at Glanaman (Carmarthenshire) of 1773, Capel Penrhiw, now at the Museum of Welsh Life (St Fagan's, Glamorgan), of 1777, the Bethesda'r Fro Chapel at Llantwit Major (Glamorgan) of 1806–7, Capel Heol Awst at Carmarthen of 1826–7, and Capel Beilidu, Pentrebach (Breconshire) of 1858. The alternative, and usually slightly later, arrangement, with the pulpit on the short wall, survives at Capel Salem, Cefncymerau (Merioneth) of 1850, and the Calvinistic Methodist chapel at Burnett's Hill (Pembrokeshire), refitted at about the same time, and there is a completely square interior of 1829 at the Welsh Baptist chapel in Hengoed (Glamorgan). An important feature of the early nineteenth-century Welsh chapel, which differentiated it from both its Anglican and its English Nonconformist counterparts, was the prominence of the *sêt fawr* (big seat) in which the deacons or elders sat, and which normally entirely enclosed the pulpit.[55]

From the late eighteenth century in England a liturgical movement was taking place aimed at giving greater prominence to the altar, and placing the pulpit and reading desk, as separate pieces of furniture, on opposite sides of the entrance to the chancel.[56] Although a number of such arrangements survive in Wales, none date from earlier than 1840: Aberdaron (Caernarfonshire) and Llanffinan (Anglesey) of 1841; Llangynfelyn (Cardiganshire), Llanarmon Dyffryn Ceiriog (Denbighshire) and Llanfihangel Nant Melan (Radnorshire) of 1846; and Manordeifi (Pembrokeshire) of 1847.[57] A slightly earlier arrangement of this type is, however, shown in the surviving plan of the alterations proposed, and indeed carried out, at Chepstow (Monmouthshire) in 1838–41. Much of the eastern part of the church had been destroyed when the central tower collapsed in 1701, leaving only a nave, into which a new chancel had been inserted, and a north aisle. The plan shows the addition of a south aisle to form a new nave, with transepts, the north transept being an extension of the existing nave and chancel, and a new chancel. The new nave was to be fitted out in two sections, with two blocks of seats in the western part, and three blocks of seats in the eastern one, similar to the surviving arrangement of 1831 at Overmonnow (Monmouthshire). There were to be three blocks of seats in each transept and there was also to be a deep west gallery in the new nave and galleries across both transepts. Pulpit and reading desk, of equal height, were to be placed on the north and south sides of the entrance to the chancel. This arrangement was destroyed when the church was partially rebuilt and substantially reordered in the late nineteenth and early twentieth centuries.[58] Only one example of a collegiate interior seems to have been built in Wales in the early nineteenth century, the new church of St Mary at Llanrwst (Denbighshire), built in 1841–2 'for the benefit of English residents and . . . visitors. . . . all the seats being made to face the central aisle'.[59] The architect, W. H. Kennedy, later built another collegiate church at Llandwrog (Caernarfonshire) in 1860, and that survives intact.[60]

The extensive programme of church building and restoration in Wales was yet another indicator of the vitality of the Established Church in the early nineteenth century, despite the numerical losses it was sustaining as a result of the Calvinistic Methodist schism of 1811 and the growth of other dissenting bodies in the principality. One would not wish to exaggerate the nature of this vitality, nor to downgrade the reform programmes of bishops such as Connop Thirlwall, Thomas Vowler Short and Alfred Ollivant, most of whose work was accomplished after 1850, but it is necessary to rescue the reputation of the Welsh Church in the pre-1850 period from the charges of lethargy, incompetence and sheer blind prejudice that have too often been alleged against it in the past.

Notes to Part III

8. Calvinistic Methodism: Growth and Schism

1 E. Evans, *Daniel Rowland and the Great Evangelical Awakening in Wales* (Edinburgh, 1985), pp. 349–53, 358–9.

2 D. E. Jenkins, *The Life of Thomas Charles BA of Bala*, 3 vols (Denbigh, 1908), I, pp. 11–474.

3 Evans, *Daniel Rowland*, pp. 354–5.

4 E. H. Hall, *A Description of Caernarvonshire (1809–1811)*, ed. E. G. Jones (Caernarfon, 1952), pp. 343–54, lists at least sixteen Calvinistic Methodist congregations in the county established before 1785; at least a further fifteen were formed in the period 1785–1805. In Cardiganshire nineteen congregations were formed between 1749 and Daniel Rowland's death in 1790, and a further nineteen between then and the formal separation of the Calvinistic Methodists from the Established Church in 1811. There was a corresponding drop in Anglican communicant figures, from 750 to 149 in four selected parishes between 1755 and 1804, with a total of only 2,157 Anglican communicants in the whole county in the latter year; see *Cardiganshire County History, Vol. III: Cardiganshire in Modern Times*, ed. G. H. Jenkins and I. G. Jones (Cardiff, 1998), p. 476. Calvinistic Methodist chapels were established in the Holywell district of Flintshire and Ysceifiog in 1775, Northop in 1778 and Caerwys in 1790; see M. V. J. Seaborne, 'The religious census of 1851 and early chapel building in north Wales: a sample survey', *NLWJ*, 26 (1989–90), 293–4.

5 R. L. Brown, 'Parsons in perplexity: Methodist clergy in and around the Vale of Glamorgan, c.1740–1811', *Morgannwg*, 37 (1983), 56–82.

6 F. C. Mather, *High Church Prophet: Bishop Samuel Horsley (1733–1806) and the Caroline Tradition in the Late Georgian Church* (Oxford, 1992), pp. 196–9.

7 S. Horsley, *The Charge . . . to the Clergy of his Diocese Delivered . . . in the Year 1790* (London, 1792), p. 30.

8 *Remarks on the Charge of the Bishop of St David's . . . by a Dissenting Minister* (London, 1791), p. 59.

9 S. Horsley, *A Charge to the Clergy . . . of St Asaph* (London, 1806), pp. 21, 24–5.

10 NLW, B/QA/14.

11 M. R. Watts, *The Dissenters: The Expansion of Evangelical Nonconformity* (Oxford, 1995), p. 385.

12 F. G. Wallace-Hadrill, *The Parish Church of St Mary, Newport, Pembrokeshire* (Cardigan, 1989), pp. 10, 25–6.

13 *Pembrokeshire County History, Vol. III: Early Modern Pembrokeshire, 1536–1815*, ed. E. Davies and B. Howells (Haverfordwest, 1987), p. 242.

14 NLW, B/PM/39 (*A Charge Delivered to the Clergy of the Diocese of Bangor*, Bangor, 1808), pp. 12–29.

15 B. I. Coleman, 'Southern England in the census of religious worship, 1851', *Southern History*, 5 (1983), 154–88.

[16] See the useful distribution maps showing areas of denominational strength and weakness in Watts, *Dissenters*, pp. 863–70.

[17] T. A. Campbell, *The Religion of the Heart: A Study of European Religious Life in the Seventeenth and Eighteenth Centuries* (Columbia, 1991), pp. 106–7.

[18] Watts, *Dissenters*, pp. 64, 122–4, 143–4, 179, 266.

[19] NLW, MS 4798E, f. 47.

[20] For the debates leading up to this decision and its repercussions see Jenkins, *Life of Thomas Charles*, II, pp. 237–333.

[21] *The History, Constitution, Rules of Discipline and Confession of Faith of the Calvinistic Methodists or the Presbyterians of Wales, adopted at the Associations of Aberystwyth and Bala, in the year 1823, translated from the Welsh* (Caernarfon, 1900), pp. 18, 32–7.

[22] Jenkins, *Life of Thomas Charles*, II, pp. 316, 321, 325, 327.

[23] Watts, *Dissenters*, pp. 115–16.

[24] *Cardiganshire in Modern Times*, pp. 469, 486.

[25] NLW, MS 4797C, f. 107.

[26] This section is based on the very full account in R. L. Brown, *The Welsh Evangelicals* (Cardiff, 1986). The quotation is on p. 46. For Bethell and Carey's position in the Hackney Phalanx see C. Dewey, *The Passing of Barchester* (London, 1991), pp. 151–3.

[27] NLW, SD/LET/1261.

[28] Brown, *Welsh Evangelicals*, pp. 47–8; A. J. Arber-Cooke, *Pages from the History of Llandovery* (Swansea, 1994), pp. 314–15; G. Borrow, *Wild Wales: Its People, Language and Scenery* (Oxford, 1920), p. 540.

[29] O. W. Jones, *Isaac Williams and His Circle* (London, 1971), pp. 92–100. See also D. E. Evans, 'Mudiad Rhydychen yng Ngogledd Sir Aberteifi', *JHSCW*, 4 (1954), 45–57.

[30] See W. N. Yates, 'The progress of ecclesiology and ritualism in Wales 1840–1875', *Archaeologia Cambrensis*, 149 (2000), 59–88. For a slightly different assessment of this impact, see D. P. Freeman, 'The influence of the Oxford Movement on Welsh Anglicanism and Welsh Nonconformity in the 1840s and 1850s' (unpublished Ph.D. thesis, University of Wales, Swansea, 1999).

[31] I. G. Jones, 'Ecclesiastic economy: aspects of church building in Victorian Wales', in *Welsh Society and Nationhood: Historical Essays presented to Glanmor Williams*, ed. R. R. Davies, R. A. Griffiths, I. G. Jones and K. O. Morgan (Cardiff, 1984), p. 222.

[32] Watts, *Dissenters*, pp. 863–70.
[33] Jones, *Congregationalism in Wales*, pp. 137–41.
[34] Ibid., pp. 144–8.
[35] Ibid., pp. 156–8.
[36] Bassett, *Welsh Baptists*, pp. 114–21.
[37] Ibid., pp. 159–71.
[38] Ibid., pp. 178–82; Jones, *Congregationalism in Wales*, pp. 153–5.
[39] D. D. Morgan, 'Smoke, fire and light: Baptists and the revitalisation of Welsh dissent', *Baptist Quarterly*, 33 (1987–8), 228–9.
[40] Watts, *Dissenters*, pp. 34, 243–5. See also G. T. Roberts, 'Methodism in Wales', in *A History of the Methodist Church in Great Britain, III*, ed. R. Davies, A. R. George and E. G. Rupp (London, 1983), pp. 253–64.
[41] See W. O. Chadwick, *The Victorian Church*, 2 vols (London, 1966–70), I, pp. 81–9, 146–58, and W. R. Ward, *Religion and Society in England 1790–1850* (London, 1972), pp. 178–89.
[42] G. I. T. Machin, 'A Welsh church rate fracas, Aberystwyth, 1832–3: the making of a political dissenter', *WHR*, 6 (1972–3), 462–8.
[43] Watts, *Dissenters*, p. 483.
[44] NLW, SD/QA/73.
[45] Watts, *Dissenters*, pp. 863–70.
[46] Jenkins, *Life of Thomas Charles*, II, p. 298.

9. A Reforming Episcopate

[1] G. F. A. Best, *Temporal Pillars: Queen Anne's Bounty, the Ecclesiastical Commission, and the Church of England* (Cambridge, 1964), p. 545.
[2] Ibid., pp. 318–19, 436–7; D. R. Thomas, *A History of the Diocese of St Asaph* (London, 1874), pp. 154–6.
[3] NLW, SA/MB/37.
[4] A. Burns, *The Diocesan Revival in the Church of England c.1800–1870* (Oxford, 1999), pp. 158, 160.
[5] Ibid., pp. 58–60, 76–8, 134; Best, *Temporal Pillars*, p. 405, who notes that Bishop Bethell of Bangor agreed to the separation of the archdeaconries of Anglesey and Bangor from the diocese during his lifetime, despite his hostility to the Ecclesiastical Commission which presented these reforms.
[6] Thomas, *History of Diocese of St Asaph*, p. 152.
[7] *DNB*, s.n. William Cleaver.

[8] NLW, B/LET/829.
[9] NLW, B/Misc/4.
[10] R. L. Brown, 'From riches to rags: the parish of Dolgellau in the nineteenth century', *Journal of the Merioneth Historical and Record Society*, 12 (1994–7), 146.
[11] E. H. Hall, *A Description of Caernarvonshire (1809–1811)*, ed. E. G. Jones (Caernarfon, 1952), p. 156; see also A. H. Dodd, *A History of Caernarvonshire* (Denbigh, 1968), pp. 344–6; it was during Cleaver's episcopate that the Bangor Diocesan Tract Society was founded in 1804.
[12] M. L. Clarke, 'John Warren, bishop of Bangor, 1783–1800', *Caernarvonshire Historical Society Transactions*, 41 (1980), 83–106, and *Bangor Cathedral* (Cardiff, 1969), pp. 47–8, 61–3, 81; Hall, *Description of Caernarvonshire*, pp. 157–8.
[13] NLW, B/PM/51 (*The Duties of the Parochial Clergy of the Church of England Considered, in a Charge delivered to the Clergy of the Diocese of Bangor* (London, 1785)), pp. 5–15.
[14] M. L. Clarke, 'A bishop of Bangor in the pre-reform era: H. W. Majendie', *Caernarvonshire Historical Society Transactions*, 30 (1969), 44–57.
[15] P. G. Yates, 'Neglect or reform? The diocese of Bangor under Bishop Henry William Majendie 1809–17' (unpublished M.Th. dissertation, University of Wales, Lampeter, 2003), especially 17–18, 31–8, 40–5, 58–66.
[16] Transcript in ibid., pp. 73–86 (NLW, B/QA/21).
[17] T. Ellis, 'Educational charities in Merioneth before 1837', *Journal of the Merioneth Historical and Record Society*, 7 (1973–6), 1–12.
[18] NLW, SA/MB/20.
[19] G. Richards, 'James Henry Cotton, dean of Bangor 1838–1868', *NLWJ*, 19 (1975–6), 147–80; Clarke, *Bangor Cathedral*, pp. 27–31, 48; Dodd, *History of Caernarvonshire*, pp. 347–8.
[20] R. W. D. Fenn, 'Richard Watson, a reappraisal', *JHSCW*, 15 (1965), 20–39; T. J. Brain, 'Some aspects of the life and works of Richard Watson, bishop of Llandaff, 1737 to 1816' (unpublished Ph.D. thesis, University of Wales, Aberystwyth, 1982), especially 152–92.
[21] Ibid., 187.
[22] R. Watson, *A Charge Delivered to the Clergy of the Diocese of Llandaff* (London, 1802), pp. 31–2.
[23] Ibid., p. 30.
[24] Guy, 'An investigation into the pattern and nature of patronage, plurality and non-residence in the old diocese of Llandaff', 173,

213–15. Of the other ten members of the chapter in 1800 one was the bishop, three held livings in the diocese and the remaining six were career pluralists.

[25] Ibid., p. 355.
[26] Ibid., p. 698.
[27] Brain, *Richard Watson*, p. 178.
[28] NLW, MS 21977C, f. 20.
[29] *The Letters of Edward Copleston, Bishop of Llandaff, 1828–1849*, ed. R. L. Brown (Cardiff, 2003), p. 10.
[30] *A Charge Delivered at the Primary Visitation of Herbert Lord Bishop of Llandaff* (Cambridge, 1817).
[31] NLW, MS 21977C, f. 18.
[32] E. A. Varley, *The Last of the Prince Bishops: William Van Mildert and the High Church Movement of the Early Nineteenth Century* (Cambridge, 1992), pp. 90–2, 203.
[33] NLW, MS 21977C, f. 20.
[34] *Copleston Letters*, pp. 47–55.
[35] W. J. Copleston and T. Phillips, *Memoir of Edward Copleston, DD, Bishop of Llandaff* (London, 1851), especially pp. 116, 131–3, 228, 230–40, 250.
[36] *Copleston Letters*, pp. 31–7, 43–7.
[37] Ibid., p. 191; see also D. R. Buttress, 'Llandaff Cathedral in the eighteenth and nineteenth centuries', 61–76.
[38] NLW, LL/Ch/704.
[39] J. R. Guy, 'Churches and churchmen in Llantrisant parish 1660–1800', *Glamorgan Historian*, 12 (n.d.), 89–90.
[40] T. J. Pritchard, 'The Anglican Church in the Rhondda from the Industrial Revolution to disestablishment' (unpublished Ph.D. thesis, University of Keele, 1981), 2–14.
[41] Thomas, *History of Diocese of St Asaph*, pp. 233–64.
[42] W. T. Morgan, 'The diocese of St David's in the nineteenth century: the unreformed Church', *JHSCW*, 21 (1971), 44–7.
[43] S. Horsley, *A Charge to the Clergy . . . of St Asaph* (London, 1806), pp. 6–8.
[44] NLW, SA/MB/20.
[45] NLW, SA/LET/312.
[46] NLW, SA/LET/315.
[47] NLW, SA/MB/20.
[48] NLW, SA/LET/627.
[49] NLW, SA/LET/648.
[50] NLW, SA/LET/650.
[51] Son of MP for Bishop's Castle (Shropshire), grandson of MP for Montgomery Boroughs, and nephew of Clive of India. Educated

at Eton and St John's College, Cambridge. Domestic chaplain to Bishop Luxmoore and the Duke of Northumberland, vicar of Welshpool 1819–65, archdeacon of Montgomery 1844–61, honorary canon of St Asaph 1849 and residentiary 1854–61, vicar of Blymhill (Staffordshire) from 1865.

52 J. E. Davies, 'Three Welshpool vicars: the clergymen of a Victorian town', *Montgomeryshire Collections*, 76 (1988), 109–14.

53 R. L. Brown, 'Making a new parish: Holy Trinity, Penrhos', *Montgomeryshire Collections*, 84 (1996), 115–22.

54 *Idem*, 'The effects of Queen Anne's Bounty and the Ecclesiastical Commission on some Montgomeryshire parishes', *Montgomeryshire Collections*, 86 (1998), 98, 100, 105–7.

55 Mather, *High Church Prophet*, pp. 163–77.

56 Burns, *Diocesan Revival*, pp. 95, 117–18, 124; see also D. T. W. Price, *Bishop Burgess and Lampeter College* (Cardiff, 1987), pp. 30–3, 36–7; see also T. Burgess, *A Charge Delivered to the Clergy of the Diocese of St David's in the year 1804* (Durham, 1805). Burgess's subsequent Charges in 1807 and 1813 followed up the reform agenda he had begun in 1804. That for 1807 covered the care of church fabrics, the necessity for clergy serving Welsh-speaking parishes to be competent in Welsh, the decent celebration of the services in church, clerical residence, the duty of catechizing, the values of clerical societies, the distribution of religious tracts and the need for clergy to continue their studies after ordination; see T. Burgess, *A Charge delivered to the Clergy of the Diocese of St David's in the year 1807* (Carmarthen, 1809). In 1813, Burgess's Charge, whilst more theological in tone than his previous Charges, contained an appendix outlining the objectives of a newly established society in Carmarthen for 'the Encouragement of Piety and Virtue, and for Preventing and Punishing of Vice, Profaneness, and Immorality' which the clergy were encouraged to support, and sections on responding to the growth of dissent and on the promotion of popular education as a means to this end; see T. Burgess, *A Charge Delivered to the Clergy of the Diocese of St David's in the Month of September 1813* (Carmarthen, 1814).

57 NLW, SD/Misc/1204.

58 NLW, SD/LET/1259.

59 D. T. W. Price, *A History of St David's University College, Lampeter, Vol I: To 1898* (Cardiff, 1977), p. 5.

60 *DWB*, p. 37; Morgan, 'Diocese of St Davids', 17–18.

[61] *Links with the Past: Swansea and Brecon Historical Essays,* ed. O. W. Jones and D. Walker (Llandybïe, 1974), pp. 170–83.
[62] *A History of the Church in Wales*, ed. D. Walker (Penarth, 1976), p. 146.
[63] Price, *History of St David's University College*, pp. 1–4, 12–14, 17–50, 204–5, 207. See also *The Saturday Magazine*, 26 October 1827, p. 156, and J. B. Jenkinson, *A Charge delivered to the Clergy of the Diocese of St David's* (London, 1828), pp. 32–4.
[64] *DWB*, pp. 633, 1009, 1051.
[65] Ibid., p. 743; D. Parry-Jones, 'Henry Thomas Payne, 1759–1832: rector of Llanbedr and archdeacon of Carmarthen', *Brycheiniog*, 5 (1959), 35–50.
[66] *DWB*, p. 171.
[67] See R. L. Brown, 'In pursuit of a Welsh episcopate', *Religion and National Identity: Wales and Scotland c.1700–2000*, ed. R. Pope (Cardiff, 2001), 84–102.
[68] Standard, unadventurous biography by J. C. Thirlwall, *Connop Thirlwall: Historian and Theologian* (London, 1936), throws little light on his episcopate. For more recent and challenging reassessments see W. T. Gibson, 'Fresh light on Bishop Connop Thirlwall of St David's (1840–1875)', *Transactions of the Honourable Society of Cymrodorion* (1992), 141–58, and M. Cragoe, *An Anglican Aristocracy: The Moral Economy of the Landed Estate in Carmarthenshire, 1832–1895* (Oxford, 1996), pp. 204–6.
[69] NLW, SD/LET/283–8.
[70] NLW, SD/LET/293.
[71] Walker, *History of the Church in Wales*, pp. 131–3.
[72] *Remains Literary and Theological of Connop Thirlwall, Vol I: Charges Delivered between the Years 1842 and 1860*, ed. J. J. S. Perowne (London, 1877), p. 68.
[73] NLW, MS 4287C.
[74] Ibid., p. 14.
[75] Ibid., p. 58.
[76] Ibid., p. 169.
[77] Ibid., p. 189.
[78] Ibid., p. 211.
[79] Ibid., p. 349.
[80] Ibid., p. 356.
[81] Ibid., p. 296.
[82] Ibid., p. 309.
[83] Ibid., p. 105.

[84] Ibid., p. 317.
[85] Ibid., pp. 190–1.
[86] Ibid., p. 299.
[87] Ibid., pp. 306–7.
[88] Ibid., p. 357.
[89] Ibid., p. 297.
[90] Ibid., p. 62.
[91] Ibid., pp. 103–4, 170, 190.
[92] Ibid., p. 177.
[93] Ibid., pp. 306–7.
[94] Ibid., p. 178.
[95] Ibid., p. 17.
[96] Ibid., p. 63.
[97] Ibid., pp. 109–10.
[98] Watts, *The Dissenters: The Expansion of Evangelical Nonconformity*, p. 125.
[99] NLW, SD/LET/1240.
[100] NLW, SD/LET/1227.
[101] D. G. Evans, 'The growth and development of organised religion in the Swansea Valley, 1820–1890' (unpublished Ph.D. thesis, University of Wales, Swansea, 1978), 75–8.
[102] Morgan, 'The diocese of St David's in the nineteenth century: the unreformed Church', 24–5, 27–8.
[103] *Cardiganshire County History, Vol. III: Cardiganshire in Modern Times*, pp. 489–90, 549.
[104] *Pembrokeshire County History, Vol. III: Early Modern Pembrokeshire*, pp. 241–2.
[105] NLW, SD/Misc/1205.
[106] NLW, SD/Misc/1081–3.
[107] NLW, SD/LET/1209.
[108] *Letters Literary and Theological of Connop Thirlwall*, ed. J. J. S. Perowne and L. Stokes (London, 1881), p. 186.
[109] NLW, B/QA/14, 23 and 26; SD/QA/62, 68, 70 and 73. All these are in the form of answers to queries on printed forms except B/QA/26 which is a visitation notebook.
[110] W. M. Jacob, 'A practice of a very hurtful tendency', *SCH*, 16 (1979), 319–26.
[111] NLW, B/LET/806.
[112] NLW, B/NR/292.
[113] Morgan, 'Diocese of St David's', 35–6.
[114] NLW, B/QA/26.
[115] W. N. Yates, *Buildings, Faith and Worship: The Liturgical*

Arrangement of Anglican Churches 1600–1900, 2nd edn (Oxford, 2000), p. 222.

10. The Welsh Church and the Welsh Language

[1] M. Cragoe, 'A question of culture: the Welsh Church and the bishopric of St Asaph, 1780–1870', *WHR*, 18 (1996–7), 237.

[2] From a sermon preached by Dean Edwards of Bangor, entitled 'Why are the Welsh people alienated from the Church', published posthumously in H. T. Edwards, *Wales and the Welsh Church* (London, 1889), pp. 313–14.

[3] R. T. Jones, 'The Church and the Welsh language in the nineteenth century', in *The Welsh Language and its Social Domains 1801–1911*, ed. G. H. Jenkins (Cardiff, 2000), pp. 215–37. The quotation is from p. 236.

[4] E. M. White, 'The Established Church, dissent and the Welsh language c.1660–1811', in *The Welsh Language before the Industrial Revolution*, ed. G. H. Jenkins (Cardiff, 1997), pp. 238.

[5] See for Ireland *A View of the Irish Language*, ed. B. Ó Cuír (Dublin, 1969); for Scotland C. W. J. Withers, *Gaelic in Scotland 1698–1981* (Edinburgh, 1984); and for the Isle of Man R. L. Thomson, 'The Manx language' and J. K. Draskau, 'The Use of Englishes', in *A New History of the Isle of Man, Vol. V: The Modern Period 1830–1999*, ed. J. Belchem (Liverpool, 2000), pp. 312–22.

[6] NLW, B/QA/14 and 26.

[7] *Cardiganshire County History, Vol. III: Cardiganshire in Modern Times*, ed. G. H. Jenkins and I. G. Jones (Cardiff, 1998), p. 488.

[8] W. T. R. Pryce, 'Approaches to the linguistic geography of north-east Wales, 1750–1846', *NLWJ*, 17 (1971–2), 356.

[9] E. T. Davies, *Religion in the Industrial Revolution in South Wales* (Cardiff, 1965), pp. 115–20.

[10] W. J. Copleston, *Memoirs of Edward Copleston, DD, Bishop of Llandaff* (London, 1851), pp. 252–67; the quotation is on pp. 254–5.

[11] *The Letters of Edward Copleston, Bishop of Llandaff, 1828–1849*, ed. R. L. Brown (Cardiff, 2003), pp. 20–5.

[12] *A History of the Church in Wales*, pp. 127, 130–3, 160.

[13] A. H. Dodd, *A History of Caernarvonshire* (Denbigh, 1968), pp. 348–9.

[14] R. L. Brown, 'The effects of Queen Anne's Bounty and the

Ecclesiastical Commission on some Montgomeryshire parishes', *Montgomeryshire Collections*, 86 (1988), 105–7.

[15] H. T. Edwards, *The Eisteddfod* (Cardiff, 1990), pp. 14–15; R. T. Jenkins and H. M. Ramage, *A History of the Honourable Society of Cymmrodorion and of the Gwyneddigion and Cymreigyddion Societies* (London, 1951), pp. 138, 169.

[16] Ibid., pp. 139–40.

[17] NLW, SD/LET/1228.

[18] Edwards, *The Eisteddfod*, p. 15.

[19] Jenkins and Ramage, *History of the Honourable Society of Cymmrodorion*, pp. 141, 143; D. Miles, *The Royal National Eisteddfod of Wales* (Swansea, 1978), pp. 46–7.

[20] For descriptions of the Carmarthen eisteddfod and its consequences see E. Humphreys, *The Taliesin Tradition* (Bridgend, 2000), pp. 128–33; T. Parry, *The Story of the Eisteddfod* (Liverpool 1963), pp. 34–6; Edwards, *The Eisteddfod*, pp. 16–20; Miles, *Royal National Eisteddfod.*, pp. 48–56; Jenkins and Ramage, *History of the Honourable Society of Cymmrodorion*, pp. 155–9; D. T. W. Price, *Bishop Burgess and Lampeter College*, pp. 42–9. For the particular contribution of the Welsh Anglican clergy to eisteddfodau see B. L. Jones, *Yr Hen Bersoniaid Llengar* (Dinbych, 1963). For the more general impact of the eisteddfod movement and Celtic antiquarianism on Welsh culture and history see especially G. A. Williams, *The Welsh in their History* (London, 1982), pp. 31–64, and *When was Wales?* (London 1985), pp. 159–67, 183–97. There is also useful material in his *Madoc: The Making of a Myth* (London, 1979), especially pp. 99–117.

[21] Jenkins and Ramage, *History of the Honourable Society of Cymmrodorion*, p. 145.

[22] See M. E. Thomas, *Afiaith yng Ngwent: Hanes Cymdeithas Cymreigyddion y Fenni 1833–1854* (Caerdydd, 1978), especially pp. 109–37.

[23] Miles, *Royal National Eisteddfod*, p. 57.

[24] Cragoe, 'A question of culture', 232–3.

[25] Price, *A History of St David's University College, Lampeter*, pp. 4, 36–8, 50, 178.

[26] Ibid., pp. 64–5. See also Jones, 'The Church and the Welsh language', 230–1.

[27] White, 'Established Church, dissent and the Welsh language', 241, 243–4, 246.

[28] NLW, B/Misc/10.

[29] White, 'Established Church, dissent and the Welsh language',

247. For the general trends in relation to the language in which services were conducted in the late eighteenth and early nineteenth centuries see ibid., 248–61.

11. *Church Building and Restoration*

[1] M. L. Clarke, 'Anglesey churches in the nineteenth century', *Anglesey Antiquarian Society and Field Club Transactions* (1961), 53–68; 'Church building and restoration in Caernarvonshire during the nineteenth century', *Caernarvonshire Historical Society Transactions*, 22 (1961), 20–31; and 'Caernarvonshire churches at the beginning of the nineteenth century', *Caernarvonshire Historical Society Transactions*, 23 (1962), 57–66. See also T. Roberts, 'Adeiladu ac atgyweirio eglwysi yn esgobaeth Bangor yn ystod y bedwaredd ganrif ar bymtheg', in *'Ysbryd Dealtwrus ac Enaid Anfarwol': Ysgrifau ar Hanes Crefydd yng Ngwynedd*, ed. W. P. Griffith (Bangor, 1999), pp. 179–89.

[2] R. Fenton, *Tours in Wales (1804–1813)*, ed. J. Fisher (London, 1917); E. H. Hall, *A Description of Caernarvonshire (1809–1811)*, ed. E. G. Jones (Caernarfon, 1952); T. Jones, *A History of the County of Brecknock*, reprinted edn (Brecon, 1898).

[3] Ibid., p. 260.

[4] Ibid., p. 341.

[5] Ibid., p. 313.

[6] Ibid., pp. 410, 450.

[7] Hall, *Description of Caernarfonshire*, p. 275.

[8] Ibid., p. 275. H. Hughes and H. L. North, *The Old Churches of Snowdonia* (Bangor, 1924), p. 159, note the survival of these dog tongs and similar examples at Bangor Cathedral, Clynnog Fawr and Llaneilian (Anglesey).

[9] Fenton, *Tours in Wales*, pp. 23, 68, 87.

[10] Details for diocese of St Asaph from D. R. Thomas, *A History of the Diocese of St Asaph* (London, 1874).

[11] Clarke, 'Church building and restoration in Caernarvonshire', 23–4; *Archaeologia Cambrensis*, 1 (1846), p. 467.

[12] W. N. Yates, 'The progress of ecclesiology and ritualism in Wales 1840–75', *Archaeologia Cambrensis*, 149 (2000), 59–88.

[13] NLW, SD/Misc/90.

[14] NLW, SA/LET/392.

[15] I. G. Jones, 'Church reconstruction in Breconshire in the nineteenth century', *Brycheiniog*, 19 (1980–1), 12.

[16] *Idem*, 'Ecclesiastical economy: aspects of church building in Victorian Wales', in *Welsh Society and Nationhood: Historical Essays presented to Glanmor Williams*, ed. R. R. Davies, R. A. Griffiths, I. G. Jones and K. O. Morgan (Cardiff, 1984), p. 230.
[17] Ibid., p. 224.
[18] *Idem*, 'Church restoration in north Cardiganshire in the nineteenth century', *NLWJ*, 20 (1977–8), 353.
[19] NLW, SD/Misc/397.
[20] University of Wales, Lampeter: University Archives H/1/1 (7).
[21] NLW, SD/Misc/3.
[22] *Pembrokeshire County History, Vol. III: Early Modern Pembrokeshire 1536–1815*, p. 239.
[23] J. W. Evans, 'St David's Cathedral: the forgotten centuries', *JWEH*, 3 (1986), 86–9.
[24] NLW, SD/Ch/B8, SD/Ch/Misc 90 and SD/Ch/LET 171–185.
[25] NLW, SD/Ch/LET 242.
[26] NLW, B/LET/650.
[27] NLW, B/LET/745.
[28] NLW, B/LET/1082–3.
[29] Hughes and North, *Old Churches of Snowdonia*, pp. 28, 238–41.
[30] NLW, SD/LET/1211.
[31] Clarke, 'Caernarvonshire churches at the beginning of the nineteenth century', 58–9.
[32] Hughes and North, *Old Churches of Snowdonia*, pp. 248, 261, 274–5.
[33] See Yates, *Buildings, Faith and Worship*, pp. 77–107.
[34] NLW, B/Maps/42.
[35] Denbighshire Record Office, PD/44/1/25.
[36] Plan in ICBS records at LPL.
[37] Yates, *Buildings, Faith and Worship*, pp. 222, 226.
[38] NLW, B/Misc/201.
[39] Yates, *Buildings, Faith and Worship*, p. 81. Contemporary plan in Denbighshire Record Office, PD/50/1/16.
[40] NLW, SD/F/140.
[41] Fenton, *Tours in Wales*, p. 114.
[42] P. D. Randall, 'The pews of St Peter's Church, Ruthin', *Denbighshire Historical Society Transactions*, 29 (1980), 169, 171.
[43] Thomas, *History of the Diocese of St Asaph*, pp. 341–3, 365.
[44] Yates, *Buildings, Faith and Worship*, pp. 102–3, 223.
[45] NLW, B/Maps/26.
[46] NLW, B/Maps/60.

[47] NLW, LL/Ch/3906.

[48] Pembrokeshire Record Office, HPR/33/3.

[49] NLW, SD/F/314.

[50] NLW, LL/Ch/3920.

[51] Yates, *Buildings, Faith and Worship*, pp. 110, 228, plate 11.

[52] D. Percival, 'Inventory of Nonconformist chapels and Sunday cchools in Cardiganshire', *Cardiganshire County History, Vol. III: Cardiganshire in Modern Times*, pp. 508–39.

[53] A. Jones, *Welsh Chapels* (Stroud, 1996), pp. 12, 21.

[54] Ibid., p. 31.

[55] Yates, *Buildings, Faith and Worship*, pp. 222–4, 226; see also Jones, *Welsh Chapels*, pp. 22–9, 34–44.

[56] Yates, *Buildings, Faith and Worhsip*, pp. 108–23.

[57] Ibid., pp. 222–6.

[58] NLW, LL/F/223; J. Newman, *Buildings of Wales: Gwent/Monmouthshire* (London, 2000), pp. 164–7, 398.

[59] Thomas, *History of the Diocese of St Asaph*, pp. 562–3.

[60] Yates, *Buildings, Faith and Worship*, p. 111, plate 12a.

[illegible]

Flintshire Record Office, [illegible]

[illegible]

[illegible] history of Nonconformist chapels and [illegible]

[illegible] (Bangor, 1994), pp. 12–[illegible].

[illegible]

ibid., pp. [illegible]

[illegible]

Part IV

1850–1920

12
The National Scene

Introduction

The period from the middle of the nineteenth century to the end of the second decade of the twentieth was, it can be argued, one of renewal and reinvention for the Anglican Church in Wales. Yet somewhat paradoxically, this seventy-year period is framed by the low point of the 1851 religious census, and the perceived crisis of the formal severance from the Church of England in 1920. As will be seen, the meaning of the 1851 census has only recently been more fully understood,[1] but as early as the 1930s, the crisis of disestablishment was acknowledged as not having been the total disaster that many had feared. Rather than obliterating Anglicanism from the face of Wales, disestablishment meant that the Church in Wales emerged as more financially self-sufficient and perhaps also more self-confident. It lost little time in re-endowing itself and in redefining its diocesan boundaries.[2] The relatively limited impact of disestablishment does not of course reduce the significance of the campaign itself, nor does it prevent the campaign from becoming a central theme in modern Welsh history. Out of this historiographical tradition emerged a largely negative interpretation of the Church as an obstructive, English institution, increasingly irrelevant to the Welsh nation in the newly emerging world of mass politics. In contrast, most recent work has questioned the culturally alien nature of the Welsh Church, and this is a theme which will be further developed in the three chapters of this part.[3] It will be argued that the Church in Wales was a thoroughly Welsh institution, which existed uneasily alongside other Christian bodies in a complex environment of religious pluralism. This chapter concentrates on the national picture, beginning with a discussion of the 1851 census and its aftermath, and moving on to investigate the impact of the disestablishment campaign. Particular attention will be given to the small but vocal group of Anglicans who actively embraced the notion of disestablishment in the face of the widespread opposition of most of their co-religionists. Chapter 13 examines the changing role of bishops and clergy in the second half of the nineteenth century, and the development of Welsh theological training. Chapter 14 is concerned with developments at parish level. The aim of these chapters is to explore the texture and shape of local church life in a way which sheds light on the manner in which Anglicanism functioned within a variety of contrasting local communities across Wales.

The 1851 Religious Census and its Aftermath

For the first and last time in British history, on Sunday 31 March 1851 an attempt was made to survey all the places of worship in Great Britain, and to count the number of those attending. The project was conceived as part of the decennial census of that year, although the data was gathered independently. It had originally been intended to make completion of the returns compulsory, but this was dropped as being of doubtful legal validity. The stated aim of the religious census was to discover whether the seating in places of worship had kept pace with the rapid growth in population, and thus the extent to which the nation's religious needs were being met by the existing church provision. Teams of census enumerators were employed to collect the names and addresses of all the ministers in their district, and then census forms – different types for Anglicans, Nonconformists and members of the Society of Friends – were sent to every place of worship. The enumerators were instructed to collect the forms, and to chase any missing ones, with a relentlessness which was intended to ensure that no worshipping community, no matter how small or informally organized, should slip through the fingers of the Registrar-General's office. Once as many completed returns as possible had been extracted, the data was sent to London where it was analysed by Horace Mann, the barrister appointed by the Registrar-General, and his team. Mann's report on the census, and the statistics which had been derived from it, were published on 3 January 1854. His findings proved controversial. The most significant were that Nonconformity was stronger than had previously been thought, and that a sizeable proportion of the British public did not worship at all. This news was predictably well or ill received by different sections of the community.[4] The impact of Mann's report was such that it is usually seen as having set the religious agenda for the second half of the nineteenth century. It gave impetus to disestablishment campaigns in both England and Wales, to the efforts to break the Anglican stranglehold on education, and to the attempts of various Christian groups to combat the effects of so-called 'unconscious secularism'.

After the flurries of mid-nineteenth-century controversy had died away, the voluminous piles of census returns gathered dust in the Public Record Office. They were subject to a 100-year closure period, and did not therefore become available to historians until the 1950s. K. S. Inglis, David Thompson and W. S. F. Pickering were the first to explore the census as a historical source, in a cluster of publications which are now always cited as the starting-points in any discussion of the census's interpretation.[5] This was followed by a number of scholarly editions of the census returns for particular counties and regions; one of the earliest was Ieuan Gwynedd Jones and David Williams's first volume, on south Wales, which appeared in 1976. Wales was also particularly well served by a number of early scholarly articles.[6] From the mid-1980s, the development of powerful computer programmes and significant research funding made possible a project which resulted in the publication in 2000 of K. D. M. Snell and Paul S. Ells's *Rival Jerusalems: The Geography of Victorian Religion*. This project subjected vast amounts of data from the census to computer analysis, and enabled scholars to look for the first time simultaneously at all parts of England and Wales, and to assess the regional strengths and weaknesses of all the denominations that existed in 1851. *Rival Jerusalems* is now the standard work on the religious census of 1851.

What does all this data tell us about the state of religion in mid-nineteenth-century Wales, and how does it compare with

England? Wales offered an enormously high level of religious provision for its population with 4,006 separate places of worship. These places contained a total of 1,005,410 sittings for a population of 1,188,914; thus overall 84.5 per cent of the population could have been seated at worship. Horace Mann described Wales as 'fortunately basking in an excess of spiritual privileges'.[7] Indeed, the counties of Merioneth and Breconshire had more seats available than population to fill them.[8] Wales also recorded much higher levels of attendance than England – equivalent to 83.4 per cent of the population in south Wales and 86.6 per cent in north Wales.[9] This renders talk of secularisation much less meaningful in mid-nineteenth-century Wales than it does on the other side of Offa's Dyke, where worship was attended by 59.1 per cent of the population. Equally, it challenges the assertion that was made by Horace Mann, and widely picked up by others, both at the time and since, that it was the working classes, the 'unconscious secularists', who stayed away from religion. Working-class Welsh people had, at this date, clearly not abandoned the practice of religion. The sheer size of Welsh Protestant dissent is another obvious and important finding; the Welsh were far more likely than the English to be Nonconformists, and Anglicans were a minority throughout the principality. In the south, the main source of rivalry for the Anglicans came from the Independents; in the north, Calvinistic Methodists were in the majority.[10] There is also evidence of an east–west split within Nonconformity, with Calvinistic Methodist and Independent congregations noticeably stronger in the Welsh-speaking west, and Wesleyan Methodism more densely clustered in the east of Wales. The strength of Nonconformity is revealed by the sheer number of their sittings, particularly in the south. The percentage share of Anglican sittings was lowest in Wales, with a dramatic decline being visible along the southern part of the English–Welsh border, between the dioceses of Hereford and St David's. The place with the lowest share of Anglican sittings anywhere in England or Wales was Merthyr Tydfil. In about half of Wales, the Anglican share was less than 30 per cent. This differentiated Wales very significantly from most of England, where large parts of the South and Midlands registered a share in excess of 60 per cent, with five registration districts in Sussex all recording well over 80 per cent. Merthyr also registered the lowest share of Anglican attendances – 6.2 per cent. Indeed, the fourteen districts with the lowest Anglican attendance were all in Wales. In parts of Hampshire, meanwhile, Anglican attendance ran at 90 per cent.[11]

It would, however, be unwise to conclude too much from these raw facts – in parts of the north of England, and the western tip of Cornwall, the Church of England was just as weak as it was in Wales. Equally, when another measurement is considered, that of the number of people per place of worship for the Church of England, a measurement which clearly favours rural areas, the Church in north Wales comes out at around or above the national average.[12] The Church of England evidently had enough provision in that part of the country, even if the north Walians chose not to make much use of it. In central and western parts of Wales, and in the south, the Established Church's provision was weak, indicating that low Anglican attendance may in some cases have been the result of lack of space in a suitable place of worship, rather than for any other reason. Welsh Anglican churches tend to be significantly smaller than their English counterparts, and often considerably less spacious than urban, galleried, Nonconformist chapels.

Mid-nineteenth-century Wales was a place in which the religious culture had undergone and was continuing to undergo sudden and rapid change. One of the most striking features to emerge from work on the 1851 data is the sheer variation in the pace of growth between Anglicans and Nonconformists. In Caernarfonshire, for instance, where the population nearly doubled in the first half of the century, there had been sixty-four places of Anglican worship in 1800, and thirty Nonconformist chapels. By 1851, there were sixty-seven Anglican churches and 221 Nonconformist chapels. This represented a growth rate for Anglicanism of less than half of 1 per cent, and for Nonconformity a growth rate in excess of 600 per cent.[13] In the second half of the century, both the rate of Nonconformist chapel building, and the rate of population expansion began to slow. Meanwhile, from the 1840s Anglicans in Caernarfonshire began to devote a considerable amount of effort to church restoration, just as the building energy of Nonconformity began to fade.[14] A similar pattern has been noted for both Denbighshire[15] and the Swansea district. At the beginning of the century there had been only seven dissenting chapels in Swansea; by the time of the census there were seventy-four. The number of Anglican churches had risen over the same period by just five; there were twenty before 1800, and twenty-five in 1851.[16] Not until 1839 had the Church responded to population growth with a building programme, by which time the Nonconformists had already erected forty-six chapels.[17] Elsewhere in Wales, the increase in Anglican provision over the first half of the nineteenth century varied from nil in Radnorshire – where no new buildings were needed, as there were no new urban or rural developments of any size – to nearly 70 per cent in Flint, which included towns such as Wrexham.[18] The patterns of correlation with Nonconformity varied from place to place. In Caernarfonshire, Nonconformist religious momentum appears to have reached a peak in the period immediately before 1850. In Swansea, however, it was sustained throughout the second half of the century. In Cardiganshire, the population increased by two-thirds in the first half of the century, and the Established Church was weak at the beginning and weaker still at the middle. Only 22.5 per cent of the worshippers on census Sunday are estimated as having attended Anglican services, and although the Anglicans could muster seventy-five places of worship across the county, large congregations were restricted to Cardigan, St Michael's Aberystwyth, Llanbadarn Fawr and Llanfihangel Genau'r-glyn.[19] In Cardiganshire, the Church of England was hugely overshadowed by Calvinistic Methodism, which claimed an estimated 38 per cent of the worshippers. Independency was also a significant rival, and it had an estimated 22 per cent of the market share. Other denominations, such as Unitarianism, tended to be confined to very specific geographical areas, and were not statistically significant across the county as a whole.[20]

Although the 1851 census is now seen as a key moment in the religious history of nineteenth-century Britain, it needs to be remembered that its publication attracted very little interest in Wales at the time. It became a controversial issue only later, when the disestablishment campaign began in earnest.[21] All four Welsh bishops delivered Charges in the mid-1850s, but the census hardly merited episcopal notice, despite the recent publication of its results. Only Alfred Ollivant of Llandaff referred to it in a Charge, and then only indirectly in a footnote, in order to extract a statistic about population growth in his diocese.[22] Aware, presumably, that parishes in his own diocese had registered the lowest Anglican attendance of anywhere in Britain, Ollivant alluded to the problems the Church faced in rather a defensive tone: 'The Church may have awoken from its slumber, but there is still a vast amount of spiritual destitution which it has not been able, and is utterly unable to reach. It has not accomplished impossibilities.'[23] Ollivant blamed the inflexibility of Church structures, an explanation which fits well with what he would have witnessed since his first arrival in Wales in 1827; the phenomenon of Nonconformist places of worship appearing with almost magical suddenness like crops of autumn mushrooms. His tendency to downplay the reality and power of dissent is more ambiguous, however:

> The same unbending rigidity of form and action which in the last century was one of the causes that drove so many from her pale, now prevents her [the Church] from opening her arms sufficiently wide to receive the multitudes who would gladly escape from the turmoils of political Dissent, and return to the Church which God is manifestly visiting with the tokens of his grace.[24]

In the same Charge, he referred to the divisions between churchmen and dissenters as 'minor differences', and commented approvingly on the help which some non-Anglicans had given to church-building projects in their parishes. Was Ollivant displaying naïve optimism, or was there in fact a better tone to interdenominational relations in south Wales than is normally assumed at this period? Or perhaps Ollivant was simply trying to smooth over some of the cracks.

Bishop Connop Thirlwall of St David's responded to the census by questioning its accuracy in a speech in the House of Lords. He claimed that the number of Anglicans had been underestimated and the number of Nonconformists overestimated.[25] This was more typical of episcopal reaction to the census than was Ollivant's position.

The Disestablishment Campaign

In both England and Wales, the most significant consequence of the 1851 census was that it gave birth to the campaign for the disestablishment of the Anglican Church. But whereas the English disestablishment campaign, orchestrated by Edward Miall and the Liberation Society, fizzled out after 1874,[26] in Wales, its effects were far-reaching, culminating in the achievement of disestablishment in 1920. The fact that a national campaign for disestablishment could build up steam relatively rapidly in the 1850s and 1860s was illustrative of the newly dynamic nature of Welsh society, with its drive for religious equality and democratic representation for all (males). Not surprisingly in view of its lengthy time-scale, the campaign went through a number of distinct phases. By the time that disestablishment was finally achieved, the central dynamic of Welsh society had moved away from its earlier seemingly all-consuming obsession with religious issues, and there was a sense of anticlimax and loss of interest.[27] For the whole of the period considered in the final three chapters of this book, however, the various phases of the campaign absorbed the energies of churchmen and Nonconformists alike, creating deep hostilities between those who, theologically and socially, were often not very far apart. As Kenneth Morgan has put it, 'Into this single theme, all the various grievances, real and imaginary, felt by Nonconformists everywhere were absorbed.'[28] The fortunes of the disestablishment campaign were also closely tied to those of the Liberal Party.

The campaign had four major phases. The first, preparatory phase began in the mid-nineteenth century, and was fuelled by a combination of pent-up rage directed at the Church, and rapid social change brought about by industrialization and urbanization and their associated population shifts. The Church was seen as implicated in the so-called 'treason of the Blue Books', the largely hostile report of the Education Commissioners in 1847, which had concluded that the Welsh were a dirty, immoral and ignorant nation.[29] Although the report was the work of a group of young English lawyers, the clergy were seen as having been complicit as witnesses, one of whom, John Jones (Tegid) acted as a translator of the English text. The overall effect of the report was to give rise to a growth in nationalist feeling, and a much more potent form of radicalism. The Church, with its English bishops and its official disapproval of popular Welsh forms of religion such as evening prayer meetings, was a natural target. It appeared rigid and Canute-like, standing immobile amongst a rising tide of relocated people, unable to respond with the speed or the creativity of the other denominations, and sometimes linguistically deficient. The publication of the 1851 census results simply confirmed the reality of the strength of Nonconformity, a fact that was obvious to all. This was the period when, in the imagination of both the Welsh and the non-Welsh, Welsh identity became increasingly strongly linked with Nonconformist religion.

The second, major phase of the disestablishment campaign began around 1868, the year in which the newly extended urban franchise produced a Liberal landslide in Wales, albeit of mainly Anglican, Gladstonian Liberals. By that year, the Liberation Society, which campaigned for the removal of state shackles on churches everywhere, had at least fifty-five branches in Wales, and had organized itself into a national movement.[30] In 1869, the Irish Church Bill was passed, setting in motion the legislation for the disestablishment of the Church of Ireland and providing an enormous boost for the Welsh disestablishment movement. In 1870, the first of what would be many disestablishment motions was put forward in the House of Commons. Arguments derived from Church history figured to an extraordinary degree. Speakers on all sides evoked and argued about the ancient Celtic Church, the works of Bede and Chaucer, the ecclesiastical policies of Henry II and Henry VIII, the issues surrounding the translation of the Bible into Welsh in 1588, and the impact of the Evangelical Revival. The debate well illustrates the extent of scholarship and religiosity in the mid-Victorian House of Commons. It also emphasizes the perceived need to identify different targets when firing at the Welsh rather than the Irish ecclesiastical establishment. Whereas parliamentary debates about the Irish Church had focused heavily on the question of disendowment, arguments about the substantially poorer Welsh Church turned to a much greater degree about its supposedly 'alien' nature.[31] All these factors gave the second phase of the campaign a much more overtly national political (as opposed to local political) dimension. This was seen again in the general election of 1885, in which a further-expanded Welsh electorate returned thirty Liberal MPs (out of a possible thirty-four), all but one of whom were pledged to the cause of Welsh disestablishment. As we shall see in the next chapter, this was also the time when the Church began to place a new emphasis on indigenous leadership. It also began to claw back something of its national popularity, although, as Morgan has pointed out, part of the growth in numbers of Easter communicants, baptisms and marriage ceremonies may be attributed to the rising population.[32]

The third phase began in 1886. By this year the future of the Welsh Church had emerged as a major issue in the context of British politics as a whole. Welsh disestablishment became officially enshrined in Liberal Party policy in 1887, and Gladstone finally committed himself to it in 1891. The Liberal Party had split over Irish Home Rule, which led to a greater prominence for Welsh members, and renewed emphasis on overtly nationalist arguments for the disestablishment of the Church in Wales. This lent an increasingly bitter tone to the rhetoric about the culturally alien nature of the Church, as examples were raked up from all periods of Church history supposedly illustrative of the Church's failings and its illegitimacy as a national institution. Rhetoric overspilled into violence as tithe riots broke out, particularly in the diocese of St Asaph, in the period from 1886 to 1891. At a time of severe downturn in agriculture, the attempted gathering of tithe payments by a Church which was only supported by a minority in the countryside, provided just the right environment to fuel a potent cocktail of religious, political, social and economic resentment. The trouble was brought to an end with the passing of the Tithe Rent Charge Recovery Act of 1891, which passed responsibility for payment of tithe from tenants to landowners. The adoption of Welsh disestablishment as official Liberal Party policy had the effect of ratcheting up pressure on the Church, as did the replacement of Gladstone – the High Church owner of a Welsh country estate – by Lord Rosebery. The first-ever Welsh Disestablishment Bill was introduced in April 1894.

Under its terms, the four Welsh dioceses would be cut away from the province of Canterbury, with the bishops excluded from the House of Lords and the clergy removed from the Convocation of Canterbury. Ecclesiastical law would cease to exist in Wales. The Church would only be allowed to keep those endowments that it had acquired since 1703; all property, graveyards, glebe and tithe vested in the Church before that time would be confiscated, and the four Welsh cathedrals would be turned into national monuments. The income from these endowments was to be turned over to the newly created county councils, with money going for the creation of a national museum, a national library and for other secular, mainly medical and educational, purposes. The bill provoked a massive outcry among the Church's defenders, and was withdrawn three months after its first reading. A second Welsh Disestablishment Bill was brought forward in 1895, this one surviving to a second reading, at which point destructive infighting broke out between the politicians of north and south Wales over the way in which secularized tithe should be allocated. This instability contributed to the fall of the Rosebery government, and an election in which the Liberals sustained heavy losses. The consequence was a major setback for the disestablishment campaign, which was prolonged for a further two decades.

The final phase of the campaign was acted out in the much-changed world of the early twentieth century. Despite the considerable, if short-lived, excitement generated by the Revival of 1904–5, it was clear by the early years of the century that Nonconformity was on the decline. In 1900 and 1901, three of the four main denominations, the Baptists, the Wesleyans and the Independents, reported a drop in numbers.[33] This was in the context of rapidly rising population across Wales. Meanwhile, between 1900 and 1908, nearly one-third of the children born in Wales were baptized as Anglicans, a statistic which hardly seemed to fit with the notion of a widespread popular rejection of, or even indifference to, the Church.[34] In 1910, an immensely detailed, multi-volume statistical analysis of religion in Wales was published by the Disestablishment Commission.[35] This revealed that the Church was indeed in a commanding position, with 25.9 per cent of the churchgoing population being Anglican communicants, making them the largest single religious body in Wales. The older interdenominational rivalries seemed increasingly out of place in the new century, and theological matters paled before the formidable agenda of pressing economic and social concerns. When the 1902 Education Act caused hostility to break out once more between Church and Chapel, it was more of an anachronistic throwback to an earlier age than the keynote for the new century. Nevertheless, negative Nonconformist reaction to the Education Act was not without an impact in determining the results of the 1906 general election. Once again there was a Liberal landslide, with every seat in Wales held by a Liberal (except the Labour seat in Merthyr Tydfil) who was pledged to disestablishment. Moreover, the arrival as chancellor of the exchequer of David Lloyd George, who had been a vehement disestablishment campaigner since the tithe wars of the 1890s, was seen as a clear indication that the issue would at last be resolved in favour of the Nonconformists. In the event, although it would be Lloyd George who took a key role in negotiating the details of the bill in its final form with Bishops Edwards and Owen, the closing stages of the campaign for Welsh disestablishment were no clearer or swifter than the earlier ones had been. The House of Lords continued to block much Liberal legislation until its powers were curbed in 1911, and Lloyd George, rather than immediately pursuing the parliamentary route, chose, in consultation with the bishops, to set up a Royal Commission to inquire into the state of religion in Wales. When the commission reported, in 1910, it showed that the Church of England was the largest religious body in Wales, and attracted over a quarter of all worshippers.[36] This was clearly a much-improved situation from the last attempt systematically to measure support for religious bodies, which had been the 1851 religious census, and it was greeted with predictable enthusiasm by Anglicans. Nevertheless, the disestablishment question could not be buried, and another bill, this one steered by the home secretary Reginald McKenna, was introduced in 1912, and began what was to be a faltering two-and-a-half-year passage through both Houses. McKenna's bill contained most of the features of its predecessors, but 1662, rather than 1703, was taken as the year from which pre-dating endowments would be seized. Church property would be transferred to a new representative body of the Church, and parochial endowments would be handed over to county councils. Yet although the politicians, both Liberal and Unionist, continued to advance the same increasingly stale arguments for and against disestablishment, in both the Nonconformist and the Anglican camps, positions were not always so clear-cut. Over 100,000 Nonconformists in Wales signed petitions against the bill, some on the grounds that to remove the Anglican establishment would greatly enhance the position of the Church of Rome.[37] Meanwhile, as we shall see shortly, some influential Anglicans came out in favour of disestablishment.

For the majority of church people, however, the attitude adopted towards the prospect of their Church being torn asunder from Canterbury and stripped of at least part of its income was one of implacable opposition. Church defence was the name given to a raft of activities designed to protect the status quo, and originally sponsored by the Church Defence Institution, formed in 1871 in opposition to the Liberation Society. The movement was at its height in the 1890s, at the time of the first two bills. Hugely well-publicized and -attended Church Congresses took place at Cardiff in 1889 and at Rhyl in 1891. It gave its last gasp at an enormous demonstration in Hyde Park on 12 June 1915. Church Defence also functioned at a parish as well as a national level, although some parochial church defence associations were founded quite late. At Meifod in Montgomeryshire, the Church Defence League was founded in 1906.[38] At its launch it claimed a membership of 112, including Nonconformists, and thirty-four were described as being Welsh, although it is not clear what 'Welsh' means in this context – presumably Welsh-speaking. At Manafon, also in Montgomeryshire, a branch of the Church Defence League was also founded in 1906, with an initial membership of eleven.[39] Events included a lantern lecture with the title 'Why am I a churchman?' delivered by Sydney H. Jarvis of Newtown.

In Church circles, opposition to disestablishment, much of it fuelled by fears of wholesale asset-stripping and a nervous desire to maintain ecclesiastical privileges at all costs, was predictable. Less predictable were the views expressed by a controversial group of Anglicans – a small but significant minority – who, in the face of the official view that disestablishment was sacrilege, actively advocated it. These Anglicans were prepared to campaign for disestablishment, and to be regarded as aberrant or subversive, sometimes at considerable personal cost.[40] They varied in their perspectives and motivations, but uniting most of them was their loyalty to the Liberal Party.[41] For Watkin Williams, foremost among the first generation of Anglican Liberal politicians who put the case for disestablishment in the early debates in the House of Commons, the arguments were at least in part couched in terms of the religious benefits which would accrue from disestablishment. He stated the classic position of the Liberation Society when he said that 'the feeling is everywhere gaining ground that establishments of religion by the State are both unscriptural and injurious to the cause of true religion'.[42] But he gave the argument a specifically Welsh twist, and was not slow to plunder church history in order to deploy nationalist arguments about the inherent superiority of the Welsh Church. Welsh Christianity originated much earlier than its English counterpart, about the middle of the second century, he claimed, and it remained untainted by Rome in a much purer form than the corrupted English version brought by Augustine to Canterbury from Rome in the sixth century.[43] Thus the Welsh Church remained independent for centuries, until 'by a combination of fraud and collusion between the Pope and the King of England the ancient Church in Wales was subjected to, though not otherwise united with, the Church of England, and in the reign of Henry VIII'.[44]

Lewis Llewelyn Dillwyn was another Anglican on the radical wing of the Liberal Party, and one of the few who supported Williams in 1870. Dillwyn opened the disestablishment debate of 1886 (once again on a motion rather than a bill) relying more on recent statistics rather than on distant church history.[45] Dillwyn's harder line and uncompromising approach were characteristic of the third phase of the campaign. There was, he said, now only one churchman for every eight dissenters in Wales.[46] To make matters worse, he claimed, some of those who attended Anglican services did so either as a result of coercion from their employers, or because they were English foreigners. Again, nationalist arguments were deployed. The Welsh were quite different from the English in thought, character and feeling, as well as in religion and language.[47] On the supposed religious benefits of disestablishment, Dillwyn took a less positive line than Watkin Williams; in this, and indeed in the next debate on the issue in May 1889, he had little good to say about his own religion. He described its clergy as prone to drunkenness and immorality, something which no doubt won the approval of the sternly teetotal elements in Welsh Nonconformity. In 1889, Dillwyn went so far as to claim that even in England the Church of England had lost so much support that it could no longer claim to be the national religion.[48]

The speeches of both Williams and Dillwyn reflect the way in which religion was moving to the edges, and politics to the centre, of the late Victorian world. The third pro-disestablishment Anglican, J. Arthur Price, also saw his religion as to some extent at the service of his politics, although this did not stop him from being a devout churchman.[49] He was a long-standing member of the congregation at St Alban's Holborn, one of the leading Anglo-Catholic churches in London, where A. H. Mackonochie and Arthur Stanton, both early and prominent members of the Liberation Society, had been the vicar and the curate. For Price, politics and religion blended perfectly. He believed that Anglo-Catholicism was a democratic force, and that its adoption would, in the first instance, make disestablishment more likely, and thereafter revitalize a disestablished Church as a truly Welsh national institution. Price was active in the third and fourth stages of the disestablishment campaign. As a young man he had been attracted to politics, but had turned instead to a legal career as a London barrister, supplementing his income with regular journalism. In old age he abandoned the Liberal Party, becoming instead a founding member of the new Welsh nationalist party, *Plaid Genedlaethol Cymru*.

Price first came to the attention of Welsh (and English) churchmen in January 1895, when, with four Anglo-Catholic clergy from north Wales, he advocated what became known as the Bangor scheme. The proposal, drafted by Price with the support of David Lloyd George, then a fairly junior Member of

Parliament, was made in the wake of the first Welsh Disestablishment Bill of 1894, a measure which had inspired a massive Church defence campaign amongst most Anglicans.[50] Unperturbed by the extreme unpopularity of his proposals, Price suggested that what was needed was compromise over disendowment, as a sweetener to make disestablishment more palatable to church people. Price tried, optimistically and unsuccessfully, to convince ardent Church defenders such as John Owen, the Principal of St David's College, Lampeter, and subsequently bishop of St David's, that as disestablishment was only a matter of time, the Church might as well settle on the best terms possible.

The much-reviled 'Bangor scheme' involved disestablishment, the abolition of lay patronage, a greater share in church management for the laity and the reform of the cathedral system. Most important was the constitution of the Church in Wales as a separate province under its own archbishop, with the restoration of its ancient national character.[51] The irony was that much of the Bangor scheme was put into effect when disestablishment was finally achieved in 1920, and that Price's services, as a lawyer, were called upon to draft part of the constitution for the new Church. But in 1895 the scheme was several decades ahead of its time, and was quickly submerged beneath the ire of the bishops, and the weight of Church defence opposition. Price was much hurt by this, and for a brief period in 1896 seriously considered converting to Rome. He had been further unsettled by *Apostolicae Curae*, the papal rejection of the validity of Anglican orders that was issued in that year. It was hard for a passionate advocate of disestablishment to remain a member of an Established Church, particularly if there were doubts over the validity of its sacraments. It was not until 1941 that the Welsh Church publicly recognized Price's considerable abilities by appointing him chancellor of the diocese of Bangor. As an eighty-year old in the final year of his life, Price was too frail to carry out any of the duties.

In 1895, the immediate significance of the Bangor scheme lay in drawing public attention to the seemingly shocking fact that there were articulate, devout Welsh churchmen, both clerical and lay, who actively favoured disestablishment. Support came from an even more unexpected source, however, in the form of the distinguished English cleric John Percival, the headmaster of Rugby. Like Watkin Williams, Dillwyn and Price, Percival was also a deeply committed supporter of the Liberal Party and champion of equality. He chose the letters page of *The Times* as the forum for his controversial views, and he framed his words in the form of an open letter to the bishops of the Church of England. He denounced the bishops' opposition to disestablishment as 'another mistake which can hardly fail to be disastrous in its consequences',[52] and went on to outline the usual reasons that were given in support of Welsh disestablishment at this period: that the Anglican Church in Wales was the religion of a minority; that the democratically elected representatives of the Welsh people in the House of Commons had agreed that the privileged and endowed position of the Church should cease; and that a disestablished Welsh Church would have a greater likelihood of spiritual power and influence.

Percival's letter elicited a shocked response. Some parents even took their sons away from Rugby. It also had a negative effect on his future advancement in the Church, costing him the expected offer of a prominent bishopric or deanery in the north of England. Lord Rosebery quickly realized that this outspoken clergyman could not be placed on such a public stage. Instead, in a shrewd political move, he decided both to curtail Percival's outspokenness and to placate the disestablishment lobby by offering him the so-called dead see, that of Hereford. Hereford diocese, small, quiet and rural, at this period contained thirteen Welsh parishes. Queen Victoria was horrified that her prime minister had offered a bishopric to a disestablisher, and did all that she could to block his nomination. Her attempts were unsuccessful, after it was pointed out to her that she could not veto Percival on the sole grounds that he was in agreement with government policy on the issue of Welsh disestablishment.[53] It was a bitter moment for a queen who believed that disestablishment was a violation of her coronation oath.

Archbishop Benson of Canterbury and Bishop Randall Davidson of Rochester, both ardent Church defenders, had hoped that Percival's move to Hereford would lead to a weakening of his support for the Welsh disestablishment question, once he was confronted by the reality of it at parish level. But this was not to be the case. Welsh disestablishment continued to elicit his strong support, and he used his position in the House of Lords to make speeches in its favour in the disestablishment debates from 1912 to 1914. His speech of 1913 reflected what he perceived as recent shifts in the debate:

> Twenty years ago when this subject was discussed, the main discussion centred around the question of Disestablishment – today the main conflict is over disendowment. During the last generation, men both inside and outside the Church have come to a different view about establishment, doubting that it is possible for any one denomination to justify establishment unless it is in accordance with the general sentiment of the people. The whole question is narrowed to this: 'Is disendowment in any sense reasonable, and if so, to what extent is it reasonable and practicable?'[54]

Percival believed that the terms of the 1913 bill were reasonable, and indeed generous, and urged the House to accept them. Whether consciously or not, Percival was drawing on the Warburtonian argument of two hundred years earlier, when he pointed out that it was only the continuing support of the majority of the people that could justify the maintenance of a religious establishment.[55] This perspective, albeit from the opposite point of view, also underpinned the arguments of those against the bill, who argued that the Welsh Church was now more popular with the people of Wales than at any point in its recent past, and it therefore did not deserve to be disestablished.[56]

The leading Church of England newspaper, the *Church Times*, which was implacably opposed to disestablishment, was disdainful of Percival. 'The robes in which the spokesman delivered his speech were certainly the rochet and chimere of Hereford, but the voice was that of Mr McKenna.'[57] The newspaper found it harder to respond to Charles Gore, bishop of Oxford, who (with Edward Lee-Hicks, bishop of Lincoln) was another English bishop who at this time became an active advocate of Welsh disestablishment. Far more controversially, Gore appeared to favour disestablishment in England as well.

Gore was a difficult target because, although the *Church Times* leader writer and most of the paper's correspondents were hostile to disestablishment, there were other elements in his speech which met with their support. Gore was also a moderate Anglo-Catholic, and thus a sympathetic figure for most *Church Times* readers. He recast the disestablishment argument in an entirely new way, arguing that de facto, disestablishment was already occurring in both Wales and England, as members of other denominations were allowed to compete on equal terms with Anglicans:

> I cannot for my own part, see any disadvantage in Disestablishment being dealt with first in one region and then in another. We have heard a great many denunciations of piecemeal Disestablishment. But there is a piecemeal disestablishment which is continually going on in England which does appear to me to be one of the most disastrous kinds of disestablishment that can be imagined. We are being disestablished in England piecemeal. We have been disestablished in the elementary schools, we have been disestablished in the universities . . . The process is continually going on, and we are finding ourselves disestablished almost everywhere except the lunatic asylums. As far as I know that is the only department of public life in which the Established Church is allowed to minister without competitors.[58]

He also suggested that the Church's obsession with the disestablishment question was effectively masking the larger and more significant question of 'doctrinal disintegration, unparalleled in our history . . . We are trying to keep the Church of England together by flying for refuge to Establishment, when we ought to be taking the trouble to assert what our principles are and saying whether we intend to stand by them.'[59] This was the kind of rhetoric that would have raised a cheer from both Anglo-Catholics and Evangelicals. Yet Gore shocked many who would have appreciated this sentiment by attempting to explode the widely cherished myth that the Church's established status allowed it to serve in a special way the poor and the needy. 'The Church of England has not succeeded in becoming the Church of the poor, as is the Roman Catholic Church in so many parts of Europe, or the Salvation Army, or

Primitive Methodism.'[60] Gore's point was that people only really value religion if they have to pay for it; if it is provided free it elicits little popular support. *The Church Times* was enraged. It did not expect an Anglo-Catholic bishop to heap praise on the Salvation Army or on Primitive Methodists. Had Gore forgotten 'that the Church remains at work in the slums when the sects have migrated to better neighbourhoods'?[61] Yet Gore's arguments were being increasingly widely supported. They were expressed in the House of Commons by Liberals like Henry Hobhouse and C. F. G. Masterman, and in Wales by A. W. Wade-Evans in his *Papers for Thinking Welshmen*. Gore's intervention in the Welsh Church debate had another unintended consequence. He had been trying to establish two new dioceses within the large diocese of Oxford for Berkshire and Buckinghamshire, in the expectation that wealthy lay people in the diocese would raise the money. But it seemed incomprehensible to the wealthy lay people that they should endow new dioceses, in the likelihood that Gore, the back-stabber of the Welsh Church, would seek to disestablish them at some later date. The scheme failed. Gore was acutely disappointed, and appeared not to have foreseen that his views on the Welsh question could rebound on an Oxford diocesan matter.[62]

In the emergency created by the outbreak of war, the Welsh Disestablishment Bill (together with the Irish Home Rule Bill) hurriedly received the royal assent on 18 September 1914, on condition that implementation would be suspended until after the end of the war. Commissioners for the Welsh Church were, however, immediately appointed, to begin the work of administering ecclesiastical endowments. Thus began a partial disestablishment which would not become complete until June 1920, when the Welsh Church began its new existence as the twentieth province within the Anglican Communion. As Kenneth Morgan put it, 'The culminating achievement of Welsh Nonconformist radicalism was thus carried out in an atmosphere of profound anticlimax, in an empty Commons and with the minds of all on the international crisis.'[63] In the almost fifty years that Welsh disestablishment had been debated in that chamber, the question had moved to the increasingly remote reaches of British politics. The Welsh Church no longer aroused strong passions. As one contemporary noted, in place of 'the old threadbare phrase of Disestablishment and Disendowment' should be substituted 'Disintegration and Disinclination'.[64] The arguments had shifted and the matter had become largely symbolic, a question of arranging a fairly dignified surrender for the Welsh Church, in a way which would permit its retreat from the battlefield without it sustaining mortal wounds. The debate had moved from arcane discussions of Wales's remote religious past, to the importance of respecting the wishes of the electorate in a region which, if not yet recognized as an independent nation, was at least no longer seen as an indistinguishable part of England. But disestablishment had become an unsatisfactory symbol for a nationalist crusade, for during the previous half-century the Welsh Church had become undeniably much more Welsh in character.[65]

In the early 1920s, J. Arthur Price made a visit to St David's cathedral, remotely located on the Pembrokeshire coast, and the historic birthplace of the Welsh Church. It was a place that he had not visited since his spiritual crisis of 1896. Then, he had been disheartened by its chilly, Low Church ambience, and by what he termed 'the common ban placed alike on the faith of the invader, and the tongue of the invaded'.[66] Now, under the friendly, Welsh-speaking High Church Dean William Williams, all was different. Price wrote: 'As I entered the Cathedral, I could not help feeling a thrill. I seemed at last to be on free ground.'[67] This was the reality of what disestablishment meant for one of the most ardent of Anglican disestablishment campaigners.

13
The Ecclesiastical Personnel

The Episcopate

The mid-nineteenth century-bishops – Alfred Ollivant, Connop Thirlwall, Christopher Bethell and Thomas Vowler Short – were all Englishmen who found themselves in Wales as the result of clerical careers which had taken them sufficiently far to reach the episcopal bench, but not far enough to propel them back towards better-endowed sees in England. In 1850, Bethell of Bangor had been the longest in office, and was the occupant of the best-endowed Welsh see. He had previously been bishop of Gloucester and for a period of less than eight months bishop of Exeter, neither of which was as profitable as Bangor. Bethell was seventy-seven in 1850, and remained at Bangor until his death at the age of eighty-six. There were clear limits on his pastoral effectiveness, particularly as a non-Welsh-speaker in a diocese that was to a very large extent monoglot Welsh, and certainly the most Welsh of the Welsh dioceses.

The other three bishops were all appointments of the 1840s. As both theologian and historian, Thirlwall was undoubtedly the most academically distinguished bishop to serve in nineteenth-century Wales. Having resigned as assistant tutor of Trinity College, Cambridge, in 1834 over his support for the admission of dissenters to university degrees, he arrived in 1840 at Abergwili from the Yorkshire living of Kirby Underdale. He was appointed by Melbourne who felt that his oratorical powers would be an asset to the House of Lords. As the historian of Greece and the translator of Schleiermacher (both works accomplished before he came to Wales), Thirlwall remained a serious scholar who spent a great many hours alone in his library. There is, however, little evidence to support

Owen Chadwick's assertion that he was 'more capable of managing the peacocks on his terrace than the clergy of his diocese',[1] an accusation which probably arises from the fact that he had more interest in theological than in pastoral matters. Thus at his visitation of 1857, he focused on contentious theology, both distant and closer to home. He devoted a portion of his Charge to condemning the dogma of the Immaculate Conception (which had been promulgated by Pope Pius IX in 1854). This cannot have been intended to be of immediate practical relevance to the listening clergy, for the chances of many of them actually meeting a Catholic were not high. St David's diocese was among the least populated by Roman Catholics of any in England and Wales; only five places of Catholic worship had been recorded in 1851.[2] Of more pressing interest to most of the clergy were the theological opinions of Rowland Williams, vice-principal of St David's College, Lampeter. Williams would later achieve national notoriety as the last Anglican clergyman to be tried for heresy in the wake of the publication of *Essays and Reviews* (1860). In 1857 the controversy that swirled around him related to clerical reaction to a series of sermons that he had published, entitled *Rational Godliness* (1855). Over seventy beneficed clergy in the diocese petitioned Thirlwall to protest at Williams's supposed attack on the supremacy and infallibility of Scripture, and on the Book of Common Prayer and the Thirty-nine Articles. They urged the bishop to use his visitorial powers to remove Williams from his particularly influential position as the major educator of Wales's future clergy.[3] Thirlwall found himself caught in the classic bishop's dilemma: his private views were similar to Williams's own, yet he dare not be explicit about them. He declined to act, and made it clear to the protesting clergy that he was concerned to protect Williams's freedom of 'thought, word and action'.[4] At the same time he declined to offer unequivocal support for Williams, much to the irascible Williams's annoyance, and the two became engaged in a pamphlet battle that erupted a few years later.[5]

Thirlwall suffered from the fact that he was appointed just at the moment when pastoral rather than professorial qualities were coming into vogue as the primary qualification for the episcopate. In Wales, there was the further complication that an increasingly vocal constituency was demanding at every episcopal vacancy that a Welsh bishop be appointed.[6] The clergy may have found him a remote and mysterious figure, but Thirlwall was in fact energetic in visiting his huge diocese (at this date second in size only to Lincoln) and in investing his money in diocesan projects of various kinds. An accomplished linguist, Thirlwall set about learning Welsh at an early point (he was taught in part by Joshua Hughes, the future bishop of St Asaph). Nevertheless, in common with Ollivant and Campbell, who were the other nineteenth-century episcopal Welsh learners, his attempts to make himself understood in the language appear to have been less successful. Thirlwall mastered an academic version of the language which bore little relation to what was spoken in the parishes of Carmarthenshire and Cardiganshire. When he used the language in services, it tended to promote consternation, not only among his English hearers, who were annoyed at not being able to understand what was going on, but among the Welsh, who found his constructions and pronunciation equally baffling.[7] The breadth of his sympathy for non-Anglicans, which had been manifested in the stand that he had taken on the admission of non-Anglicans to Cambridge degrees, should have made him well suited to leading a minority denomination in St David's, but it seems merely to have antagonized church people.[8] Thirlwall may also have manifested some genuine eccentricities, but the myths which have gathered round him make it difficult to be sure what may genuinely be attributed to him, and what has been embroidered in the telling.[9] The overall impression is of an isolated scholar, whom it would have been kinder to rescue from Abergwili (where he remained for thirty-four years until his retirement in 1874) and nominate to a regius professorship. Nineteenth-century protocol prevented the moving of bishops back to the academy, however, and Thirlwall's political and theological opinions prohibited his being moved to a more congenial English see.

Thomas Vowler Short had spent his early years in the West Country, and after a successful spell as an Oxford college tutor, where his pupils included both Gladstone and Pusey, he devoted himself to the parochial ministry in Devon and then London, at St George's Bloomsbury, before becoming bishop of the tiny diocese of Sodor and Man. In varied ministerial contexts, he was clearly pastorally effective, and his *Parochialia* (1842) provided a blueprint for the management of a large urban parish. After five years on the Isle of Man, Short went to St Asaph in 1846, one factor in his decision being that his wife needed medical treatment that was not available on the island. Short presents something of a paradox. His episcopal Charges make him sound much more obviously pastoral than the other mid-nineteenth-century English and Welsh bishops. His 1856 Charge, for example, had none of the tone of a lofty lecture which was more typical of the episcopal communications of this period. He urged his clergy to holiness and pastoral depth, and displayed an engaging candour about the pressures of episcopal ministry. He lamented that the nature of much of a bishop's work was likely to render him unspiritual, and he informed his clergy that when he reviewed them mentally, he divided them into 'such as I should like to have around my bed, if I were dying, and such as I should more readily consult on any other occasion'.[10] It might have seemed rather blunt, but it was a perfect mid-Victorian metaphor for Episcopal–clerical relations, and he made it plain that he saw himself and his clergy as a collective 'us'.

Short was not, however, a particularly popular figure in his diocese, and he made some bitter and vociferous enemies amongst those clergy who disliked both his Englishness and his tendency to make harsh judgements about disputed matters before he had taken account of all of the evidence.[11] In his autobiography, Robert Roberts provided a somewhat satirical account of the way in which Short conducted himself at Roberts's ordination examination and the subsequent dinner. 'The extreme servility [of his dinner companions] struck me at once . . . The bishop was vain, and liked flattery . . . it was not given to him in infinitesimal doses, but shovelled over him.'[12] Unlike Thirlwall, Short made no attempt to master the Welsh language, although according to Roberts,

> The Bishop prided himself upon his knowledge of the origin of names of places and though he knew very little Welsh and could not pronounce half a dozen words in that language

> intelligibly, he told us that he had an ambition to be reckoned an authority on such matters.[13]

In reality, he made little attempt to disguise his dislike of all things Welsh. Thus Short was entirely the wrong person to be raised to the Welsh episcopate, at a time when both nationalist sentiments and concern about the survival of the language were growing.

Another sore point was patronage. Nationally, there was a notable trend at this period for increasing amounts of patronage to be vested in the bishops.[14] Historically, the bishop of St Asaph had long had a very considerable amount at his disposal – 117 benefices in total, although not all were in the diocese. This made him the single most important patron in the Welsh Church. It was natural that the bishop of St Asaph's exercise of patronage should always be a matter of sensitive interest, and Short's practices, with a noted tendency to promote Englishmen to Welsh parishes and to overlook the claims of the diocesan clergy, caused much unfavourable comment. For reasons which are less clear, Short's commitment to parochial education also made him unpopular in some quarters. He was described by one clerical enemy as seeking to change 'every Clergyman into a State-Schoolmaster, and degrading the Church itself, the Ministry of Souls, into a Commercial Academy'.[15] Robert Roberts noted that he had complained to him: 'I can hardly ever find a candidate [for ordination] who knows anything about fractions.'[16] After his death, the *Carnarvon and Denbigh Herald* lampooned the late bishop as one who had 'run about the diocese with a *birch rod* in one hand, and *vulgar fractions* in the other'.[17] In fact, the provision of schools in the diocese was so ample that W. E. Forster, the originator of the 1870 Education Act, argued that his office as president of the Board of Education would scarcely have been necessary if all the dioceses of England were as well provided with schools as was St Asaph.[18] In 1857, a petition, apparently originating from some people in Mold, was got up to attempt to remove Short from the diocese. A counter-petition, signed by nearly 200 clergy in the diocese, noted their high estimation of the bishop, and offered their sympathy and support.[19] An anecdote related by A. G. Edwards nicely illustrates something of

Short's character, as well as the problems caused by his inability in Welsh. As a small boy, the future archbishop encountered Short on a number of occasions in the 1840s and 1850s, when he visited his father's parishes first at Llanymawddy and then at Llangollen. He remembered him being driven by his coachman, himself so stately in powdered wig and silk stockings that he was sometimes mistaken for the bishop. According to Edwards, during one visit Short examined the Sunday school boys, and questioned them on the subject of 'besetting sins'. What, he asked them, did they think was the bishop's own besetting sin? 'Drunkenness, sir', was the response of the boldest child, perhaps struggling to name a sin in English. 'No, not drunkenness but vanity', was the bishop's disarming reply.[20]

Originally from Manchester, Alfred Ollivant had arrived in Wales in 1827 to take up the post of vice-principal at the newly opened St David's College, Lampeter. From there he went back to Cambridge as Regius Professor of Divinity. He was nominated to Llandaff in 1849, which was one of the most challenging dioceses in England and Wales, combining huge social problems with very poor financial resources. Ollivant's first Charge, delivered in 1851 two years after his arrival in the diocese, indicates that while he was cautiously optimistic about the prospects for improvement, he was also realistic about the 'inadequacy of [the Church's] ministrations for the spiritual multitudes who had so unexpectedly thronged into our seaports, and taken possession of our rugged mountains and sequestered vales'.[21] It is the 'unexpectedly' which is the most interesting word here – Ollivant's Charge vividly conveys the sense of the Church overwhelmed by rapid social and economic change on a scale not witnessed hitherto. South Wales had indeed been plunged very rapidly into the Industrial Revolution, beginning in the mid-eighteenth century with ironworks developing across north Glamorgan and north Monmouthshire, and then, within a few years of Ollivant's remarks, with deep coal mining from the 1860s. The appointment of Ollivant indicated that the government, in this case Russell's, had at least understood the importance of bishops appointed to Welsh sees being Welsh-speaking, even if they had as yet failed to understand the difference between a native Welsh-speaker and a non-Welsh learner. Ollivant was represented as having learned Welsh at Lampeter, although the extent and fluency of his mastery of the language remained a matter of debate.[22] The real benefit that he derived from his time at Lampeter was that he had trained a good proportion of the future clergy of his diocese. Ollivant emerges as a conscientious bishop, who devoted himself very assiduously to the challenges of Llandaff, which he served for thirty-three years. He is deservedly regarded as one of Llandaff's greatest diocesans.

This mid-century group of bishops were, it turned out, the last generation of Englishmen to administer the Welsh Church. In 1859 the aged Bethell was replaced at Bangor by a Scot who had previously been rector of Merthyr Tydfil, James Colquhoun Campbell. Known as 'doleful Jim', Campbell had at least the advantages of not being English, and of being promoted from within Wales. He had a smattering of Welsh, but could not use it confidently. Campbell was succeeded in 1890 by a former schoolmaster from Brecon, a fluent Welsh-speaker called Daniel Lewis Lloyd. Meanwhile in the south of the country Ollivant was replaced by Richard Lewis in 1882, and Thirlwall by William Basil Jones in 1874. As a former archdeacon of York and a scholarly figure who was well rooted in the minor aristocracy, Jones was the kind of man who might have looked plausible on the late nineteenth-century English bench. He had some familiarity with the Welsh language and was clearly Welsh, despite having ill-advisedly suggested at his primary visitation that Wales was no more than a 'geographical expression', the remark for which he is best remembered.[23] It was a remark he developed further at a later visitation, when he commented: 'Wales is neither politically nor geographically distinct from England, and so far as there is an ethnical distinction between the two countries, it is not greater than that which divides the Highlands from the Lowlands of Scotland.'[24] The point of this remark was to strengthen his argument for maintaining the established religion on both sides of Offa's Dyke. Jones was a trenchant supporter of establishment, and a vehement opponent of Nonconformity, believing that the way to defeat it was not by attempting to outpreach it but by providing better pastoral support. He adopted much of the standard mid-nineteenth-century Anglican agenda, although rather later than most other diocesans. This included a large emphasis on the desirability of two full Sunday services,[25] and the launch of a diocesan conference which provided a framework in which clergy and laity could discuss the issues of the day.[26] Like other bishops who pioneered diocesan conferences rather earlier, such as E. H. Browne of Ely, and G. A. Selwyn of Lichfield, Jones saw the potential for tapping the expertise of the laity, and particularly that of the middle-class professional male.[27]

J. C. Campbell, Richard Lewis and Basil Jones were all non-Englishmen who possessed a bit of Welsh, but lacked native fluency. The prime ministers who appointed these individuals had supposed that in doing so they were discharging adequately their responsibilities to the Welsh Church, but they had failed to appreciate the strength of opinion, expressed both by individuals within Wales, and by pressure groups such as the Association of Welsh Clergy of the West Riding of Yorkshire, who demanded a fluent, native episcopate. A few years before the appointment of Lewis and Jones, the issue had come to a crescendo with the appointment of Joshua Hughes to St Asaph. The exiled Welshmen in Yorkshire had been petitioning prime ministers on the language issue since 1835, and such was the head of steam that had developed by 1870, when a vacancy arose at St Asaph, that enormous interest was taken in every detail of the appointment of the new bishop.[28] This time Gladstone was the prime minister, and he was far more conscious than his predecessors had been of the need to appoint a proper, Welsh-speaking Welshman.[29] But on whom should the honour fall? The field of possible candidates was diminished as various individuals were rejected on the grounds of social inadequacy or previous scandal. Eventually the choice fell on Joshua Hughes, the incumbent of Llandovery, a Pembrokeshire man and an Evangelical, a fluent Welsh preacher whose wife was the daughter of a baronet. Gladstone clearly felt that he had at last found a man who fulfilled all the criteria. Then it emerged that he had misunderstood Hughes's academic attainments. Hughes had not graduated as a BA in 1842 from Queens' College Cambridge as his entry in *Crockford's Clerical Directory* indicated; indeed he was exposed as never having been at Cambridge. Hughes's higher education, it emerged, had been received at St David's College, Lampeter, where he had obtained the degree of BD. Gladstone was shocked by his mistake, because whatever could be said in favour of Lampeter, it was not seen at this date as providing suitable formation for a future bishop. Hughes claimed that he knew nothing of his misleading *Crockford's* entry. He said that rather than using *Crockford's*, he preferred to rely on the other clerical reference book, the *Clergy List*, but it seems odd that anyone's entry should contain such a significant error for so many years without him noticing, or having it pointed out to him. It was, however, too late to revoke Hughes's appointment, and he found himself having to manage the most aristocratic of the Welsh sees. He was despised by the gentry clergy – despite his wife's connections – and not respected by the *gwerin* clergy as his antecedents were too similar to their own.[30] Like Basil Jones, he was, however, an efficient administrator who managed his diocese well. Naturally, his utterances on the language issue aroused particular interest, but he was not as forthright as some might have expected him to be. In fact, he took a similar line to every previous nineteenth-century Welsh bishop. At his first visitation in 1871 he wrestled with the issue of the two languages, acknowledging the needs of the 'influx' of English-speaking residents, whilst at the same time urging the clergy not to ignore the needs of the Welsh by failing to provide two full Welsh services each Sunday for them.[31] By 1877, he was recommending that both children and adults in the bilingual parishes should be taught to read the Bible and the Prayer Book in both languages, yet the emphasis seemed to be on the Welsh acquiring English rather than the English acquiring Welsh.

> If this were done, it would not only facilitate the acquisition of the English language, by supplying an easy interpretation of words and sentences difficult to understand, but also enable child and adult to join intelligently in the service of the Church, and to appreciate its beauty.[32]

Hughes always argued for the importance of Welsh children being taught to read and speak English fluently in school, whilst at the same time being able to worship in their native tongue. In fact, as the graph at Table 13.1 shows, what

Table 13.1 Sunday services in English and Welsh in St Asaph Diocese, 1871–1910

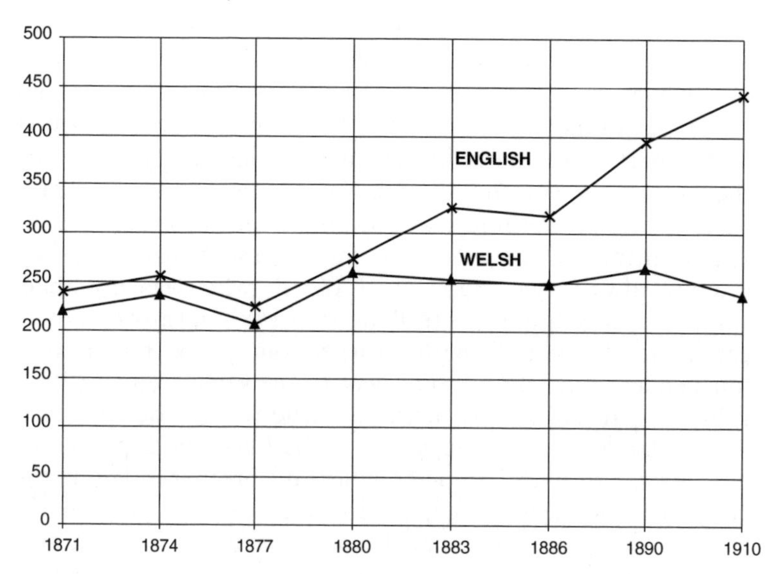

Sources: NLW St Asaph Parochial Records: Berriew 101 (for the years 1871–90) and PP 1910, XIV, Royal Commission on the Church of England and Other Religious Bodies in Wales and Monmouthshire, 1910, vol. I, p. 20 (for the year 1910).

happened in the diocese of St Asaph was that from 1880 English began rapidly to outstrip Welsh as the language of worship.

Into this increasingly Anglophone world came the last generation of leaders of the Established Church, all ardently pro-establishment Welshmen, who were later, like poachers turned gamekeepers, to become the first generation of leaders of the disestablished Church. Most notorious was Hughes's successor A. G. Edwards, bishop of St Asaph from 1889, and archbishop of Wales from 1920 to 1934. Edwards, described recently by Roger Brown as 'a petty, vicious and unprincipled schoolmaster',[33] was a sharp political operator who worked hard – and shamelessly – to promote those of whom he approved and block those whom he disliked. As Brown has noted, once it became clear that episcopal appointments were to be limited to the much narrower pool of Welsh-speaking Welshmen, many began to believe that the new situation was one which they could use in their own favour, or to the advantage of their friends. By the 1880s, Edwards had formed a little party – variously known as the 'Llandovery clique' or the 'St Asaph syndicate' – which was designed to ensure that a small group of Welshmen would obtain all the senior clerical appointments in Wales. As is the way with such schemers, they did not always succeed. Daniel Lloyd, who was not their candidate, was appointed to Bangor in 1890; meanwhile their candidate, Watkin Williams, turned out to be remarkably independent after his appointment to the same see in 1899.[34] Edwards particularly favoured men who were associated with either Llandovery College, where he had been both pupil and headmaster, or with Lampeter, where his brother-in-law Francis Jayne had been principal. Edwards worked particularly closely with Jayne, who had become bishop of Chester, and with one of his protégés, John Owen, another former principal of Lampeter who, as Edwards ensured, became bishop of St David's.

Owen, a weaver's son from Ysguborwen on the Lleyn peninsula, was clearly in a different mould from his predecessors. For the first time, hostile detractors questioned a bishop's ability to make himself understood in English, although any difficulties that were experienced should be attributed to his north Walian accent and to his lisp rather than to any hesitancy in the language – Owen clearly had complete fluency in English, and never spoke Welsh either to his students or to the clergy.[35] This curious point of principle indicates much about the mentality of the late nineteenth-century Welsh Church; it was a genuinely Welsh-led institution, and yet it seemed oddly equivocal about such unambiguous tokens of Welsh identity as the language itself. The defining policy of all who were appointed under Edwards's influence was that they wanted the Church to remain an integral part of the province of Canterbury. This goes at least some way to explaining how it was that the Church – officially at least – adopted such an entrenched position on the disestablishment question for so long. It was deeply ironic that it was eventually to be A. G. Edwards, sometimes in company with John Owen, who sat down with Lloyd George in order to negotiate the details of the implementation of the disestablishment, in moments Lloyd George snatched from the Paris Peace Conference in 1919.

The Clergy

The nineteenth-century Welsh clergy were particularly susceptible to varying forms of hostile stereotyping. On the one hand, they were viewed by the guardians of the nationalist cause as either the local lackeys of the alien religion, or as ineffectual English monoglots addicted to English forms of social exclusiveness and to the elimination of the Welsh language. On the other, they were seen by English observers as little more than ordained peasants; quarrelsome, poorly educated and prone to 'scandalous and degrading vice'.[36] These opposing – and equally misleading – caricatures have been responsible for the construction of two very different views of the Welsh clergy. It will be argued here that the Welsh clergy were an educationally and socially diverse body, more so than their English equivalents, and to understand them it is necessary to understand the extent to which they were controlled by the expectations and limitations imposed on them by a number of different educational processes. It will be suggested that the Welsh clergy's educational background prior to ordination to a large degree shaped the course of their future ministerial career. Although the English clergy were by no means educationally or socially monochrome, they were the products of different educational processes to a far lesser extent. Alan Haig has shown that in the province of Canterbury in 1865 (excluding the four Welsh dioceses) 78 per cent of ordinands had been educated at Oxbridge and only 3 per cent were literates (i.e. without university degrees); the remaining 19 per cent had been educated at a variety of newer institutions. In the province of York, 46 per cent had been to Oxbridge and 4 per cent were literates, with the remaining 49 per cent educated elsewhere. In Wales, however, the picture was very different. 25 per cent were Oxbridge-educated, 20 per cent were ordained as literates and

55 per cent had been educated elsewhere – the majority would have been at Lampeter.[37] In the 1860s, therefore, the newly ordained Welsh clergy came from three distinctively different educational backgrounds. This was not a new trend, and it was one which was to continue for many years.

The applications of fifty men who applied for ordination in St David's diocese between August 1874 and December 1875 were analysed in order to provide a detailed picture both of the kinds of men who sought ordination, and of what happened to them in the first twenty-five years of their ministry (see Table 13.2). As would be expected in St David's, the percentage breakdown of educational backgrounds is rather different from the figures that Haig provides for the whole of Wales a few years earlier. It was the case that most of the Oxbridge-educated gravitated to the better-paid curacies in Bangor and St Asaph – and thence to the richer livings – so the lower percentage of Oxbridge applicants, 14 per cent of the total – causes little surprise. Haig does not differentiate between Lampeter applicants and those educated elsewhere, but my higher figure, 72 per cent, which comprises 48 per cent educated at Lampeter and 24 per cent educated at other colleges, is not unexpected in view of the fact that St David's College was located in the heart of the diocese, and had a primary mission to educate men for the diocese. My figure for non-college-educated literates, 14 per cent, is just a few points lower than Haig's figure. The men in this sample have been divided into four different categories – Oxbridge, Lampeter, college-educated literates and non-college-educated literates, and they exhibit some interestingly different trends.[38] Some are entirely unsurprising, such as that any Oxbridge graduate was bound to be ordained, whereas a man like Evan Evans, a former pupil of Dolgellau National School who had worked as an agent in an ironworks, and who had failed the Welsh composition part of the ordination exam, was not. Other conclusions could not have been anticipated. The large proportion of men who had been employed in some capacity before ordination, usually as schoolmasters or tutors, is interesting. Once in the parish these men should, at least, have felt comfortable catechizing children and overseeing their National School. Lampeter men typically spent their entire ministry in Wales, and could reasonably

Table 13.2 Ministerial experiences of fifty candidates who applied for ordination in the diocese of St David's, August 1874–December 1875, classified by educational background

	Oxbridge	Lampeter	College-educated literates	Non-college-educated literates	Totals
Total number from each educational background	7[1]	24	12[2]	7[3]	50
Ordained in St David's, or other Welsh diocese	6	22	9	3	40
Ordained in England or the colonies	1[4]	0	1[5]	1[6]	3
Rejected	0	2	2	3	7
Had been employed before ordination	3[7]	16[8]	5[9]	6[10]	30
Spent whole ministry in Wales (up until 1900)	3	20	5	2	30
Achieved beneficed status (before 1900)	5	17	6	2	30
Still in ministry in 1900	4	14	5	4	27

Sources: NLW, SD/Misc/B/80 St David's Diocesan ordinands book; *Crockford's Clerical Directory*, 1900.

Notes:
[1] Includes 3 from Jesus College Oxford.
[2] Comprises 4 from St Bees, Cumberland, 3 from Queen's College, Birmingham, 1 from St Aidan's, Birkenhead, 1 from Bala Dissenting

College, 1 from Didsbury Wesleyan College, 1 from Western College, Plymouth, 1 from Royal Naval College, Portsmouth.
[3] Comprises 2 who had had National School education only, 3 who had had grammar school education only, and 2 who had studied privately with clergymen.
[4] Ordained for Gloucester and Bristol, 1874.
[5] Ordained for York, 1877.
[6] Ordained for Tobago, 1876.
[7] All had been either schoolmasters or tutors.
[8] 13 had been schoolmasters or tutors, 1 had been a printer, 1 a draper's assistant, and 1 had worked on the family farm.
[9] 1 had been a naval commander, 1 a probationary Wesleyan minister, 1 an office clerk, 2 had been Congregationalist ministers, of whom 1 had previously worked in the grocery trade.
[10] 3 had been schoolmasters (and 2 of the 3 had combined this with being lay readers), 1 had been an agent at an ironworks, 1 had been a Wesleyan minister, and previously a draper's assistant, and 1 had been a Congregationalist missionary.

expect to achieve beneficed status during the first twenty-five years of their ministry. A larger sample would be needed before very firm conclusions could be drawn about the prospects of those in the other categories, although it seems likely that the Oxbridge group found it easier to move to benefices in England. The literates were less likely to get over the first hurdle, ordination, and if they did so, they were more likely to have to be content with a string of poorly paid curacies within Wales.

One important finding relates to the average age of the men seeking ordination. The average for the whole cohort is thirty years and three months. As might be expected this breaks down into a slightly more youthful profile for the Oxbridge and Lampeter men, but it is not very marked. The average Oxbridge applicant was 28½. The average Lampeter man was just past his 29th birthday.[39] The average for a college-educated literate was 32. The average non-college literate was 30½. The striking finding is that in the diocese of St David's in the early 1870s, candidates seeking ordination were likely to be about six years older than their English equivalents. Obtaining ordination was a long haul, and was often embarked on as a 'second career' after the youthful years had been spent in teaching or in a trade. It would be interesting to know what the diocesan authorities regarded as 'too old' for ordination. William John Wooding was accepted for Fishguard at the Lent ordination in 1876 at the age of forty-five. Thomas James Morgan was turned down for Laugharne on account of his age at Michaelmas 1876. He was forty-seven.

The bishop's examining chaplain was Archdeacon Henry de Winton, who had been a distinguished classicist at Trinity College, Cambridge.[40] He reported on the candidates' health, their personal qualities, their conduct whilst deacons (if appropriate) and their academic abilities. He was generally satisfied with the intellectual achievements of the Oxbridge and the Lampeter men, reserving his most scathing comments for the candidates who had studied at St Bees. One such was David Davies, who had been ordained by Ollivant for a parish near Merthyr Tydfil in 1869. As was common in the case of an intellectually weak candidate, Davies was given a five-year diaconate, and thus did not present himself for priest's orders until August 1874, by which point he had moved to a curacy in Llanrhidian near Swansea. De Winton described his preaching and reading as 'sing-song', his command of the Old Testament as 'meagre', his New Testament as 'weak' and his grasp of doctrine as 'weak and defective with much error'. Liturgy, pastoralia and church history were also all 'weak'. His health was not strong, and his rector considered him lacking in energy and timid. Nevertheless, perhaps feeling that he was unlikely to improve by being sent away for a further period of study, it was decided that he was adequate to be priested at Michaelmas 1874. Davies held a further curacy after Llanrhidian, and died in the 1880s. Another St Bees student who had also been ordained to a five-year diaconate in 1869 was Daniel Jones, curate of Meline, Pembrokeshire, who in August 1874 was a candidate for the vacant incumbency of that parish. His general health, and his reading and preaching were better than Davies's – 'not so much amiss; very Welsh', although de Winton judged his theological performance equally poor and confused – 'Cannot write English.' He too was ordained at the Michaelmas ordination, and became the rector of Meline, where he died some years later.

More pleasing to de Winton were candidates like William Williams, who after a brief spell as a schoolmaster won a scholarship to St David's College in 1871. He was fast-tracked into deacon's orders on the title of St Peter's Lampeter in 1872, perhaps as a way of providing some extra financial help for this bright but impoverished student. Thirlwall had made it a condition that he obtain his degree before he was admitted to the priesthood, and he duly achieved first-class honours in the summer of 1874. He had little trouble with the theological papers in the ordination examination; his reading and preaching were described as 'good', and his references were 'very good'. Williams went on to what may be described as a typical Lampeter graduate's career. It was all spent in Wales, he was beneficed by the age of twenty-eight, and in 1900 he was serving in Pembrokeshire as the vicar of St David's. This gave him a decent house and a gross income of £292 per annum, which was a mid-range stipend by the standards of the early-twentieth-century Welsh Church.[41] One other candidate who applied to the examining chaplain in August 1874 is worth singling out for special notice. He was Alfred George Edwards, who had just graduated from Jesus College, Oxford. He hoped to be ordained on the title of Llandingat, the parish church of Llandovery, on a stipend of just £10 per annum. In view of the limited stipend, it was hardly surprising that the future archbishop should have immediately taken up the post of second master at Llandovery College; he was promoted to warden within a year. At the time of his ordination examination, his health was described as 'good', and his reading and preaching as 'fair'. His performance in the Old Testament paper was 'fair and full', and his ability in New Testament was judged to be 'fair but *vague*'. Francis Jayne had, characteristically, supplied a reference that was '*very* satisfactory'. However, not all was well. De Winton noted that Edwards was 'Not to be licensed to preach in Welsh before further examination. He may read prayers.' It was an interesting judgement to make on someone who, in his autobiography, claimed that he had been appointed as the headmaster of Llandovery College because his spoken Welsh had so much impressed Lady Llanover, who was one of the school's trustees.[42] Edwards made much of his Welshness, but probably lacked the facility in the language enjoyed by his elder brother, H. T. Edwards, dean of Bangor. The language of the Edwards family home had almost certainly been English. Their father was a Welsh-speaker, but their mother was English, although she apparently learned the language well enough to speak to her servants, to visit parishioners and to help in the Sunday school.[43] H. T. Edwards commented that when he went to Oxford he realized that his Welsh was so poor that he needed to work at it every day, reading aloud and committing passages to memory. 'I made up my mind that I should never be put in the shade by reason of not being able to express my thoughts in the language of the people.'[44] His younger brother seems to have had no such realization. Indeed, one of the abiding memories that he carried into old age was of hearing a lecture delivered in Welsh in a Methodist chapel by the Congregationalist minister Kilsby Jones. The lecturer concluded: 'Boys, if you want to succeed in the world, learn English. Remember, Welsh is a barley-bread language.'[45] A. G. Edwards also believed that the boys from Welsh-speaking homes whom he taught at Llandovery were at an educational disadvantage.[46]

It is clear from the analysis of the careers of the men who appear in the St David's diocesan ordinands book that ministry in the Welsh Church typically took one of several predictable patterns, depending largely upon the individual's educational starting-point. Evan Evans (the rejected applicant from Dolgellau National School), David Davies (the curate from St Bees), William Williams (the incumbent from St David's College, Lampeter) and A. G. Edwards (the bishop from Jesus College, Oxford) all exemplify the kinds of outcomes that men of their background might reasonably expect. That is not to say that able men without the benefit of a college education could never progress. The best example of one who did is David Howell, who was ordained at Llandaff in 1855 straight from Abergavenny Grammar School. Howell had been born in the vale of Glamorgan in 1831. He attended only a dame school, and spent his early years working the family farm, marrying at the age of nineteen after his sixteen-year-old girlfriend became pregnant. He also embarked on a private study of the Welsh language, moving from a working knowledge to a literary ability.[47] An Evangelical conversion swiftly followed his marriage, and Howell was persuaded by the local curate that he should seek ordination. His father eventually agreed to support him financially, and at the age of twenty David Howell entered the Eagle Academy in Cowbridge in order to gain an elementary knowledge of classics, studying alongside boys half his age. He then moved to a crammer's in Merthyr to prepare for Abergavenny's entrance examination. Howell studied at Abergavenny Grammar School from February 1853 until August 1855, renting a cottage in the town for his wife and by now three children. He described the experience as 'reading for my life, as it were, pouring over my books for as many as twelve or fifteen hours every day, in anticipation of the ordeal I shall have to undergo' (i.e., the ordination examination).[48] But despite his heavy workload, Howell maintained a prodigious literary output, submitting poetry to Welsh magazines and making substantial and regular contributions to the Welsh-language Church periodical *Yr Haul.* He adopted the bardic name *Llawdden* and wrote essays and poetry for eisteddfodau.

When David Howell was ordained at the age of twenty-five, he was already a well-known figure on the Welsh literary scene. For Bishop Ollivant, he may have been 'merely' a non-college literate, a farm boy who had transformed himself into a curate in the space of five years, but such a disparaging view would have been based on a misunderstanding of Howell's own standing within Welsh-speaking south Wales. As his ministry unfolded, he became a leading Anglican Evangelical and a national figure in the principality, occupying a number of important posts including the archdeaconry of Wrexham and finally the deanery of St David's. As a Welsh-speaking Welshman with considerable gifts and some influential friends, he was discussed for every see vacant in Wales between 1870 and 1897, but the episcopate eluded him. The problem was threefold.[49] First, there was his perceived lack of education. In later life, Howell bitterly regretted that the curate who had encouraged his vocation had not persuaded his parents to send him to one of the ancient universities. Secondly, there was his wife, whose lowly social origins meant that she was not seen as bishop's-wife material. Thirdly, there was the prenuptial conception of his first son, which at the hands of A. G. Edwards became magnified into a secret illegitimate child. Howell is an excellent example of a man who was blocked by Edwards and his clique, largely because he failed to share their implacable opposition to disestablishment, and had positive views about

Nonconformists. But even without the effectiveness of the St Asaph muckraking operation, it seems that Howell had hit the glass ceiling as far as the advancement of a 'literate' in the Welsh Church was concerned. A deanery was possible, but a bishop's palace was not.

The Development of Welsh Theological Training

Until the foundation of St Michael's College, Aberdare in 1892, St David's College, Lampeter, was the only institution especially dedicated to preparing clergy for the realities of life in Welsh parishes. With this in mind, Lampeter offered a broad curriculum and an impressive array of extracurricular activities which were designed not only to protect its graduates from the charge of 'narrowness' (an accusation which was frequently levelled at the alumni of institutions such as St Bees) but also to provide them with resources on which to draw in the years that lay ahead. In 1849, Sir Thomas Phillips drew out the intended consequences of the 'liberal' education offered at Lampeter:

> By accustoming them [the students] to habits of self-respect and communicating to them tastes for liberal studies, they will also be preserved from those habits of intemperance, on the one hand, and that spirit of despondency or indolent apathy on the other, which are not uncommonly produced or perpetuated in the solitary parishes so often the dwelling place of a Welsh clergyman.[50]

Phillips recognized that the sheer isolation of many Welsh parishes was likely to be the greatest challenge that many clergy faced, a theme that will be explored further in the next chapter.

St Michael's, Aberdare, also marketed itself explicitly as providing preparation for future ministry in Wales. Despite its location close to the urban and more Anglophone environment of Aberdare, it made much of the opportunities that it provided for students to improve their fluency in the Welsh language and to worship regularly through the medium of Welsh. This was at the time when Principal John Owen had virtually banished the use of the Welsh tongue from Lampeter. The foundation of St Michael's was part of the nationwide approach that was adopted to Anglican theological training from the middle of the nineteenth century. This approach emphasized the importance of a period of residence and professional formation, normally of one year, in a theological college after the ordinand had graduated from university. To meet this need, many theological colleges were founded in England, often in close proximity to cathedrals. St Michael's was the only such institution to be founded in Wales, and was very much the creation of the wealthy benefactor Olive Emma Talbot, a mineral magnate from Margam. She was enthusiastically supported by Bishop Richard Lewis of Llandaff, who was delighted to have such an institution in his most difficult of dioceses. The first warden was Henry Robert Johnson, a Cambridge graduate who had been trained at Cuddesdon.

Olive Talbot's involvement illustrates well the role which the wealthy industrialist could have in shaping the religion of south Wales. She was typical of several such people whose families had become very wealthy by exploiting the raw materials and industrial potential of the Valleys.[51] Not only did she meet most of the college's running costs, she also funded a very generous bursary scheme which allowed many of the students to be remitted the whole of their £70 annual fee. For many men, it was in effect an entirely free year of education, an extraordinary privilege at this period. It was recognized that many students had already taxed themselves to the utmost by putting themselves through a degree course, and that without very significant financial incentives, any attempt to introduce postgraduate theological training to Wales would be destined to failure. By 1906, St Michael's boasted of being the only theological college for graduates which offered a year's additional training 'at whatever fees a man can afford to pay'.[52] It followed that those who took Miss Talbot's money were expected not only to become benefactors of the college once they were established in their parishes, but also to minister in Wales. From the outset, the college's authorities made it explicitly clear that its students were expected to work in Wales, and in almost every issue of the annual report, ritual abuse was poured on those who had succumbed to the temptations of ministry in England. According to the warden, the St Michael's man should only leave his first curacy at the end of two years if requested to do so by the incumbent; in any other circumstances to move on so soon encouraged

> the idea, already too prevalent, that the only duty of the clergy is to preach, and that, like a Salvation captain who moves on when he has said all that he has to say, the priest's message is delivered and he is eager to be saved the trouble of further preparation of sermons. It must, too, in justice to the College be pointed out that when uncongenial surroundings or lack of 'society' lead the men who have benefited by St Michael's to seek greener pastures, or larger stipends, in England, they are going contrary to the conditions upon which they were admitted to the College. All profiting by the training here are expected to remain in one of the four Welsh dioceses for at least five years. The difficulties of the Church in Wales are overwhelming enough without being made a training ground for the comparatively raw recruit . . . It is rather pitiable to find so much patriotism which ends in mere vague affection for everything Welsh, except work in a Welsh diocese.[53]

Patagonia was the only place outside Wales where a St Michael's student could work with pride. Nevertheless, the records show that after the first curacy, there was a steady drift of men to English parishes.

In common with the ordinands in the diocese of St David's in 1874–5, the first intakes of St Michael's men were rather older than would have been expected in England. Thirty-two of the first forty-eight students were over the age of 23 when they applied for admission to the College, but a more detailed picture of their age profile unfortunately cannot be reconstructed. In the early years the majority of the students had previously studied at Lampeter. Of the 88 students who had been ordained by 1898, 46 had come from Lampeter, 9 were graduates of Oxford, 4 had come from Cambridge, 5 from Dublin, Durham and London, 14 had (rather curiously) previously studied at other theological colleges, 8 were non-graduates who had been admitted to a two-year course in Aberdare, and 2 had passed the Oxbridge theological preliminary examination and were received as if they were graduates.

Their first destinations are also interesting. Forty-four went to parishes in the diocese of Llandaff, 13 went to St David's, 12 to St Asaph, 6 to Bangor, 11 to England and 2 went abroad. The warden noted dryly that of those who had gone to England, 'some have gone by the advice of those who know them best; it is to be hoped that such advice has been wisely given.'[54] The fact that precisely half the students were ordained for Llandaff seems to weaken Bishop Lewis's claim that St Michael's was 'not merely diocesan'.[55] It was clearly fulfilling much of the function that Lampeter had for decades been performing for the diocese of St David's.

St Michael's overdependence on attracting students from Lampeter created tensions, and at times the two institutions clearly strained to fish from the same pool. For over sixty years, a two- or three-year course at St David's College had been considered a perfectly sound preparation for ministry in the Welsh Church. Suddenly, men for whom the educational process had often been long, arduous and expensive, were being told that they should undergo a further year of training, with the associated loss of income, in an avowedly High Church institution in the Valleys. In the first few years a combination of the lure of the Talbot bursaries with pressure from Lewis (and perhaps the other bishops) seems to have made Lampeter graduates willing to extend their education. Disaster struck in 1899, however, when only three of the forty students who had graduated from Lampeter in the June of that year proved willing to sign up for the Aberdare course. The newly arrived Principal Bebb invited Warden Johnson to visit 'to explain the theological college and try to remove some of the prejudices which somehow or other had found a way into a good number of men's minds'.[56] Meanwhile, fearing the total collapse of his student numbers, Johnson began to soften his tone with regard to men with aspirations to work in England. He observed that it was 'unquestionably good for some Welshmen to go to England, and perhaps equally advantageous for some Englishmen to go to Wales – though not just because they cannot get an English bishop to ordain them'.[57] Johnson's more vigorous approach to student recruitment – in addition to an annual visit to Lampeter he also began to address regular meetings of Welsh ordinands in Oxford and Cambridge –

seems to have paid off. Within a few years, the college was once more able to fill its twenty-five places, and in 1903 the decision was made to relocate it to Llandaff close to the cathedral, to a site which had been given by one of the college's long-standing supporters, W. S. de Winton (almost certainly a relative of the former archdeacon of Brecon and St David's examining chaplain, Henry de Winton). Here St Michael's flourished, and moved in a somewhat more Anglo-Catholic direction under the influence of Timothy Rees, a future bishop of Llandaff. A former student of both Lampeter and St Michael's, Rees was chaplain and tutor for several years at the beginning of the twentieth century, before joining the Community of the Resurrection. The next major development came in 1910, when the college opened a church hostel in Cardiff Road, to accommodate those students at University College Cardiff who might be contemplating holy orders. This was in response to a recommendation from the bishops of the southern province that clerical training ought to embrace first a university degree in the arts or the sciences, before a two-year professional training in a theological college. The enthusiasm with which this suggestion was taken up by the staff at St Michael's says much about the vigour and liveliness of the Welsh Church on the eve of disestablishment.

14

Developments in the Parishes

Building Parish Plant: Churches, Parsonages and Schools

There was of course no such thing as a typical Welsh parish. Size, and whether it was in an urban or a rural setting, made for the greatest contrasts in the second half of the nineteenth century. The most obvious differences were between the vast and teeming populations of the south Wales Valleys, and the remote and tiny parishes in places like Anglesey. Thus to be ordained for Llandaff was to set a young man on a completely different track than would be the case if he were ordained for a rural parish in any of the other three dioceses. In 1851, the population of Wales was 1,163,139; by 1914, it was 2,523,500, an increase of 117 per cent in sixty-three years. In 1914, almost half of these people lived on the south Wales coalfield. The general trend was therefore a movement of people into the south from the central and western Welsh counties, and from England, as the male labour force switched from agriculture, which had employed 35 per cent of them in 1851, to the coal industry, which employed the same percentage in 1914. But there was also significant population growth in the north. This was linked with slate quarrying in the north-west, where 60,000 people lived, and coal mining in the north-east, where 100,000 had settled. Later on in the century, there was also a significant increase in the populations of the northern seaside towns from Llanfairfechan to Prestatyn, as the tourist industry began to develop.[1]

In 1851, the parish of Merthyr Tydfil was reeling from the effects of a population increase of a little over 500 per cent in the previous fifty years, and the parish of Aberdare had experienced growth of over 900 per cent in the same period. A large proportion of the members of this new society were immigrants; in the case of the two parishes mentioned above they were mainly Welsh people who had moved in from the hinterland and from the rural west. In the case of the more easterly county of Monmouthshire, which had also seen massive growth, 12,245 of the people recorded in the 1851 census had been born in an English county. Of the 25,866 Monmouthshire dwellers who had been born in a Welsh county, many had moved in from the north and the west, and thus regarded themselves as 'strangers' in south-east Wales.[2] All facilities were stretched to breaking point. The existing churches were completely unable to accommodate even a small proportion of these rapidly rising numbers, and in most cases they were unsuitably located – with the exception of Merthyr Tydfil and Aberdare, the churches in the Valleys region had been built at the tops of mountains, whereas the population was settling alongside the industry in the valley floor. In these circumstances, it was hardly surprising that all the Nonconformist denominations continued to flourish well into the second half of the century. As we have seen (p. 236) Bishop Copleston had taken the view that providing for the pastoral needs of Llandaff's growing parishes was of greater importance than repairing the cathedral. Nevertheless, the fact that Llandaff Cathedral was not fully restored from its previously ruinous condition until 1869, had the effect of sending a negative message, particularly to casual observers, about the state of the entire diocese; it was one which Bishop Ollivant was at pains to refute. He used his first charge to criticize the *Quarterly Review* for implying that the condition of the cathedral was typical of the diocese as a whole.

> *We* in this diocese, do *not* hear of the Church in Wales 'of some churches without doors and others without windows, of yawning chasms frequent in the roof, of the inside wet, as if just rinsed with water'. The general condition of our parish churches is utterly at variance with such a representation.[3]

Although Ollivant's churches may have been few in number and poorly located, his point was that they were in a generally decent condition.

What was needed was a new parochial structure which would permit new building, and vast amounts of money and men. The process of creating new ecclesiastical districts in south Wales was begun by the Ecclesiastical Commissioners at an early stage in their existence. Dowlais was the first one in 1837, and then Rhymney, Tredegar, Penmaen, Cyfarthfa, Nant-y-glo and Beaufort, all of which followed over the next nine years. The creation of new districts did not, however, gather pace until the episcopates of Lewis and Hughes. Twenty-five were created under Lewis (1883–1905) and a further twenty-five under Hughes (1905–31).[4] The rising numbers of new ecclesiastical districts prompted the need for changes in the boundaries of the rural deaneries and archdeaconries, and thus in the period from 1850 to 1910, the diocese of Llandaff was significantly restructured.[5] It would be wrong, however, to assume that the slowness in carving out new ecclesiastical territories had meant that, before the arrival of Lewis in the 1880s, the industrial districts had been widely ignored. In fact, Ollivant had adopted a missionary strategy, which was not hidebound by the more high and dry Anglican conventions. He encouraged the clergy to take an active approach to pastoral work, and to hold services in any suitable buildings, such as parish rooms, schools and even inns. Considerable use was also made of temporary iron structures, and the bishop was willing to consecrate temporary buildings, as well as unfinished permanent ones, in order to bring them into immediate use. The Llandaff Diocesan Church Extension Society, which was founded in 1850 and wound up in 1911, coordinated many of these activities. It had four specific objectives: to contribute to curates' stipends in populous places; to contribute to the costs of building churches and licensed places of worship; to contribute to the costs of other objects bearing on the welfare and progress of the Church; and to endeavour to increase the supply of educated Welsh clergymen. Its financial fortunes were however extremely chequered, with annual donations varying from £5,122. 18*s.* 6*d.* in the first year of its existence, to just £13 some years later.[6] Although significant sums were raised from within parishes, or donated by wealthy Welsh industrialists, much of the work was funded directly from London by the Ecclesiastical Commissioners, the Queen Anne's Bounty and national Church charities such as the Church Pastoral Aid Society and the Additional Curates Society. By 1883, however, the funds of the Llandaff Diocesan Extension Society were virtually exhausted, and Bishop Lewis, as one of his first acts, had to inaugurate the 'Bishop of Llandaff's Fund' with an appeal for £50,000. By the end of his episcopate in 1905, 201 projects involving a total expenditure of £362,817 had been set in train, with £30,570 being drawn down in the form of grants from the fund.[7]

In the period from 1850 to the beginning of the twentieth century, the Church in the diocese of Llandaff was completely transformed. The rural deanery of Aberdare had seen its population increase from 14,999 in 1851 to 65,949 in 1901. The number of churches had risen from three to twenty-seven, and the number of clergy from two to twenty-five. The number of Anglican Sunday services had risen from five in 1848, to sixty-one in 1906. In Merthyr Tydfil, the population had increased from 46,378 in 1851 to 70,999 in 1901. The number of churches had risen from four to twenty-four, and the number of clergy increased from four to twenty-two. The number of Sunday services had risen from eleven in 1848, to fifty-three in 1906.[8] In both places the proportion of communicants as an overall percentage of the population remained fairly low; in Aberdare it was 6.2 per cent, and in Merthyr 5.8 per cent. This was not, however, out of line with national trends.[9]

The experience of the diocese of Llandaff, which had the fastest-growing population of anywhere in Britain at this period, was clearly unique. In the other dioceses, whilst significant efforts were put into restoring existing churches and erecting new ones, nothing was required on the scale discussed above. Nevertheless, the amount of building and restoration was impressive. In 1883, Basil Jones noted that whereas under his predecessor, Bishop Thirlwall, the diocese of St David's had witnessed an average of one church consecration a year, it had now reached an average of five a year.[10] Bishop Hughes noted in 1874 that in the forty years that the St Asaph Church Building Society had been in existence, it had given financial assistance towards the building of fifty new churches and (rather surprisingly) thirty-two school chapels. It had helped with the rebuilding of eighteen old churches, and the restoration of twenty-nine others.[11] As in Llandaff, there were problems in St Asaph with churches being poorly located for developing centres of population. The ancient church had often been built at one end of the parish, while the population was either scattered over a huge area, or concentrated in an area several miles away.[12] Between 1851 and 1910, 347 new churches were built in Wales, and almost all the old churches, nearly 1,000 of them, were renovated or rebuilt.[13]

It was not, however, just a restored or newly built church that was at the heart of the ideal mid-nineteenth-century parish. Equally important in making the ideal a reality was the existence of a suitable parsonage, and a school managed under the auspices of the National Society (the National Society for Promoting the Education of the Poor in the Principles of the Established Church). A stock of well-maintained parsonages was essential for implementing the policy of clerical residence which had been legally enforced since the passing of the Pluralities Act in 1838. Every parish needed a house for the incumbent. If a curate was employed, it was acceptable for him to live in lodgings. Later on, in the few Anglo-Catholic parishes that began to emerge in the urban south, where clergy were expected to be unmarried, several might live together in a clergy house. An example of this was in the parish of St Mary's in Cardiff, but such arrangements were highly untypical. Far more usual was the provision of upper-middle-class, family-sized accommodation, which for Victorians tended to mean at least five bedrooms. In 1852, Bishop Bethell of Bangor gave the incumbent of Llandudno permission to live in his own house, on account of the parsonage 'being very small containing only four bedrooms'.[14] The generally more humble social origins of the Welsh clergy do not seem to have made them noticeably more tolerant than their English brethren of modest or poor parsonages. Expectations of what was suitable for a clerical family were changing. A house which in 1850 might have seemed commodious to an incumbent, was likely to be perceived as in need of major extension and modernization by his successors. In 1900, the incumbent of the Anglesey parish of

Llanfihangel yn Nhowyn lamented that although his house had been repaired, it was still 'only a glebe cottage'.[15]

The history of the vicarage at Aberdare provides an illuminating example of changing expectations. In 1832, the resident curate had lived in a house rented at £9 per annum, probably next to a public house in Green Street. In 1846, the Marquis of Bute, as patron, agreed to a scheme by which a house would be built, financed from a £400 lump sum, and repayments that he agreed to make on a £600 mortgage on the living. The Queen Anne's Bounty also contributed. The house was constructed as rapidly and cheaply as possible – so rapidly and cheaply, in fact, that within twenty years it was regarded by the then incumbent, H. T. Edwards (elder brother of A. G. Edwards) as unfit for habitation. It was very damp, the roof leaked, and there was an insufficient number of bedrooms (only four, with dressing rooms). It was estimated that £1,000 would be required to put it into good order, and that the work needed included repairs, a new roof, better servants' rooms, an enlarged entrance hall, a new staircase and an extended kitchen. The Ecclesiastical Commissioners offered £500 towards this work, on condition that a further £500 was found from a non-ecclesiastical source. No such donation was forthcoming, and the house began to deteriorate further. In the 1870s, the vicar, Wynne Jones, was obliged to spend £136 of his own money on urgent repairs, and to obtain a mortgage of £596 from the Queen Anne's Bounty to cover the rest. In 1893 Charles Green – later to be the Church in Wales's second archbishop – became vicar of Aberdare. At first he lived in the house in the Anglo-Catholic style with three of his six curates. His marriage, in 1899, ended this arrangement, and Green took out a £200 mortgage in order to make the house more suitable for his wife, who was the daughter of Sir William Thomas Lewis, Lord Merthyr. He wanted repairs, extra bedrooms and a reslated roof. Nine years later, Green contacted the Bounty again in order to begin what were to be a series of protracted negotiations aimed at making the vicarage rather grander. He was seeking another mortgage, and hoped to spend £943 improving the property. The governors of the Bounty clearly thought that Green was being extravagant, and wondered, among other things, whether a second staircase was really necessary. The proposed alteration was obviously symbolic of the division of the house into a back thoroughfare for servants and coal, and a grander arena for Green and his family. The Bounty finally gave in to Green's demand for a second staircase, but the vicar was still not satisfied, and was outraged that the Bounty's architect seemed to think it acceptable for the top of the staircase to be placed opposite the bathroom door, where anyone ascending the stairs might witness a lady emerging from the bathroom. Green seemed to be pushing the official parsonage architects to accept new definitions of what was suitable and decorous in early-twentieth century clergy housing. Green left the parish in 1914, six years after the improvements had been completed. Both the size of the newly enlarged house, and the size of the outstanding mortgage, which cost £54 per annum, proved a burden to his successors.[16] Aberdare vicarage was a house with a chequered history, which at no time seemed quite to satisfy the needs (or aspirations) of its occupants.

In the rest of the diocese of Llandaff, the transformation in clerical housing was probably not as extreme as in Aberdare, but almost all of the old rural parsonage houses were replaced by solid and imposing vicarages in the years between 1850 and 1910.[17] In urban areas, the clergy sometimes began their work by living in houses provided by wealthy industrialists – examples being at Dowlais, where accommodation was provided by Lady Charlotte Guest, and at Beaufort, where it was provided by one of the ironmasters – almost certainly the Blaina Iron Company, who also paid for the rebuilding of St Peter's church. In time, the industrialists were sometimes prevailed upon to give land for a parsonage, and to contribute towards the costs of its construction, as the Talbot family did at Margam.

Bangor too saw a huge programme of parsonage construction over these years. Out of sixty-three parishes in the archdeaconry of Bangor in 1856 for which records survive, only thirty-six (57 per cent) had a house in which lived the incumbent, or occasionally, a curate. Twenty-five parishes had no house at all, and two parishes (Llandudno and Bangor with Pentir) had a house, but the incumbent had been given permission to live elsewhere. In 1856, the proportion of resident clergy was higher on Anglesey than it was on the mainland. Of the thirty-five Anglesey parishes recorded, twenty-three had a resident minister.[18] By 1900, out of eighty-one parishes for which records survive in the Bangor archdeaconry, sixty-eight (84 per cent) had a house with a resident minister.[19] Interestingly, only three of the mainland parishes were still without clerical accommodation, and any housing shortage that existed was now on Anglesey. But what at first sight appears to be non-residence may usually be attributed to the union of very small benefices, with the minister living in one parish whilst serving two. The populations, and the distances involved on the island, were extremely small. In one parish, Bodewryd, Robert Jones explained that there was no glebe house, but he lived 'in a rented house close to Bodewryd church, which to all intents and purposes for the last forty years has been used as a vicarage'.[20]

In St Asaph in the late 1870s, the provision of houses appears to have been as good as it was becoming in Bangor. In a sample of seventy-one parishes in that diocese for which the reports of rural deans in 1879 survive, sixty-one (86 per cent) had an incumbent residing in the parsonage, and fifty-nine had a parsonage that was described as in good repair. The implication was that although the incumbent resided, in two cases the house was regarded as substandard.[21] It is likely that one of these houses may have been the one at Llanmerewig, which had existed as early as 1689, and had been described in 1874 as 'but a poor, straw-thatched, clay-floor cottage'.[22]

That parsonage houses such as the one at Llanmerewig were becoming increasingly shocking and noteworthy is a revealing tribute to the unselfishness of the mid-nineteenth-century generation of Welsh clergy. These men were generally willing to mortgage their livings in order to engage in major building projects or new builds, which were intended to benefit not only themselves, but several generations of their successors. Although it was the case that since 1838, bishops had been able legally to compel clergy to mortgage their livings under clause 62 of the Pluralities Act, this was very much a matter of last resort. Whereas the National Society put money into school buildings, and the Incorporated Church Building Society and the various diocesan building societies gave funds for the construction, extension and restoration of churches, with the exception of the Queen Anne's Bounty and the Ecclesiastical Commissioners, there were no equivalent large funding bodies to pay for parsonages, although some diocesan societies, like the one in Llandaff, included grants towards the costs of work on houses as within the general remit of promoting the work of the Church. The Queen Anne's Bounty and the Ecclesiastical Commissioners, useful though they were, imposed careful limits on the extent of the help that they would allow themselves to give, as we have seen in the case of Aberdare. They tended to refuse aid unless an equivalent amount had been raised through subscriptions, and the Bounty declined to assist parishes where building work had already started. This could leave clergy in the very uncomfortable position of having to live in clearly dilapidated houses, whilst they engaged in lengthy and sometimes fruitless fund-raising exercises and correspondence. It was hardly surprising that Evan Lewis, one of the mid-nineteenth-century vicars of Aberdare and a future dean of Bangor, suffered severely with rheumatic fever, which he attributed to the dampness of the vicarage.[23] Another source of financial help was dilapidations payments – the charge that a new incumbent could make upon his predecessor, or his predecessor's estate, for putting the house into a good state of repair. This was an important, although precarious, source for funding work on parsonages. Although, as we have seen, grants could be applied for, and patrons and parishioners could sometimes be generous, in most cases improvements to a parsonage meant the individual sacrifice of reduced income, as a consequence of taking out a mortgage on the living. This sacrifice was felt more keenly in Wales because the average value of livings was lower than in England. The experience of Henry Rogers, the rector of Melverley in the diocese of St Asaph, illustrates the plight which could befall the inadequately housed incumbent. His living was worth only £172 per annum. As there had been no parsonage when he arrived in the parish, Rogers had taken on the largest mortgage permitted by the Queen Anne's Bounty – £520, roughly three years of his income. The whole of this sum, and ten pounds besides, had been spent on building a house. The erection of outbuildings, and the architect's fees, had taken a further £100. Meanwhile, the value of the living had been reduced to £137. Rogers had no private means, and was in a desperate state. He launched a public appeal, begging the help of the parish landowners, and the friends of the Church.[24] There was a vicious circle here. Until the value of livings could be improved, it was unrealistic to mortgage them with a view to improving clerical housing. Henry Rogers was one of many clergy who was caught in a dreadful trap.

The provision of day schools and Sunday schools had long been a central element in the well-run Anglican parish. Indeed, the curate of Wrexham had such strong views on the subject that he told the bishop that it was 'almost useless' holding public worship, unless there was also high-quality catechetical instruction taking place in the parish school.[25] Across Wales, educational provision became ever more central in the period discussed here, expanding from the elementary schools under the auspices of the Anglican National Society and the non-denominational British and Foreign Society, to the foundation of additional grammar schools, intermediate county schools and university colleges.[26] These new establishments gave Wales a network of provision which, by the end of the nineteenth century, was considerably in advance of what was available in England. Furthermore, as Kenneth Morgan has suggested, the education movement moved to the centre of the political stage, and became the major force in transforming what had been a sense of regional vitality into a national consciousness.[27]

As we have already seen, in the northern dioceses, and particularly St Asaph, church schools were well established by the middle of the nineteenth century. The president of the Board of Education regarded St Asaph under Bishop Short as a model of good practice, which could well have been emulated by the English dioceses (p. 334). By the turn of the twentieth century, no less than 50 per cent of the children in the diocese of St Asaph were being educated in church schools, far above the figure for Wales as a whole, where the proportion was only 16 per cent.[28] In some other places, educational provision also remained almost entirely Anglican until 1902. These included the counties of Breconshire, Denbighshire, Flintshire, Pembrokeshire and Radnorshire.[29] That this was so says much about the very generous provision of church schools which had been made in the mid-nineteenth century, which had made the need for the erection of Board schools in the years after the 1870 Education Act far less pressing than in the south of the country. The lack of alternatives to Anglican education was, however, a state of affairs that was bound to bring many Nonconformists into direct conflict with the Church. In many parishes, they had no alternative but to educate their children in Anglican schools. At the time when many of these schools were established, Nonconformists had been happy to give them moral and financial support. But as denominational identities began to sharpen, and as the Anglican Church came increasingly to be seen as having been subject to an onslaught from non-Protestant forces, church schools as the sole educational provision in a community became increasingly less acceptable.

Bishop Short received plenty of letters from his clergy on the subject of church schools, indicating that the provision of day schools seems to have been regarded as of greater importance than either clerical housing or church restoration. Certainly, Welsh schools developed further and faster in the second half of the nineteenth century than at any time before or since. At the beginning of the period, there continued to be some ramshackle parochial schoolrooms that were outside the auspices of the National Society, although it is evident that the days of such failing institutions were numbered. One example was at Llandysilio near Llangollen in 1847, where the only school in the parish was kept in a transept, boarded off from the body of the church. It had existed since 1834, and was supported entirely by voluntary subscriptions and the 'weekly pence' of the children. The master, who was eighteen and a half years old, was paid only £13 per annum. Although there were thirty-six children on the books, the average attendance was just twenty. 'I attribute the paucity of the number of scholars entirely to the youth and inexperience of the master. The small farmers send their children to schools three and four miles from Llandysilio, [*sic*] owing to their want of confidence in our Master.'[30] The incumbent believed that the school could be turned round by securing a larger salary for a more competent teacher. Another school that was at a turning-point was Bala Free Grammar School, which had had new buildings in 1840. The issue was whether raising the academic standards required for entry was compatible with the intentions of the founder.

The school had been founded in 1712, and was funded with an endowment that Edmund Meyricke, the then treasurer of St David's, had vested in Jesus College, Oxford. His intention was to maintain six scholars and six exhibitioners, and to teach thirty poor boys from north Wales. Jesus College gave the master, T. Z. Davies, £80 per annum, and the boys two entire suits of clothes. The master wanted to admit only those boys who could read a little, but the 'gentlemen from this neighbourhood' who made decisions about who should be admitted objected to this 'on the grounds that a better class of boys would thus gain the benefit of a charity, intended, as they suppose, for the very poorest orders'.[31] The bishop favoured selecting the boys on the basis of a competitive examination. Thus the old world of slavish respect for the intentions of pious donors began to come into conflict with the new world of measurable inputs and outcomes. In the decades that followed, the grammar school retained its link with Jesus College, Oxford, and appears to have thrived.

Education was also something which had interested successive bishops of Bangor (p. 230). The widespread provision of schools is attested in the visitation returns for the archdeaconry of Bangor in 1856. Of the sixty-three parishes, only ten were lacking in any kind of day-school provision, and seven of these were small Anglesey parishes where pupils could normally travel to schools in neighbouring parishes.[32] The island was well provided with both day schools and Sunday schools that were, in theory at least, being run in connection with the Church, although the extent to which some of them emphasized Anglican teachings fell rather short of what the National Society would have expected. In the parish of Llanfachraeth near Holyhead, the incumbent reported that there was a school for twenty-five to thirty children, and 'a Dame School at Llanfwrog wherein thirty to forty children attend who learn the Catechism and are of all Denominations various'.[33] The incumbent of Pentraeth commented that he had two parochial schools, one with twenty-five children at Pentraeth, and the other with fifty at Llanbedrgoch. 'The schools are not strictly speaking in close connection with the Church of England, and more on the plan of schools in older times, yet they are useful in their way, as the children are taught to read and to write well.'[34] The greatest number of pupils in the archdeaconry were being educated in the mainland parish of Llanbeblig, which included Caernarvon. Here there were six National schools with over 900 pupils, and four Sunday schools, with 750 scholars.[35] A couple of respondents noted that their Sunday schools were attended by adults as well as children, indicating that this Welsh tradition was not confined to Nonconformity.[36] It is likely that adult Sunday school attendance was at this date fairly widespread, and not something to which incumbents felt that they needed to make particular reference.

By 1900, the educational landscape had changed out of all recognition. In the visitation returns of that year, the Bangor incumbents were asked to provide much more detailed information about their schools, including the average number of pupils in the day and Sunday schools, the breakdown between English and Welsh schools, and whether there were infant and night schools. They were also asked whether they taught in their schools themselves, whether they were involved in the religious instruction of the pupil teachers, whether a school board had been established in their parish, whether the school had been transferred to it, and if so, to what extent they were able to deliver the religious instruction offered. In the eighteen parishes of the mainland deanery of Arllechwedd, every parish without exception had a Welsh-medium Sunday school, and all the clergy were involved in teaching in it to some extent. Fourteen of the parishes also ran an English-medium Sunday school, and the same number could muster a day school. Four had infant schools, and six had night schools.[37] Morris Roberts, the incumbent of Penmachno, commented that he found it hard to get adults to attend the (Welsh) Sunday school. Perhaps as he also ran a night school with an average attendance of twenty-five, those adults in his parish with an interest in education with an Anglican flavour had transferred to that.[38] None of the parish schools in the deanery had been transferred to boards, and it appeared that relatively few boards had been established in the area. The setting up of school boards had been a provision of the 1870 Education Act, to allow for schools to be established more systematically in places where they were absent or inadequate. Membership of the local school boards was by election, and provided the opportunity for a trial of strength between the denominations, as they vied with each other to stamp their own influence on the schools' religious provision. In 1899 it was reported that of 320 school boards across Wales, 62 had no religious instruction, 118 taught the Bible without comment, and almost all had no religious examination.[39] In the Bangor parish of Trefriw, there was no parish school, and a Board school had been established. John Gower, the incumbent, noted that his giving religious instruction in the Board school was 'tolerated'.[40] In Llanbedr-y-Cennin, a Board school existed in the absence of a National school, but the Revd Edward Hughes's offer to teach in it had been rejected.[41] In Arvon, the other mainland deanery in the archdeaconry of Bangor, fewer National schools had survived, and five had been transferred to school boards, to be run at state expense. In all cases, the clergy had been required to withdraw from involvement in what had formerly been 'their' schools. 'We do not meddle with the Board Schools', noted Thomas Johns of Llanrûg. At Llanaelhaearn, the school had been transferred back in 1870. The clergy were, however, still allowed access to the slate works school, although they were forbidden to give regular religious instruction there.[42]

In terms of sheer numbers of people being educated, the most active parishes in the Arllechwedd deanery were, unsurprisingly, the largest ones of Llandudno and Glanogwen (which included Bethesda), but the trends in these two parishes pointed in different directions. The Church was struggling in Llandudno, where the population had risen from 6,061 in the 1891 census, to an estimated 10,000 in 1900. This had produced, predictably, a great variety of non-Anglican places of worship – 5 Calvinistic Methodist (including 1 English-speaking congregation), 4 Wesleyan, 2 Independent, 4 Baptist, and 2 Roman Catholic. Although the church day school had 306 pupils and the infant school 90, it was apparent that the Anglicans were educating only a small proportion of the children of the town, and there was no night school. In Glanogwen, the population was 5,000 and there was considerable competition in the form of 12 Nonconformist chapels – 5 Calvinistic Methodist, 5 Independent, 1 Baptist and 1 Wesleyan – but the picture was rather different from Llandudno. The church day school was attended by 245 pupils, and the

Sunday school by 240, 'practically all Welsh'. Eighty-one were in the infants school and sixty-one attended the night school – the vicar, Richard Thomas Jones, taught church history between October and Easter, as well as Prayer Book classes for young men and boys. He did not teach in the day school, however, remarking: 'not yet as I want to gain the confidence of all parents'; something which he evidently thought himself capable of achieving .[43]

The other large parishes in the archdeaconry make an interesting comparison. Llanbeblig with Caernarfon in the deanery of Arfon, which in 1856 had educated over 900 pupils in six National schools, and had had 750 Sunday scholars in four Sunday schools, had clearly lost the position which it had enjoyed at the middle of the century. In 1900, the National schools only had 155 in the infants' department, 184 in the boys' school and 182 in the girls' school. There were 160 children in the English Sunday school, and 373 in the Welsh Sunday school. The population was 10,138, making it a similar size to Llandudno. The religious mix of the town was similar, and included Roman Catholicism, although there were fewer Nonconformist chapels than in Llandudno – ten, in comparison with Llandudno's fifteen. The Bangor parishes, which in 1856 had boasted seven church schools of varying sizes and types, had by 1900 been reduced to three.[44] Another large community located between Bangor and Caernarfon, Llanddeiniolen, with a population in the civil parish of 6,212 in 1900, seemed to be experiencing a similar trend. Back in 1856, the rector of Llanddeiniolen had reported that a school in connection with the Church of England was 'lately completed', and that it was large enough for 400 scholars. By 1900, this school appears to have been transferred to the school board, and it was educating just sixty pupils.

On the eve of the 1902 Education Act, National schools had lost ground badly to the Board schools. A total of 71,940 pupils were being educated in Anglican National schools, and 171,507 children were attending Board schools.[45] The Act itself created local education authorities and gave them control over all types of school, thus collapsing the distinction between Board and voluntary schools. It also provided for all schools to be partially funded from the rates, irrespective of their denominational standpoint. This caused enormous hostility among Nonconformists throughout England and Wales, who objected to what was commonly termed 'Rome on the rates'. Opposition to the Act took a very different form in Wales from the form it took in England. In England, the emphasis was upon individual Nonconformist 'passive resisters' withholding that part of their rates that was considered likely to be used for educational purposes, and facing the legal consequences, which were usually the distraint of goods, and sometimes imprisonment.[46] In Wales, the opposition, which was organized by Lloyd George, took place at an institutional rather than an individual level, with fourteen of the sixteen Welsh LEAs simply refusing to implement the Act.[47] The government retaliated with the Education (Local Authority Default) Act, intended to circumvent local revolts, which was passed, but little enforced. Had the government not fallen, it is difficult to know how they would have resolved matters in the light of the virtual shut-down of the schools system by most local authorities. Thus the 1902 Education Act had two different meanings on either side of the national boundary. In England, the Act was the last, curiously anachronistic, occasion in which one Christian group – the largely Anglican magistracy and political establishment – could contemplate prosecuting another Christian group, on account of the strength of their religious views. In Wales, it played out differently, and with a seemingly less bitter legacy and certainly a less heavy footprint on the historical record. By 1902, Nonconformists had taken their place among the local government establishment, and Anglicans maintained a lower profile during the course of the dispute.[48] Anglican–Nonconformist bitterness existed, but remained relentlessly focused on the disestablishment campaign. In any event, Wales had an educational system of which it could be proud, which could educate pupils from elementary level through to university graduation.

Developing Parish Life: Worship, Language and Culture

Despite the powerful rhetoric about 'Rome on the rates' that was asserted in the wake of the 1902 Education Act, in Wales it was a charge which objectively was hard to make plausible. If there was a complaint that could be justifiably upheld about religious education in Wales, it was that Welsh children were being made to read the Bible in English, rather than that they were being indoctrinated with Catholic devotions. The prevailing culture of parish life was, as we shall see, Low Church and Protestant. Anglo-Catholicism was rare, and because it was so unusual, in the places where it existed it tended to make ripples. In May 1899, Charles F. Reeks, the vicar of Monmouth, received a petition signed by forty-five parishioners objecting to the Catholic nature of eight different liturgical practices that had been observed in his church. These included 'undue elevation' of the bread and wine at communion, the use of wafer bread, the lighting of candles when not required to give light, the introduction of a second holy table in the church and the wearing of unauthorized eucharistic vestments. Reeks took the unusual step of sending a printed questionnaire to each of the complainants, to ascertain how much they really knew about what went on in his church, and to find out whether he still had the confidence of any of them.[49] It turned out that most of the respondents did have confidence in him, although one submitted the rather cryptic reply: 'If as a Church of England minister – yes. If as a sacerdotal priest – no.'

Three months later in August, the vicar of St Mary's Cardiff was also the recipient of a long letter about liturgical practices.[50] It was from his churchwardens, written on behalf of the churchgoers. But unlike the Monmouth parishioners, the Cardiff worshippers were full of praise for the 'beautiful and symbolical adjuncts to Divine worship' that had been introduced by their vicar. They were particularly distressed that the bishop of Llandaff had called for a ban on the use of incense, which they described as 'one of those innocent and scriptural accessories to divine worship'.[51] But opinion in Cardiff was mixed, and there is some evidence of violent hostility. Indeed, it remained a feature of British life in the late nineteenth century that anti-Catholic sentiment was sometimes articulated in visceral and semi-literate form. It is seen in the words of an anonymous correspondent who wrote to Bishop Lewis:

> what is being practiced in Cardiff especially at St Mary's is what the Bishop should put a stop to as its *illegal* not according to the Prayer Book . . . we can easily make it a *topic* at the next general Election *which will be done* . . . there is not the shadow of a doubt but it will end in a *great row*, I should be very sorry to see it you know its the *Protestantism* of this *land we* want to *preserve* if that is not done down we go.[52]

Whether intentionally or not, the author of this letter was conjuring up the powerful image of a tidal wave of (Roman) Catholicism gathering strength to sweep across the English Channel and engulf Protestant Britain. The presence of incense and altar lights in an Anglican church in Cardiff was thought to be contributing to this possibility. St Mary's Cardiff, and the twelve other parishes in the diocese of Llandaff (including Aberdare) that were in the patronage of the Bute family, as well as apparently destabilizing Protestantism, offered rare sanctuary to Anglo-Catholic clergy. The third Marquis of Bute, whose family were major landowners in south Wales, became a Roman Catholic in 1868, when he came of age and succeeded to the title.[53] As a Catholic the third marquis was, however, legally prevented from exercising his rights as patron. Rather than allowing his rights to lapse the marquis shrewdly appointed a group of his Anglican High Church friends to act on his behalf. Naturally, they appointed very High Church men to the Bute parishes, and thus Anglo-Catholicism entered the Cardiff area by this means.[54]

These parishes were, in reality, a few Catholic drops in a Protestant ocean.[55] By 1874, only 3 Welsh churches used vestments, 3 had daily communion, 23 had communion on holy days and 32 had communion every Sunday.[56] This is in the context of there being nearly 1,000 parishes in Wales. Communion every Sunday was regarded as the hallmark of advanced High Churchmanship at this date. Ritualism established itself more easily in the city of Cardiff, in some of the large industrial parishes in the south Wales Valleys and in the English-speaking parts of Pembrokeshire, rather than in the Welsh-speaking rural areas. The strength of ritualism in the fashionable seaside resort of Tenby, in south-west Wales, also parallels the ritualist strongholds on parts of the English south coast. The overall picture, however, was of an odd religious phenomenon that was spread thinly, and limited to parishes that were often isolated from others espousing similar views. It was a movement which would not come into its own in Wales until the third decade of the twentieth century.

For Welsh Anglicans in the early twentieth century, much more significant than the Catholic revival was the impact of the Evan Roberts Revival of 1904–5. This was the last major such event to occur in Britain, and unlike earlier Revivals such as that of 1859, which manifested itself in England, Scotland, Ireland and Wales, the 1904–5 Revival occurred only in Wales. Although chiefly an event supported by Nonconformists, the Protestant Evangelical atmosphere of much of Welsh Anglicanism meant that many church people were open to its effects. In his 1905 visitation articles, Bishop Watkin Williams of Bangor, who was personally sympathetic,[57] asked his clergy to respond to the question, 'Please give any information you may have as to the effect of the recent Revival within the Parish under your charge'.[58] In sixty parishes surveyed, only nine declined to provide any answer in the large space provided on the form. Not all incumbents viewed it positively, although the majority undoubtedly did so. Among those who were sceptical, the most frequent observations were that its effects had been short-lived. At the height of the Revival, which began in November 1904, congregations everywhere experienced significant increases, but by August 1905, when these forms were being filled in, there had generally been something of a decline in the number of worshippers. 'In this parish church [Llanddeiniolen] we saw very little difference, except the visible increases in attendance at public worship, and at season [*sic*] for Holy Communion. There are still traces of this improvement . . . but I think we are fairly normal all round now.'[59] 'There is a good deal of singing, but I fear the results will not be permanent.'[60] At Bangor, it was claimed that the Revival had lacked spontaneity and divine action. 'It was galvanised into existence by a desire to emulate what was taking place elsewhere. It only affected the lowest and most ignorant of the community, with disastrous effect in the case of weak intellects, several have been removed to Denbigh asylum.'[61]

Of the fifty-one clergy in the sample who responded to the question, forty-seven had something positive to say about the Revival, even if in some cases their answers also contained elements of criticism. The most generally reported good effects were that there had been significant increases in worshippers, particularly communicants and those seeking confirmation, that drunkenness had declined, that people were more serious, and that youths in particular had become more willing to discuss religious matters and become involved in church activities. At Llanllechid,

> Young men come forward more readily to take part in prayer meetings and to open and close the Sunday schools. The attendance at the services are [*sic*] better and more devout. Some of the laymen of their own accord visit the sick and pray with them. Men and women come forward more readily to teach in the Sunday schools, and the attendance particularly at week night services is much improved.[62]

A similar observation was made about Newborough: 'Over 20 of all ages have come out to speak in public at our weekly meetings and are now glad to take part in prayer meetings.'[63] The Revival evidently gave opportunities to normally passive Anglican worshippers that would previously have been only found within Nonconformity. The incumbent of Aber reported a similar impact on the young people, but struck a note of caution:

> One effect has been to make the young people easier to talk to on Religious subjects. Here, as elsewhere, they had come to think of nothing but sport and amusements: but now they will listen to and take part in religious conversation. But still I am afraid that in the Dissenting chapels they have made rather too much of the excitement, and rather neglected to press the sense of duty upon those affected. Some that I have spoken to appeared to think that it was but a small matter to neglect or shirk some of their daily work in order that they might be able to attend the chapel revival services and keep late hours thereat.[64]

Clearly the revivalist mentality did not always sit easily with the Anglican temperament. Not surprisingly, one of the most positive evaluations came from the Anglesey parish of Llanddona, where Evan Roberts had held a meeting in the church on 1 July 1905. 'The formalist has been wonderfully awakened to a higher sense of the realities of spiritual life; and many indifferent and hardened sinners have been brought to seek salvation.'[65]

Across Wales, at least in the years before the Revival, the staple of Anglican worship was morning and evening prayer, with at least one sermon every Sunday, and very often an elaborate rotation between the two languages. At Holyhead, where there were two churches, the parish church and St Seiriol's, the curate Charles Williams reported on the arrangements in 1856. On Sundays at ten there was Welsh in one church and at eleven English in the other; at two there was Welsh at St Seiriol's, and at six there was English when there had been Welsh in the morning, and Welsh when there had been English in the morning. An additional Welsh service with sermon was provided in a licensed room two miles from the town, and a further Welsh service was provided in the parish church on a Wednesday.[66] Communion services were held about twenty times a year. Eucharistic provision was more frequent at Holyhead than in the surrounding area, and this may be attributed to duplication caused by the need to give careful attention to the needs of both language communities. It is likely that Williams would have regarded ten to twelve times a year as the 'normal' frequency, and doubled this in order to provide equally for both English- and Welsh-speakers. In the other thirty-four Anglesey parishes for which records survive for 1856, fifteen had communion services monthly and at the great festivals, and eighteen held them between four and six times a year. The only island parish that had more frequent eucharistic worship than Holyhead was Beaumaris, which had an unusually 'advanced' pattern of thirty-five communion services a year, three Sunday sermons, and daily morning prayer.[67] In the 28 parishes in the mainland archdeaconry of Bangor for which records for 1856 survive, 8 retained the old pattern of quarterly communion, 2 held it every two months, 17 held it monthly and 1 held it fortnightly.[68]

The 1900 visitation records indicate that Welsh-medium worship held its ground in Bangor. In a sample of thirty-five mainland parishes, sixteen used Welsh for the majority of their services, and a further ten used Welsh exclusively.[69] In the more Anglicized diocese of St Asaph, however, it is apparent that even within a relatively compact geographical area, distinctly different patterns of liturgical language use may be discerned as early as the mid-nineteenth century. In Montgomeryshire, for example, forty-eight Anglican places of worship may be identified from the 1851 census.[70] Of these, 17 only held services in English, 19 only used Welsh and 12 used both English and Welsh, although the two languages were not mixed (officially at least) at the same service. A clear picture of liturgical language use in the county at mid-century emerges. Welsh only was used in the parishes around Llanidloes in the south-west and Pennant Melangell in the north-west. The parishes in the Newtown area and eastwards into Shropshire used English exclusively. Parishes on the border, such as Llandyssil, Berriew and Welshpool, also used English. The parishes in Llanfyllin registration district, in the north-east and central regions of the county, were most likely to provide services in both languages. Here the most common pattern was to offer services alternately in English and Welsh, in a similar pattern to that noted on Anglesey a few years later. Meifod, in the north of Montgomeryshire, was typical of a parish making this form of provision. The vicar, Richard Richards, reported on his census form: 'The morning congregation, whether Welsh or English, is always largest.'[71]

This pattern of more or less equal provision of services in Welsh and English was sustained in the diocese of St Asaph for the next thirty years until 1880, when there began to be a dramatic increase in the amount of English used, as Table 13.1 makes clear. In 1880, 274 English Sunday services were recorded as having taken place in St Asaph, and 259 in Welsh – a mere fifteen more. By 1890, 394 English Sunday services were recorded, a sharp contrast with the 264 Welsh ones – 130 more.[72] Another ten years would see an even greater acceleration in English-medium worship, with an accompanying drop in provision for Welsh-speakers. In 1910 the number of English services in the diocese was recorded as 443, and the number of

Welsh as 236 – 207 more.[73] The increase in the amount of English used at worship was naturally more marked in the more Anglicized county of Montgomeryshire, where 52 per cent of the population were monoglot English-speakers by 1901, than in the more solidly Welsh-speaking parts of the diocese, such as the county of Denbigh, and parts of Merioneth and Caernarfonshire. The pattern of language shift may be traced through individual Montgomeryshire parishes: Bettws Cedewain, near Newtown, where two services in Welsh had been held at mid-century, had entirely switched to using English by 1871, and by 1895 it was very firmly part of the English-language belt;[74] Llanwddyn had also only used Welsh at mid-century, and had introduced an English service in addition to the Welsh at some point between 1877 and 1880.[75] They experimented with bilingual worship; by 1891 four Sunday services were being held, with six different liturgical combinations used in rotation.[76] Change did not always come this early, however. Llangadfan, a parish with a population of 354 in the west of the county, may have been among the last Anglican churches in Montgomeryshire to abandon a Welsh-only policy. English services were introduced for the first time in 1913.[77]

The increasing use of English liturgy was not the only significant change of this period. During the 1890s and 1900s, it became increasingly common for services to be held on Ash Wednesday and Ascension Day. It also became more usual to mark major saints' days with an early communion service. The typical Sunday pattern remained Morning Prayer at about eleven and Evening Prayer at about six, a monthly service for children and a monthly communion service. The most obvious trend at the turn of the century was the gradual introduction of weekly or fortnightly communion. As in England, the enthusiasm of the clergy for more communion services was often not shared by the laity,[78] and there were sometimes twice as many people at the service as there were communicants. At Llanwddyn, 1900 was the year when weekly communion was introduced, and the communicants' register reveals that of the approximately sixty-five communicants in the parish, only four began to receive three or four times a month. They were the vicar, a female member of his family, the parish clerk and another female worshipper.[79] In nearby Bettws Cedewain in 1895, there were usually fewer than ten communicants at the fortnightly service, although over 100 (out of a population of 500) would be present for evensong.[80] In Montgomeryshire, the service of choice of the majority of Church worshippers was undoubtedly choral evensong.[81]

The biggest event in Montgomeryshire's annual liturgical cycle was not Easter but harvest festival. The largest crowds were reserved for harvest festivals, which in the late nineteenth century were sometimes large communal celebrations which lasted for several days. In November 1880, the Berriew parish magazine reported that the church had been 'tastefully decorated' with evergreens, corn, fruit, vegetables, flowers and bread and butter.[82] Everywhere, worshippers thronged the churches.[83] At Llanllwchaiarn, the attendance at the 1885 harvest festival was described as the 'largest congregation ever seen in this church within the memory of man' and in 1894 it was described as 'overflowing'.[84] At Bettws Cedewain there were usually about 300 at the principal service on Friday evening; in the late 1890s there was never any standing room, and crowds gathered in the churchyard. The year 1896 was typical: the church's celebrations began on Friday 18 September, with two communion services, one at 8.30 and one at 11, producing between them 102 communicants; there was luncheon in the schoolroom, and then an intoned litany at 3, followed by an organ recital with sacred solos and quartets. Tea followed, and then at 6.30 evensong, a service at which there was not even standing room. On Saturday, there was a mission service, with magic lantern, at the schoolroom, which raised money for the Church Army. On Sunday the harvest festival services of the previous Friday were repeated, with another large crowd attending in the evening. This was followed by a final mission meeting organized by the Church Army.

The vicar of Bettws Cedewain was William Gwynne Vaughan, a youthful and energetic graduate of St David's College. His approach to his parishioners' enthusiasm for harvest celebrations was supportive, but he also tried to steer it in an ecclesiastical direction. Thus harvest became an occasion for the best-attended communion services of the year, and also an occasion to raise awareness of missionary work. Many of the Welsh clergy were the sons of farmers, and most had been brought up in rural Wales, so that they were naturally in sympathy with the harvest-time mood of their parishioners.[85] In this part of mid-Wales, Advent and Christmas were less keenly observed than either harvest or Easter, although it varied from parish to parish. There were no special services in the days immediately before Christmas, and the number of Christmas Day communicants was often quite small; at Bettws Cedewain on Christmas Day 1895, there were thirty-five communicants out of the fifty-three who came to church. Much more important in Welsh society were *Dydd Calan* (New Year's Day) and *Calan Hen* (old New Year's Day on 12 January).[86] Bettws Cedewain was probably not the only church which held social events and bell ringing to see in the new year, and in many places carols were sung at Epiphany.

By the late nineteenth century, many Welsh parishes had developed quite complex social networks which involved both a well-established pattern of annual celebrations and observances, and an array of weekly or monthly activities sponsored by parish clubs and societies.[87] At his visitation in 1900, Bishop Watkin Williams of Bangor asked his clergy detailed questions about their parish organizations. Was there a parish association to aid foreign or home missions, or other church causes? Was there a branch of the Church of England Temperance Society, or the Church of England Purity Society? Was there a young men's association for mutual improvement? Was there a branch of the Girls' Friendly Society? Was there a branch of the Mothers' Union? Was there a parochial library or institute? Was there a society for visiting and relieving the poor? In a sample of thirty-five of the mainland Bangor parishes, many had at least several of these organizations. The most common were associations to raise money for mission work or related charities, young men's organizations and the Girls' Friendly Society. Thirteen of the parishes had some sort of parish library or institute, although at Llanbeblig with Caernarfon this was not felt to be necessary because, significantly, the churchmen chiefly belonged to the Conservative Club.[88] Visiting the sick and poor was conducted in a highly organized fashion in some places, such as Llandudno and

Llanfairfechan, which each deployed sixteen women as district visitors. Elsewhere, visiting was carried out by the clergy or the clergy's family. Nevertheless, whilst the traditional notion that members of the religious establishment had a duty to relieve the suffering of the sick poor was generally maintained, there is evidence that it was breaking down in places. Thomas Edwards of Llanllyfni in the heart of the quarrying district on the Llŷn peninsula commented pointedly that the Calvinistic Methodists had a Dorcas Society: 'they are the rich people here.'[89]

Over a quarter of the parishes in the Bangor sample had their own branch of the Church of England Temperance Society (CETS), thus revealing the enormous influence of the temperance movement in the second half of the nineteenth century not simply on Nonconformity and Catholicism, but on Anglicanism as well.[90] Thomas Edwards of Llanllyfni claimed that over 100 people in his parish had taken the pledge (out of a total population of considerably more than 5,000), but lamented that 'very few have paid any subscription as yet'. We may assume that quite a significant proportion of the 5,000 parishioners would have been non-drinkers on account of their Nonconformist principles – there were nineteen Nonconformist chapels in the parish. Nevertheless, Edwards saw drink as the major social evil in Llanllyfni, and he had organized a temperance mission in the previous year. He noted that 'spending Saturday afternoon or evening in worldly pleasure and excess tells materially on places of worship on Sundays'.[91]

Across Wales, senior churchmen gave prominent support to the temperance movement. In 1873, Bishop Hughes of St Asaph recommended that every parish should establish a branch of the CETS, and by 1883, a diocesan branch had been formed in St David's.[92] John Owen, principal of St David's College, noted with satisfaction that in the Michaelmas term of 1894, of the 130 men in residence at Lampeter, ninety-five were total abstainers.[93] H. T. Edwards was another prominent teetotaller who was enlisted to address large public gatherings on the issue, and whose intervention was credited with having aided the passage of the Welsh Sunday Closing Act of 1881.[94] There was an element of irony in this, because the passing of the Welsh Sunday Closing Act helped to establish the principle of separate legislation for Wales, thus easing the path towards disestablishment legislation. Although there was considerable pressure on the Welsh clergy to embrace teetotalism, it was clearly resisted by some, often with arguments that neither Jesus nor St Paul had condemned the modest consumption of wine. Nevertheless, the biographers of G. Arthur Jones, the celebrated Cardiff Anglo-Catholic, still found it necessary to devote four pages to explaining how it was that Father Jones 'liked a glass of wine, made no secret of it, and knew no reason why he should not enjoy it'.[95] Whereas Jones was prepared to administer the pledge to parishioners who came to St Mary's for that purpose, William Edwards of St James's Bangor refused to have a branch of CETS in his parish: 'We teach that the Church itself is the Society instituted by Christ to cope with evil and bring souls to God.'[96] Everywhere, the arguments about temperance versus teetotalism remained lively. At Bettws Cedewain in 1897, the parish debating society drew its largest crowd for a debate on total abstinence.[97]

The evident, although barely acknowledged, reliance on women to do pastoral work in the Bangor parishes, whether as district visitors or as members of organizations like the Glanogwen needlework guild, which supplied maternity items to women in Bethesda, raises the issue of the role which the late nineteenth-century Welsh Church envisaged for its lay members. In 1883, Basil Jones of St David's devoted a lengthy portion of his Charge to the need for 'the employment of fit, but unordained persons to assist the clergy wherever this can be done'.[98] In fact, Jones claimed that such men were already being 'extensively resorted to' despite the lack of sanction from the Prayer Book or the Articles. Somewhat controversially, Jones appeared not to be advocating lay readers, of whom there was no mention, but a type of subdeacon: 'the institution of a separate and inferior order of the ministry which should not be regarded as indelible, and the exercise of whose functions should not be regarded as incompatible with secular avocations'.[99] The revival of the office of subdeacon, to enable the Church's minor orders to be opened to society's lower orders was something that was much discussed in the nineteenth century, but always resisted. In reviving the topic again, Jones was showing his radical commitment to extending the

Church's ministry. He was even willing to suggest that laymen should be permitted to preach in consecrated buildings.

Whilst not going as far as Jones, the other bishops were also swift to articulate the importance of incorporating lay people more fully. Bishop Hughes of St Asaph reminded his clergy that they alone did not constitute the Church, although in 1871 he appeared not to have thought further than occupying laymen in the traditional roles of churchwarden and sidesman.[100] Campbell of Bangor told the Canterbury Convocation in 1884 that what was needed were 'Christian men who can bridge over the gap between the different classes of society; who being in close communication with the clergyman on the one hand and the industrious masses on the other, can interpret each to each'.[101] In Llandaff, Ollivant advocated the closer cooperation of clergy and laymen at parish level through the setting up of church councils. Under certain constraints, most notably that it should not be seen as a passport to ordination for the poorly educated, he also favoured the recognition of lay readers, as a type of parallel ministry to the lay preachers on whom the Nonconformists relied so heavily. The first six lay readers for the diocese of Llandaff were licensed by Ollivant in his private chapel on 27 April 1870, five for the parish of Gelligaer, and one for Dowlais.[102]

Lay ministry in Llandaff proved popular, and between 1880 and 1924 422 people were licensed.[103] The vast majority were men, but there were also a handful of women, who became lay workers or deaconesses. A few, socially elite men were given general licenses which enabled them to operate anywhere within the diocese, with the incumbent's permission. One was Wilfred Seymour de Winton, a wealthy resident of Llandaff who gave the site on which St Michael's College was built.[104] Another was Edmund Palmer-Bott, a naval officer who lost his reader's badge when the ship he was commanding sank during the First World War. (Rather curiously, Palmer-Bott felt that without the badge he could not take services, despite the wartime conditions.)[105] The majority of readers were recommended by their parish clergy, and were given a licence that was valid in that parish only. This rankled with some; Emmanuel Barson ARCO wrote to the diocesan registrar to express surprise that he had been licensed only for Blaenavon;

he seems to have felt that an Associate of the Royal College of Organists should have been given a freer range. He was told that if he was invited to minister in any other parish, he must obtain the bishop's permission on every single occasion.[106] The occupational background of many of the readers was professional. They included a doctor, several teachers, a Lloyds bank cashier, a solicitor and an ordinand from St Michael's. The only one in a sample of 110 who could be unambiguously identified as a miner was Albert Bradley of Abercynon. The 10*s.* 6*d.* fee for Bradley's licence was paid by a well-wisher, who wrote to the registrar to point out that 'Mr Bradley is engaged in the mine, and works from 7 to 3 pm. I suppose it will mean that he must lose a day when at Llandaff for his license, unless it is at 5pm.'[107] This highlighted a problem, which affected several readers, including the bank cashier. The bishop held his licensings at noon, and then entertained the readers to lunch. But staff at the palace were slow to appreciate that events involving males in employment really needed to be held in the evening or at the weekend. Whereas Bradley appears to have lost a day's pay in order to appear at noon, others were less compliant. 'I am a very busy person,' wrote Samuel Arthur in 1917, 'especially so in the mornings.' He then proceeded to give the registrar the times at which he could appear at the palace. His request was accommodated.[108]

Once licensed, readers were empowered to read, preach and say prayers in unconsecrated buildings, and to read the lessons in church when required by the incumbent. They were also able to engage in visiting under the direction of the incumbent, and 'such other duties as may be lawfully assigned' by him or the bishop. This vagueness seems to have led to uncertainty about what was permissible, for by the 1930s the licence was endorsed on the back with what was not included: readers were not to celebrate Holy Communion, baptize, conduct funerals, enter the sanctuary to present alms, give a blessing or church women. It is not clear what training was required before licensing, but it is evident that some of the less well educated candidates were expected to pass an exam, and this may have encompassed all candidates. Various courses were offered under the auspices of the SPCK, and also by the diocese of London. By the early twentieth century, there had emerged within Llandaff diocese a group of highly mobile and fairly young men who appeared to be making a career out of lay ministry. Thirty-five-year-old George Brown of Aberdare had been trained at the SPCK College in Stepney, 'having passed out successfully and holding the college certificates'. Before Aberdare, he had been a reader at All Saints, Fishponds, Bristol, and he described himself as experienced in mission work, having spent two seasons acting as a missioner to hop-pickers in Kent under the auspices of the CETS. Brown was originally from Cardiff – 'I am one of the Revd A. Henderson's Cardiff confirmation boys.'[109] Frederick Tellett Dickson, aged thirty-six, had obtained his reader's licence in London, where he had studied some church history, Christian evidences and a course entitled 'How we got our Bible', all apparently run by the London diocese. He had been a reader in Norfolk and Hertfordshire, and had come to Wales in order to work for the Taff Vale Railway. In March 1906 he was put in charge of a mission church at Coychurch near Bridgend, and applied for a Llandaff reader's licence after a few months there.[110] Lay workers sponsored by the Missions to Seamen, sometimes known as marine readers, were another highly mobile group who moved from station to station along the diocese's coastline.

Church life in the diocese of Llandaff changed more dramatically between 1850 and 1920 than at any other period. With the fastest-growing population anywhere in Britain at mid-century, it was the diocese which faced the greatest challenges. As we have seen, new churches were built, the number of clergy grew rapidly, and the parochial boundaries and diocesan structures were completely overhauled. Thanks to a wealthy benefactor, the diocese was even able to found its own graduate theological college, and to offer free education to those who could not afford to pay. By the end of the nineteenth century it had realized that part of the strategy for its future success would depend on the proper deployment of lay aid, and it was making use of men of all social classes, and of women to a more limited extent (officially at least). Llandaff's problems had required and received a particularly robust response. The other three Welsh dioceses had encountered different problems: depopulation (in places), tense relations with Nonconformity, with particular bitterness over tithes, education and disestablishment, and the increasing challenge of accommodating the needs of two language communities, who often seemed to exist in isolation from each other, even in quite small parishes. By the early twentieth century, to a remarkable degree, the Welsh Church had adjusted to all of these complexities. When disestablishment eventually came, it too turned out to be nothing that had needed to be feared. In the final analysis, disestablishment was the lion that failed to roar.

Notes to Part IV

12. The National Scene

1 Of particular relevance here is K. D. M. Snell and Paul S. Ells, *Rival Jerusalems: The Geography of Victorian Religion* (Cambridge, 2000). It provides the most important findings to date on the comparisons between religion in Wales and in England in the mid-nineteenth century. The work is a useful companion to Ieuan Gwynedd Jones's editions of the Census in Wales – I. G. Jones and D. Williams (eds), *The Religious Census of 1851: A Calendar of the Returns Relating to Wales, Vol. I: South Wales* (Cardiff, 1976) and I. G. Jones (ed.), *The Religious Census of 1851: A Calendar of the Returns Relating to Wales, Vol. II: North Wales* (Cardiff, 1981). For more on the major themes discussed in this chapter, see I. G. Jones, *Explorations and Explanations: Essays in the Social History of Victorian Wales* (Llandysul, 1981), especially chapters 6 and 7.

2 D. Densil Morgan, *The Span of the Cross: Christian Religion and Society in Wales 1914–2000* (Cardiff, 1999), p. 81.

3 For the earlier period, see especially Philip Jenkins, 'Church, nation and language: the Welsh Church, 1660–1800', in Jeremy Gregory and Jeffrey S. Chamberlain, *The National Church in Local Perspective: The Church of England and the Regions, 1660–1800* (Woodbridge, 2003), as well as the other contributors to this volume. See also Frances Knight, 'The cultural aspirations of the Welsh clergy', in David Bebbington and Timothy Larsen (eds), *Modern Christianity and Cultural Aspirations* (Sheffield, 2003).

[4] For good general accounts of the way in which the census was conducted, see Snell and Ells, *Rival Jerusalems*, pp. 23–53, and Owen Chadwick, *The Victorian Church*, Part 1, 3rd edn (London, 1971), pp. 363–9.

[5] K. S. Inglis, 'Patterns of religious worship in 1851', *Journal of Ecclesiastical History*, 11 (1960), 74–86; David M. Thompson, 'The 1851 religious census: problems and possibilities', *Victorian Studies*, 11 (1967), 87–97; W. S. F. Pickering, 'The 1851 religious census – a useless experiment?', *British Journal of Sociology*, 18 (1967), 382–407. Other relevant publications are listed in Snell and Ells, *Rival Jerusalems*, pp. 23–4.

[6] David Williams, 'The census of religious worship of 1851 in Cardiganshire', *Ceredigion*, 4, 2 (1961), 113–28; Ieuan Gwynedd Jones, 'Denominationalism in Swansea and district: a study of the ecclesiastical census of 1851', *Morgannwg*, 12 (1968), 67–96; Ieuan Gwynedd Jones, 'Denominationalism in Caernarvonshire in the mid-nineteenth century as shown in the religious census of 1851', *Transactions of the Caernarvonshire Historical Society*, 31 (1970), 78–110; Ieuan Gwynedd Jones, 'The religious condition of the counties of Brecon and Radnor', in O. W. Jones and David Walker, *Links with the Past* (Llandysul, 1974), pp. 185–214; W. T. R. Pryce, 'The 1851 census of religious worship: an introduction to the unpublished schedules for Denbighshire', *Transactions of the Denbighshire Historical Society*, 23 (1974), 147–80. More recent has been the publication of M. Seaborne, 'The religious census of 1851 and early chapel building in north Wales', *NLWJ*, 26 (1990), 281–310.

[7] Ieuan Gwynedd Jones, *Mid-Victorian Wales: The Observers and the Observed* (Cardiff, 1992), p. 131.

[8] Jones, 'Denominationalism in Caernarvonshire', 82–3.

[9] John Wolffe, *God and Greater Britain: Religion and National Life in Britain and Ireland 1843–1945* (London, 1994), p. 66.

[10] Jones, 'Denominationalism in Caernarvonshire', 88–9. See also John Davies, *A History of Wales* (London, 1993), pp. 424–6 which provides a very helpful set of maps indicating all the places of worship recorded in the 1851 census for Anglicans, Congregationalists, Baptists, Calvinistic Methodists, Wesleyan Methodists, Catholics, Unitarians and Mormons.

[11] Snell and Ells, *Rival Jerusalems*, pp. 55–8.

[12] Snell and Ells, *Rival Jerusalems*, p. 64.

[13] Jones, 'Denominationalism in Caernarvonshire', 97.

[14] Jones, 'Denominationalism in Caernarvonshire', 98, 100.

[15] Pryce, 'The 1851 Census for Denbighshire', 174–6.
[16] Jones, 'Denominationalism in Swansea and district', 94.
[17] Jones, 'Denominationalism in Swansea and district', 83–4.
[18] Jones, 'Denominationalism in Caernarvonshire', 97.
[19] Williams, 'Census in Cardiganshire', 119–21.
[20] Williams, 'Census in Cardiganshire', 121–7
[21] Jones, *Census: Calendar of Returns* (1976), p. xxiv.
[22] Alfred Ollivant, *A Charge Delivered to the Clergy of the Diocese of Llandaff, at his Second Visitation, August 1854* (London, 1854), p. 43.
[23] Ollivant, *Charge 1854*, p. 43
[24] Ollivant, *Charge 1854*, p. 43.
[25] Williams, 'Census in Cardiganshire', 114.
[26] Gerald Parsons, *Religion in Victorian Britain, Vol. II: Controversies* (Manchester, 1988), p. 155.
[27] The standard accounts of the disestablishment campaign have been provided by Kenneth O. Morgan, *Freedom or Sacrilege? A History of the Campaign for Welsh Disestablishment* (Penarth, 1966), republished as 'The campaign for Welsh disestablishment', in *Modern Wales: Politics, Places and People* (Cardiff, 1995), pp. 142–76, and P. M. H. Bell, *Disestablishment in Ireland and Wales* (London, 1969). It also features strongly in Kenneth O. Morgan, *Wales in British Politics 1868–1922*, 3rd edn (Cardiff, 1991).
[28] Morgan, *Modern Wales*, p. 147.
[29] Ieuan Gwynedd Jones, '1848 and 1868: "Brad y Llyfrau Gleision" and Welsh Politics', in *Mid-Victorian Wales*, pp. 103–65.
[30] Morgan, *Modern Wales*, p. 148. The Liberation Society had achieved the status of a national movement by 1862.
[31] Bell, *Disestablishment in Ireland and Wales*, p. 236.
[32] Morgan, *Modern Wales*, p. 151.
[33] Morgan, *Modern Wales*, p. 161.
[34] Bell, *Disestablishment in Ireland and Wales*, p. 274.
[35] PP 1910 XIV, *Royal Commission on the Church of England and Other Religious Bodies in Wales and Monmouthshire* (London, 1910). The statistics relating to the Church in Wales are found in vol. V. For more on this see R. Tudur Jones, *Faith and the Crisis of a Nation: Wales 1890–1914*, trans. Sylvia Prys Jones, (ed.) Robert Pope (Cardiff, 2004), pp. 10–13.
[36] PP 1910 XIV, *Royal Commission*, Vol. I, p. 20.
[37] Morgan, *Modern Wales*, p. 169; Bell, *Disestablishment in Ireland and Wales*, p. 246.

[38] NLW, St Asaph Parish Records Meifod 28 – Meifod Church Defence Notebook.

[39] NLW, St Asaph Parish Records Manafon 6 – Manafon Ready Reference Register.

[40] Roger L. Brown, 'Traitors and compromisers: the shadow side of the Church's fight against disestablishment', *The Journal of Welsh Religious History*, 3 (Welshpool, 1995), pp. 35–53. Brown divides the pro-disestablishment Anglicans into 'traitors', 'compromisers' and 'peacemakers'.

[41] All the churchmen discussed in this section were strongly associated with the Liberal Party except Charles Gore. He never belonged to a political party, but according to his biographer 'most of the measures which he advocated on grounds of justice happened also to be included in the political programmes of Liberal and Labour representatives' (G. L. Prestige, *The Life of Charles Gore* (London, 1935), p. 274).

[42] Hansard's *Parliamentary Debates*, Third Series, 201, col. 1276, 24 May 1870.

[43] Hansard, Third Series, 201, cols. 1277–9.

[44] Hansard, Third Series, 201, col. 1280.

[45] Morgan, *Wales in British Politics*, pp. 67–8.

[46] Hansard, Third Series, 303, col. 306, 9 March 1886.

[47] Handard, Third Series, 303, col. 309.

[48] Hansard, Third Series, 336, cols. 70–1.

[49] Frances Knight, 'Welsh nationalism and Anglo-Catholicism: the politics and religion of J. Arthur Price (1861–1942)', in Robert Pope (ed.), *Religion and National Identity: Wales and Scotland c.1700–2000* (Cardiff, 2001), pp. 103–22.

[50] Morgan, *Modern Wales*, p. 159.

[51] Eluned E. Owen, *The Early Life of Bishop Owen* (Llandysul, 1958), pp. 179–81.

[52] John Percival to *The Times*, 4 May 1894. Cited in Jeremy Potter, *Headmaster: The Life of John Percival, Radical Autocrat* (London, 1998), pp. 202–3.

[53] Potter, *Headmaster*, pp. 205–7.

[54] Hansard, Fifth Series: Lords, 1912–13, vol. XIII, col. 1111.

[55] A central argument in William Warburton's *The Alliance between Church and State, or The Necessity and Equity of an Established Religion and a Test Law* (1736) had been that the authority of a religious establishment rested upon its maintaining numerical supremacy amongst the population at large.

[56] See for example the speeches by the bishop of St Asaph and the

archbishop of Canterbury, Hansard, Fifth Series: Lords, 1912–13, cols 1056, 1148–9.

57 *Church Times*, 14 February 1913, 207.

58 Hansard, Fifth Series: Lords, 1912–13, vol. XIII, col. 1200.

59 Hansard, Fifth Series: Lords, 1912–13, vol. XIII, col. 1203.

60 Hansard, Fifth Series: Lords, 1912–13, vol. XIII, col. 1201.

61 *Church Times* 21 February 1913, 213.

62 Prestige, *Gore*, pp. 353–6.

63 Morgan, *Wales in British Politics*, p. 271.

64 *Church Times*, 28 February 1913, 280.

65 Morgan, *Modern Wales*, p. 173.

66 J. Arthur Price, 'The home of St David' *The Welsh Outlook* (March 1917), 113.

67 J. Arthur Price, 'St David's Revisited' in *The Welsh Outlook* (March 1923), 80.

13. The Ecclesiastical Personnel

1 Owen Chadwick, *The Victorian Church*, Part 1, 3rd edn (London, 1971), p. 470.

2 There were Catholic places of worship at Swansea, Carmarthen, Haverfordwest, Pembroke and Brecon.

3 For a full discussion of this episode, see Owain W. Jones, *Rowland Williams: Patriot and Critic* (Llandysul, 1991), pp. 45–59.

4 Connop Thirlwall, *A Charge Delivered to the Clergy of the Diocese of St David's, at his Sixth Visitation, October 1857* (London, 1857), p. 63.

5 Rowland Williams, *An Earnestly Respectful Letter to the Lord Bishop of St David's* (London, 1860); Connop Thirlwall, *Letter to the Revd Rowland Williams* (London, 1860); Rowland Williams, *A Critical Appendix upon the Lord Bishop of St David's Reply* (London, 1861).

6 See Roger Lee Brown, *In Pursuit of a Welsh Episcopate: Appointments to Welsh Sees 1840–1905* (Cardiff, 2005). Brown has investigated the circumstances surrounding each episcopal vacancy in great detail. The 1840 vacancy at St David's was the first in which the Welsh lobby attempted to canvass for a Welsh candidate, although the campaign was not sufficiently well organized to yield the desired result.

7 Brown, *Welsh Episcopate*, p. 58.

8 In addition to supporting the admission of dissenters to Cambridge in 1834, Thirlwall supported the Maynooth grant in

1845, the admission of Jews to Parliament in 1858 and the disestablishment of the Irish Church in 1869.

[9] See for example, John Connop Thirlwall, Jr, *Connop Thirlwall: Historian and Theologian* (London, 1936) and Jones, *Rowland Williams*, p. 55.

[10] Thomas Vowler Short, *A Charge Delivered to the Clergy of the Diocese of St Asaph, July 1856*, p. 21.

[11] Brown, *Welsh Episcopate*, pp. 72–7.

[12] Robert Roberts, *A Wandering Scholar: The Life and Opinions of Robert Roberts*, ed. John Burnett and H. G. Williams (Cardiff, 1991), p. 378.

[13] Roberts, *Wandering Scholar*, p. 380.

[14] As a consequence of the Dean and Chapter Act (1840), and the efforts of the bishops themselves, the bishops' share of patronage rose from 12 to 20 per cent of the total in the period from 1835 to 1878. See Alan Haig, *The Victorian Clergy* (London and Sydney, 1984), p. 249, and Frances Knight, *The Nineteenth Century Church and English Society* (Cambridge, 1995), pp. 159–60.

[15] R. W. Morgan, perpetual curate of Tregynon, Montgomeryshire, *The Church and Its Episcopal Corruptions in Wales*, 2nd edn (London, 1855), pp. 66–7.

[16] Roberts, *Wandering Scholar*, p. 378. Short evidently prided himself in having written a mathematical textbook which he believed to be superior to Colenso's.

[17] *Carnarvon and Denbigh Herald*, 9 July 1859, cited by Brown, *Welsh Episcopate*, p. 108.

[18] Brown, *Welsh Episcopate*, p. 78.

[19] Brown, *Welsh Episcopate*, p. 77.

[20] A. G. Edwards, *Memories* (London, 1927), pp. 80–1.

[21] Alfred Ollivant, *A Charge Delivered to the Clergy of the Diocese of Llandaff, at his Primary Visitation, September 1851* (London, 1851), p. 9.

[22] Brown, *Welsh Episcopate*, pp. 92–4.

[23] For Basil Jones, see Matthew Cragoe, *An Anglican Aristocracy: The Moral Economy of the Landed Estate in Carmarthenshire 1832–1895* (Oxford, 1996), pp. 207–10.

[24] William Basil Jones, *Charge at his Third Triennial Visitation to the Clergy of the Diocese of St David's* (London, 1883), p. 71.

[25] Jones, *Charge* (1883), p. 24, in which he triumphantly reported that in only about seventeen parishes (out of around 500) was anything less than two full services held every Sunday. This compared with ninety-three in 1877.

[26] St David's was one of the last dioceses in England and Wales to adopt a diocesan conference (in 1882).

[27] Jones, *Charge* (1883), p. 56.

[28] See Brown, *Welsh Episcopate*, ch. 6, and Matthew Cragoe, 'A question of culture: the Welsh Church and the bishopric of St Asaph, 1870', *Welsh History Review*, 18 (1996), 228–54. Brown also provides much detailed information about those involved in the campaign for the Welsh episcopate.

[29] It is well known that he took meticulous care with all ecclesiastical appointments, and his diary reveals that he read extensively in Welsh history before making the St Asaph appointment. H. C. G. Matthew (ed.), *The Gladstone Diaries with Cabinet Minutes and Prime-Ministerial Correspondence, Vol. VII: January 1869–June 1871* (Oxford, 1982), entries from 12 January to 11 March 1870, pp. 219–53.

[30] Brown, *Welsh Episcopate*, p. 153.

[31] Joshua Hughes, *Primary Charge Delivered to the Clergy of the Diocese of St Asaph at his Primary Visitation, October 1871* (London, 1871), pp. 8–12.

[32] Joshua Hughes, *A Charge Delivered to the Clergy of the Diocese of St Asaph, at his Third Visitation, October 1877* (London, 1877), p. 6.

[33] Roger L. Brown, *David Howell: A Pool of Spirituality* (Denbigh, 1998), p. 233.

[34] Brown, *Welsh Episcopate*, pp. 239, 272.

[35] Eluned E. Owen, *The Early Life of Bishop Owen: A Son of Lleyn* (Llandysul, 1958), p. 135. Owen's lisp was more apparent in Welsh than in English, and may explain his reluctance to use his native tongue in formal situations.

[36] W. J. Conybeare, 'The Church of England in the mountains', *Edinburgh Review*, 97 (1853), pp. 342–79. I discuss both these views more fully in Frances Knight, 'The cultural aspirations of the Welsh clergy', in David Bebbington and Timothy Larsen (eds), *Modern Christianity and Cultural Aspirations* (Sheffield, 2003), pp. 124–7. For more on the reality of what it was like to be a clergyman thought to conform to 'the worst sort', see Roberts, *Wandering Scholar*. Robert Roberts had been brought up in extreme poverty, but after lengthy employment as a schoolmaster, eventually managed to graduate from St Bees. His career in the Church was terminated by a drink problem, and he escaped to Australia.

[37] Haig, *Victorian Clergy*, p. 118.

[38] All the data relating to the men who applied for ordination

1874–6 has been extracted from NLW SD/Misc/B/80 – the St David's diocesan ordinands book.

[39] This gives some substance to the otherwise rather baffling remark of Mrs Rowland Williams that the students she remembered at Lampeter in the 1850s were 'men advanced in years, broken-down farmers, blacksmiths, Wesleyan preachers' (*The Life and Letters of Rowland Williams DD*, edited by his wife, 2 vols (London, 1874), I, p. 167.

[40] A senior optime, he was ranked third in the classical tripos in 1846, and had won Sir William Brown's medal for a Greek ode in 1845.

[41] In the period before disestablishment, clerical stipends in Wales had ranged from about £120 to over £1,000 per annum. Following disestablishment, they were balanced out so that no one received less than £200, or more than £600 (P. M. T. Bell, *Disestablishment in Ireland and Wales* (London, 1969), p. 325).

[42] A. G. Edwards, *Memories* (London, 1927), p. 89.

[43] Edwards, *Memories*, p. 76; J. Vyrnwy Morgan, *Welsh Religious Leaders of the Victorian Era* (London, 1905), p. 58.

[44] Morgan, *Welsh Religious Leaders*, p. 59.

[45] Edwards, *Memories*, p. 13.

[46] Edwards, *Memories*, pp. 92–5.

[47] Brown, *David Howell*, p. 10.

[48] NLW, MS 964E, f. 130 Howell to Thomas Stephens, 6 August 1855. Cited by Brown, *David Howell*, p. 16.

[49] Brown, *David Howell*, pp. 199–210.

[50] Sir Thomas Phillips, *Wales: The Language, Social Conditions, Moral Character and Religious Opinions of the People, Considered in their Relation to Education* (London, 1849), p. 326.

[51] Other examples would include the third Marquis of Bute, a convert to Roman Catholicism, who presented Anglo-Catholic clergy to the thirteen livings in the Llandaff diocese that were in his gift, and the Cory family, prominent ship and colliery owners, who disliked Catholic forms of religion, and encouraged instead organizations like the Salvation Army.

[52] *St Michael and All Angels Theological College Aberdare, Report for 1904–6.*

[53] *St Michael and All Angels Theological College Aberdare, Report for 1895–6.* The reference to the 'Salvation captain' probably reflects the fact that Aberdare was an early centre for Salvation Army activity in Wales, the target of evangelism by Pamela Shepherd and her daughters from 1878. See Glenn K. Horridge,

The Salvation Army: Origins and Early Days (Godalming, 1993), pp. 208, 211–12, 218.

54 *St Michael and All Angels Theological College Aberdare, Report for 1897–98*, p. 7.

55 *St Michael and All Angels Theological College Aberdare, Report for 1892–94*, p. 6.

56 *St Michael and All Angels Theological College Aberdare, Report for 1898–99.*

57 *St Michael and All Angels Theological College Aberdare, Report for 1898–99.*

14. Developments in the Parishes

1 John Davies, *A History of Wales* (London, 1993), pp. 398–9. A map which indicates the locations of the main slate quarries in north Wales is on p. 405.

2 E. T. Davies, *Religion in the Industrial Revolution in South Wales* (Cardiff, 1965), pp. 8–9. In 1851, the population of the parish of Merthyr was 46,378, and of Aberdare, 14,999.

3 Alfred Ollivant, *A Charge Delivered at his Primary Visitation, September 1851*, p. 11.

4 Davies, *Religion in South Wales*, pp. 112–14.

5 Davies, *Religion in South Wales*, p. 114.

6 Davies, *Religion in South Wales*, pp. 103–4.

7 Davies, *Religion in South Wales*, pp. 105–6.

8 Davies, *Religion in South Wales*, pp. 139–40.

9 Frances Knight, *The Nineteenth-Century Church and English Society* (Cambridge, 1995), pp. 35–6.

10 Basil Jones, *A Charge at the Third Triennial Visitation to the Clergy of the Diocese of St David's October 1883* (London, 1883), p. 18.

11 Joshua Hughes, *A Charge Delivered to the Clergy of the Diocese of St Asaph at his Second Visitation, September and October 1874* (London, 1874), pp. 3–4.

12 Joshua Hughes, *Primary Charge Delivered to the Clergy of the Diocese of St Asaph at his Primary Visitation, October 1871* (London, 1871), p. 4.

13 Davies, *History of Wales*, p. 435.

14 NLW, B/QA/28 Bangor Visitation Records 1856 – Llandudno.

15 NLW, B/QA/33 Bangor Visitation Records 1900 – Llanfihangel yn Nhowyn.

16 Roger Brown, *Reclaiming the Wilderness: Some Aspects of*

Parochial Life and Achievements of the Diocese of Llandaff during the Nineteenth Century (Welshpool, 2001), pp. 62–6.

17 Davies, *Religion in South Wales*, p. 115.

18 NLW, B/QA/28 Bangor Visitation Records 1856.

19 NLW, B/QA/33 Bangor Visitation Records 1900.

20 NLW, B/QA/33 Bangor Visitation Records 1900 – Bodewryd.

21 NLW, SA/RD/53.

22 D. R. Thomas, *The Diocese of St Asaph* (Oswestry, 1874), p. 335.

23 Brown, *Reclaiming the Wilderness*, p. 63.

24 NLW, SA/LET/386 Henry Rogers, undated (but late 1840s) appeal for financial assistance.

25 NLW, SA/LET/338 Edward Edwards to Vowler Short, 30 September 1847.

26 Under the Endowed Schools Act (1869) twenty-seven grammar schools were endowed in Wales, in which two-thirds of the pupils were Anglican. The Welsh Intermediate Education Act (1889) laid the foundation for the development of county secondary schools. Both developments provided the all-important source of students for the new university colleges at Bangor, Aberystwyth and Cardiff, which had emerged in the 1880s as the nucleus of the new University of Wales.

27 Kenneth O. Morgan, *Wales in British Politics 1868–1922* (Cardiff, 1991), p. 53.

28 Morgan, *Wales in British Politics*, p. 188. Morgan was citing a figure in the *Church Times* for 1 May 1903.

29 Morgan, *Wales in British Politics*, p. 46.

30 NLW, SA/LET/310 John W. Kirkham to Vowler Short, 16 April 1847.

31 NLW, SA/LET/260 T. Z. Davies to Vowler Short, 12 March 1847.

32 NLW, B/QA/28 Bangor Visitation Records 1856.

33 NLW, B/QA/28 Bangor Visitation Records 1856 – Llanfachraeth.

34 NLW, B/QA/28 Bangor Visitation Records 1856 – Pentraeth.

35 NLW, B/QA/28 Bangor Visitation Records 1856 – Llanbeblig.

36 NLW, B/QA/28 Bangor Visitation Records 1856 – Llanfairfechan and Llanrûg.

37 NLW, B/QA/33 Bangor Visitation Records 1900.

38 NLW, B/QA/33 Bangor Visitation Records 1900 – Penmachno.

39 Morgan, *Wales in British Politics*, p. 45.

40 NLW, B/QA/33 Bangor Visitation Records 1900 – Trefriw.

[41] NLW, B/QA/33 Bangor Visitation Records 1900 – Llanbedr-y-Cennin.

[42] NLW, B/QA/33 Bangor Visitation Records 1900 – Arfon deanery parishes. The parishes in which church schools had been transferred to boards were Llanaelhaearn, Llanddeiniolen, Llandwrog, Llanllyfni and Llanrûg.

[43] NLW, B/QA/33 Bangor Visitation Records 1900 – Glanogwen.

[44] NLW, B/QA/28 and B/QA/33 Bangor Visitation Records 1856 and 1900. In 1856, Bangor with Pentir had a National School with 100 boys and 100 girls, an infant school with 150 boys and girls and two other parochial schools with 110 pupils. Bangor St Mary's had one National School and two other county schools supported by subscribers. By 1900, Bangor St Mary's had one school with 352 pupils, Bangor St James, the parish which included the cathedral, had another with 233 pupils and Bangor Pentir had the third school with just 82 on the roll.

[45] Morgan, *Wales in British Politics*, p. 183.

[46] James Munson, *The Nonconformists: In Search of a Lost Culture* (London, 1991), pp. 244–89.

[47] Morgan, *Wales in British Politics*, pp. 181–98. The two 'renegade' counties were Breconshire and Radnorshire.

[48] A. G. Edwards, bishop of St Asaph, attempted to act as a mediatorial figure, although his fellow bishops were less conciliatory on this occasion.

[49] NLW, LL/Misc/237–42. Alleged ritual irregularities at St Mary's Monmouth, May 1899.

[50] The vicar was G. Arthur Jones, the subject of a biography written by two of his curates, H. W. Ward and H. A. Coe, *Father Jones of Cardiff: A Memoir* (London, 1907).

[51] NLW, LL/Misc/458 Edwin Dobbin and Henry Thatcher to G. Arthur Jones, 27 August 1899.

[52] NLW, LL/Misc/459 letter from 'a Churchman not ritual [*sic*]' to the bishop of Llandaff, 23 May 1899.

[53] John Davies, *Cardiff and the Marquesses of Bute* (Cardiff, 1981).

[54] Roger L. Brown, 'The Bute church patronage in Glamorgan: a legal note on *pro hac vice* patronage', *The Journal of Welsh Religious History*, 5 (Welshpool, 1992), 92–8.

[55] Nigel Yates, 'The progress of ecclesiology and ritualism in Wales', *Archaeologica Cambrensis*, 149 (2000), 59–88.

[56] Nigel Yates, *Anglican Ritualism in Victorian Britain 1830–1910* (Oxford, 1999), p. 115.

[57] Raymond Renowden, *A Genial, Kind Divine: Watkin Herbert Williams 1845–1944* (Denbigh, n.d.), pp. 135–42.
[58] NLW, B/QA/34 Bangor Visitation Records 1905.
[59] NLW, B/QA/34 Bangor Visitation Records 1905 – Llanddeiniolen.
[60] NLW, B/QA/34 Bangor Visitation Records 1905 – Glanadda.
[61] NLW, B/QA/34 Bangor Visitation Records 1905 – Bangor St Mary.
[62] NLW, B/QA/34 Bangor Visitation Records 1905 – Llanllechid.
[63] NLW, B/QA/34 Bangor Visitation Records 1905 – Newborough.
[64] NLW, B/QA/34 Bangor Visitation Records 1905 – Aber.
[65] NLW, B/QA/34 Bangor Visitation Records 1905 – Llanddona.
[66] NLW, B/QA/28 Bangor Visitation Records 1856 – Holyhead.
[67] NLW, B/QA/28 Bangor Visitation Records 1856 – Llandegfan with Beaumaris. The rector reported that 1,868 had communicated at Beaumaris in 1855. Presumably this was the total number of communions made, not the total number of individual communicants.
[68] NLW, B/QA/28 Bangor Visitation Records 1856.
[69] NLW, B/QA/33. Six parishes used English for the majority of their services, and three parishes used English and Welsh equally. No parishes in the sample used English exclusively.
[70] Data derived from Ieuan Gwynedd Jones (ed.), *The Religious Census of 1851: A Calendar of the Returns Relating to Wales, Vol. II: North Wales* (Cardiff, 1981). The 1851 census did not ask questions about the language in which services were conducted, but this deficiency has been overcome in Jones's edition of the census by means of the incorporation of data taken from a government report of 1849, entitled *Number of Services Performed in each Church and Chapel [in Wales]*. See Jones, *The Religious Census of 1851: A Calendar of Returns Relating to Wales, Vol. I: South Wales* (Cardiff, 1976), p. xxxii.
[71] Jones, *Census of 1851: North Wales*, p. 83. It is also worth noting that 85 per cent of the parishes in Montgomeryshire were recorded as holding two or more Sunday services in 1851.
[72] NLW, St Asaph Parish Records: Berriew 101.
[73] *Royal Commission on the Church of England and Other Religious Bodies in Wales and Monmouthshire*, 1910, vol. I, p. 20.
[74] Jones, *Census of 1851: North Wales*, p. 38, and NLW St Asaph Parish Records: Berriew 101. The switch of language may have occurred in 1854 when Henry James Marshall of Corpus Christi

College, Oxford became vicar. See D. R. Thomas, *A History of the Diocese of St Asaph* (London 1874), p. 319.

[75] NLW, St Asaph Parish Records: Berriew 101.

[76] NLW, St Asaph Parish Records: Llanwddyn 4 Service Register 1891–9. No foliation. The rotation was Welsh mattins and sermon; English Holy Communion with litany and sermon; English evensong and Welsh sermon; Welsh litany, ante-communion and sermon; English mattins and sermon and Welsh evensong and English sermon.

[77] NLW, St Asaph Parish Records: Llangadfan 6: Service Register 1910–31. No foliation.

[78] Knight, *The Nineteenth Century Church and English Society*, pp. 35–6, 81 and 203.

[79] NLW, St Asaph Parish Records: Llanwddyn Service Register 1899–1907. No foliation. Many of the service registers contain communicants' registers at the back, and they were often diligently completed by the clergy.

[80] NLW, St Asaph Parish Records: Bettws Cedewain 93, Service Register 1895–1901. No foliation.

[81] Frances Knight, 'Anglican worship in late nineteenth-century Wales: a Montgomeryshire case study', in Robert Swanson (ed.), *Studies in Church History*, 35 (Woodbridge, 1999), 409–19. This article explores the twin musical traditions that are evident in Montgomeryshire church life. Great enthusiasm was shown both for the development of English choral music and for traditional Welsh musical events such as the *plygain* and the *cymanfa ganu*.

[82] NLW, St Asaph Parish Records: 119 Beriew Parish Magazine November 1880.

[83] The desire to celebrate harvest was not confined to the countryside. Jeffrey Cox has shown that harvest festival was also the most popular service in inner Lambeth at this period. Jeffrey Cox, *The English Churches in a Secular Society: Lambeth 1870–1930* (Oxford, 1982), pp. 103–4.

[84] NLW, St Asaph Parish Records: Llanllwchaiarn 12 Service Register 1884–1901. No foliation.

[85] Throughout the period 1827–97 more of the students admitted to St David's College Lampeter were the sons of farmers than any other occupational category. See D. T. W. Price, *A History of St David's University College, Vol. I: To 1898* (Cardiff, 1977), pp. 207–10. See also D. Parry-Jones,

Welsh Country Upbringing (London, 1948), pp. 77–8 for an account of Anglican harvest celebrations in Carmarthenshire in the 1890s.

[86] Trefor M. Jones, *Welsh Folk Customs* (Cardiff, 1959), pp. 41–7; Parry-Jones, *Welsh Country Upbringing*, pp. 75–6, 78–9.

[87] The St Asaph Parochial Records in the NLW for parishes such as Berriew, Bettws Cedewain, Llangadfan, Llanwddyn and Manafon give a full sense of the liveliness of church-centred social and cultural events in these places in the late nineteenth century.

[88] NLW, B/QA/33 Bangor Visitation Records 1900 – Llanbeblig with Caernarfon.

[89] NLW, B/QA/33 Bangor Visitation Records 1900 – Llanllyfni.

[90] Frances Knight, 'The pastoral ministry in the Anglican Church in England and Wales *c.*1840–1950', *The Pastor Bonus: Dutch Review of Church History*, 83 (Leiden, 2004), pp. 416–19. The Church of England Temperance Society was founded in 1862 as the Church of England Total Abstinence Society, and changed its name in 1873, partly in order to broaden its support to include non-abstainers. The CETS was happy to sanction the use of wine at Holy Communion, and by 1877 had developed a network of diocesan branches and parochial associations that covered England and Wales.

[91] NLW, B/QA/33 Bangor Visitation Records 1900 – Llanllyfni.

[92] Joshua Hughes, *Charge delivered to the Clergy of St Asaph at his Second Visitation* (London, 1874), p. 15; Basil Jones, *Charge at the Third Triennial Visitation of the Clergy of the Diocese of St David's* (London, 1883), p. 41.

[93] Eluned E. Owen, *The Early Life of Bishop Owen, a Son of Lleyn* (Llandysul, 1958), p. 197.

[94] J. Vyrnwy Morgan (ed.), *Welsh Religious Leaders in the Victorian Era* (London, 1905), p. 81.

[95] Ward and Coe, *Father Jones*, p. 112.

[96] NLW, B/QA/22 Bangor Visitation Returns 1900 – Bangor Cathedral and St James.

[97] NLW, St Asaph Parish Records: Bettws Cedewain 93. No foliation. Other topics for debate between 1897 and 1899 included 'Is marriage preferable to singleness?' 'Is the use of tobacco justifiable?' 'Ought women to be on [*sic*] equality with men?' 'Strikes: are they justifiable?' 'Is a club better for the working man than a bank?' 'The docking of horses: should it be abolished?' and 'Is the Transvaal war justifiable?' Only for this

last debate was the vote recorded. Twenty thought that the war was justifiable, fourteen were against.

[98] Jones, *Charge* (1883), p. 45.

[99] Jones, *Charge* (1883), p. 47.

[100] Joshua Hughes, *Primary Charge Delivered to the Clergy of the Diocese of St Asaph at his Primary Visitation, October 1871* (London, 1871), pp. 30–1. The forms for churchwardens' presentments for St Asaph in 1882 contained a printed note that 'it is thought advisable in many parishes to restore the ancient office of sidesman'. Few parishes, however, seemed to have more than one sidesman, and many none at all. Parishes with between six and twelve sidesmen included Denbigh, Llangollen, Oswestry, Rhosymedre and Rhyl.

[101] Rhoda Hiscox, *Celebrating Reader Ministry: 125 Years of Lay ministry in the Church of England* (London, 1991), p. 15.

[102] E. T. Davies, *Religion in the Industrial Revolution in South Wales* (Cardiff, 1965), pp. 125–6.

[103] NLW, Diocese of Llandaff Lay Clergy Papers LL/LC/1–422.

[104] NLW, LL/LC/87.

[105] NLW, LL/LC/18.

[106] NLW, LL/LC/14.

[107] NLW, LL/LC/20.

[108] NLW, LL/LC/6.

[109] NLW, LL/LC/26.

[110] NLW, LL/LC/88.

Select Bibliography

This bibliography includes only the more recent and authoritative books cited by the respective authors in their chapters. Details of older books, articles in journals and edited collections, unpublished theses, archives and manuscripts used by the respective authors are cited in the footnotes to each chapter.

(1) General Histories of Wales

Davies, J., *Cardiff and the Marquis of Bute* (Cardiff, 1981).
Davies, J., *A History of Wales* (London, 1993).
Howell, D., *The Rural Poor in Eighteenth-Century Wales* (Cardiff, 2000).
Jenkins, G. H., *The Foundations of Modern Wales 1642–1780* (Oxford, 1987).
Jenkins, P., *A History of Modern Wales, 1536–1990* (London, 1992).
Jones, I. G., *Explorations and Explanations: Essays in the Social History of Wales* (Llandysul, 1981).
Jones, I. G., *Mid-Victorian Wales: The Observers and the Observed* (Cardiff, 1992).
Jones, T. M., *Welsh Folk Customs* (Cardiff, 1959).
Morgan, K. O., *Wales in British Politics 1868–1922*, 3rd edn (Cardiff, 1991).
Morgan, K. O., *Modern Wales: Politics, Places and People* (Cardiff, 1995).
Thomas, J. D. H., *A History of Wales, 1435–1660* (Cardiff, 1972).
Thomas, W. S. K., *Stuart Wales* (Llandysul, 1988).

(2) General Religious Histories

Green, I. M., *The Christian's ABC: Catechism and Catechising in England c1530–1740* (Oxford, 1996).
O'Day, R. and Heal, F. (eds), *Princes and Paupers in the English Church 1500–1800* (Leicester, 1981).

Pope, R. (ed.), *Religion and National Identity: Wales and Scotland c1700–2000* (Cardiff, 2001).
Thomas, K., *Religion and the Decline of Magic* (London, 1971).
Williams, G., *Religion, Language and Nationality in Wales* (Cardiff, 1979).
Williams, G., *The Welsh and their Religion* (Cardiff, 1991).

(a) The Seventeenth and Eighteenth Centuries

Bullock, F. W. B., *Voluntary Religious Societies 1520–1799* (St Leonards-on-Sea, 1963).
Evans, G. W., *Religion and Politics in Mid-Eighteenth Century Anglesey* (Cardiff, 1963).
Griffith, W. P., *Learning, Law and Religion, 1540–1640* (Cardiff, 1976).
Jenkins, G. H., *Literature, Religion and Society in Wales 1660–1730* (Cardiff, 1978).
Jones, R. M. and Davies, G., *The Christian Heritage of Welsh Education* (Bridgend, 1986).
Rupp, E. G., *Religion in England 1688–1791* (Oxford, 1986).
Tyacke, N., *Anti-Calvinists: The Rise of English Arminianism c1590–1640* (Oxford, 1987).
Williams, G. A., *Ymryson Edmwnd Prys a Wiliam Cynwal* (Caerdydd, 1986).

(b) The Nineteenth and Twentieth Centuries

Bell, P. M. H., *Disestablishment in Ireland and Wales* (London, 1969).
Chadwick, W. O., *The Victorian Church*, 2 vols (London, 1966–70).
Davies, E. T., *Religion in the Industrial Revolution in South Wales* (Cardiff, 1965).
Jones, B. L., *Yr Hen Bersoniaid Llengar* (Dinbych, 1963).
Jones, I. G. and Williams, D. (eds), *The Religious Census of 1851: A Calendar of the Returns Relating to Wales*, 2 vols (Cardiff, 1976–81).
Jones, R. T., *Faith and the Crisis of a Nation: Wales 1890–1914* (Cardiff, 2004) (English translation and edition by Robert Pope of *Ffydd ac Argyfwng Cenedl*, 2 vols (Abertawe, 1981–2)).
Morgan, D. D., *The Span of the Cross: Christian Religion and Society in Wales 1914–2000* (Cardiff, 1999).
Snell, K. D. M. and Ell, P. S., *Rival Jerusalems: the Geography of Victorian Religion* (Cambridge, 2000).

Thomas, M. E., *Afiaith yng Ngwent* (Caerdydd, 1978).
Ward, W. R., *Religion and Society in England 1790–1850* (London, 1972).
Wolffe, J., *God and Greater Britain: Religion and National Life in Britain and Ireland 1843–1945* (London, 1994).

(3) The Established Church

Best, G. F. A., *Temporal Pillars: Queen Anne's Bounty, The Ecclesiastical Commission and the Church of England* (Cambridge, 1964).
Guy, J. R. and Nealy, W. G. (eds), *Contrasts and Comparisons: Studies in Irish and Welsh Church History* (Llandysul, 1999).
Jones, O. W. and Walker, D. (eds), *Links with the Past: Swansea and Brecon Historical Essays* (Llandybie, 1974).
Perkins, M. (ed.), *Directory of the Parochial Libraries of the Church of England and the Church in Wales* (London, 2004).
Temperley, N., *The Music of the English Parish Church* (Cambridge, 1978).
Walker, D. (ed.), *A History of the Church in Wales* (Penarth, 1976).
Yates, W. N., *Buildings, Faith and Worship: The Liturgical Arrangement of Anglican Churches 1600–1900*, 2nd edn (Oxford, 2000).

(a) The Seventeenth and Eighteenth Centuries

Clarke, W. K. L., *A History of the SPCK* (London, 1959).
Clement, M. (ed.), *Correspondence and Minutes of the SPCK Relating to Wales 1699–1740* (Cardiff, 1952).
Clement, M., *The SPCK and Wales 1699–1740* (Aberystwyth, 1954).
Clement, M. (ed.), *Correspondence and Minutes of the SPG Relating to Wales 1701–1750* (Cardiff, 1973).
Green, I. M., *The Re-establishment of the Church of England 1660–1663* (Oxford, 1978).
Gregory, J. and Chamberlain, J. S. (eds), *The National Church in Local Perspective: The Church of England and the Regions* (Woodbridge, 2003).
Griffiths, G. M. (ed.), *A Report of the Deanery of Penllyn and Edeirnion by the Revd John Wynne* (Merioneth Historical and Record Society, 1955).
Guy, J. R. (ed.), *The Diocese of Llandaff in 1763: The Primary Visitation of Bishop Ewer* (South Wales Record Society, 1991).

Hart, A. T., *William Lloyd: Bishop, Politician, Author and Prophet 1627–1717* (London, 1952).

Jacob, W. M., *Lay People and Religion in the Early Eighteenth Century* (Cambridge, 1996).

Mather, F. C., *High Church Prophet: Bishop Samuel Horsley (1733–1806) and the Caroline Tradition in the Late Georgian Church* (Oxford, 1992).

Snape, M., *The Church in an Industrialised Society* (Woodbridge, 2003).

Spurr, J., *The Restoration Church of England 1646–1689* (New Haven and London, 1991).

Trevor-Roper, H. R., *Archbishop Laud*, 2nd edn (London, 1962).

(b) The Nineteenth and Twentieth Centuries

Brown, R. L., *Reclaiming the Wilderness: Some Aspects of Parochial Life and Achievements of the Diocese of Llandaff during the Nineteenth Century* (Welshpool, 2001).

Brown, R. L. (ed.), *The Letters of Edward Copleston, Bishop of Llandaff, 1828–1849* (South Wales Record Society, 2003).

Brown, R. L., *In Pursuit of a Welsh Episcopate: Appointments to Welsh Sees 1840–1905* (Cardiff, 2005).

Burns, A., *The Diocesan Revival in the Church of England c1800–1870* (Oxford, 1999).

Cragoe, M., *An Anglican Aristocracy: The Moral Economy of the Landed Estate in Carmarthenshire, 1832–1895* (Oxford, 1996).

Dewey, C., *The Passing of Barchester* (London, 1991).

Haig, A., *The Victorian Clergy* (London and Sydney, 1984).

Hiscox, R., *Celebrating Reader Ministry: 125 Years of Lay Ministry in the Church of England* (London, 1991).

Jones, O. W., *Isaac Williams and His Circle* (London, 1971).

Jones, O. W., *Rowland Williams: Patriot and Critic* (Llandysul, 1991).

Knight, F., *The Nineteenth Century Church and English Society* (Cambridge, 1995).

Owen, E. E., *The Early Life of Bishop Owen* (Llandysul, 1958).

Price, D. T. W., *Bishop Burgess and Lampeter College* (Cardiff, 1987).

Varley, E. A., *The Last of the Prince Bishops: William Van Mildert and the High Church Movement of the Early Nineteenth Century* (Cambridge, 1992).

Yates, W. N., *Anglican Ritualism in Victorian Britain 1830–1910* (Oxford, 1999).

(4) *Catholic Recusancy and Puritanism*

Acheson, R. J., *Radical Puritanism in England, 1550–1640* (London, 1990).
Ellis, T. P., *The Catholic Martyrs of Wales, 1535–1680* (London, 1955).
Hill, C., *The World Turned Upside Down* (London, 1975).
Jones, E. G., *Cymru a'r Hen Ffydd* (Caerdydd, 1951).
Jones, R. T., *Vavasor Powell* (Abertawe, 1971).
Jenkins, G. H., *Protestant Dissenters in Wales, 1639–1689* (Cardiff, 1992).
Nuttall, G. F., *The Welsh Saints 1640–1660* (Cardiff, 1957).
Nuttall, G. F., *The Puritan Spirit* (London, 1967).

(5) *Protestant Nonconformity*

Barnes, D. R., *People of Seion: Patterns of Nonconformity in Cardiganshire and Carmarthenshire in the Century before the Religious Census of 1851* (Llandysul, 1995).
Bassett, T. M., *The Welsh Baptists* (Swansea, 1977).
Horridge, G. K., *The Salvation Army: Origins and Early Days* (Godalming, 1993).
Jones, R. T., *Congregationalism in Wales* (Cardiff, 2004) (English translation and edition by Robert Pope of *Hanes Annibynwyr Cymru* (Abertawe, 1968)).
Munson, J., *The Nonconformists: In Search of a Lost Culture* (London, 1991).
Watts, M. R., *The Dissenters from the Reformation to the French Revolution* (Oxford, 1978).
Watts, M. R., *The Dissenters: The Expansion of Evangelical Nonconformity* (Oxford, 1995).

(6) *The Evangelical Revival*

Brown, R. L., *The Welsh Evangelicals* (Cardiff, 1986).
Brown, R. L., *David Howell: A Pool of Spirituality* (Denbigh, 1998).
Campbell, T. A., *The Religion of the Heart: A Study in European Religious Life in the Seventeenth and Eighteenth Centuries* (Columbia, 1991).
Clarkson, G. E., *George Whitefield and Welsh Calvinistic Methodism* (Lewiston, 1996).

Evans, E., *Daniel Rowland and the Great Evangelical Awakening in Wales* (Edinburgh, 1985).
Hughes, G. T., *Williams Pantycelyn* (Cardiff, 1983).
Jones, D. C., *'A Glorious Work in the World': Welsh Methodism and the International Evangelical Revival, 1735–1750* (Cardiff, 2004).
Morgan, D. L., *The Great Awakening in Wales* (London, 1988).
Morgan, D. L., *Pobl Pantycelyn* (Llandysul, 1986).
Nuttall, G. F., *Howell Harris 1714–1773: The Last Enthusiast* (Cardiff, 1965).
Tudur, G., *Howell Harris: From Conversion to Separation 1735–1750* (Cardiff, 2000).
Ward, W. R., *The Protestant Evangelical Awakening* (Cambridge, 1992).
White, E. M., *'Praidd Bach y Bugail Mawr': Seiadau Methodistaidd De-Orllewin Cymru 1737–50* (Llandysul, 1996).
Williams, A. H., *John Wesley in Wales 1739–90* (Cardiff, 1971).

Index